Who Else
writes like ...

A readers' guide to fiction authors

Fifth edition

Edited by
Roy and Jeanne Huse

LISU Research & consultancy
for performance management
Information, cultural & academic services

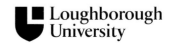
Loughborough
University

HUSE, Roy and Jeanne, Editors

Who Else Writes Like ...? A readers' guide to fiction authors

First published 1993, 5th edition 2005

ISBN-13: 978-1-901786-897

ISBN-10: 1-901786-897

Cover design by
Mary Ashworth & Sharon Fletcher, LISU
and Paul Atkins, Media Services, Loughborough University

Inside pages designed and typeset in Gill Sans and Verdana by
Mary Ashworth & Sharon Fletcher, LISU

Printed by
Alltrade Printers (Sales) Ltd
2 Ringway Business Park, Richard Street,
Birmingham, West Midlands B7 4AA

Published and distributed by
LISU
Loughborough University, Loughborough, LE11 3TU
Tel: +44 (0)1509 635680 Fax: +44 (0)1509 635699
E-mail: lisu@lboro.ac.uk
Web: www.lboro.ac.uk/departments/dis/lisu

Contents

Acknowledgements

As we have said for every previous edition, this publication could not have been produced without the active help of a small group of enthusiastic advisors. They have made significant contributions to create a bigger and better edition for the 21st century. The editors are grateful to:

Ian Baillie	*West Dunbartonshire Council*
Neil Davies	*London Borough of Newham*
Debbie Hicks	*The Reading Agency*
Carolyn Huckfield	*Herefordshire County Libraries*
John Lake	*City of London Library*
Marion Phillips	*Belfast City Library*
Bob Sharpe	*Dorset County Library*
Briony Train	*University of Sheffield*

With special thanks to Ian and Maggie Sumner; freelance authors and researchers

We would also again like to thank Dr Jim Parker, the Registrar of Public Lending Right, and his colleagues for supplying the statistics upon which the core list of authors is based. The staff of West Sussex Libraries have, as always, been very supportive, particularly Louise Withington and her colleagues at the Bognor Regis and Willowhale libraries. We are also most grateful for advice given by Karen Aveyard, Reader Development Librarian. Special thanks to the staff of the Brighton Library, part of the Bayside Library Service in Melbourne, Australia, for their enthusiasm and technical assistance. Our sincere thanks go, as ever, to Eric Pascal for his invaluable computer expertise.

We have relied, as for every edition, upon the help and support of our publishers: LISU and its current Director, Dr Eric Davies. Our special thanks go to Mary Ashworth and Sharon Fletcher who continue to maintain their own personal interest and enthusiasm, which has helped to ensure its continuing success.

Finally we would like to dedicate this 5th edition to the memory of John Sumsion (1928–2004), former Director of LISU from 1991–1996, whose idea it was to revise and re-publish *The Readers' Guide to Fiction Authors*, edited by Peter Mann, and originally issued in 1985. We hope he would be pleased with this latest edition.

Roy and Jeanne Huse
Aldwick

March 2005

Introduction

Who Else Writes Like ...? was first published under this title in 1993. It is designed to help library users who have read all the books by their favourite authors and are seeking new names to try. Of course, no author writes exactly like another, but the selection of alternatives under each author should help to narrow the choices from the hundreds of titles available on the shelves of the average public library. While today's modern technology can produce sophisticated reading lists, the advantage of this guide lies in its simplicity and portability. It can be taken around the shelves by a reader or by a member of the library staff; and for this reason, the editors, advisors and publishers all hope that the guide will be prominently displayed, readily available to encourage maximum use. While this guide is compiled by librarians for librarians, it is of equal value to bookshops and to their customers.

The basis for the initial selection of authors continues to be those who are the most borrowed according to the lists compiled by the Registrar of Public Lending Right. These are supplemented with names suggested by a small team of advisors based in libraries in different parts of the United Kingdom. This fifth edition lists more authors than ever, with some 430 new authors replacing the 350 that have been deleted mainly because their books are no longer represented on the shelves. In this way, the 1,875 authors in this edition should reflect a good cross-section of the stock and the current borrowing trends of public libraries across the UK. At the same time efforts have been made to retain the compact nature of this guide.

There are several detailed changes in this edition. The number of alternative authors has, in general, been limited to nine, although this has been extended to 12 for many of the most popular writers. Since the publication of the last edition, the number of authors with their own website has greatly increased. These sites have been included, where known, and are correct at the time of going to press. The list of Literary Prizes has been updated, but only entries from 1990 are now shown, as earlier winners can be found in the 4th edition. Some minor amendments have been made to the subgenre headings and the two lists of Western and Romance authors have been deleted, as almost all libraries display these books in separate sequences. The Crime genre has been split into more subgenres to reflect the growing number of overseas authors and locations, as well as catering for the increasing popularity of 'historical crime'. Finally, the guide concludes with a short list of books and websites which should help all readers further explore the wonderfully diverse world of fiction.

How to Use this Guide

The main list of authors is in alphabetical order. Each name is followed by a list of suggested alternatives. So pick out an author whose books you like, and see which other writers are recommended underneath. For instance, if you like **Michelle de Kretser**, *Who Else Writes Like ...?* suggests that you might also like **Regi Claire**, **Arthur Golden**, and so on.

Additional information is given with many of the author entries:

- author's dates of birth and death, where known
- nationality (or place of birth) of authors who are not English, where known (see abbreviations used on page vi)
- the genre and/or subgenre, or type of novel (eg **Crime: Historical - C17th** or **General**)
- name of main character(s), preceded by ⚓ (eg **Countess Ashby-de-la-Zouche**)
- environment and/or occupation (eg **C17th London** or '**Kingsmarkham**' — quotation marks ('xxx') indicate a fictional environment — and **maid**)
- pseudonym(s): **also writes as** or **is**
- author's own website (eg **www.fidelismorgan.com**) or websites with more details about an author and their books (eg **www.fantasticfiction.co.uk**)
- prizes won with dates (see abbreviations used on page vi)

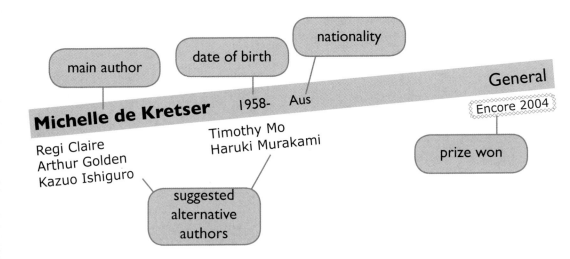

An increasing number of established authors are writing in alternative genres. These are shown in the main sequence as well as in the genre listings at the end of the book. Where an author writes under the same name but under two different genres, we have given two entries: for example, **June Drummond** *(Adventure/Thriller)* and **June Drummond** *(Historical)*.

Authors who usually write in one category may occasionally produce a book in a quite different genre — so if genre is important to you, check the jacket details of a book before you read it.

If you want to start by consulting a list of authors who write in a particular category, go to **Authors listed by Genre** beginning on page 288. Some of the genres are further sub-divided — for instance, *Crime* is divided into *Humour*, *Private investigator (PI)*, and so on. Authors classified as *General* have not been listed.

You may remember a character's name but cannot remember the author's name, so there is an index of **Characters**, **Series** and **Families**, listed alphabetically by surname, beginning on page 303.

Another possible starting point is to look at the lists of prize-winning books in **Literary Prizes and Awards**, which begin on page 320.

Who Else Writes Like ...? apart, there is an increasing number of guides to novelists and their works. Some of these are listed in **Further Reading** with Books on pages 342 and 343 and some useful Websites on page 344.

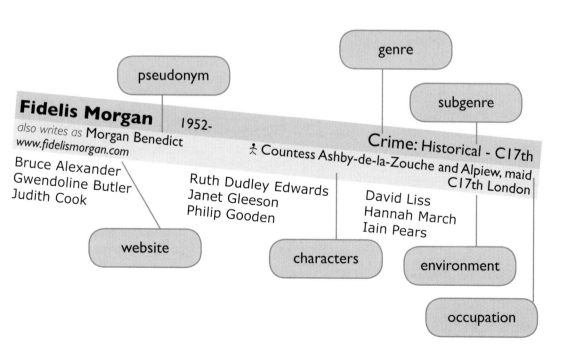

v

Abbreviations

Nationality or Place of Birth

The nationality or place of birth (where known) of those authors who are not English is indicated in the main list by an abbreviation or, in a few places, by the name of the country in full. The following is a full list of these countries.

Arg	Argentina	Ire	Ireland	Sco	Scotland
Aus	Australia	Isr	Israel	Sing	Singapore
Belg	Belgium	It	Italy	Spain	Spain
Braz	Brazil	Ja	Japan	Sri Lan	Sri Lanka
Can	Canada	Leb	Lebanon	Swe	Sweden
Carib	Caribbean	Mex	Mexico	Switz	Switzerland
Chile	Chile	Neth	Netherlands	Tai	Taiwan
China	China	NZ	New Zealand	Thai	Thailand
Col	Colombia	Nigeria	Nigeria	US	United States
Cuba	Cuba	Nor	Norway		of America
Den	Denmark	Peru	Peru	Wales	Wales
Fr	France	Pol	Poland	Zam	Zambia
Ger	Germany	Rus	Russia	Zan	Zanzibar
Guy	Guyana	SA	South Africa	Zim	Zimbabwe
Ind	India				

Literary Prizes and Awards

The following are the abbreviations used in the main body of the guide for winners of prizes. Most are listed in full with their descriptions in the list of Literary Prizes and Awards (pages 320–341).

Authors	Authors' Club First Novel Award
Black	James Tait Black Memorial Prizes
Booker	Booker Prize for Fiction
British Fantasy	British Fantasy Awards
BSFA	British Science Fiction Association Awards
Arthur C Clarke	Arthur C Clarke Award
Commonwealth	Commonwealth Writers Prize
CWA	Crime Writers' Association
Encore	Encore Award
Faber	Geoffrey Faber Memorial Prize
Guardian	Guardian Fiction Prize / First Book Award
Hawthornden	Hawthornden Prize
Higham	David Higham Prize for Fiction (listed in 4th ed)
Holtby	Winifred Holtby Memorial Prize
IMPAC	International IMPAC Dublin Literary Award
Independent	Independent Foreign Fiction Award
Irish Times	Irish Times International Fiction Prize
Mail	Mail on Sunday / John Llewellyn Rhys Prize
Man Booker	Man Booker Prize for Fiction
S Maugham	Somerset Maugham Awards
McKitterick	McKitterick Prize
Orange	The Orange Prize
Pulitzer	Pulitzer Prize for Fiction
Romantic	Foster Grant Romantic Novel of the Year
Saga for Wit	Saga Award for Wit
Sagittarius	Sagittarius Prize
WHSmith	WHSmith Literary Award
Sunday Times	Sunday Times Young Writer of the Year Award
TGR	Thumping Good Read Book Award
Betty Trask	Betty Trask Awards
Whitbread	Whitbread Book of the Year and Literary Awards
Wingate	Jewish Quarterly / Wingate Literary Prize for Fiction

The Readers' Guide
An Alphabetical List

Jeff Abbott US   Adventure/Thriller: Legal/financial
www.jeffabbott.com   Texas

Harlan Coben   James Grippando   George P Pelecanos
Robert Crais   David Michie

Keith Russell Ablow US Adventure/Thriller: Psychological
www.keithablow.com   ♣ Dr Frank Clevenger

Alice Blanchard   Jeffery Deaver   Jonathan Kellerman
Robin Cook   Thomas Harris

Dan Abnett   Science Fiction: Space opera
www.fantasticfiction.co.uk/authors/Dan_Abnett.htm

Lois McMaster Bujold Ben Counter   Jonathan Green
Chris Bunch   David A Drake   Tanith Lee

Peter Ackroyd 1949-   General
www.contemporarywriters.com/authors/?p=auth148

John Banville   John Fowles   S Maugham 1984
Julian Barnes   Maggie Gee   Guardian 1985
Anthony Burgess Robert Nye   Whitbread 1985
Christopher Fowler Iain Sinclair   Jill Paton Walsh

Paul Adam 1958-   Adventure/Thriller
www.fantasticfiction.co.uk/authors/Paul_Adam.htm

Paul Carson   Robert Harris   Leah Ruth Robinson
Robin Cook   Roy Lewis
Len Deighton   Ken McClure

Douglas Adams 1952-2001   Science Fiction: Humour
www.douglasadams.com

Jasper Fforde   Rob Grant   Terry Pratchett
Neil Gaiman   Tom Holt   Robert Rankin

Go to back for lists of:
Authors by Genre • Characters and Series • Prize Winners • Further Reading

1

James Adams 1951- Adventure/Thriller

Ted Allbeury
James Buchan
Stephen Coonts

Clive Egleton
James Follett
John Lawton

James Long
Terence Strong
Robert Wilson

Jane Adams 1960- Crime: Psychological

www.jane-adams.co.uk

⚐ DI Mike Croft • DS Ray Flowers - Norfolk
Naomi Blake, Blind ex-policewoman

Lisa Appignanesi
Hilary Bonner
Deborah Crombie

Frances Fyfield
P D James
Ed O'Connor

Danuta Reah
Alison Taylor
Margaret Yorke

Jessica Adams 1964- Aus Chick Lit

www.fantasticfiction.co.uk/authors/Jessica_Adams.htm

Cecelia Ahern
Susie Boyt
Sarah Harvey

Serena Mackesy
Chris Manby
Carole Matthews

Alexandra Potter
Fiona Walker

Elizabeth Adler Saga

www.elizabethadler.com

Lisa Appignanesi
Charlotte Bingham
Rose Boucheron

Barbara Taylor Bradford
Anita Burgh

Sidney Sheldon
Penny Vincenzi

Cecelia Ahern Ire Chick Lit

www.ceceliaahern.ie

Jessica Adams
Susie Boyt
Rebecca Campbell

Jenny Colgan
Jill Mansell
Sue Margolis

Elizabeth Noble
Morag Prunty
Daisy Waugh

Catherine Aird 1930- Crime: Police work - UK

is Kim Hamilton McIntosh
www.catherineaird.com

⚐ DI Sloan & DS Crosby
'Calleshire'

Vivien Armstrong
M C Beaton
Pauline Bell

W J Burley
Agatha Christie

Ann Cleeves
Gladys Mitchell

Rennie Airth 1935- SA Crime: Historical

www.fantasticfiction.co.uk/authors/Rennie_Airth.htm

⚐ DI John Madden - Surrey

Boris Akunin

Eric Ambler
Stephen Booth

Agatha Christie
Peter Robinson

Rosemary Aitken   1942-   Saga

also writes as **Rosemary Rowe**
www.raitken.wyenet.co.uk

Philip Boast	Elizabeth Ann Hill	Susan Sallis
Gloria Cook	Malcolm Ross	Barbara Whitnell
Winston Graham		

Boris Akunin   1956-   Rus   Crime: Historical - C19th

is **Grigory Chkhartishvili**   ⚐ Erast Fandorin, Tsarist agent
www.fantasticfiction.co.uk/authors/Boris_Akunin.htm

Rennie Airth	Barbara Cleverly	George Macdonald Fraser
Tom Bradby	David Dickinson	Michael Pearce
Agatha Christie	Arthur Conan Doyle	Barrie Roberts

Maggie Alderson   Aus   Chick Lit

www.fantasticfiction.co.uk/authors/Maggie_Alderson.htm

Sarah Ball	Melissa Nathan	Jennifer Weiner
Alexandra Carew	Freya North	Deborah Wright
Jenny Colgan		

Brian W Aldiss   1925-   Science Fiction: Space and time

www.brianwaldiss.com

Isaac Asimov	Joe Haldeman	BSFA 1982 & 1985
Greg Bear	Robert A Heinlein	
Arthur C Clarke	Brian Herbert	Kurt Vonnegut
Harlan Ellison	Frank Herbert	John Wyndham

Bruce Alexander   1932-2003   US   Crime: Historical - C18th

was **Bruce Cook**   ⚐ Sir John Fielding, Bow Street magistrate
C18th London

Gwendoline Butler	Janet Laurence	Hannah March
Janet Gleeson	David Liss	Fidelis Morgan
Deryn Lake		

Vanessa Alexander   Saga

also writes as **Anna Apostolou, Michael Clynes,
PC Doherty, Paul Harding**
is **Paul Doherty**

Aileen Armitage	Margaret Bacon	Helen Cannam
Elizabeth Aston	Louise Brindley	Elizabeth Darrell

Monica Ali   1967-   General
www.fantasticfiction.co.uk/authors/Monica_Ali.htm

Bernardine Evaristo   Hanif Kureishi   Salman Rushdie
Michel Faber   Andrea Levy   Zadie Smith
Abdulrazak Gurnah   Arundhati Roy   Meera Syal

Thalassa Ali   General
www.thalassaali.com

Barbara Cleverly   Rohinton Mistry   Carolyn Slaughter
M M Kaye   Paul Scott

Ted Allbeury   1917-   Adventure/Thriller
also writes as Richard Butler, Patrick Kelly
www.fantasticfiction.co.uk/authors/Ted_Allbeury.htm

James Adams   Len Deighton   Brian Freemantle
Eric Ambler   Clive Egleton   John Lawton
Evelyn Anthony   Colin Forbes   Robin White

Isabel Allende   1942-   Chile   General
www.isabelallende.com

Gail Anderson-Dargatz   Carlos Fuentes   Tomas Eloy Martinez
Louise Erdrich   Gabriel Garcia Márquez   Mario Vargas Llosa
Laura Esquivel   Shifra Horn

Margery Allingham   1904-66   Crime: Amateur sleuth
www.margeryallingham.org.uk   ⚹ Albert Campion

Agatha Christie   Michael Innes   Josephine Tey
Barbara Cleverly   Ngaio Marsh   Patricia Wentworth
Elizabeth Ferrars   Dorothy L Sayers

Catherine Alliott   Chick Lit
www.fantasticfiction.co.uk/authors/Catherine_Alliott.htm

Anita Anderson   Alexandra Campbell   Carole Matthews
Lisa Armstrong   Sarah Harvey   Amanda Murphy
Sarah Ball   Sue Margolis   Fiona Walker

> Go to back for lists of:
> Authors by Genre
> Characters and Series
> Prize Winners
> Further Reading

Karin Alvtegen 1966- Swe   Crime: Psychological

www.karinalvtegen.com

Karin Fossum	Pernille Rygg	Barbara Vine
Patricia Highsmith	Maj Sjöwall and	Minette Walters
Henning Mankell	Per Wahlöö	Laura Wilson

Eric Ambler 1909-1998   Adventure/Thriller

www.fantasticfiction.co.uk/authors/Eric_Ambler.htm

Rennie Airth   Joseph Kanon   CWA 1972
Ted Allbeury   Robert Littell
John Buchan   Charles McCarry
Ian Fleming   Robin White
John Gardner

David Ambrose 1943-   Horror

www.davidambrose.com

Jonathan Aycliffe   Chaz Brenchley   Rupert Thomson
Clive Barker   Peter James

Kingsley Amis 1922-95   General

www.fantasticfiction.co.uk/authors/Kingsley_Amis.htm

Malcolm Bradbury   David Nobbs   Booker 1986
Joseph Connolly   Alan Sillitoe
Michael Frayn   Keith Waterhouse
David Lodge   A N Wilson
Stanley Middleton

Martin Amis 1949-   General

http://martinamis.albion.edu

Paul Auster	Justin Cartwright	James Joyce
J G Ballard	David Flusfeder	Vladimir Nabokov
Iain Banks	Tobias Hill	D B C Pierre
Saul Bellow	Sean Hughes	Virginia Woolf

Anita Anderson   Chick Lit

Catherine Alliott	Sarah Harvey	Fiona Walker
Valerie-Anne Baglietto	Donna Hay	Jane Wenham-Jones
Alexandra Carew	Shari Low	

Barbara Anderson 1926- NZ General
www.bookcouncil.org.nz/writers/andersonb.html

Anita Brookner	Margaret Drabble
Raymond Carver	Bernice Rubens

Kevin J Anderson 1962- US Science Fiction: Space opera
www.wordfire.com

Iain M Banks	Frank Herbert	Alastair Reynolds
Simon R Green	Michael P Kube-McDowell	Dan Simmons
Peter F Hamilton	Larry Niven	

Poul Anderson 1926-2001 US Science Fiction: Space opera
www.fantasticfiction.co.uk/authors/Poul_Anderson.htm

Isaac Asimov	John Brosnan	Charles Stross
Stephen Baxter	Harlan Ellison	Roger Zelazny
Ray Bradbury	Jack McDevitt	

Gail Anderson-Dargatz Can General
www.randomhouse.ca/catalog/author.pperl?authorid=642

Isabel Allende	Alice Munro
Barbara Kingsolver	Anne Tyler

Colin Andrews 1946- US Adventure/Thriller
also writes as **F Paul Wilson**

Jonathan Aycliffe	Michael Crichton	Michael Palmer
Robin Cook	Ken McClure	Morris West

Lyn Andrews 1943- Saga
previously wrote as **Lynn M Andrews**
http://authorpages.hoddersystems.com/LynAndrews/author.htm Liverpool Irish

Anne Baker	June Francis	Maureen Lee
Donna Baker	Ruth Hamilton	Lynda Page
Josephine Cox	Joan Jonker	Margaret Thornton

Russell Andrews 1952- US Adventure/Thriller
also writes as **Peter Gethers**; *is* **David Handler**
www.fantasticfiction.co.uk/authors/Russell_Andrews.htm

Campbell Armstrong	Clive Cussler	Stanley Pottinger
Harlan Coben	William Diehl	P J Tracy
Michael Connelly	John Katzenbach	

Virginia Andrews   1923-86   US   General

also wrote as V C Andrews (with Andrew Neiderman)
www.fantasticfiction.co.uk/authors/Virginia_Andrews.htm

| Susan Hill | Judith Kelman | Anne Worboys |
| Gwen Hunter | Nora Roberts | |

Evelyn Anthony   1928-   Adventure/Thriller: Spy

www.fantasticfiction.co.uk/authors/Evelyn_Anthony.htm   🏃 Davina Graham

| Ted Allbeury | Clare Francis | Lindsay Townsend |
| Colin Forbes | Alan Furst | |

Mark Anthony   1966-   US   Fantasy: Epic

www.thelastrune.com

Chaz Brenchley	Stephen Donaldson	Robert Jordan
Steven Brust	David Farland	Guy Gavriel Kay
Jonathan Carroll	Terry Goodkind	

Piers Anthony   1934-   US   Fantasy: Humour

is Piers Anthony Dillingham Jacob
www.hipiers.com

| Steven Brust | Craig Shaw Gardner | William Sarabande |
| Alan Dean Foster | Terry Pratchett | |

Lisa Appignanesi   1946-   Pol   General

www.fantasticfiction.co.uk/authors/Lisa_Appignanesi.htm

| Elizabeth Adler | Helen Dunmore | Josephine Hart |
| Sally Beauman | Lesley Glaister | Judith Krantz |

Lisa Appignanesi   1946-   Pol   Adventure/Thriller: Psychological

www.fantasticfiction.co.uk/authors/Lisa_Appignanesi.htm

| Jane Adams | Nicci French | |
| Clare Francis | Robert Goddard | |

Diana Appleyard   Aga saga

Charlotte Bingham	Nina Dufort	Mary Sheepshanks
Cindy Blake	Sarah Grazebrook	Joanna Trollope
Victoria Clayton	Stevie Morgan	

Go to back for lists of:
Authors by Genre • Characters and Series • Prize Winners • Further Reading

A

Geoffrey Archer   1944-   Adventure/Thriller
www.geoffreyarcher.co.uk   🏃 Sam Packer

Stephen Coonts	Stephen Leather	Julian Jay Savarin
Graham Hurley	Mike Lunnon-Wood	Tim Sebastian
Philip Kerr	Chris Ryan	Craig Thomas

Jeffrey Archer   1940-   General
www.fantasticfiction.co.uk/authors/Jeffrey_Archer.htm

Nicholas Coleridge	Philip Hensher	Lawrence Sanders
Michael Dobbs	David Mason	Michael Shea
Colin Harrison	Peter Rawlinson	Sidney Sheldon

Aileen Armitage   1930-   Saga
🏃 Eva Bower • Hawksmoor Series
Yorkshire

Vanessa Alexander	Louise Brindley	Kay Stephens
Jessica Blair	Helen Cannam	Elizabeth Walker
Philip Boast		

Simon Armitage   1963-   Lad Lit: Humour
www.simonarmitage.co.uk

Mark Barrowcliffe	Ben Hatch	Willy Russell
Nick Earls	Tim Lott	

Campbell Armstrong   1944-   Sco   Adventure/Thriller
www.campbellarmstrong.com/index.php   🏃 DS Lou Perlman - Glasgow

Russell Andrews	Glenn Meade	Julian Jay Savarin
Harold Coyle	David Morrell	Tim Sebastian
Colin Forbes		

Kelley Armstrong   1968-   Can   Horror
www.kelleyarmstrong.com

Poppy Z Brite	Laurell K Hamilton	Phil Rickman
Nancy Collins	Tanya Huff	

Lisa Armstrong   Chick Lit

Catherine Alliott	Jane Green	Melissa Nathan
Emily Barr	Wendy Holden	Deborah Wright
Victoria Corby		

Vivien Armstrong

Crime: Police work - UK

www.fantasticfiction.co.uk/authors/Vivien_Armstrong.htm

*DS Roger Hayes - Oxfordshire
DI Ian Preston & DS Judith Pullen -
Great Yarmouth

A

Catherine Aird	Brian Cooper	P D James
Stephen Booth	Geraldine Evans	Susan B Kelly
Ken Bruen		

Jake Arnott   1961

Crime: Hardboiled

www.contemporarywriters.com/authors/?p=auth166

Nicholas Blincoe	Thomas Kelly	David Peace
Jeremy Cameron	Simon Kernick	John B Spencer
Jeff Gulvin	Toby Litt	Mark Timlin

Sarah Ash

Fantasy: Epic

www.sarah-ash.com

Joanne Bertin	Robin Hobb	Robert Newcomb
James Clemens	Anne McCaffrey	Melanie Rawn
David Eddings	Juliet Marillier	Cecilia Dart-Thornton

Jane Asher   1946-

General

Julia Hamilton	Shena Mackay
Elizabeth Jane Howard	Deborah Moggach

Michael Asher

Adventure/Thriller
North Africa

www.lost-oasis.org

Tom Clancy	John Nichol	Wilbur Smith
John Fullerton	Chris Ryan	

Neal Asher   1961-

Science Fiction: Near future

http://freespace.virgin.net/n.asher

Iain M Banks	Richard Morgan	Alastair Reynolds
Peter F Hamilton	Larry Niven	Dan Simmons

Jeffrey Ashford   1926-

Crime: Police work - UK

is Roderic Jeffries
www.fantasticfiction.co.uk/authors/Jeffrey_Ashford.htm

Hilary Bonner	J M Gregson	Bill Knox
Martin Edwards	Bill James	Roy Lewis
Kate Ellis		

Trisha Ashley · Chick Lit

Victoria Corby	Dorothy Koomson	Adele Parks
Nina Dufort	Jill Mansell	Victoria Routledge
Louise Harwood	Sarah Mason	

Sherry Ashworth · 1953- · Humour

Anne Atkins	Helen Fielding	Kate O'Riordan
Victoria Colby	Kathy Lette	Arabella Weir

Isaac Asimov · 1920-92 · US · Science Fiction: Space and time

www.asimovonline.com

Brian W Aldiss	Ben Bova	Robert A Heinlein
Poul Anderson	Arthur C Clarke	Larry Niven
Gregory Benford	Philip K Dick	John Wyndham

Richard Asplin · 1972- · Lad Lit: Humour

Paul Burke	Danny King	Damien Owens
James Delingpole	Mil Millington	Paul Reizin

Robert Asprin · 1946- · US · Fantasy: Epic

also writes as **Robert Lynn Asprin**
www.fantasticfiction.co.uk/authors/Robert_Asprin.htm

Jasper Fforde	Andrew Harman	Martin Scott
Alan Dean Foster	Tom Holt	Freda Warrington
Craig Shaw Gardner	Terry Pratchett	

Judy Astley · Aga saga

www.fantasticfiction.co.uk/authors/Judy_Astley.htm

Raffaella Barker	Rebecca Gregson	Stevie Morgan
Anne Doughty	Santa Montefiore	Sophia Watson
Nina Dufort	Charlotte Moore	Madeleine Wickham

Elizabeth Aston · 1948- · Historical

also writes as **Elizabeth Pewsey**

Vanessa Alexander	Margaret Bacon	Barbara Erskine
Jane Austen	Elizabeth Chadwick	Georgette Heyer

Ace Atkins   c1971-   US

Crime: Amateur sleuth

www.aceatkins.com

⚹ Nick Travers, Blues historian - New Orleans **A**

Charlotte Carter	Ron Ellis	Michael McGarrity
Thomas H Cook	G M Ford	James Sallis
Stephen Donaldson	Jonathon King	Stuart Woods

Anne Atkins

Aga saga

Sherry Ashworth	Charlotte Moore	Diana Saville
Marika Cobbold	Ann Purser	Rebecca Shaw
Hazel Hucker	Pam Rhodes	Madeleine Wickham

Meg Elizabeth Atkins   1932-

Crime: Police work - UK

⚹ DI Sheldon Hunter - 'Chatfield', Cheshire

Pauline Bell	Georgie Hale	Sally Spencer
Freda Davies	Roy Hart	Peter Turnbull
J M Gregson	Dorothy Simpson	

Kate Atkinson   1951-

General

www.geocitles.com/kateatkinson14

Beryl Bainbridge	Laura Esquivel	Whitbread 1995
Kate Bingham	Margaret Forster	
Angela Carter	Anne-Marie MacDonald	
Maureen Duffy	Charlotte Mendelson	Alice Sebold
Leif Enger	Mary Morrissy	Ali Smith

Margaret Atwood   1939-   Can

General

www.owtoad.com

Joan Barfoot	Valerie Martin	Arthur C Clarke 1987
Anthony Burgess	David Mitchell	Booker 2000
Clare Chambers	George Orwell	
Nadine Gordimer	Annie Proulx	Rachel Seiffert
Aldous Huxley	Jane Rogers	Donna Tartt

Jean M Auel   1936-   US

Historical

www.jeanmauel.co.uk

Louise Cooper	Christian Jacq	William Sarabande
Diana Gabaldon	Edward Rutherfurd	Manda Scott
Pauline Gedge		

Go to back for lists of:
Authors by Genre • Characters and Series • Prize Winners • Further Reading

Jane Austen 1775-1817 General
www.austen.com

Elizabeth Aston	Georgette Heyer	Barbara Trapido
Charles Dickens	Alison Lurie	Edith Wharton
Penelope Fitzgerald	Emma Tennant	

Paul Auster 1947- US General
www.paulauster.co.uk

Martin Amis	Don Delillo	D B C Pierre
Nicola Barker	E L Doctorow	Thomas Pynchon
Julian Barnes	Haruki Murakami	Adam Thorpe

Jonathan Aycliffe 1949- Horror
also writes as **Daniel Easterman**
is **Denis McEoin**
www.fantasticfiction.co.uk/authors/Jonathan_Aycliffe.htm

David Ambrose	Clive Barker	Richard Matheson
Colin Andrews	Graham Joyce	Kim Newman
Richard Bachman	Stephen Laws	Anne Rice

Steve Aylett 1967- Science Fiction: Near future
www.steveaylett.com

J G Ballard	Gwyneth Jones	Neal Stephenson
Eric Brown	Ken MacLeod	Bruce Sterling
William Gibson	Jeff Noon	Tad Williams

Trezza Azzopardi 1961- Wales General
www.fantasticfiction.co.uk/authors/Trezza_Azzopardi.htm

Maggie Gee	Rachel Seiffert	Faber 2001
Ann Patchett	Carol Shields	

Marian Babson 1929 US Crime: Amateur sleuth
is **Ruth Stenstreem**

♁ Trixie Dolan & Evangeline Sinclair, Actresses
Douglas Perkins & Gerry Tate, PR consultants
London

Lilian Jackson Braun	Anthea Fraser	Simon Shaw
Simon Brett	Alison Joseph	Charles Spencer
Sarah Caudwell	Charlotte MacLeod	

Richard Bachman   1947-   US   Horror

is Stephen King
www.fantasticfiction.co.uk/authors/Richard_Bachman.htm

Jonathan Aycliffe	James Herbert	Mark Morris
Douglas Clegg	Peter James	Dan Simmons
Muriel Gray	Dean R Koontz	Peter Straub

Margaret Bacon   Historical

Vanessa Alexander	Maeve Binchy	Robin Pilcher
Elizabeth Aston	Elizabeth Jane Howard	Rosamunde Pilcher

Anita Rau Badami   1962-   Can   General

Jhumpa Lahiri	Cauvery Madhavan	Bharati Mukherjee
Sharon Maas	Amulya Malladi	Anita Nair

David Baddiel   1964-   Lad Lit

www.fantasticfiction.co.uk/authors/David_Baddiel.htm

Mark Barrowcliffe	Rob Grant	Matt Thorne
Robert Chalmers	Ben Hatch	Nigel Williams
Ben Elton	Sean Thomas	

Andrea Badenoch   1951-2004   Crime: Psychological

www.andreabadenoch.org.uk   NE England

Carol Anne Davis	Julie Parsons	Barbara Vine
Denise Mina	Danuta Reah	Minette Walters
Gemma O'Connor	Carol Smith	Laura Wilson

Desmond Bagley   1923-83   Adventure/Thriller

www.fantasticfiction.co.uk/authors/Desmond_Bagley.htm

Jon Cleary	Ken Follett	Hammond Innes
Clive Cussler	John Gardner	Alistair MacLean
James Follett	Jack Higgins	

Valerie-Anne Baglietto   1971-   Chick Lit

Anita Anderson	Victoria Corby
Emily Barr	Jane Wenham-Jones
Lynne Barrett-Lee	

Go to back for lists of:
Authors by Genre • Characters and Series • Prize Winners • Further Reading

13

Louise Bagshawe 1972- Chick Lit
www.fantasticfiction.co.uk/authors/Louise_Bagshawe.htm

Celia Brayfield	Olivia Goldsmith	Marian Murphy
Imogen Edwards-Jones	Christina Jones	Robyn Sisman
Lucy Ellman	Susan Lewis	Fiona Walker

B

Hilary Bailey 1936- General
www.fantasticfiction.co.uk/authors/Hilary_Bailey.htm

Nina Bawden	Jane Gardam	Hilary Mantel
Charlotte Bingham	Henry James	Emma Tennant
Maureen Duffy	Angela Lambert	

Beryl Bainbridge 1934- General
www.contemporarywriters.com/authors/?p=auth10

Kate Atkinson	Mary Morrissy	
Pat Barker	Bernice Rubens	
Penelope Fitzgerald	Teresa Waugh	
Linda Grant	Fay Weldon	

Guardian 1974
Whitbread 1977 & 1996
Black 1998
WHSmith 1999

Anne Baker Saga
Liverpool
www.fantasticfiction.co.uk/authors/Anne_Baker.htm

Lyn Andrews	Helen Forrester	Margaret Mayhew
Donna Baker	Audrey Howard	Elizabeth Murphy
Katie Flynn	Maureen Lee	Lynda Page

Donna Baker 1939- Saga
also writes as **Lilian Harry**   Weavers Series • Glassmakers Series - Kidderminster

Lyn Andrews	Meg Hutchinson	Susan Sallis
Anne Baker	Marie Joseph	Sally Spencer
Jean Chapman	Annie Murray	Sue Sully

John Baker 1942- Crime: PI
www.johnbakeronline.co.uk   Sam Turner - York • Stone Lewis - Hull

Adam Baron	Martin Edwards	Iain McDowall
Eileen Dewhurst	Reginald Hill	Stuart Pawson
Alan Dunn	Lynda La Plante	Cath Staincliffe
Robert Edric	Frank Lean	Martyn Waites

Nicholson Baker 1957- US Humour
www.fantasticfiction.co.uk/authors/Nicholson_Baker.htm

Malcolm Bradbury	Tom Sharpe
Glen Duncan	Keith Waterhouse

David Baldacci   1960-   US   Adventure/Thriller

www.david-baldacci.com

Nelson DeMille	Craig Holden	David Michie
Joseph Finder	Paul Kilduff	David Morrell
Alan Folsom	Brad Meltzer	Sabin Willett

TGR 1997

B

Sarah Ball   1973-   Chick Lit

www.sarahball.co.uk

Maggie Alderson	Amanda Lees	Carmen Reid
Catherine Alliott	Marissa Mackle	Laura Wolf
Sue Haasler	Claudia Pattison	Deborah Wright

J G Ballard   1930-   Science Fiction: Technical

www.fantasticfiction.co.uk/authors/J_G_Ballard.htm

Steve Aylett	Frank Herbert	
Ray Bradbury	James Lovegrove	
Philip K Dick	Christopher Priest	
Joe Haldeman	Kurt Vonnegut	Ian Watson

BSFA 1979
Black 1984
Guardian 1984

J G Ballard   1930-   General

www.fantasticfiction.co.uk/authors/J_G_Ballard.htm

Martin Amis	Tobias Hill	Will Self
Peter Carey	Stewart Home	

Melissa Bank   US   General

Jane Green	Marian Keyes
Wendy Holden	Sophie Kinsella

Ashok K Banker   1966-   Ind   Fantasy: Myth

www.epicindia.com

Kate Elliott	Juliet Marillier	Caiseal Mor
Robert Jordan	George R R Martin	Sarah Zettel

Iain Banks   1954-   Sco   General

also writes as Iain M Banks
www.iainbanks.net

Martin Amis	Jeremy Dronfield	Duncan McLean
Peter Benson	Gordon Legge	Ruaridh Nicoll
Douglas Coupland	Ian McEwan	Alan Warner

Iain M Banks   1954-   Sco   Science Fiction: Space opera
also writes as **Iain Banks**
www.iainbanks.net

Kevin J Anderson   Ken MacLeod
Neal Asher   John Meaney
Greg Bear   Charles Stross
Peter F Hamilton   Ian Watson   David Zindell

B

Lynne Reid Banks   1929-   General
www.lynnereidbanks.com

Margaret Drabble   Penelope Lively   Libby Purves
Nadine Gordimer   Edna O'Brien   Muriel Spark

Jo Bannister   1951-   Crime: Police work - UK
www.fantasticfiction.co.uk/authors/Jo_Bannister.htm   ⚘ DCI Frank Shapiro
DI Liz Graham & DS Cal Donovan - 'Castlemere'
Brodie Farrell, PI - South Coast, England
Clio Rees, Doctor

Simon Brett   Liz Evans   Priscilla Masters
Deborah Crombie   Jill McGown   Peter Turnbull
Marjorie Eccles   Barry Maitland

John Banville   1945-   Ire   General
www.contemporarywriters.com/authors/?p=auth13

Peter Ackroyd   John McGahern
Dermot Bolger   Vladimir Nabokov
Peter Carey   Darin Strauss
James Hamilton-Paterson   William Trevor   Barry Unsworth

James Barclay   1965-   Fantasy: Epic
www.jamesbarclay.com

Stephen Donaldson   Kate Jacoby   George R R Martin
Steven Erikson   Greg Keyes   Caiseal Mor
Jude Fisher   Juliet E McKenna   Stan Nicholls
David Gemmell   John Marco   Freda Warrington

Tessa Barclay   1928-   Sco   Saga
is **Jean Bowden**   ⚘ Craigallan, Corvill & Tramont Families

Emma Blair   Margaret Graham   Nicola Thorne
Betty Burton   Pamela Oldfield   T R Wilson
Brenda Clarke   Frances Paige   Janet Woods

Joan Barfoot 1946- Can   General
www3.sympatico.ca/jbarfoot

Margaret Atwood	Margaret Drabble	Anne Tyler
Isla Dewar	Carol Shields	

Clive Barker 1952-   Horror **B**
www.clivebarker.com

David Ambrose	Simon Clark	Richard Laymon
Jonathan Aycliffe	Christopher Fowler	Bentley Little
Jonathan Carroll	Neil Gaiman	Dan Simmons

Nicola Barker 1966-   General
www.fantasticfiction.co.uk/authors/Nicola_Barker.htm

Paul Auster	Jenny Diski	Higham 1993
Julian Barnes	Candia McWilliam	Mail 1996
Saul Bellow	Marcia Muller	IMPAC 2000
Regi Claire	J D Salinger	

Pat Barker 1943-   General
www.fantasticfiction.co.uk/authors/Pat_Barker.htm

Beryl Bainbridge	Valerie Martin	Guardian 1993
Louis de Bernières	Mary Morrissy	Booker 1995
Linda Grant	Erich Maria Remarque	
Anne-Marie MacDonald	Bernhard Schlink	Charles Todd

Raffaella Barker 1964-   General
www.fantasticfiction.co.uk/authors/Raffaella_Barker.htm

Judy Astley	Louise Doughty	India Knight
Alexandra Campbell	Kate Fenton	Polly Samson
Victoria Clayton	Julie Highmore	Isabel Wolff

Robert Barnard 1936-   Crime: Police work - UK
www.fantasticfiction.co.uk/authors/Robert_Barnard.htm

🏃 Supt Perry Trethowan - London
Det Supt Oddie & DC Charlie Peace - Yorkshire

Pauline Bell	John Harvey	Peter Robinson
Colin Dexter	Reginald Hill	Simon Shaw
Jonathan Gash	Stuart Pawson	Peter Turnbull
Patricia Hall	Nicholas Rhea	R D Wingfield

Go to back for lists of:
Authors by Genre • Characters and Series • Prize Winners • Further Reading

Julian Barnes   1946-   General

also writes as **Dan Kavanagh**
www.julianbarnes.com

Peter Ackroyd	Bruce Chatwin	
Paul Auster	Tim Parks	
Nicola Barker	Rachel Seiffert	
Peter Benson	Graham Swift	A N Wilson

S Maugham 1981
Faber 1985

Linda Barnes   1949-   US   Crime: PI

www.lindabarnes.com   ⚐ Carlotta Carlyle - Boston, Mass.

Stella Duffy	Lauren Henderson	Dana Stabenow
Janet Evanovich	Marcia Muller	Sarah Strohmeyer
Meg Gardiner	Sara Paretsky	

Zoë Barnes   Chick Lit

www.zoebarnes.supanet.com

Maria Barrett	Donna Hay	Elizabeth Noble
Cindy Blake	Serena Mackesy	Tyne O'Connell
Dawn Cairns	Carole Matthews	Lesley Pearse

Adam Baron   Crime: PI

www.fantasticfiction.co.uk/authors/Adam_Baron.htm   ⚐ Billy Rucker - London

John Baker	Stephen Donaldson	Frank Lean
Jeffery Deaver	Alan Dunn	Martyn Waites

Emily Barr   Chick Lit

http://authorpages.hoddersystems.com/EmilyBarr

Lisa Armstrong	India Knight	
Valerie-Anne Baglietto	Adele Parks	
Alexandra Carew	Fiona Walker	

WHSmith 2001

Maria Barrett   Glitz & Glamour

www.fantasticfiction.co.uk/authors/Maria_Barrett.htm

Zoë Barnes	Roberta Latow	Una-Mary Parker
Celia Brayfield	Susan Lewis	Lynne Pemberton

Lynne Barrett-Lee   1959-   Chick Lit

Valerie-Anne Baglietto	Amanda Lees	Marian Murphy
Rebecca Campbell	L McCrossan	Sheila Norton
Imogen Edwards-Jones	Tara Manning	Andrea Semple

Mark Barrowcliffe

Lad Lit

www.fantasticfiction.co.uk/authors/Mark_Barrowcliffe.htm

Simon Armitage	Matthew Branton	Alex George
David Baddiel	Nick Earls	Danny King
Matthew Beaumont	Mike Gayle	Damien Owens

B

Dave Barry   1947-   US

Crime: Humour

Florida

Colin Bateman	Carl Hiaasen	Zane Radcliffe
Tim Dorsey	Danny King	Laurence Shames
Bill Fitzhugh	Douglas Lindsay	

Colin Bateman   1962-   Ire

Humour

🏃 Dan Starkey, Journalist

http://authorpages.hoddersystems.com/ColinBateman

Betty Trask 1994

Dave Barry	Danny King	
Marc Blake	Douglas Lindsay	
Marius Brill	Toby Litt	
Christopher Buckley	Malcolm Pryce	Mike Ripley
Peter Guttridge	Zane Radcliffe	John B Spencer

Susannah Bates   1970-

Chick Lit

www.fantasticfiction.co.uk/authors/Susannah_Bates.htm

Lisa Jewell	Sharon Mulrooney	Penny Vincenzi
Sophie Kinsella	Kathy Rodgers	Sarah Webb
Jacinta McDevitt		

Nina Bawden   1925-

General

www.ninabawden.net

Hilary Bailey	Caro Fraser	Alison Lurie
Rachel Billington	Jane Gardam	Elizabeth Pewsey
Margaret Drabble	Penelope Lively	Muriel Spark

Stephen Baxter   1957-

Science Fiction: Technical

www.cix.co.uk/~sjbradshaw/baxterium/baxterium.html

BSFA 1995

Poul Anderson	China Miéville
Ben Bova	Robert Reed
Wil McCarthy	Ian Watson
Jack McDevitt	H G Wells
Ian McDonald	

Go to back for lists of:
Authors by Genre • Characters and Series • Prize Winners • Further Reading

Greg Bear 1951- US Science Fiction: Technical
www.gregbear.com

Brian W Aldiss	C J Cherryh	Wil McCarthy
Iain M Banks	Arthur C Clarke	John Meaney
Gregory Benford	Harlan Ellison	Kim Stanley Robinson
David Brin		

M C Beaton 1936- Sco Crime: Police work - UK
also writes as **Marion Chesney** ⚐ PC Hamish MacBeth - Scotland
www.fantasticfiction.co.uk/authors/M_C_Beaton.htm Agatha Raisin, Retired advertising executive

Catherine Aird	Margaret Duffy	Carolyn G Hart
Pauline Bell	Gerald Hammond	Joyce Holms
Clare Curzon	Janis Harrison	Bill Knox

Simon Beaufort 1958- Crime: Historical - Medieval
also writes as **Susanna Gregory** ⚐ Sir Geoffrey Mappestone &
is **Elizabeth Cruwys** Roger of Durham
www.fantasticfiction.co.uk/authors/Simon_Beaufort.htm C12th England

Alys Clare	Michael Jecks	Candace Robb
Paul Doherty	Edward Marston	Joan Wolf
Sylvian Hamilton	Ellis Peters	

Sally Beauman 1944- Glitz & Glamour
also writes as **Vanessa James**

Lisa Appignanesi	Susan Lewis	Una-Mary Parker
Julie Ellis	Judith Michael	Lynne Pemberton
Judi James	Hilary Norman	Caroline Upcher

Matthew Beaumont Lad Lit

Mark Barrowcliffe	Alex George	William Sutcliffe
Nick Earls	Tim Lott	Matt Whyman
Mike Gayle		

Pauline Bell 1938- Crime: Police work - UK
www.fantasticfiction.co.uk/authors/Pauline_Bell.htm ⚐ DI Benny Mitchell - 'Cloughton', Yorkshire
CI Browne & DC Jennie Taylor

Catherine Aird	Janie Bolitho	Patricia Hall
Meg Elizabeth Atkins	Brian Cooper	Stuart Pawson
Robert Barnard	Eileen Dewhurst	Peter Robinson
M C Beaton	Marjorie Eccles	Peter Turnbull

Saul Bellow   1915-2005   US   General

www.saulbellow.org

Martin Amis	Philip Roth	Pulitzer 1976
Nicola Barker	Isaac Bashevis Singer	
Joseph Heller	William Styron	
Amos Oz	John Updike	
Frederic Raphael		

B

Gregory Benford   1941-   US   Science Fiction: Technical

also writes as **Sterling Blake**
www.fantasticfiction.co.uk/authors/Gregory_Benford.htm

Isaac Asimov	Paul J McAuley	BSFA 1980
Greg Bear	Wil McCarthy	
Ben Bova	Brian Stableford	
C J Cherryh	Ian Watson	
Arthur C Clarke		

Anne Bennett   Saga

www.annebennett.co.uk

Julia Bryant	Patricia Grey	Kay Stephens
Jean Chapman	Mary Minton	Janet Woods
Brenda Clarke		

Maggie Bennett   1931-   Saga

www.fantasticfiction.co.uk/authors/Maggie_Bennett.htm

Emma Blair	Margaret Thomson Davis	Meg Hutchinson
Philip Boast	Evelyn Hood	Frances Paige

Peter Benson   1956-   General

Iain Banks	Graham Swift	Authors 1987
Julian Barnes	Colm Toibin	Guardian 1987
Robert Edric		Encore 1990
		S Maugham 1991

Raymond Benson   1955-   US   Adventure/Thriller

also writes as **David Michaels**   ⃛ James Bond
www.raymondbenson.com

Tom Clancy	James Follett	John R Maxim
Ian Fleming	John Gardner	

Go to back for lists of:
Authors by Genre • Characters and Series • Prize winners • Further reading

Carol Berg   1948-   US   Fantasy: Epic
www.sff.net/people/carolberg

Joanne Bertin	Robin Hobb	Robert Newcomb
Sara Douglass	Mercedes Lackey	Melanie Rawn
Terry Goodkind		

B

Elizabeth Berg   1948-   US   General
www.fantasticfiction.co.uk/authors/Elizabeth_Berg.htm

Suzanne Berne	Laurie Graham	Anita Shreve
Fannie Flagg	Jacquelyn Mitchard	Adriana Trigiani
Patricia Gaffney	Anna Quindlen	

Suzanne Berne   US   Adventure/Thriller: Psychological
www.fantasticfiction.co.uk/authors/Suzanne_Berne.htm

Elizabeth Berg	Annie Proulx	Orange 1999
Kate Grenville	Anita Shreve	
Shirley Hazzard	Donna Tartt	
Harper Lee	Adriana Trigiani	Minette Walters

William Bernhardt   1960-   US   Crime: Legal/financial
www.williambernhardt.com

D W Buffa	John Grisham	Phillip Margolin
William Diehl	John Le Carré	Lisa Scottoline
James Grippando	John T Lescroart	

Joanne Bertin   US   Fantasy: Epic
www.weredragon.com

Sarah Ash	James Clemens	Anne McCaffrey
Carol Berg	Jude Fisher	Robert Newcomb

Mark Billingham   Crime: Police work - UK
www.markbillingham.com   ⚑ DI Tom Thorne - London

Stephen Booth	Russell James	Chris Simms
Ken Bruen	Simon Kernick	Boris Starling
Joy Fielding	Val McDermid	Tony Strong
Mo Hayder	Barry Maitland	P J Tracy

Rachel Billington   1942-   General

Nina Bawden	Anne Fine	Elizabeth Jane Howard
Rachel Cusk	Penelope Fitzgerald	Penelope Lively
		Alison Lurie

Maeve Binchy   1940-   Ire

Aga saga

www.maevebinchy.com

Ireland

Margaret Bacon	Adèle Geras	
Sarah Challis	Erin Kaye	
Anne Christie	Geraldine O'Neill	
Anne Doughty	Imogen Parker	Mary Ryan
Rose Doyle	Liz Ryan	Alice Taylor

B

Tim Binding   1947-

Adventure/Thriller

www.contemporarywriters.com/authors/?p=auth167

Francis Cottam	David Lodge
Louis de Bernières	Tim Pears

Charlotte Bingham   1942-

General

www.charlottebingham.com

Elizabeth Adler	Lucinda Edmonds	
Diana Appleyard	Maeve Haran	
Hilary Bailey	Sarah Harrison	
Elizabeth Buchan	Helen Humphreys	Sally Spencer

Harry Bingham   1967-

Adventure/Thriller: Legal/financial

www.fantasticfiction.co.uk/authors/Harry_Bingham.htm

Jonathan Davies	John T Lescroart	Christopher Reich
Reg Gadney	John McLaren	Michael Ridpath
Paul Kilduff	Steve Martini	

Kate Bingham

General

Kate Atkinson	Sue Gee
Margaret Forster	Carol Shields

Carol Birch   1951-

General

Helen Dunmore	Catherine Merriman	
Lesley Glaister	Deborah Moggach	

Cara Black   US

Crime: PI

www.carablack.com

⚘ Aimée Leduc - Paris

Denise Danks	Frank Lean	Zoë Sharp
Liz Evans	Marcia Muller	Cath Staincliffe
Sue Grafton	Sara Paretsky	

Ingrid Black   Ire   Crime: Psychological

www.fantasticfiction.co.uk/authors/Ingrid_Black.htm

Ken Bruen	Mo Hayder	Margaret Murphy
Sarah Diamond	Theresa Monsour	Minette Walters

B Emma Blair   1942-   Sco   Saga

is Iain McPhee   ☃ Drummond Family - Scotland

www.fantasticfiction.co.uk/authors/Emma_Blair.htm

Tessa Barclay	Nora Kay	Eileen Ramsay
Maggie Bennett	Elisabeth McNeill	Jessica Stirling
Christine Marion Fraser	Isobel Neill	

Jessica Blair   1923-   Saga

is William J Spence

www.jessicablair.co.uk

Aileen Armitage	Margaret Graham	Eileen Townsend
Helen Cannam	Eileen Ramsay	Elizabeth Walker
Iris Gower	Margaret Thornton	

Cindy Blake   General

Diana Appleyard	Susie Boyt
Zoë Barnes	Mary Sheepshanks

Marc Blake   Crime: Humour

www.fantasticfiction.co.uk/authors/Marc_Blake.htm

Colin Bateman	Janet Evanovich	Chris Niles
Nicholas Blincoe	Peter Guttridge	Zane Radcliffe
Matthew Branton	Carl Hiaasen	

Alice Blanchard   US   Adventure/Thriller

www.fantasticfiction.co.uk/authors/Alice_Blanchard.htm

Keith Russell Ablow	Stuart Harrison	Scott Smith
John Gilstrap	Paullina Simons	Boston Teran

Faith Bleasdale   Humour

www.faithbleasdale.com

Maggie Gibson	Sue Limb	Linda Taylor
Sarah Grazebrook	Chris Manby	Isabel Wolff
Wendy Holden		

Nicholas Blincoe

Crime: Hardboiled
Manchester

CWA 1998

Jake Arnott	Jeremy Cameron	Kevin Sampson
Marc Blake	Paul Johnston	Mark Timlin
Christopher Brookmyre	Nick Oldham	

Lawrence Block   1938-   US

Crime: Hardboiled

also writes as Chip Harrison,
Paul Kavanagh
www.lawrenceblock.com

☆ Matthew Scudder, Retired policeman
Bernie Rhodenbarr, Burglar
John Keller, Hit man
New York

Raymond Chandler	Elmore Leonard	Reggie Nadelson
Loren D Estleman	John D Macdonald	Robert B Parker
Dashiell Hammett	Ross Macdonald	

Giles Blunt   1952-   Can

Crime: Police work - Canada

www.gilesblunt.com

☆ Det John Cardinal & Det Lisa Delorme - 'Algonquin Bay'

Michael Connelly	Henning Mankell	Ridley Pearson
Steve Hamilton	Archer Mayor	Kathy Reichs
Donald Harstad	Theresa Monsour	Dana Stabenow
Barry Maitland	Jonathan Nasaw	Jess Walter

Philip Boast   1952-

Saga

www.fantasticfiction.co.uk/authors/Philip_Boast.htm

☆ Ben London - London

Rosemary Aitken	Harry Cole	Beryl Kingston
Aileen Armitage	Patricia Grey	Victor Pemberton
Maggie Bennett	Lena Kennedy	Elizabeth Waite

Dermot Bolger   1959-   Ire

General

www.fireandwater.com/authors/default.aspx?id=596

John Banville	Colum McCann	Glenn Patterson
Roddy Doyle	Brian Moore	Colm Toibin
Patrick McCabe	Joseph O'Connor	Niall Williams

Janie Bolitho   1950-

Crime: Police work - UK

www.fantasticfiction.co.uk/authors/Janie_Bolitho.htm

☆ DCI Ian Roper
Rose Trevelyan, Painter
Cornwall

Pauline Bell	Kate Ellis	Peter Robinson
W J Burley	Ann Granger	Betty Rowlands
Agatha Christie	J M Gregson	Sally Spencer
Freda Davies	Roy Hart	Alison Taylor

25

B

Hilary Bonner 1949- Crime: Psychological

www.fantasticfiction.co.uk/authors/Hilary_Bonner.htm ⚲ DCI Rose Piper - Devon

Jane Adams
Jeffrey Ashford
Stephen Booth
Robert Goddard
Gregory Hall
Morag Joss
Iain McDowall
Sarah Rayne
Alison Taylor

Martin Booth 1944-2004 Adventure/Thriller

www.fantasticfiction.co.uk/authors/Martin_Booth.htm

James Clavell
Bryce Courtenay
Peter May
William Rivière

Stephen Booth 1957- Crime: Psychological

www.stephen-booth.com ⚲ DC Ben Cooper & DS Diane Fry - Peak District

Rennie Airth
Vivien Armstrong
Mark Billingham
Hilary Bonner
Iain McDowall
Jill McGown
Barry Maitland
Priscilla Masters
Ed O'Connor
Danuta Reah
Alison Taylor
Minette Walters

Alice Borchardt US Fantasy: Myth

www.fantasticfiction.co.uk/authors/Alice_Borchardt.htm

Poppy Z Brite
Mark Chadbourn
Storm Constantine
Sylvie Germain
Katharine Kerr
Megan Lindholm
Holly Lisle
Juliet Marillier
S P Somtow

Rose Boucheron Saga

Elizabeth Adler
Julia Bryant
Anita Burgh
Josephine Cox
Sarah Harrison
Elizabeth Jane Howard
Beryl Kingston
Janet Woods

Anthony Bourdain 1956- US Crime: Hardboiled

www.anthonybourdain.com

Tim Dorsey
Bill Fitzhugh
Kinky Friedman
Vicki Hendricks
Simon Kernick
Danny King
Joe R Lansdale
José Latour
Chuck Palahniuk
Laurence Shames
John B Spencer
Sarah Strohmeyer

Ben Bova 1932- US Science Fiction: Space and time

www.benbova.net

Isaac Asimov
Stephen Baxter
Gregory Benford
Greg Egan
Larry Niven
Kim Stanley Robinson

Elizabeth Bowen   1899-1973   Ire   General

www.fantasticfiction.co.uk/authors/Elizabeth_Bowen.htm

Anita Brookner   Penelope Lively   Iris Murdoch
Graham Greene   Candia McWilliam   William Trevor
Jennifer Johnston

B

David Bowker   Horror

www.fantasticfiction.co.uk/authors/David_Bowker.htm   ⚘ CS Vernon Lavelle

Ramsey Campbell   Christopher Fowler
John Farris   Phil Rickman

Harry Bowling   1931-1999   Saga
                                            Tanner Trilogy - London

Harry Cole   Anna King   Victor Pemberton
Josephine Cox   Elizabeth Lord   Mary Jane Staples
Emma Dally   Margaret Pemberton   Elizabeth Waite

C J Box   US   Crime: Amateur sleuth

www.cjbox.net   ⚘ Joe Pickett, National warden - 'Saddlestring', Wyoming

James Lee Burke   Donald Harstad   Michael McGarrity
Loren D Estleman   Tony Hillerman   Dana Stabenow
Steve Hamilton

William Boyd   1952-   General

www.contemporarywriters.com/authors/?p=auth17

Margaret Elphinstone   Matthew Kneale   Whitbread 1981
Giles Foden   Alistair MacLeod   Mail 1982
Alan Gurganus   Simon Mawer   S Maugham 1982
Philip Hensher   Tim Parks   Black 1990
Christopher Hope   Richard Powers
Alan Isler   James Robertson

Clare Boylan   1948-   Ire   Saga

www.fantasticfiction.co.uk/authors/Clare_Boylan.htm

Michael Collins   Mary Ryan   Peta Tayler
Edna O'Brien   Diana Saville   Alice Taylor
Wendy Perriam   Patricia Scanlan   Sue Townsend

Go to back for lists of:
Authors by Genre • Characters and Series • Prize Winners • Further Reading

T Coraghessan Boyle   1948-   US   Humour
www.tcboyle.com

Don DeLillo	Jay McInerney	Evelyn Waugh
Gabriel Garcia Márquez	Paul Micou	Tom Wolfe

B Susie Boyt   1969-   Chick Lit
www.susieboyt.com

Jessica Adams	Jenn Crowell	Lesley Pearse
Cecelia Ahern	Lucy Ellman	Lynne Truss
Cindy Blake	Julie Highmore	Fiona Walker

Malcolm Bradbury   1932-2000   General
www.fantasticfiction.co.uk/authors/Malcolm_Bradbury.htm

Kingsley Amis	Michael Frayn	Keith Waterhouse
Nicholson Baker	John Mortimer	A N Wilson
Melvyn Bragg	Nicholas Shakespeare	

Ray Bradbury   1920-   US   Science Fiction: Space and time
www.raybradbury.com

Poul Anderson	Robert A Heinlein	Ken MacLeod
J G Ballard	Aldous Huxley	George Orwell
Harlan Ellison	H P Lovecraft	Roger Zelazny

Tom Bradby   Adventure/Thriller
www.fantasticfiction.co.uk/authors/Tom_Bradby.htm

Boris Akunin	Alan Folsom	A J Quinnell
Daniel Easterman	Stephen Leather	Tim Sebastian
Clive Egleton	Robert Ludlum	Gerald Seymour

Barbara Taylor Bradford   1933-   Saga
www.barbarataylorbradford.com   ⚹ Emma Harte

Elizabeth Adler	Sidney Sheldon	Nicola Thorne
Frankie McGowan	Danielle Steel	Penny Vincenzi
Una-Mary Parker	Rosie Thomas	Elizabeth Walker

Marion Zimmer Bradley   1930-1999   US   Fantasy: Epic
www.mzbfm.com

Barbara Hambly	Holly Lisle	Caiseal Mor
Robert Holdstock	Morgan Llywelyn	Melanie Rawn
Helen Hollick	Juliet Marillier	Jan Siegel
Tanith Lee	Julian May	Sheri S Tepper

Rita Bradshaw — Saga

NE England

Catherine Cookson
Ruth Hamilton
Una Horne

Meg Hutchinson
Freda Lightfoot

Annie Murray
Lynda Page

B

Melvyn Bragg 1939- — General

www.contemporarywriters.com/authors/?p=auth237

Malcolm Bradbury
A S Byatt
Margaret Drabble
Sarah Hall

Thomas Hardy
Catherine Merriman
Stanley Middleton
Andrew O'Hagan

WHSmith 2000

Matthew Branton 1969- — General

home.hawaii.rr.com/matthewbranton/feedyourhead.html

Mark Barrowcliffe
Marc Blake

Bret Easton Ellis
Alex Garland

William Sutcliffe

Lilian Jackson Braun 1916- US — Crime: Amateur sleuth

www.fantasticfiction.co.uk/authors/Lilian_Jackson_Braun.htm

🏃 Jim Qwilleran, Journalist
& Yum Yum & Koko, Siamese cats -
'Moose County', US

Marian Babson
Paula Gosling

Janis Harrison
Carolyn G Hart

Charlotte MacLeod
Margaret Maron

Celia Brayfield 1945- — Glitz & Glamour

Louise Bagshawe
Maria Barrett
Jackie Collins

Jilly Cooper
Barbara Delinsky
Lucinda Edmonds

Judith Michael
Hilary Norman
Victoria Routledge

Chaz Brenchley 1959- — Horror

www.chazbrenchley.co.uk

David Ambrose
Mark Anthony
Simon Clark
Nancy Collins

Sara Douglass
Stephen Gallagher
Andrew Klavan
David Martin

British Fantasy 1998

K J Parker

Go to back for lists of:
Authors by Genre
Characters and Series
Prize Winners
Further Reading

Simon Brett 1945-

www.fantasticfiction.co.uk/authors/Simon_Brett.htm

Crime: Amateur sleuth

🏃 Charles Paris, Actor • Mrs Pargeter
Carole Seddon - 'Fethering'
Sussex

B

Marian Babson	Jonathan Gash	Simon Shaw
Jo Bannister	Carolyn G Hart	Charles Spencer
Sarah Caudwell	Veronica Heley	Stella Whitelaw

Gene Brewer US

Fantasy: Contemporary

www.genebrewer.com

Bill Fitzhugh	Jeff Noon	Michael Marshall Smith
John Meaney	Adam Roberts	

Marius Brill

Humour

Colin Bateman	Carl Hiaasen
Jasper Fforde	Malcolm Pryce

Dougie Brimson

Lad Lit

www.brimson.net

Paul Burke	Cy Flood	Kevin Sampson
Colin Butts	John King	

David Brin 1950- US

Science Fiction: Space opera

www.davidbrin.com

Greg Bear	Alan Dean Foster	Robert Reed
John Brosnan	Brian Herbert	Dan Simmons
C J Cherryh	Frank Herbert	Robert Charles Wilson

Louise Brindley

Saga
Tanquillan Series

Vanessa Alexander	Susan Sallis	Margaret Thornton
Aileen Armitage	Titia Sutherland	Janet Woods
Sara Hylton		

André Brink 1935- SA

General

J M Coetzee	Nadine Gordimer
Jim Crace	Christopher Hope

Go to back for lists of:
Authors by Genre • Characters and Series • Prize Winners • Further Reading

Poppy Z Brite   1964-   US   Horror
www.poppyzbrite.com

Kelley Armstrong	Tom Holland	Kim Newman
Alice Borchardt	Tanya Huff	Anne Rice
Nancy Collins	Brian Lumley	S P Somtow

B

Suzanne Brockmann   US   Adventure/Thriller
🏃 US Navy 'Seal' teams
www.suzannebrockmann.com

John Case	Vince Flynn	Stanley Pottinger
Nelson DeMille	David Hagberg	

Po Bronson   1964-   US   Crime: Legal/financial

Linda Davies	Brad Meltzer
Paul Kilduff	Michael Ridpath

Amanda Brookfield   1960-   Aga saga
www.fantasticfiction.co.uk/authors/Amanda_Brookfield.htm

Erica James	Karen Nelson	Titia Sutherland
Kate Long	Elizabeth Palmer	Sophia Watson
Santa Montefiore	Elizabeth Pewsey	Madeleine Wickham

Christopher Brookmyre   1968-   Sco   Crime: Humour
🏃 Jack Parlabane, Journalist - Scotland
www.brookmyre.co.uk

Nicholas Blincoe	Christopher Fowler	Douglas Lindsay
Christopher Buckley	Jack Harvey	Malcolm Pryce
Jeremy Cameron	James Hawes	Zane Radcliffe
Bill Fitzhugh	Carl Hiaasen	Kevin Sampson

Anita Brookner   1928-   General
www.contemporarywriters.com/authors/?p=auth19

Barbara Anderson	Charlotte Mendelson	Booker 1984
Elizabeth Bowen	Gwendoline Riley	
A S Byatt	Bernice Rubens	
Penelope Fitzgerald	Salley Vickers	

Geraldine Brooks   US   Historical
www.geraldinebrooks.com

Tracy Chevalier	Anita Diamant
Will Davenport	Rose Tremain

Terry Brooks 1944- US Fantasy: Epic

www.terrybrooks.net

James Clemens	David Gemmell	Mickey Zucker Reichert
Kate Elliott	John Marco	J R R Tolkien
Raymond E Feist	Elizabeth Moon	Margaret Weis
Maggie Furey	Stan Nicholls	Tad Williams

John Brosnan 1947-2005 Aus Science Fiction: Space opera

also wrote as Simon Childer, James Blackstone, Harry Adam Knight, John Raymond
www.fantasticfiction.co.uk/authors/John_Brosnan.htm

Poul Anderson	Harlan Ellison	Larry Niven
David Brin	Colin Greenland	Robert Reed
C J Cherryh		

Benita Brown Saga

C19th Tyneside

Catherine Cookson	Mary McCarthy	Elizabeth Murphy
Joan Jonker	Beryl Matthews	Mary Jane Staples
Margaret Kaine		

Dale Brown 1956- US Adventure/Thriller

www.megafortress.com ⚡ Patrick McLanahan - Aviation

Richard Herman	Kyle Mills	Julian Jay Savarin
Graham Hurley	John J Nance	James Siegel
Gordon Kent	Patrick Robinson	Robin White

Dan Brown 1964- US Adventure/Thriller

www.danbrown.com ⚡ Professor Robert Langdon - Harvard University

Lincoln Child	Vince Flynn	John J Nance
Michael Cordy	Alan Folsom	Douglas Preston
Michael Crichton	David Hagberg	A J Quinnell
Sean Flannery	Tobias Hill	P J Tracy

Eric Brown 1960- Science Fiction: Near future

www.ericbrown.co.uk

Steve Aylett	Paul Johnston	Justina Robson
Pat Cadigan	James Lovegrove	Neal Stephenson
William Gibson	Adam Roberts	Bruce Sterling
K W Jeter		

Go to back for lists of:
Authors by Genre • Characters and Series • Prize Winners • Further Reading

Sandra Brown 1948- US Glitz & Glamour

also writes as **Laura Jordan, Rachel Ryan, Erin St Claire**
www.sandrabrown.net

Candace Bushnell	Jayne Ann Krentz	Nora Roberts
Olivia Goldsmith	Roberta Latow	Penny Vincenzi
Judi James	Harold Robbins	

B

Ken Bruen 1951- Ire Crime: Hardboiled

www.modestyarbor.com/kenbruen.html

🏃 DCI Roberts & DS Brant - London
Jack Taylor, Former policeman - Galway

Vivien Armstrong	Robert Edric	Russell James
Mark Billingham	Barry Eisler	Simon Kernick
Ingrid Black	Patricia Hall	David Peace
Paul Charles	Bill James	Martyn Waites

Steven Brust 1955- US Fantasy: Epic

www.dreamcafe.com

Mark Anthony	Elizabeth Haydon	Janny Wurts
Piers Anthony	Margaret Weis	Roger Zelazny

Julia Bryant Saga

www.juliabryant-online.com

🏃 Forrest Family - Portsmouth

Anne Bennett	Elizabeth Elgin	Anna Jacobs
Rose Boucheron	June Francis	Janet Woods

Elizabeth Buchan 1948- Aga saga

www.elizabethbuchan.com

Charlotte Bingham	Angela Huth	Romantic 1994
Kate Fenton	Anna Maxted	
Olivia Goldsmith	Juliette Mead	
Eileen Goudge	Fay Weldon	Sarah Woodhouse

James Buchan 1954- Adventure/Thriller

James Adams	John Le Carré	Guardian 1984 & 1985
Alan Judd	Gerald Seymour	Higham 1984
		Whitbread 1995

John Buchan 1875-1940 Sco Adventure/Thriller

www.johnbuchansociety.co.uk

Eric Ambler	Joseph Conrad	Robert Goddard
Jon Cleary	Ian Fleming	

Edna Buchanan   1939-   US   Crime: Amateur sleuth

www.ednabuchanan.com   ⚸ Britt Montero, Journalist - Miami

Alafair Burke	James Hall	Laura Lippman
Jan Burke	Denise Hamilton	Liza Marklund
Sue Grafton	Sparkle Hayter	Sara Paretsky

B

Christopher Buckley   1952-   US   Crime: Humour

www.fantasticfiction.co.uk/authors/Christopher_Buckley.htm

Colin Bateman	Bill Fitzhugh	Malcolm Pryce
Christopher Brookmyre	Carl Hiaasen	Zane Radcliffe

D W Buffa   US   Crime: Legal/financial

www.dwbuffa.com   ⚸ Joseph Antonelli, Lawyer - Portland, Oregon

William Bernhardt	John Grisham	Lisa Scottoline
Alafair Burke	Phillip Margolin	Susan R Sloan
Linda Fairstein	Perri O'Shaughnessy	Robert K Tanenbaum
James Grippando	Richard North Patterson	Scott Turow

Lois McMaster Bujold   1947-   US   Science Fiction: Space opera

www.dendarii.com   ⚸ Lord Miles Vorkosigan

Dan Abnett	David Feintuch	Anne McCaffrey
Orson Scott Card	Colin Greenland	Elizabeth Moon
C J Cherryh	Peter F Hamilton	Charles Stross
Ben Counter		

Chris Bunch   1943-   US   Fantasy: Epic

www.fantasticfiction.co.uk/authors/Chris_Bunch.htm

Dan Abnett	David Feintuch	John Marco
C J Cherryh	Maggie Furey	Harry Turtledove
Ben Counter	Robert Jordan	Janny Wurts
David A Drake		

John Burdett   Adventure/Thriller: Legal/financial

www.fantasticfiction.co.uk/authors/John_Burdett.htm

Tom Clancy	Robert Ludlum
John Le Carré	Gerald Seymour

Anthony Burgess   1917-93   General

www.fantasticfiction.co.uk/authors/Anthony_Burgess.htm

Peter Ackroyd	William Golding	George Orwell
Margaret Atwood	Niall Griffiths	Salman Rushdie
Gabriel Garcia Márquez	Vladimir Nabokov	Angus Wilson

Anita Burgh   1937-   Saga

also writes as **Annie Leith**
www.anitaburgh.com

Elizabeth Adler	Teresa Crane	Claire Rayner
Rose Boucheron	Winston Graham	Sue Sully

B

Alafair Burke   US   Adventure/Thriller: Legal/financial

www.alafairburke.com   ◟ DDA Samantha Kincaid - Portland, Oregon

Edna Buchanan	Sue Grafton	Nancy Taylor Rosenberg
D W Buffa	Steve Martini	John Sandford
Linda Fairstein	Perri O'Shaughnessy	

James Lee Burke   1936-   US   Crime: Hardboiled

www.jamesleeburke.com   ◟ Dave Robicheaux, Policeman - New Iberia, Louisiana
Billy-Bob Holland, Attorney - Texas; Montana

C J Box	William Heffernan	CWA 1998
Michael Connelly	Tony Hillerman	
James Crumley	Jonathon King	
Barry Eisler	Michael Malone	James Sallis
James Hall	George P Pelecanos	John Sandford

Jan Burke   1953-   US   Crime: Amateur sleuth

www.janburke.com   ◟ Irene Kelly, Journalist - California

Edna Buchanan	Denise Hamilton	Claire McNab
Caroline Carver	Faye Kellerman	Liza Marklund
Meg Gardiner	Laurie King	Margaret Maron
Sue Grafton	Laura Lippman	Chris Niles

Paul Burke   Lad Lit: Humour

◟ Frank Dempsey

Richard Asplin	Cy Flood	Mil Millington
Dougie Brimson	John King	Kevin Sampson

W J Burley   1914-2002   Crime: Police work - UK

www.fantasticfiction.co.uk/authors/W_J_Burley.htm   ◟ Supt Wycliffe - Cornwall

Catherine Aird	Freda Davies	Roy Hart
Janie Bolitho	Kate Ellis	June Thomson
Ann Cleeves		

Go to back for lists of:
Authors by Genre • Characters and Series • Prize Winners • Further Reading

35

Mark Burnell 1964- Adventure/Thriller

www.fantasticfiction.co.uk/authors/Mark_Burnell.htm 🏃 Stephanie Patrick - Northumberland

| Robin Cook | Patricia Hall | Tim Wilson |
| John Fullerton | Jefferson Parker | |

B

Betty Burton Saga

www.bettyburton.co.uk 🏃 Lu Wilmott - London • Nugent Family - Hampshire

Tessa Barclay	Harriet Hudson	Sally Stewart
Elizabeth Daish	Freda Lightfoot	Alison Stuart
Elizabeth Darrell	Pamela Oldfield	

Candace Bushnell 1959- US Glitz & Glamour

www.fantasticfiction.co.uk/authors/Candace_Bushnell.htm

| Sandra Brown | Barbara Delinsky | Jayne Ann Krentz |
| Jackie Collins | Olivia Goldsmith | Nora Roberts |

Gwendoline Butler 1922- Crime: Police work - UK

also writes as **Jennie Melville** 🏃 Com John Coffin - London
www.fantasticfiction.co.uk/authors/Gwendoline_Butler.htm Major Mearns & Sgt Denny - C18th England

Bruce Alexander	Deryn Lake	CWA 1973
Paul Charles	Janet Laurence	Romantic 1981
Ann Cleeves	David Liss	
Janet Gleeson	Hannah March	Iain Pears
Cynthia Harrod-Eagles	Fidelis Morgan	David Pirie

Robert Olen Butler 1945- US General

www.fantasticfiction.co.uk/authors/Robert_Olen_Butler.htm

| Pete Dexter | Richard Ford | Pulitzer 1993 |
| Andre Dubus | David Guterson | |

Ron Butlin 1949- Sco General

www.contemporarywriters.com/authors/?p=auth02C19L040412626885

| A L Kennedy | Ruaridh Nicoll | Ali Smith |
| Duncan McLean | Paul Sayer | Alan Warner |

Colin Butts Lad Lit

www.fantasticfiction.co.uk/authors/Colin_Butts.htm

| Dougie Brimson | Cy Flood | Kevin Sampson |
| Ben Elton | John King | Sean Thomas |

A S Byatt   1936-   General

www.asbyatt.com

Melvyn Bragg	Penelope Fitzgerald	Booker 1990
Anita Brookner	Penelope Lively	Irish Times 1990
Angela Carter	Candia McWilliam	
Margaret Drabble	Marianne Wiggins	Angus Wilson

B
C

Colette Caddle   Ire   Chick Lit

Martina Devlin	Monica McInerney	Kate O'Riordan
Sabine Durrant	Amanda Murphy	Morag Prunty
Tara Heavey	Anita Notaro	Kate Thompson

Pat Cadigan   1953-   US   Science Fiction: Near future

www.fantasticfiction.co.uk/authors/Pat_Cadigan.htm

Eric Brown	James Lovegrove	Arthur C Clarke 1992 & 1995
Greg Egan	Ian McDonald	
Jon Courtenay Grimwood	Jeff Noon	
K W Jeter	J D Robb	

Dawn Cairns   Ire   Chick Lit

Zoë Barnes	Marissa Mackle	Kathy Rodgers
Louise Kean	Sharon Mulrooney	Patricia Scanlan
Shari Low	Sheila O'Flanagan	

Brian Callison   1934-   Sco   Sea: Modern

www.fantasticfiction.co.uk/authors/Brian_Callison.htm

Alexander Fullerton	Justin Scott	Antony Trew
James Pattinson	Terence Strong	Richard Woodman
Douglas Reeman		

Claire Calman   Chick Lit

Alexandra Carew	Sarah Mason	Kate Saunders
Maeve Haran	Sheila Norton	Isabel Wolff
Christina Jones	Tyne O'Connell	Liz Young

Jeremy Cameron   Crime: Hardboiled
www.fantasticfiction.co.uk/authors/Jeremy_Cameron.htm   ⚘ Nicky Burkett - London

Jake Arnott	Martina Cole	Danny King
Nicholas Blincoe	James Hawes	Mark Timlin
Christopher Brookmyre	Paul Johnston	

Andrea Camilleri 1925- It
Crime: Police work - Italy
www.fantasticfiction.co.uk/authors/Andrea_Camilleri.htm

⚐ Insp Salvo Montalbano - Sicily

Michael Dibdin	David Hewson	Georges Simenon
Luiz Alfredo Garcia-Roza	Donna Leon	Qiu Xiaolong
Juan Goytisolo	Arturo Perez-Reverte	

Alexandra Campbell
Glitz & Glamour

Catherine Alliott	Jilly Cooper	Madge Swindells
Raffaella Barker	Olivia Goldsmith	Caroline Upcher

C

Ramsey Campbell 1946-
Horror
www.ramseycampbell.com

David Bowker	H P Lovecraft	British Fantasy 1991 & 1994
Jonathan Carroll	S P Somtow	
Christopher Fowler	Whitley Strieber	
Stephen Laws	T M Wright	

Rebecca Campbell
Chick Lit
www.fantasticfiction.co.uk/authors/Rebecca_Campbell.htm

Cecelia Ahern	Lisa Jewell	Shari Low
Lynne Barrett-Lee	Josie Lloyd & Emlyn Rees	Jane Wenham-Jones

Trudi Canavan 1969- Aus
Fantasy: Epic
www.spin.net.au/~trudi/canavan.htm

Sara Douglass	Ursula K Le Guin	William Nicholson
Terry Goodkind	Juliet Marillier	Garth Nix

Ethan Canin 1960- US
General

E L Doctorow	Jonathan Franzen	Sue Miller
Jeffrey Eugenides	Henry James	John Updike
F Scott Fitzgerald	Garrison Keillor	

Helen Cannam
Saga

Vanessa Alexander	Elizabeth Elgin	Kay Stephens
Aileen Armitage	Sheelagh Kelly	Eileen Townsend
Jessica Blair	Elvi Rhodes	Elizabeth Walker

Go to back for lists of:
Authors by Genre • Characters and Series • Prize Winners • Further Reading

Stephen J Cannell
1941- US   Adventure/Thriller

www.cannell.com   ⚘ Det Shane Scully - Los Angeles Police Dept

Nelson DeMille	Robert Littell	David Mason
John Lawton	James Long	Martin Cruz Smith

Lorenzo Carcaterra
1954- US   Adventure/Thriller

www.fantasticfiction.co.uk/authors/Lorenzo_Carcaterra.htm

Jeff Gulvin	Thomas Kelly	Sidney Sheldon
George V Higgins	Mario Puzo	

C

Orson Scott Card
1951- US   Science Fiction: Space opera

www.hatrack.com

Lois McMaster Bujold	Joe Haldeman	Charles Stross
David Feintuch	Michael P Kube-McDowell	David Zindell
Alan Dean Foster	Dan Simmons	

Alexandra Carew
Chick Lit

Maggie Alderson	Emily Barr	Francesca Clementis
Anita Anderson	Claire Calman	

Helen Carey
Saga

www.helencarey.co.uk   ⚘ Lavender Road Series - London

Harry Cole	Anna King	Mary Jane Staples
Pamela Evans	Margaret Mayhew	Elizabeth Waite
Lilian Harry	Sally Spencer	Dee Williams

Peter Carey
1943- Aus   General

www.fantasticfiction.co.uk/authors/Peter_Carey.htm

J G Ballard	Thomas Keneally	Booker 1988 & 2001
John Banville	David Malouf	Commonwealth 1998 & 2001
Robert Drewe	Patrick White	
Gabriel Garcia Márquez	Tim Winton	
Tobias Hill		

Irene Carr
1920s-   Saga

NE England

Elizabeth Gill	Sheila Jansen	Wendy Robertson
Una Horne	Brenda McBryde	Janet MacLeod Trotter
Anna Jacobs	Denise Robertson	

Jaye Carroll   Ire   Chick Lit

Suzanne Higgins
Jacinta McDevitt
Jill Mansell

Freya North
Adele Parks

Carmen Reid
Kathy Rodgers

Jonathan Carroll   1949-   US   Horror

www.jonathancarroll.com

Clive Barker
Ramsey Campbell
James Cobb

Christopher Fowler
Graham Joyce
Peter Straub

British Fantasy 1992

C

Jonathan Carroll   1949-   US   Fantasy: Dark

www.jonathancarroll.com

Mark Anthony
Ben Counter
John Crowley

Stephen Donaldson
Michael Moorcock

Janny Wurts
Jonathan Wylie

Michael Carson   1946-   General

Jonathan Coe
Alan Gurganus

Alan Hollinghurst
Evelyn Waugh

Edmund White

Paul Carson   1949-   Ire   Crime: Medical

www.paulcarson.net

Paul Adam
Robin Cook
Patricia D Cornwell

Tess Gerritsen
Ken McClure

Michael Palmer
Leah Ruth Robinson

Angela Carter   1940-92   General

www.fantasticfiction.co.uk/authors/Angela_Carter.htm

Kate Atkinson
A S Byatt
Alison Fell
Ben Okri

Michèle Roberts
Iain Sinclair
Fay Weldon
Jeanette Winterson

Black 1984

Charlotte Carter   US   Crime: Amateur sleuth

www.fantasticfiction.co.uk/authors/Charlotte_Carter.htm

🏃 Nanette Hayes, Saxophonist
New York

Ace Atkins
Kinky Friedman

Sara Paretsky
James Sallis

Alexander McCall Smith
Valerie Wilson Wesley

Justin Cartwright 1945- SA General

www.fantasticfiction.co.uk/authors/Justin_Cartwright.htm

Martin Amis	William Nicholson
J M Coetzee	John Updike
Graham Greene	Evelyn Waugh
Christopher Hope	Rebecca Wells

Caroline Carver Adventure/Thriller: Amateur sleuth

www.carolinecarver.com

⚐ India Kane, Journalist - Australia

C

Jan Burke	G M Ford	Hazel Holt
Sarah Diamond	Denise Hamilton	Sarah Rayne

Raymond Carver 1939-88 US General

www.fantasticfiction.co.uk/authors/Raymond_Carver.htm

Barbara Anderson	Philip Hensher	Haruki Murakami
Richard Ford	Alice Munro	Joyce Carol Oates
Ernest Hemingway		

John Case 1943- US Adventure/Thriller

also writes as James Eliot; *is* Jim & Carolyn Hougan
www.fantasticfiction.co.uk/authors/John_Case.htm

Suzanne Brockmann	Lury Gibson	Gareth O'Callaghan
Michael Cordy	Jean-Christophe Grangé	Douglas Preston
Daniel Easterman	Bill Napier	Mark T Sullivan

Sarah Caudwell 1939-2000 Crime: Amateur sleuth

was Sarah Cockburn

⚐ Hilary Tamar, Law professor

www.fantasticfiction.co.uk/authors/Sarah_Caudwell.htm

Marian Babson	Ruth Dudley Edwards	Hazel Holt
Simon Brett	Jonathan Gash	Simon Shaw

Mark Chadbourn 1960- Fantasy: Contemporary

www.markchadbourn.com

Alice Borchardt	David Eddings	Katharine Kerr
Charles de Lint	Terry Goodkind	Jan Siegel
Stephen Donaldson	Guy Gavriel Kay	David Zindell

Elizabeth Chadwick Historical

also writes as Nancy Herndon
www.elizabethchadwick.com

Elizabeth Aston	Barbara Erskine	Rosalind Laker
Will Davenport	Georgette Heyer	Sharon Penman
Dorothy Dunnett		

Sarah Challis — Aga saga

Maeve Binchy	Rebecca Gregson	Santa Montefiore
Anne Christie	Julie Highmore	Rosamunde Pilcher
Patricia Fawcett	Sarah MacDonald	Peta Tayler

Robert Chalmers — General

David Baddiel	Nick Hornby
James Delingpole	Willy Russell

C

Clare Chambers   1966- — General
www.fantasticfiction.co.uk/authors/Clare_Chambers.htm

Margaret Atwood	Elizabeth Pewsey
Katie Fforde	Mary Wesley

Joy Chambers   Aus — Historical
www.joychambers.com

Elizabeth Darrell	Julie Garwood	Wilbur Smith
June Drummond	Juliette Mead	

Raymond Chandler   1888-1959   US — Crime: PI
www.bookreporter.com/authors/au-chandler-raymond.asp

🏃 Philip Marlowe • John Delmas
Los Angeles

Lawrence Block	Stuart M Kaminsky	George P Pelecanos
James Hadley Chase	John D Macdonald	James Sallis
Harlan Coben	Ross Macdonald	John Shannon
Robert Crais	Reggie Nadelson	Robert Wilson

Jean Chapman — Saga
www.leicesterwriters.org.uk/LWC-JeanChapman.htm

Donna Baker	Elizabeth Gill	Annie Murray
Anne Bennett	Una Horne	Denise Robertson
June Francis	Rosalind Laker	Wendy Robertson

Paul Charles — Crime: Police work - UK
www.fantasticfiction.co.uk/authors/Paul_Charles.htm

🏃 DI Christy Kennedy - London

Ken Bruen	Colin Dexter	Russell James
Gwendoline Butler	Patricia Hall	Susan B Kelly
Brian Cooper	Graham Hurley	Maureen O'Brien
Judith Cutler	Graham Ison	Martyn Waites

Jerome Charyn   1937-   US   Crime: Hardboiled

www.jeromecharyn.com   ⚐ Det Isaac Sidel - New York

David Cray   Thomas Laird   George P Pelecanos
James Ellroy   Dennis Lehane   Jim Thompson
George V Higgins   Carol O'Connell   Jess Walter

James Hadley Chase   1906-85   US   Crime: Hardboiled

also wrote as James L Docherty, Ambrose Grant,   ⚐ Dave Fenner • Vic Malloy
Raymond Marshall; *was* René Brabazon Raymond   Steve Harmas • Frank Terrell
www.fantasticfiction.co.uk/authors/James_Hadley_Chase.htm   Mark Girland • Helga Rolfe

Raymond Chandler   Stuart M Kaminsky   Ross Macdonald
Dashiell Hammett   John D Macdonald   Robert B Parker
Vicki Hendricks

Bruce Chatwin   1940-1989   General

www.brucechatwin.com

Julian Barnes   Patrick McGrath   Black 1982
Margaret Elphinstone   Robert Nye   Whitbread 1982
John Fowles   Barry Unsworth
Patrick McCabe

Amit Chaudhuri   1962-   Ind   General

www.contemporarywriters.com/authors/?p=auth21

John Masters   Arundhati Roy   Betty Trask 1991
Gita Mehta   Salman Rushdie   Encore 1994
Rohinton Mistry   Vikram Seth
R K Narayan   Zadie Smith

Mavis Cheek   Humour

www.fantasticfiction.co.uk/authors/Mavis_Cheek.htm

Isla Dewar   Sue Limb   Lynne Truss
Catherine Feeny   Shena Mackay   Arabella Weir
Jane Green   Ben Richards

C J Cherryh   1942-   US   Science Fiction: Space opera

www.cherryh.com

Greg Bear   John Brosnan   Alan Dean Foster
Gregory Benford   Lois McMaster Bujold   Colin Greenland
David Brin   David Feintuch   Peter F Hamilton

Go to back for lists of:
Authors by Genre • Characters and Series • Prize Winners • Further Reading

C J Cherryh 1942- US — Fantasy: Myth

www.cherryh.com

Chris Bunch
Kate Elliott
Sylvie Germain
Barbara Hambly

Stephen R Lawhead
Tanith Lee
Megan Lindholm

George R R Martin
L E Modesitt Jr
Sheri S Tepper

Marion Chesney 1936- Sco — Historical

also writes as M C Beaton
www.fantasticfiction.co.uk/authors/Marion_Chesney.htm

Catherine Coulter
Jude Deveraux

Georgette Heyer
Amanda Quick

Tracy Chevalier 1962- US — Historical

www.tchevalier.com

Geraldine Brooks
Will Davenport
Stevie Davies
Maggie Gee

Anne Haverty
Andrew Miller
Christopher Peachment
Maureen Peters

James Runcie
Jane Stevenson
Salley Vickers
Susan Vreeland

Lee Child 1954- — Adventure/Thriller

www.leechild.com

♀ Jack Reacher, ex Military policeman - Florida

TGR 1999

Conor Cregan
William Diehl
John Gilstrap
James Hall

Graham Hurley
Donald James
Michael Marshall
Gareth O'Callaghan

Lincoln Child 1957- US — Adventure/Thriller

also writes jointly with Douglas Preston
www.prestonchild.com

Dan Brown
Daniel Easterman

Douglas Preston
A J Quinnell

Agatha Christie 1890-1976 — Crime: Amateur sleuth

also wrote as Mary Westmacott
www.agathachristie.com

♀ Miss Marple
Hercule Poirot

Catherine Aird
Rennie Airth
Boris Akunin
Margery Allingham

Janie Bolitho
Natasha Cooper
Ngaio Marsh
Gladys Mitchell

David Roberts
Dorothy L Sayers
June Thomson
Patricia Wentworth

Anne Christie   Sco   General

Maeve Binchy	Adèle Geras	
Sarah Challis	Sarah MacDonald	

Regi Claire   Switz   General

Nicola Barker	Janice Galloway	Amy Tan
Michelle de Kretser	Catherine Lim	

Tom Clancy   1947-   US   Adventure/Thriller **C**

www.fantasticfiction.co.uk/authors/Tom_Clancy.htm   ☆ Jack Ryan • Net Force Explorers

Michael Asher	David Hagberg	Gordon Kent
Raymond Benson	Brian Haig	Kyle Mills
John Burdett	Eric L Harry	John J Nance
Duncan Falconer	Paul Henke	James Thayer

Alys Clare   1944-   Crime: Historical - Medieval

also writes as **Elizabeth Harris**   ☆ Abbess Helewise & Josse D'Acquin
www.alysclare.com   C12th Kent, 'Hawkenlye Abbey'

Simon Beaufort	Michael Jecks	Candace Robb
Paul Doherty	Bernard Knight	Kate Sedley
Margaret Frazer	Viviane Moore	Peter Tremayne
Sylvian Hamilton	Ellis Peters	Joan Wolf

Lucy Clare   1949-   Aga saga

Patricia Fawcett	Hazel Hucker	Mary Sheepshanks
Kate Fenton	Erica James	Peta Tayler
Katie Fforde		

Candida Clark   1970-   General

Josephine Hart	Libby Purves	Louise Voss
Sian James	Rosie Thomas	

Carol Higgins Clark   1956-   US   Crime: PI

www.carolhigginsclark.com   ☆ Regan Reilly - Missouri

Sue Grafton	Margaret Maron	Sara Paretsky
Laura Lippman	Marcia Muller	Nancy Taylor Rosenberg

Go to back for lists of:
Authors by Genre • Characters and Series • Prize Winners • Further Reading

Mary Higgins Clark 1929- US Adventure/Thriller: Psychological

www.maryhigginsclark.com

Joy Fielding
Carol Goodman
Fiona Mountain

Gloria Murphy
Hilary Norman

Liz Rigbey
Christina Schwarz

Simon Clark 1958- Horror

www.bbr-online.com/nailed

Clive Barker
Chaz Brenchley
Muriel Gray

Shaun Hutson
Bentley Little
Mark Morris

British Fantasy 2002

C

Arthur C Clarke 1917- Science Fiction: Technical

also writes as E G O'Brien, Charles Willis

www.clarkefoundation.org/arthurclarke/biography.html

Brian W Aldiss
Isaac Asimov
Greg Bear
Gregory Benford

Michael P Kube-McDowell
Jack McDevitt
Robert Reed
Robert Silverberg

Dan Simmons

BSFA 1973

Brenda Clarke 1926- Saga

also writes as Kate Sedley

Midlands • West Country

Tessa Barclay
Anne Bennett
Margaret Graham

Mary Minton
Connie Monk

Eileen Stafford
Caroline Stickland

Shaun Clarke War: Modern

Andy McNab
John Nichol

Chris Ryan
James Webb

James Clavell 1924-94 US Adventure/Thriller

Martin Booth
Colin Falconer
Giles Foden

Humphrey Hawksley
Amin Maalouf
David Malouf

Christopher Nicole
Laura Joh Rowland
Alan Savage

Victoria Clayton Aga saga

www.fantasticfiction.co.uk/authors/Victoria_Clayton.htm

Diana Appleyard
Raffaella Barker
Anne Doughty

Katie Fforde
Elizabeth Jane Howard
Karen Nelson

Imogen Parker
Rosamunde Pilcher
Mary Wesley

Jon Cleary   1917-   Aus   Adventure/Thriller: Police work - Australia

www.kirjasto.sci.fi/jcleary   🏃 Insp Scobie Malone - Sydney

Desmond Bagley	Colin Forbes	Gavin Lyall
John Buchan	Hammond Innes	Claire McNab
June Drummond	John Lawton	Nevil Shute

Ann Cleeves   1954-   Crime: Police work - UK

www.fantasticfiction.co.uk/authors/Ann_Cleeves.htm   🏃 DI Stephen Ramsay - Northumberland
George & Molly Palmer-Jones, Ornithologists
DI Vera Stanhope

C

Catherine Aird	Judith Cutler	Gay Longworth
W J Burley	Georgie Hale	Iain McDowall
Gwendoline Butler	Patricia Hall	Andrew Taylor
John Connor	Lesley Horton	David Williams

Douglas Clegg   Horror

www.douglasclegg.com

Richard Bachman	Scott Nicholson	Rupert Thomson
Nancy Collins	John Saul	
Stephen King		

James Clemens   1961-   US   Fantasy: Epic

www.jamesclemens.com

Sarah Ash	Cecilia Dart-Thornton	Robert Newcomb
Joanne Bertin	Robin Hobb	Ricardo Pinto
Terry Brooks	Anne McCaffrey	

Francesca Clementis   1958-   Chick Lit

Alexandra Carew	Jill Mansell	Sarah Webb
Wendy Holden	Carole Matthews	Liz Young
Laura Lockington	Melissa Nathan	

Barbara Cleverly   Crime: Historical - C20th

www.barbaracleverly.com   🏃 Insp Joe Sandilands - 1920s India

CWA 2004

Boris Akunin	Graham Ison	
Thalassa Ali	Laurie King	
Margery Allingham	Gillian Linscott	
David Dickinson	Ngaio Marsh	Elizabeth Peters
Martha Grimes	Michael Pearce	David Roberts

Go to back for lists of:
Authors by Genre • Characters and Series • Prize Winners • Further Reading

Michael Clynes

Crime: Historical - C16th

also writes as **Vanessa Alexander, Anna Apostolou, P C Doherty, Paul Harding**
is **Paul Doherty**

🏃 Sir Roger Shallot
Henrician England

Judith Cook	Philip Gooden	C J Sansom
Patricia Finney	John Pilkington	Peter Tonkin

Lynn Coady   Can

General

www.lynncoady.com

Jane Hamilton	Alice McDermott	Alice Munro
Mary Lawson	Anne-Marie MacDonald	Carol Shields

James Cobb   US

Sea: Modern

www.fantasticfiction.co.uk/authors/James_H_Cobb.htm

🏃 Com Amanda Lee Garrett
Destroyer USS Cunningham

Jonathan Carroll	Richard Herman	Patrick Robinson
Duncan Harding	James Pattinson	Justin Scott
Eric L Harry	Douglas Reeman	

Marika Cobbold   Swe

Aga saga

www.bloomsbury.com/Authors/microsite.asp?id=335&section=1&aid=0

Anne Atkins	Kate Long	Ann Purser
Rachel Cusk	Santa Montefiore	Amanda Eyre Ward
Karen Hayes	Elizabeth Noble	Jane Yardley

Harlan Coben   1962-   US

Crime: Amateur sleuth

www.harlancoben.com

🏃 Myron Bolitar, Sports agent
New York

TGR 2003

Jeff Abbott	Loren D Estleman	
Russell Andrews	G M Ford	
Raymond Chandler	Stuart Harrison	
Michael Connelly	John Katzenbach	Robert B Parker
Robert Crais	Jonathan Kellerman	Gillian White

Tim Cockey   US

Crime: Amateur sleuth

www.timcockey.com

🏃 Hitchcock Sewell, Mortician
Baltimore

Tim Dorsey	Lauren Henderson	Laura Lippman
Janet Evanovich	Elmore Leonard	Rebecca Tope

Go to back for lists of:
Authors by Genre • Characters and Series • Prize Winners • Further Reading

Jonathan Coe   1961-   Humour

www.contemporarywriters.com/authors/?p=auth22

Michael Carson   David Nicholls   Mail 1994
Joseph Connolly   Geoff Nicholson
John Irving   Tim Pears
John Lanchester   Nigel Williams
Magnus Mills

Paulo Coelho   1947-   Braz   General

www.paulocoelho.com.br/engl/index.html

C

Umberto Eco   Mark Haddon
Gabriel Garcia Márquez   Steve Martin

J M Coetzee   1940-   SA   General

www.fantasticfiction.co.uk/authors/J_M_Coetzee.htm

André Brink   Christopher Hope   Faber 1981
Justin Cartwright   Pamela Jooste   Booker 1983 & 1999
Jim Crace   Doris Lessing   Irish Times 1995
Nadine Gordimer   Amanda Prantera   Commonwealth 2000

Victoria Colby   Chick Lit

Sherry Ashworth   Dorothy Koomson   Victoria Routledge
Sarah Harvey   Freya North   Fiona Walker
Veronica Henry   Sheila Norton

Harry Cole   1931-   Saga
                                                       London

Philip Boast   Patricia Grey   Elizabeth Waite
Harry Bowling   Anna King   Dee Williams
Helen Carey   Mary Jane Staples   Sally Worboyes

Martina Cole   Crime: Hardboiled

http://authorpages.hoddersystems.com/MartinaCole2/author.htm
                                              ⚘ DI Kate Burrows
                                                 East End, London

Jeremy Cameron   Lynda La Plante   Hilary Norman
Colin Falconer   Peter May   Stuart Woods
Mandasue Heller

Nicholas Coleridge   1957-   Adventure/Thriller

www.fantasticfiction.co.uk/authors/Nicholas_Coleridge.htm

Jeffrey Archer   Ken Follett
John Gordon Davis   Alan Furst

Eoin Colfer 1965- Ire

Fantasy: Epic

http://homepage.eircom.net/~eoincolfer65

♟ Artemis Fowl

William Nicholson
Terry Pratchett

Philip Pullman
J K Rowling

Jenny Colgan 1972- Sco

Chick Lit

www.jennycolgan.com

Cecelia Ahern
Maggie Alderson
Jenny Eclair

Imogen Edwards-Jones
Marissa Mackle
Marian Murphy

Tina Reilly
Stephanie Theobald
Jane Wenham-Jones

C

Catrin Collier 1948- Wales

Saga

www.fantasticfiction.co.uk/authors/Catrin_Collier.htm ♟ Heart of Gold Series - Pontypridd, Wales

Elizabeth Daish
Sara Fraser
Iris Gower

Catrin Morgan
Cynthia S Roberts

Sarah Shears
Grace Thompson

Jackie Collins 1941-

Glitz & Glamour

www.jackiecollins.com

Celia Brayfield
Candace Bushnell
Joan Collins

Judith Krantz
Roberta Latow
Judith Michael

Fern Michaels
Harold Robbins
Madge Swindells

Joan Collins 1933-

Glitz & Glamour

www.joancollins.net

Jackie Collins
Jude Deveraux
Judith Gould

Veronica Henry
Judi James
Judith Krantz

Frankie McGowan
Harold Robbins

Max Allan Collins 1948- US

Crime: Forensic

www.maxallancollins.com

♟ Gil Grissom - Las Vegas

Patricia D Cornwell
Lisa Gardner
Tess Gerritsen

Iris Johansen
Keith McCarthy
Nigel McCrery

Kathy Reichs
Karin Slaughter

Michael Collins 1964- Ire

General

Clare Boylan
Michael Cunningham

Louise Erdrich
Alice Hoffman

Tim O'Brien

Go to back for lists of:
Authors by Genre • Characters and Series • Prize Winners • Further Reading

Nancy Collins   1959- US   Horror

Kelley Armstrong	Douglas Clegg	Anne Rice
Chaz Brenchley	Laurell K Hamilton	Dan Simmons
Poppy Z Brite	Tom Holland	S P Somtow

Michael Connelly   1956- US   Crime: Police work - US
www.michaelconnelly.com   ⚐ Harry Bosch • Terry McCaleb, Retired FBI Agent
                                                                   Los Angeles

Russell Andrews	G M Ford	Thomas Laird
Giles Blunt	William Heffernan	Reggie Nadelson
James Lee Burke	J A Jance	John Sandford
Harlan Coben	John Katzenbach	John Shannon

Tom Connery   1944-   Sea: Historical
is David Donachie   ⚐ George Markham, Lieut of Marines - C18th

David Donachie	Jan Needle	Dudley Pope
Alexander Kent	Patrick O'Brian	Victor Suthren
Allan Mallinson	Dan Parkinson	Richard Woodman

John Connolly   1968- Ire   Crime: Psychological
www.johnconnolly.co.uk   ⚐ Charlie 'Bird' Parker, Retired policeman - New England

Thomas H Cook	Mo Hayder	Jefferson Parker
Jeffery Deaver	Jonathan Kellerman	Boris Starling
Joy Fielding	Dennis Lehane	P J Tracy

Joseph Connolly   1950-   Humour

| Kingsley Amis | Charles Higson | Tom Sharpe |
| Jonathan Coe | Geoff Nicholson | Evelyn Waugh |

Alexandra Connor   Saga
www.alexandra-connor.co.uk   Lancashire

Ruth Hamilton	Freda Lightfoot	Kay Stephens
Anna Jacobs	Annie Murray	Margaret Thornton
Joan Jonker		

John Connor   Crime: Police work - UK
                                         ⚐ DC Karen Sharpe - West Yorkshire

Ann Cleeves	Lesley Horton	Priscilla Masters
Brian Cooper	Lynda La Plante	Ed O'Connor
Roger Jon Ellory	Gay Longworth	Danuta Reah
Patricia Hall	Iain McDowall	Cath Staincliffe

C

51

Joseph Conrad   1857-1924   General
www.kirjasto.sci.fi/jconrad.htm

John Buchan	James Hamilton-Paterson	W Somerset Maugham
Louis de Bernières	Ernest Hemingway	V S Naipaul
Abdulrazak Gurnah	Henry James	Virginia Woolf

Pat Conroy   1945-   US   General
www.patconroy.com

Pete Dexter	Harper Lee	Paullina Simons
Nicholas Evans	Larry McMurtry	William Styron
Winston Graham	Anne Rivers Siddons	Paul Theroux

C

Storm Constantine   1956-   Fantasy: Dark
www.grebo-heights.wox.org/bast/home.htm

Alice Borchardt	Juliet Marillier	Judith Tarr
Mary Gentle	Anne Rice	Freda Warrington

Gloria Cook   Historical
                                                                 Cornwall

Rosemary Aitken	Elizabeth Ann Hill	Malcolm Ross
Iris Gower	Malcolm Macdonald	Susan Sallis
Winston Graham	Cynthia S Roberts	E V Thompson

Judith Cook   1933-   Crime: Historical - C16th
www.judithcook.co.uk   ☇ Dr Simon Forman & John Bradedge - C16th England
                                          John Latymer, Retired policeman

Michael Clynes	C C Humphreys	C J Sansom
Patricia Finney	Edward Marston	Kate Sedley
Margaret Frazer	Fidelis Morgan	Martin Stephen
Philip Gooden	John Pilkington	Peter Tonkin

Robin Cook   1940-   US   Adventure/Thriller: Medical
www.fantasticfiction.co.uk/authors/Robin_Cook.htm

Keith Russell Ablow	Mark Burnell	Ken McClure
Paul Adam	Paul Carson	Michael Palmer
Colin Andrews	Michael Crichton	Leah Ruth Robinson

Thomas H Cook   1947-   US   Crime: Psychological
www.fantasticfiction.co.uk/authors/Thomas_H_Cook.htm   ☇ Frank Clemons, PI

Ace Atkins	Roger Jon Ellory	David Lindsey
John Connolly	Thomas Harris	Michael Malone
		John Sandford

Sophie Cooke   Sco   General

Esther Freud   Maggie O'Farrell   Alexandra Raife

Catherine Cookson   1906-1998   Saga

also wrote as **Catherine Marchant**   ⚲ Mary Ann Shaughnessy ⎫ NE England
www.fantasticfiction.co.uk/authors/Catherine_Cookson.htm   Tilly Trotter • Bill Bailey ⎭

Rita Bradshaw   Audrey Howard   Denise Robertson
Benita Brown   Sheila Jansen   Grace Thompson
Ruth Hamilton   Beryl Matthews   Janet MacLeod Trotter
Una Horne   Sheila Newberry   Valerie Wood

C

Stephen Coonts   1946-   US   Adventure/Thriller

www.stephencoonts.com   ⚲ Rear Admiral Jake Grafton

James Adams   David Hagberg   Matthew Reilly
Geoffrey Archer   Richard Herman   Julian Jay Savarin
Vince Flynn   John R Maxim

Brian Cooper   1919-   Crime: Police work - UK

www.fantasticfiction.co.uk/authors/Brian_Cooper.htm   ⚲ CI MikeTench & DCI John Lubbock
                                                                          Norfolk

Vivien Armstrong   John Connor   Geraldine Evans
Pauline Bell   Colin Dexter   P D James
Paul Charles

Jilly Cooper   1937-   Glitz & Glamour

www.jillycooper.co.uk

Celia Brayfield   Veronica Henry   Lesley Pearse
Alexandra Campbell   Christina Jones   Caroline Upcher
Judith Gould   Judith Krantz

Louise Cooper   1952-   Fantasy: Epic

www.louisecooper.com

Jean M Auel   L E Modesitt Jr   Melanie Rawn
Barbara Hambly   Michael Moorcock   Janny Wurts
Robert Jordan

Natasha Cooper   1951-   Crime: Amateur sleuth

also writes as **Clare Layton**; *is* **Daphne Wright**   ⚲ Willow King, Civil servant ⎫ London
www.lydmouth.demon.co.uk/us/natasha/cooper.htm   Trish Maguire, Barrister ⎭

Agatha Christie   Susan B Kelly   Veronica Stallwood
Frances Fyfield   Marianne Macdonald   Leslie Thomas
Joyce Holms   Betty Rowlands

Victoria Corby — Chick Lit

www.fantasticfiction.co.uk/authors/Victoria_Corby.htm

Lisa Armstrong	Helen Fielding	Adele Parks
Trisha Ashley	India Knight	Andrea Semple
Valerie-Anne Baglietto	Melissa Nathan	Daisy Waugh

Michael Cordy — Adventure/Thriller

Dan Brown	Daniel Easterman	Douglas Preston
John Case	Lury Gibson	A J Quinnell
Michael Crichton	Bill Napier	

C

Bernard Cornwell 1944- — War: Historical

also writes as **Susannah Kells**
www.bernardcornwellbooks.com

🏃 Richard Sharpe
Nathaniel Starbuck

Garry Douglas	C C Humphreys	Steven Pressfield
Daniel Hall	Sam Llewellyn	Patrick Rambaud
Richard Howard	Allan Mallinson	Edward Rutherfurd

Patricia D Cornwell 1956- US — Crime: Forensic

www.patriciacornwell.com

🏃 Kay Scarpetta, Pathologist } Virginia
Judy Hammer & Andy Brazil, State Police }

CWA 1990 & 1993

Paul Carson	Keith McCarthy	
Max Allan Collins	Nigel McCrery	
Lynn Hightower	Peter May	
Tami Hoag	Jonathan Nasaw	Karin Slaughter
Iris Johansen	Kathy Reichs	P J Tracy

Francis Cottam 1957- — War: Modern

www.fantasticfiction.co.uk/authors/Francis_Cottam.htm

Tim Binding	Douglas Kennedy	Robert Ryan
Sebastian Faulks	Derek Robinson	Paul Watkins
Andrew Greig		

Catherine Coulter US — Historical

www.catherinecoulter.com

Marion Chesney	Victoria Holt	Amanda Quick
Teresa Crane	Genevieve Lyons	Nora Roberts
Julie Garwood	Judith McNaught	

Go to back for lists of:
Authors by Genre • Characters and Series • Prize Winners • Further Reading

Ben Counter

Dan Abnett	Jonathan Carroll	Tanith Lee
Lois McMaster Bujold	David A Drake	Freda Warrington
Chris Bunch	Jonathan Green	

Douglas Coupland   1961-   Can

General

www.coupland.com

Iain Banks	John McCabe	Ben Richards
Bret Easton Ellis	Chuck Palahniuk	Rupert Thomson
Alex Garland		

C

Bryce Courtenay   1933-   Aus

Adventure/Thriller

www.brycecourtenay.com

Martin Booth	Eric Lustbader	Wilbur Smith
June Drummond	Amin Maalouf	Peter Watt

Josephine Cox   1938-

Saga

also writes as **Jane Brindle**
www.josephinecox.co.uk

Lyn Andrews	Katie Flynn	Joan O'Neill
Rose Boucheron	Sara Fraser	Lynda Page
Harry Bowling	Erin Kaye	Wendy Robertson

Harold Coyle   1952-   US

Adventure/Thriller

www.fantasticfiction.co.uk/authors/Harold_Coyle.htm

Campbell Armstrong	Jack Higgins	Matthew Reilly
Clive Cussler	Leo Kessler	James Thayer
W E B Griffin	Stephen Leather	Craig Thomas

Jim Crace   1946-

General

www.jim-crace.com

André Brink	Yann Martel	Guardian 1986
J M Coetzee	David Mitchell	Higham 1986
E L Doctorow	Rupert Thomson	Whitbread 1986 & 1997
Jim Harrison	Barry Unsworth	Holtby 1994
Alistair MacLeod		

Amanda Craig   1959-

General

www.amandacraig.com

Janice Galloway	A L Kennedy	Amanda Prantera
Jane Gardam	Allison Pearson	Barbara Trapido
Laurie Graham		

Maggie Craig   Sco   Saga

Margaret Thomson Davis   Meg Henderson   Jessica Stirling
Inga Dunbar   Evelyn Hood   Mary Withall
Margaret Graham   Eileen Ramsay

Robert Crais   1953-   US   Crime: PI
www.robertcrais.com   ⚞ Elvis Cole - Los Angeles

Jeff Abbott   G M Ford   John Shannon
Raymond Chandler   Joe R Lansdale   Don Winslow
Harlan Coben   Reggie Nadelson

Teresa Crane   Historical

Anita Burgh   Sara Hylton   Belva Plain
Catherine Coulter   Genevieve Lyons Judith Saxton
Elizabeth Falconer   Elisabeth McNeill Eileen Townsend

David Cray   US   Crime: Hardboiled
is Stephen Solomita   New York
www.fantasticfiction.co.uk/authors/David_Cray.htm

Jerome Charyn   Thomas Laird   Reggie Nadelson
William Heffernan   Dennis Lehane   George P Pelecanos
Lynn Hightower   Ed McBain   Jess Walter

Conor Cregan   1962-   Ire   Adventure/Thriller
www.fantasticfiction.co.uk/authors/Conor_Cregan.htm

Lee Child   Greg Iles   David Mason
Alan Folsom   Donald James   Chris Ryan
Alan Furst   Robert Ludlum

Candida Crewe   1964-   General

Catherine Feeny   Alice Hoffman   Deborah Moggach
Kate Grenville   Hilary Mantel   Anne Tyler

Michael Crichton   1942-   US   General
also writes as Jeffrey Hudson, John Lange
www.crichton-official.com

Colin Andrews   Michael Cordy   Ken McClure
Dan Brown   William Gibson   Richard Morgan
Robin Cook   Philip Kerr   Bill Napier

Deborah Crombie US Crime: Police work - UK

http://64.70.139.77/welcome/welcome.html
    🏃 Supt Duncan Kincaid & Sgt Gemma James
London

Jane Adams
Jo Bannister
Margaret Duffy

Elizabeth George
Paula Gosling
Martha Grimes

Cynthia Harrod-Eagles
Priscilla Masters
R D Wingfield

Neil Cross 1969- General

www.fantasticfiction.co.uk/authors/Neil_Cross.htm

Sarah Hall
Tim Lott

Julie Parsons
Tony Parsons

Matt Thorne

C

Jenn Crowell 1978- US Glitz & Glamour

Susie Boyt
Lucinda Edmonds
Lucy Ellman

Judi James
Roberta Latow
Johanna Lindsey

Freya North
Sheila O'Flanagan

Elaine Crowley Ire Saga

www.fantasticfiction.co.uk/authors/Elaine_Crowley.htm
    🏃 O'Hara Family - Ireland

Frank Delaney
Rose Doyle
Mary A Larkin

Genevieve Lyons
Joan O'Neill
D M Purcell

Liz Ryan
Mary Ryan

John Crowley 1942- US Fantasy: Contemporary

www.michaelscycles.freeserve.co.uk/crowl1.htm

Jonathan Carroll
Charles de Lint
Sara Douglass

Neil Gaiman
Stephen King

Michael Marshall Smith
Gene Wolfe

James Crumley 1939- US Crime: PI

www.fantasticfiction.co.uk/authors/James_Crumley.htm
    🏃 C W Sughrue - Texas
Milo Milodragovitch - Montana

CWA 2002

James Lee Burke
James Ellroy
Robert Ferrigno
Ross Macdonald

George P Pelecanos
Jason Starr
Boston Teran
Jim Thompson

Jenny Crusie 1949- US Chick Lit

www.sff.net/people/jennifercrusie/home.html

Jenny Eclair
Janet Evanovich
Fannie Flagg

Sophie Kinsella
Chris Manby

Jill Mansell
Jennifer Weiner

Claudine Cullimore   Ire   Chick Lit

Martina Devlin	L McCrossan	Sheila O'Flanagan
Cathy Kelly	Anita Notaro	Morag Prunty

Michael Cunningham   1952-   US   General
http://literati.net/Cunningham

Michael Collins	Jonathan Franzen	Pulitzer 1999
Helen Dunmore	Tim O'Brien	
Richard Ford		

C
D

Clare Curzon   1922-   Crime: Police work - UK
is Rhona Petrie and Marie Buchanan
www.fantasticfiction.co.uk/authors/Clare_Curzon.htm

🏃 Supt Mike Yeadings & DS Angus Mott - Thames Valley
Lucy Sedgwick - Early C20th England

M C Beaton	Veronica Heley	Elizabeth Peters
Caroline Graham	Gillian Linscott	Dorothy Simpson

Rachel Cusk   1967-   General
www.fantasticfiction.co.uk/authors/Rachel_Cusk.htm

Rachel Billington	Anne Fine	Hilary Mantel
Marika Cobbold	Esther Freud	

Clive Cussler   1931-   US   Adventure/Thriller
www.numa.net/clive_cussler.html

🏃 Dirk Pitt • Kurt Austin

Russell Andrews	David Hagberg	Matthew Reilly
Desmond Bagley	Paul Henke	Julian Jay Savarin
Harold Coyle	Hammond Innes	Justin Scott
Duncan Falconer	James Pattinson	James Thayer

Judith Cutler   1946-   Crime: Amateur sleuth
www.judithcutler.com

🏃 Sophie Rivers, Lecturer • DS Kate Power
Birmingham

Paul Charles	Priscilla Masters	Michelle Spring
Ann Cleeves	Nick Oldham	Scarlett Thomas
Martin Edwards	Barrie Roberts	Stella Whitelaw

Fred D'Aguiar   1960-   General
www.contemporarywriters.com/authors/?p=auth26

Patricia Duncker	William Golding	Higham 1994
Rumer Godden	Pauline Melville	Whitbread 1994
	Caryl Phillips	
	Barry Unsworth	

Janet Dailey   1944-   US   Saga
www.janetdailey.com   ⚐ Calder Family

Jayne Ann Krentz	Judith Saxton	LaVyrle Spencer
Belva Plain	Anne Rivers Siddons	Barbara Wood
Nora Roberts		

Elizabeth Daish   Saga
⚐ Emma - London • Coppins Bridge Series - Isle of Wight

Betty Burton	Lilian Harry	Sally Stewart
Catrin Collier	Harriet Hudson	Sally Worboyes
Elizabeth Darrell	Joan Jonker	

Emma Dally   1954-   Saga   D

Harry Bowling	Ruth Hamilton	Margaret Pemberton
Pamela Evans	Gilda O'Neill	Linda Sole

Denise Danks   US   Crime: Amateur sleuth
www.fantasticfiction.co.uk/authors/Denise_Danks.htm   ⚐ Georgina Powers, Computer journalist
London

Cara Black	Simon Shaw	Don Winslow
Zoë Sharp	Cath Staincliffe	

Elizabeth Darrell   Saga
also writes as **Emma Drummond**   ⚐ Sheridan Family

Vanessa Alexander	Elizabeth Daish	Angela Huth
Betty Burton	June Drummond	Juliette Mead
Joy Chambers		

Cecilia Dart-Thornton   Aus   Fantasy: Myth
http://members.optushome.com.au/neptune5/homepage.html

Sarah Ash	Robin Hobb	Caiseal Mor
James Clemens	Juliet Marillier	J R R Tolkien

Kavita Daswani   Ind   General

Manju Kapur	Sharon Maas
Jhumpa Lahiri	Preethi Nair

Go to back for lists of:
Authors by Genre • Characters and Series • Prize Winners • Further Reading

Will Davenport · Historical

is James Long

Geraldine Brooks
Elizabeth Chadwick
Tracy Chevalier

Stevie Davies
Daphne Du Maurier
Margaret George

Matthew Kneale
Christopher Peachment
Sharon Penman

Doris Davidson · 1922- · Sco · Saga
Scotland

Margaret Thomson Davis
Nora Kay
Gwen Kirkwood

Elisabeth McNeill
Frances Paige
Eileen Ramsay

Jessica Stirling
Anne Vivis

D · Freda Davies · Crime: Police work - UK
🏃 DI Keith Tyrell - Gloucestershire

Meg Elizabeth Atkins
Janie Bolitho
W J Burley

Kate Ellis
Caroline Graham
Ann Granger

Georgie Hale
Roy Hart
Hazel Holt

Jonathan Davies · 1944- · Crime: Legal/financial

www.fantasticfiction.co.uk/authors/Jonathan_Davies.htm
🏃 Jeremy Scott, Barrister

Harry Bingham
Frances Fyfield

John McLaren
Michael Ridpath

Linda Davies · 1963- · US · Adventure/Thriller: Legal/financial

www.ex.ac.uk/~RDavies/arian/linda.html

Po Bronson
John Grisham

Jill McGown
Carol O'Connell

Michael Ridpath

Murray Davies · Adventure/Thriller

www.fantasticfiction.co.uk/authors/Murray_Davies.htm

Johnny 'Two Combs'
   Howard

Andy McNab
John Nichol

Chris Ryan

Stevie Davies · 1946- · Wales · General

also writes as **Stephanie Davies**
www.steviedavies.com

Tracy Chevalier
Will Davenport

Salley Vickers
Sarah Waters

Carol Anne Davis 1976- Sco Crime: Psychological

www.carolannedavis.co.uk

Andrea Badenoch	Phil Lovesey	Minette Walters
Roger Jon Ellory	Barbara Vine	Laura Wilson

John Gordon Davis SA Adventure/Thriller

Nicholas Coleridge	Daniel Easterman	Alan Furst
Nelson DeMille	Ken Follett	Wilbur Smith
June Drummond		

Lindsey Davis 1949- Crime: Historical - Ancient

www.lindseydavis.co.uk

🏃 Marcus Didius Falco - Ancient Rome

Margaret Doody	Simon Scarrow	Authors 1989
Conn Iggulden	Marilyn Todd	CWA 1999
Rosemary Rowe	Peter Tremayne	
Laura Joh Rowland	David Wishart	
Steven Saylor		

D

Margaret Thomson Davis 1926- Sco Saga

🏃 Andrina McPherson • Monkton Family • Breadmakers Series
Scotland

Maggie Bennett	Christine Marion Fraser	Isobel Neill
Maggie Craig	Meg Henderson	Alexandra Raife
Doris Davidson	Marie Joseph	Jessica Stirling

Jill Dawson 1962- General

www.jilldawson.co.uk

Catherine Feeny	Zoë Heller	Elizabeth Pewsey
Shirley Hazzard	Deborah Moggach	

Louis de Bernières 1954- General

www.contemporarywriters.com/authors/?p=auth2

Pat Barker	Yann Martel	CWA 1995
Tim Binding	David Mitchell	
Joseph Conrad	Nicholas Shakespeare	
Tibor Fischer	Mario Vargas Llosa	
James Hamilton-Paterson		

Michelle de Kretser 1958- Aus General

Regi Claire	Timothy Mo	Encore 2004
Arthur Golden	Haruki Murakami	
Kazuo Ishiguro		

Charles de Lint 1951- Can · Fantasy: Contemporary

www.sfsite.com/charlesdelint

Mark Chadbourn	Neil Gaiman	Juliet Marillier
John Crowley	Robert Holdstock	Caiseal Mor
Sara Douglass	Guy Gavriel Kay	

Jeffery Deaver 1950- US · Crime: Forensic

www.jefferydeaver.com

⚐ Lincoln Rhyme, Forensic scientist
Rune, Film maker - New York
John Pellam, Film location scout

Keith Russell Ablow	Michael Marshall	TGR 2001
Adam Baron	Jonathan Nasaw	CWA 2004
John Connolly	James Patterson	
Mo Hayder	Ridley Pearson	Paullina Simons
John Katzenbach	Kathy Reichs	Stephen White

D

Len Deighton 1929- · Adventure/Thriller

www.fantasticfiction.co.uk/authors/Len_Deighton.htm

⚐ Bernard Samson

Paul Adam	Donald James	Anthony Price
Ted Allbeury	John Lawton	Nigel West
Clive Egleton	Gavin Lyall	

Frank Delaney 1942- Ire · Saga

www.fantasticfiction.co.uk/authors/Frank_Delaney.htm

⚐ Kane Family

Elaine Crowley	Joan O'Neill	Liz Ryan
Rose Doyle	D M Purcell	Mary Ryan
Mary A Larkin		

R F Delderfield 1912-72 · Saga

www.mcbooks.com/Historical/DelderfieldPage/delderfield.html

⚐ Craddock Family • Swann Family

John Galsworthy	J B Priestley	E V Thompson
Winston Graham	Michael Taylor	Nigel Tranter
Malcolm Macdonald		

Don DeLillo 1936- US · General

also writes as **Cleo Birdwell**

Paul Auster	Chuck Palahniuk	Irish Times 1989
T Coraghessan Boyle	Richard Powers	
Jonathan Franzen	Thomas Pynchon	
Norman Mailer	Tobias Wolff	
Haruki Murakami		

James Delingpole
Lad Lit: Humour

Richard Asplin
Robert Chalmers

Ben Hatch
Nick Hornby

Mil Millington
Paul Reizin

Barbara Delinsky   1945-   US
General

also writes as **Billy Douglass, Bonnie Drake**
www.barbaradelinsky.com

Celia Brayfield
Candace Bushnell
Penny Jordan

Judith McNaught
Una-Mary Parker
Belva Plain

LaVyrle Spencer
Danielle Steel

Nelson DeMille   1943-   US
Adventure/Thriller

www.nelsondemille.net
⚶ Det John Corey & Kate Mayfield

David Baldacci
Suzanne Brockmann
Stephen J Cannell

John Gordon Davis
Daniel Easterman
Ken Follett

Robert Littell
Stanley Pottinger
Wilbur Smith

D

Anita Desai   1937-   Ind
General

www.contemporarywriters.com/authors/?p=auth124

Chitra Banerjee
  Divakaruni
Ruth Prawer Jhabvala
Lee Langley

Amulya Malladi
Gita Mehta
Bharati Mukherjee

R K Narayan
Salman Rushdie
Amy Tan

Jude Deveraux   1947-   US
Glitz & Glamour

www.fantasticfiction.co.uk/authors/Jude_Deveraux.htm

Marion Chesney
Joan Collins
Johanna Lindsey

Fern Michaels
Belva Plain

Nora Roberts
Danielle Steel

Martina Devlin   Ire
Chick Lit

www.martinadevlin.com

Colette Caddle
Claudine Cullimore
Anna Maxted

Claire Naylor
Sheila O'Flanagan
Kate O'Riordan

Adele Parks
Patricia Scanlan
Kate Thompson

Isla Dewar   Sco
General

Joan Barfoot
Mavis Cheek
Kate Fenton

L McCrossan
Carole Matthews
Anna Maxted

Agnes Owens
Zoë Strachan
Lynne Truss

63

Eileen Dewhurst   1929-   Crime: Amateur sleuth

www.fantasticfiction.co.uk/authors/Eileen_Dewhurst.htm

🚶 Phyllida Moon, Doctor
DI Tim Le Page - Guernsey

John Baker   Caroline Graham
Pauline Bell   Ann Granger

Colin Dexter   1930-   Crime: Police work - UK

www.fantasticfiction.co.uk/authors/Colin_Dexter.htm

🚶 DI Morse - Oxford

Robert Barnard   Susan B Kelly   CWA 1979, 1981,
Paul Charles   Henning Mankell   1989 & 1992
Brian Cooper   M R D Meek
Kate Ellis   Peter Robinson   Veronica Stallwood
Reginald Hill   Sally Spencer   Fred Vargas

D

Pete Dexter   1943-   US   General

Robert Olen Butler   Richard Ford   Jim Harrison
Pat Conroy   David Guterson   William Kennedy

Anita Diamant   1951-   US   General

www.anitadiamant.com/default.htm

Geraldine Brooks   Anita Shreve   Susan Vreeland
Jenny Diski   Salley Vickers   Sarah Willis
Alice Sebold

Sarah Diamond   1976-   Crime: Psychological

www.fantasticfiction.co.uk/authors/Sarah_Diamond.htm

Ingrid Black   Julie Parsons   Barbara Vine
Caroline Carver   Sarah Rayne   Gillian White
Gemma O'Connor   Carol Smith   Laura Wilson

Michael Dibdin   1947-   Crime: Police work - Italy

www.contemporarywriters.com/authors/?p=auth28

🚶 Aurelio Zen

CWA 1988 & 1990

Andrea Camilleri   David Hewson
Dan Fesperman   Donna Leon
Leslie Forbes   Manuel Vázquez   Barbara Nadel
Luiz Alfredo Garcia-Roza   Montalbán   Eliot Pattison
Juan Goytisolo   Magdalen Nabb   Daniel Pennac

Go to back for lists of:
Authors by Genre
Characters and Series
Prize Winners
Further Reading

Philip K Dick 1928-82 US Science Fiction: Space and time

www.philipkdick.com

Isaac Asimov	Michael Moorcock	BSFA 1978
J G Ballard	Tim Powers	
Robert A Heinlein	Christopher Priest	
K W Jeter	Kurt Vonnegut	John Wyndham

Charles Dickens 1812-70 General

Jane Austen	Sheri Holman	Iain Sinclair
Emma Donoghue	W Somerset Maugham	Anthony Trollope
Michel Faber	Rohinton Mistry	Tom Wolfe

David Dickinson Ire Crime: Historical - C20th

www.fantasticfiction.co.uk/authors/David_Dickinson.htm
⚉ Lord Francis Powerscourt
Edwardian England

Boris Akunin	Michael Pearce	David Pirie
Barbara Cleverly	Anne Perry	Barrie Roberts
Jane Jakeman	Elizabeth Peters	

Margaret Dickinson 1942- Saga

also writes as **Everatt Jackson**
www.fantasticfiction.co.uk/authors/Margaret_Dickinson.htm
⚉ Kate Hilton - Lincolnshire

Lilian Harry	Sybil Marshall	Mary E Pearce
Elizabeth Jeffrey	Catrin Morgan	Linda Sole
Mary Mackie	Sharon Owens	T R Wilson

William Diehl 1924- US Crime: Legal/financial

⚉ Martin Vail

Russell Andrews	Ed McBain	Richard North Patterson
William Bernhardt	Phillip Margolin	Joseph Wambaugh
Lee Child	David Morrell	

Des Dillon 1960- Sco General

www.contemporarywriters.com/authors/?p=auth02C26N470412627142

Anne Donovan	Gordon Legge	Alan Spence
James Kelman	Duncan McLean	Irvine Welsh

Jenny Diski 1947- General

www.contemporarywriters.com/authors/?p=auth29

Nicola Barker	Maggie Gee	Frances Hegarty
Anita Diamant	Lesley Glaister	Joyce Carol Oates
David Flusfeder		

Chitra Banerjee Divakaruni   1956-   Ind   General

www.chitradivakaruni.com

Anita Desai   Gita Mehta   V S Naipaul
Jhumpa Lahiri   Bharati Mukherjee   Meera Syal

Michael Dobbs   1948-   General

www.fantasticfiction.co.uk/authors/Michael_Dobbs.htm   ⚘ Tom Goodfellow, MP
Francis Urquhart Trilogy, MP

Jeffrey Archer   Peter Rawlinson
Philip Hensher   Michael Shea

D

E L Doctorow   1931-   US   General

www.fantasticfiction.co.uk/authors/E_L_Doctorow.htm

Paul Auster   F Scott Fitzgerald   William Kennedy
Ethan Canin   Craig Holden   John Updike
Jim Crace   Thomas Keneally

Edward Docx   1972-   General

www.edwarddocx.com

Howard Jacobson   Philip Roth   Adam Thirlwell
Rod Liddle   Donna Tartt

Paul Doherty   1946-   Crime: Historical

also writes as **Vanessa Alexander,**   ⚘ Sir Hugh Corbett & Brother Athelstan - C13th England
Anna Apostolou, Michael Clynes,   Alexander the Great & Telamon, Physician -
P C Doherty, Paul Harding   C3rd BC Greece
Amerotke - Ancient Egypt

Simon Beaufort   Susanna Gregory   Edward Marston
Alys Clare   Michael Jecks   Viviane Moore
Margaret Doody   Bernard Knight   Ellis Peters

David Donachie   1944-   Sco   Sea: Historical

also writes as **Tom Connery**   ⚘ Harry Ludlow, Privateer
www.fantasticfiction.co.uk/authors/David_Donachie.htm

Tom Connery   Jan Needle   Dan Parkinson
C S Forester   James L Nelson   Dudley Pope
Alexander Kent   Patrick O'Brian   Julian Stockwin

Anabel Donald   1944-   Crime: Amateur sleuth

www.fantasticfiction.co.uk/authors/Anabel_Donald.htm   ⚘ Alex Tanner, TV Researcher

Anne Fine   Veronica Stallwood
Susan Isaacs   Leslie Thomas

Stephen Donaldson   1947-   US   Fantasy: Epic
also writes as **Stephen R Donaldson, Reed Stephens**
www.stephendonaldson.com

Mark Anthony	Steven Erikson	Julian May
James Barclay	Raymond E Feist	Robert Newcomb
Jonathan Carroll	Ian Irvine	Sean Russell
Mark Chadbourn	Paul Kearney	David Zindell

Stephen Donaldson   1947-   US   Crime: PI
also writes as **Stephen R Donaldson, Reed Stephens**   ☆ Ginny Fistoulari &
www.stephendonaldson.com   Mick Axbrewder

Ace Atkins	James Ellroy
Adam Baron	Walter Mosley

D

Sara Donati   Historical
is **Rosina Lippi**
www.saralaughs.com

Daphne Du Maurier	Sheri Holman	Anya Seton
Susan Hill	Victoria Holt	

Emma Donoghue   1969-   Ire   General
www.emmadonoghue.com

Charles Dickens	Sheri Holman	Alice Walker
Joanne Harris	Sarah Kate Lynch	Jeanette Winterson
Anne Haverty	Michèle Roberts	

Anne Donovan   Sco   General
www.fantasticfiction.co.uk/authors/Anne_Donovan.htm

Des Dillon	Agnes Owens	Zoë Strachan
Gordon Legge	Alan Spence	

Margaret Doody   1939-   Can   Crime: Historical - Ancient
www.nd.edu/~mdoody   ☆ Aristotle, Philospher, & Stephanos, Citizen -
                                                                     Ancient Athens

Lindsey Davis	Rosemary Rowe	Marilyn Todd
Paul Doherty	Steven Saylor	David Wishart

Tim Dorsey   1961-   US   Crime: Humour
www.timdorsey.com   ☆ Serge Storms - Florida

Dave Barry	Bill Fitzhugh	Douglas Lindsay
Anthony Bourdain	Kinky Friedman	Scott Phillips
Tim Cockey	Vicki Hendricks	Donald E Westlake

Anne Doughty   Ire   Aga saga

www.contemporarywriters.com/authors/?p=auth176

Judy Astley	Nina Dufort	Julia Hamilton
Maeve Binchy	Patricia Fawcett	Kate Long
Victoria Clayton	Kate Fenton	Joanna Trollope

Louise Doughty   General

www.contemporarywriters.com/authors/?p=auth176

Raffaella Barker	Lesley Glaister	Margaret Yorke
Janet Evanovich	Jenny Maxwell	

D

Garry Douglas   1941-   War: Historical

also writes as **Garry Kilworth**   ⚔ Sgt Jack Crossman
www.fantasticfiction.co.uk/authors/Garry_Kilworth.htm   Crimean War

Bernard Cornwell	Allan Mallinson
Richard Howard	Patrick Rambaud

Sara Douglass   1957-   Aus   Fantasy: Epic

www.saradouglass.com

Carol Berg	John Crowley	Kate Jacoby
Chaz Brenchley	Charles de Lint	Gwyneth Jones
Trudi Canavan	Julia Gray	Megan Lindholm

Clare Dowling   Ire   Chick Lit

Suzanne Higgins	Shari Low	Sheila O'Flanagan
Melissa Hill	Monica McInerney	Sarah Webb
Marian Keyes	Amanda Murphy	

Arthur Conan Doyle   1859-1930   Crime: PI

www.sherlockholmesonline.com   ⚔ Sherlock Holmes & Dr John Watson

Boris Akunin	Anne Perry	Norman Russell
Laurie King	David Pirie	June Thomson
Alanna Knight	Barrie Roberts	M J Trow
Peter Lovesey	Roberta Rogow	Gerard Williams

Roddy Doyle   1958-   Ire   Humour

www.fantasticfiction.co.uk/authors/Roddy_Doyle.htm   ⚔ Henry Smart

Dermot Bolger	Magnus Mills	Booker 1993
Stephen Fry	David Nobbs	
Niall Griffiths	Joseph O'Connor	
Patrick McCabe	Tom Sharpe	Irvine Welsh

Rose Doyle   Ire   General

Maeve Binchy   Frank Delaney   Joan O'Neill
Elaine Crowley   Mary A Larkin   D M Purcell

Margaret Drabble   1939-   General

Barbara Anderson   Nina Bawden   Bernice Rubens
Lynne Reid Banks   Melvyn Bragg   Virginia Woolf
Joan Barfoot   A S Byatt

David A Drake   1945-   US   Fantasy: Epic
www.david-drake.com

Dan Abnett   Ian Irvine   R A Salvatore
Chris Bunch   George R R Martin   Margaret Weis
Ben Counter   L E Modesitt Jr   Tad Williams
Terry Goodkind

D

Robert Drewe   1943-   Aus   General

Peter Carey   David Malouf   Patrick White
Thomas Keneally   Peter Watt

Jeremy Dronfield   1965-   Wales   Adventure/Thriller: Psychological
www.fantasticfiction.co.uk/authors/Jeremy_Dronfield.htm

Iain Banks   Ian McEwan
Nicci French   Barbara Vine

June Drummond   1923-   SA   Adventure/Thriller

Jon Cleary   John Gordon Davis
Bryce Courtenay   Wilbur Smith

June Drummond   1923-   SA   Historical

Joy Chambers   Winston Graham   Jane Aiken Hodge
Elizabeth Darrell   Cynthia Harrod-Eagles Barbara Michaels

Daphne Du Maurier   1907-89   General
www.dumaurier.org/index.html

Will Davenport   Joanna Hines   Charlotte Lamb
Sara Donati   Susan Howatch   Anya Seton
Susan Hill   Susanna Kearsley   Sue Sully

Brendan Dubois
US Adventure/Thriller

www.brendandubois.com

🏃 Lewis Cole

Robert Harris	Kyle Mills	James Siegel
Robert Ludlum	Lawrence Sanders	Daniel Silva

Andre Dubus
1936-1999 US General

www.fantasticfiction.co.uk/authors/Andre_Dubus.htm

Robert Olen Butler	Jane Hamilton	Anne Tyler
Richard Ford	J Robert Lennon	

Margaret Duffy
1942- Sco Crime: Police work - UK

www.fantasticfiction.co.uk/authors/Margaret_Duffy.htm

🏃 Insp James Carrick • Patrick Gillard
Ingrid Langley, Novelist • Joanna Mackenzie, PI
Bath

M C Beaton	Caroline Graham	Priscilla Masters
Deborah Crombie	Bill Knox	

D

Maureen Duffy
1933- General

Kate Atkinson	Zoë Fairbairns	Marge Piercy
Hilary Bailey	Margaret Forster	Amanda Prantera

Stella Duffy
1963- NZ Crime: PI

www.fantasticfiction.co.uk/authors/Stella_Duffy.htm

🏃 Saz Martin - London

Linda Barnes	Lauren Henderson	Claire McNab
Sparkle Hayter	Frank Lean	Marcia Muller

Nina Dufort
Aga saga

Diana Appleyard	Anne Doughty	Katie Fforde
Trisha Ashley	Elizabeth Falconer	Kate Fielding
Judy Astley	Kate Fenton	Sarah MacDonald

Inga Dunbar
Sco Saga

Maggie Craig	Evelyn Hood	Kay Stephens
Barbara Erskine	Frances Paige	Reay Tannahill
Diana Gabaldon	Elvi Rhodes	Valerie Wood

Glen Duncan
1965- General

www.fantasticfiction.co.uk/authors/Glen_Duncan.htm

Nicholson Baker	A L Kennedy	Will Self
Graham Greene	Tim Pears	Evelyn Waugh

Patricia Duncker   1951-   General

www.contemporarywriters.com/authors/?p=auth33

Fred D'Aguiar	William Golding	Pauline Melville
Alison Fell	Graham Greene	

Anne Dunlop   1969-   Ire   Chick Lit

Amy Jenkins	Amanda Murphy	Sarah Webb
Monica McInerney	Carmen Reid	Jane Wenham-Jones
Louise Marley	Kathy Rodgers	

Helen Dunmore   1952-   General

www.contemporarywriters.com/authors/?p=auth103

Lisa Appignanesi	David Flusfeder	McKitterick 1994
Carol Birch	Nikki Gemmell	Orange 1996
Michael Cunningham	Catherine Merriman	
Suzannah Dunn	Maggie O'Farrell	Gillian White

D

Alan Dunn   Crime: Hardboiled

www.fantasticfiction.co.uk/authors/Alan_Dunn.htm   ♟ Billy Oliphant, Security consultant
                                                           NE England

John Baker	Robert Edric	Mike Ripley
Adam Baron	Frank Lean	Martyn Waites

Suzannah Dunn   1963-   General

Helen Dunmore	Sian James	Anne Tyler
Esther Freud	Lorrie Moore	

Catherine Dunne   1954-   Ire   General

Catherine Fox	Joan O'Neill	Anne Tyler
Jane Hamilton	Joanna Trollope	

Dorothy Dunnett   1923-2001   Sco   Historical

also wrote as **Dorothy Halliday**   ♟ Francis Crawford of Lymond
www.dorothydunnett.co.uk   C15th England

Elizabeth Chadwick	Mary Renault	Reay Tannahill
Diana Gabaldon	Edward Rutherfurd	Nigel Tranter
Sharon Penman	Jane Stevenson	

Go to back for lists of:
Authors by Genre • Characters and Series • Prize Winners • Further Reading

Sabine Durrant · Chick Lit

www.fantasticfiction.co.uk/authors/Sabine_Durrant.htm

Colette Caddle	Marissa Mackle	Tina Reilly
Shari Low	Louise Marley	Kathy Rodgers
Jacinta McDevitt	Anna Maxted	

Nick Earls · 1963- · Aus · Lad Lit

www.nickearls.com

Simon Armitage	Matthew Beaumont	Danny King
Mark Barrowcliffe	Mike Gayle	

Daniel Easterman · 1949- · Adventure/Thriller

also writes as Jonathan Aycliffe; *is* Denis McEoin
www.fantasticfiction.co.uk/authors/Daniel_Easterman.htm

Tom Bradby	Michael Cordy	Sean Flannery
John Case	John Gordon Davis	Amin Maalouf
Lincoln Child	Nelson DeMille	John R Maxim

Marjorie Eccles · 1927- · Crime: Police work - UK

also writes as Judith Bordill, Jennifer Hyde
www.fantasticfiction.co.uk/authors/Marjorie_Eccles.htm

🏃 DI Abigail Moon & Supt Gil Mayo - Midlands
DI Tom Richmonds - Yorkshire

Jo Bannister	Elizabeth George	Priscilla Masters
Pauline Bell	Patricia Hall	Betty Rowlands
Geraldine Evans		

Jenny Eclair · Chick Lit

Jenny Colgan	Sophie Kinsella	Jill Mansell
Jenny Crusie	Kathy Lette	Deborah Wright
Tara Heavey	Chris Manby	

Umberto Eco · 1932- · It · General

www.themodernword.com/eco

Paulo Coelho	Ross King	Arturo Perez-Reverte
Jostein Gaarder	Lawrence Norfolk	Jill Paton Walsh
William Golding		

Go to back for lists of:
Authors by Genre
Characters and Series
Prize Winners
Further Reading

David Eddings   1931-   US   Fantasy: Epic

www.harpercollins.co.uk/microsites/eddings

Sarah Ash	Robert Jordan	Robert Silverberg
Mark Chadbourn	Stan Nicholls	J R R Tolkien
Elizabeth Haydon	Ricardo Pinto	Tad Williams
Ian Irvine	Mickey Zucker Reichert	Sarah Zettel

Lucinda Edmonds   1966-   Glitz & Glamour

Charlotte Bingham	Johanna Lindsey	Fern Michaels
Celia Brayfield	Judith Michael	Fiona Walker
Jenn Crowell		

Robert Edric   1956-   Historical

Black 1985

Peter Benson	Simon Kernick
Alan Dunn	Chris Paling
Giles Foden	Tim Pears
Janice Graham	Donna Tartt

E

Robert Edric   1956-   Crime: PI

🏃 Leo Rivers - Hull

John Baker	Graham Hurley	Martyn Waites
Ken Bruen	Simon Kernick	

Martin Edwards   1955-   Crime: Amateur sleuth

www.fantasticfiction.co.uk/authors/Martin_Edwards.htm   🏃 Harry Devlin, Solicitor - Liverpool

Jeffrey Ashford	Ron Ellis	M R D Meek
John Baker	Bill James	Barrie Roberts
Judith Cutler	Jim Kelly	Gillian Slovo

Ruth Dudley Edwards   1944-   Ire   Crime: Amateur sleuth

www.ruthdudleyedwards.co.uk   🏃 Robert Amiss & Baroness Troutbeck

Sarah Caudwell	Fidelis Morgan
Bartholomew Gill	Tom Sharpe

Imogen Edwards-Jones   1959-   Chick Lit

www.fantasticfiction.co.uk/authors/Imogen_Edwards-Jones.htm

Louise Bagshawe	Melissa Hill	Arabella Weir
Lynne Barrett-Lee	Louise Marley	Jane Wenham-Jones
Jenny Colgan	Tina Reilly	

Greg Egan   1961-   Aus   Science Fiction: Near future
http://gregegan.customer.netspace.net.au

Ben Bova	Ian McDonald	Nick Sagan
Pat Cadigan	Ken MacLeod	Neal Stephenson
Jon Courtenay Grimwood	Robert Reed	David Wingrove

Clive Egleton   1927-   Adventure/Thriller
www.fantasticfiction.co.uk/authors/Clive_Egleton.htm   ⋏ Peter Ashton

James Adams	Len Deighton	Anthony Price
Ted Allbeury	Colin Forbes	Kenneth Royce
Tom Bradby	Frederick Forsyth	

Thomas Eidson   1944-   US   General

Nicholas Evans	Scott Phillips	TGR 1995
Charles Frazier	Annie Proulx	
Cormac McCarthy	Jane Smiley	
Stewart O'Nan	Jane Urquhart	

E

Barry Eisler   1964-   US   Adventure/Thriller
www.barryeisler.com   ⋏ John Rain, Assassin

Ken Bruen	Ian Fleming
James Lee Burke	Jefferson Parker

Elizabeth Elgin   Saga
www.fantasticfiction.co.uk/authors/Elizabeth_Elgin.htm   ⋏ Sutton Family - Yorkshire

Julia Bryant	Beryl Matthews	Susan Sallis
Helen Cannam	Margaret Mayhew	Kay Stephens
Anna Jacobs	Wendy Robertson	June Tate

Kate Elliott   1958-   US   Fantasy: Epic
is Alis A Rasmussen
www.sff.net/people/kate.elliott

Ashok K Banker	Raymond E Feist	Paul Kearney
Terry Brooks	Maggie Furey	Holly Lisle
C J Cherryh	J V Jones	Elizabeth Moon

Bret Easton Ellis   1964-   US   General
www.fantasticfiction.co.uk/authors/Bret_Easton_Ellis.htm

Matthew Branton	Haruki Murakami	Richard Price
Douglas Coupland	Chuck Palahniuk	Will Self
Stewart Home	Tim Parks	Tom Wolfe

Julie Ellis   1933-   US   Glitz & Glamour
www.julieellis.net

Sally Beauman	Carole Matthews	Fern Michaels
Judi James	Judith Michael	Una-Mary Parker
Judith Krantz		

Kate Ellis   1953-   Crime: Police work - UK
www.kateellis.co.uk   ♁ DS Wesley Peterson - West Country

Jeffrey Ashford	Freda Davies	P D James
Janie Bolitho	Colin Dexter	Roy Lewis
W J Burley	Roy Hart	

Ron Ellis   1941-   Crime: Amateur sleuth
www.ronellis.co.uk   ♁ Johnny Ace, Disc jockey - Liverpool

| Ace Atkins | Chris Niles | Cath Staincliffe |
| Martin Edwards | Robert T Price | |

E

Harlan Ellison   1934-   Science Fiction: Space and time
www.harlanellison.com/home.htm

| Brian W Aldiss | Greg Bear | John Brosnan |
| Poul Anderson | Ray Bradbury | Joe Haldeman |

Lucy Ellman   1956-   US   General

Louise Bagshawe	Joanne Harris	Guardian 1988
Susie Boyt	Sarah Kate Lynch	
Jenn Crowell	Pauline Melville	
Anne Fine	Lynne Truss	

Roger Jon Ellory   1965-   Crime: Psychological
www.fantasticfiction.co.uk/authors/Roger_Jon_Ellory.htm

| John Connor | Carol Anne Davis | Jim Kelly |
| Thomas H Cook | Karin Fossum | George P Pelecanos |

James Ellroy   1948-   US   Crime: Hardboiled
www.fantasticfiction.co.uk/authors/James_Ellroy.htm   ♁ DS Lloyd Hopkins - Los Angeles

Jerome Charyn	Stuart M Kaminsky	Jason Starr
James Crumley	Chuck Palahniuk	Boston Teran
Stephen Donaldson	Richard Price	Jim Thompson
Loren D Estleman	John B Spencer	Joseph Wambaugh

Margaret Elphinstone 1948- Sco — Historical

www.hybrasil.demon.co.uk

William Boyd	Barbara Erskine	Matthew Kneale
Bruce Chatwin	Julie Garwood	James Robertson

Ben Elton 1959- — Lad Lit

www.fantasticfiction.co.uk/authors/Ben_Elton.htm

CWA 1996

David Baddiel	Charles Higson
Colin Butts	Robert Llewellyn
Stephen Fry	John McCabe
James Hawes	Keith Waterhouse

Leif Enger 1961- US — General

Kate Atkinson	Charles Frazier	Adriana Trigiani
Nicholas Evans	Haven Kimmel	

E Louise Erdrich 1954- US — General

Isabel Allende	Barbara Kingsolver	Stewart O'Nan
Michael Collins	Alison Lurie	Annie Proulx
Fannie Flagg	Lorrie Moore	Rebecca Wells

Steven Erikson 1959- Can — Fantasy: Epic

is Steve Rune Lundin
www.tor.com/erikson

James Barclay	Jude Fisher	John Marco
Stephen Donaldson	David Gemmell	Ricardo Pinto
Raymond E Feist	Greg Keyes	Sean Russell

Barbara Erskine 1944- — Historical

is Barbara Hope-Lewis
www.fantasticfiction.co.uk/authors/Barbara_Erskine.htm

Elizabeth Aston	Inga Dunbar	Helen Hollick
Elizabeth Chadwick	Margaret Elphinstone	Reay Tannahill

Laura Esquivel 1951- Mex — General

www.fantasticfiction.co.uk/authors/Laura_Esquivel.htm

Isabel Allende	Gabriel Garcia Márquez	Jeanette Winterson
Kate Atkinson	Shifra Horn	

Loren D Estleman   1952-   US   Crime: PI

www.lorenestleman.com   ♱ Amos Walker - Detroit • Peter Macklin, Hitman

Lawrence Block	James Ellroy	Jon A Jackson
C J Box	Steve Hamilton	Reggie Nadelson
Harlan Coben	Dashiell Hammett	Robert K Tanenbaum

Jeffrey Eugenides   1960-   US   General

www.jeffreyeugenides.com

Ethan Canin	Siri Hustvedt	Pulitzer 2003
Michel Faber	Rick Moody	
Jonathan Franzen	Richard Powers	
Andrew Sean Greer	Donna Tartt	John Updike

Janet Evanovich   1943-   US   Crime: Humour

also writes as **Steffie Hall**   ♱ Stephanie Plum, Bail bondswoman - Newark, New Jersey
www.evanovich.com   Max Holt • Alexander Barnaby

Linda Barnes	Liz Evans	CWA 1995 & 1997
Marc Blake	Sparkle Hayter	
Tim Cockey	Pauline McLynn	
Jenny Crusie	Zoë Sharp	Scarlett Thomas
Louise Doughty	Sarah Strohmeyer	Valerie Wilson Wesley

E

Geraldine Evans   1953-   Crime: Police work - UK

also writes as **Geraldine Hartnett**   ♱ DI Joe Rafferty & Sgt D Llewellyn
www.geraldineevans.com   DCI Casey & Thomas Catt

Vivien Armstrong	Caroline Graham	Reginald Hill
Brian Cooper	Ann Granger	Jill McGown
Marjorie Eccles	J M Gregson	

Liz Evans   Crime: PI

is **Patricia Grey**   ♱ Grace Smith -
http://lizevans.net   'Seatoun', South Coast, England

Jo Bannister	Joyce Holms	Sarah Strohmeyer
Cara Black	Pauline McLynn	Scarlett Thomas
Janet Evanovich	Zoë Sharp	Rebecca Tope
Sparkle Hayter	Michelle Spring	Stella Whitelaw

Nicholas Evans   1950-   General

www.randomhouse.com/features/nickevans

Pat Conroy	Charles Frazier	Larry McMurtry
Thomas Eidson	Jim Harrison	Nicholas Sparks
Leif Enger	Stuart Harrison	Robert James Waller

Pamela Evans

www.fantasticfiction.co.uk/authors/Pamela_Evans.htm

Saga
London

Helen Carey	Elizabeth Lord	Alison Stuart
Emma Dally	Victor Pemberton	Elizabeth Waite
Elizabeth Hawksley	Sally Spencer	Jeanne Whitmee

Bernardine Evaristo

www.contemporarywriters.com/authors/?p=auth179

General

Monica Ali	Arundhati Roy
Hanif Kureishi	Vikram Seth

Michel Faber   1960-   Neth

www.fantasticfiction.co.uk/authors/Michel_Faber.htm

General

Monica Ali	Alasdair Gray	W Somerset Maugham
Charles Dickens	James Kelman	Magnus Mills
Jeffrey Eugenides	A L Kennedy	Rupert Thomson

E

F

Zoë Fairbairns   1948-

www.zoefairbairns.co.uk

General

Maureen Duffy	Kate Hatfield	Kate Saunders
Philippa Gregory	Susan Howatch	Titia Sutherland

Linda Fairstein   1947-   US

www.lindafairstein.com

Crime: Legal/financial
⚐ Alexandra Cooper, Assistant DA
New York

D W Buffa	Steve Martini	Lisa Scottoline
Alafair Burke	Perri O'Shaughnessy	Karin Slaughter
Lisa Gardner	Kathy Reichs	Susan R Sloan
John T Lescroart	Nancy Taylor Rosenberg	Robert K Tanenbaum

Colin Falconer   1953-

www.fantasticfiction.co.uk/authors/Colin_Falconer.htm

Adventure/Thriller

James Clavell	Eric Lustbader
Martina Cole	Christopher Nicole

Duncan Falconer

www.fantasticfiction.co.uk/authors/Duncan_Falconer.htm

Adventure/Thriller

Tom Clancy	Paul Henke	John Nichol
Clive Cussler	Andy McNab	Chris Ryan

Elizabeth Falconer
Aga saga

Teresa Crane
Nina Dufort
Rebecca Gregson

Elizabeth Pewsey
Amanda Prantera
Alexandra Raife

Joanna Trollope
Mary Wesley

David Farland   1957-   US
Fantasy: Epic

is **Dave Wolverton**
www.fantasticfiction.co.uk/authors/David_Farland.htm

Mark Anthony
Kate Jacoby

J V Jones
Robert Jordan

Juliet E McKenna
Jane Welch

John Farris   1936-   US
Horror

also writes as **Steve Brackeen**
www.fantasticfiction.co.uk/authors/John_Farris.htm

David Bowker
Stephen Gallagher
Stephen King

Richard Laymon
H P Lovecraft
Robert McCammon

Graham Masterton
Peter Straub
Whitley Strieber

Howard Fast   1914-2003   US
General

also wrote as **E V Cunningham**
www.fantasticfiction.co.uk/authors/Howard_Fast.htm

Winston Graham
Robert Graves
Georgette Heyer

James A Michener
Mary Renault

Nigel Tranter
Leon Uris

F

William Faulkner   1897-1962   US
General

www.kirjasto.sci.fi/faulkner.htm

Connie May Fowler
James Joyce
Cormac McCarthy

Carson McCullers
Toni Morrison
Joyce Carol Oates

Amos Oz
William Styron

Sebastian Faulks   1953-
General

www.contemporarywriters.com/authors/?p=auth3

Francis Cottam
Giles Foden
Andrew Greig

Laurent Joffrin
Alice McDermott
Simon Mawer

Juliette Mead
Chris Paling
Erich Maria Remarque

Patricia Fawcett
Aga saga

Sarah Challis
Lucy Clare
Anne Doughty

Kate Fielding
Adèle Geras
Charlotte Moore

Rebecca Shaw
Peta Tayler

Catherine Feeny 1957- General

Mavis Cheek
Candida Crewe
Jill Dawson

Anne Fine
Kathy Lette

Deborah Moggach
Elizabeth Pewsey

David Feintuch US Science Fiction: Space opera
www.cris.com/~writeman

Lois McMaster Bujold
Chris Bunch

Orson Scott Card
C J Cherryh

Joe Haldeman
Harry Turtledove

Raymond E Feist 1945- US Fantasy: Epic
www.raymondfeistbooks.com

Terry Brooks
Stephen Donaldson
Kate Elliott
Steven Erikson

Maggie Furey
Paul Kearney
John Marco
Stan Nicholls

Ricardo Pinto
Mickey Zucker Reichert
Jan Siegel
Janny Wurts

Alison Fell 1944- Sco General
www.contemporarywriters.com/authors/?p=auth158

Angela Carter
Patricia Duncker

Janice Graham
Alice Hoffman

Nancy Thayer

F

Kate Fenton 1954- Aga saga
www.katefenton.com

Raffaella Barker
Elizabeth Buchan
Lucy Clare

Isla Dewar
Anne Doughty
Nina Dufort

Katie Fforde
Sue Limb
Mary Sheepshanks

Elizabeth Ferrars 1907-95 Crime: Amateur sleuth
was Morna Doris Brown
www.fantasticfiction.co.uk/authors/Elizabeth_Ferrars.htm

🏃 Andrew Basnett
Felix Freer

Margery Allingham
Anthea Fraser
Alison Joseph

Ngaio Marsh
Maureen O'Brien
June Thomson

Patricia Wentworth
Margaret Yorke

Robert Ferrigno 1948- US Crime: Hardboiled
www.robertferrigno.com

🏃 Jimmy Gage, Reporter
Los Angeles

James Crumley
James Hall

Tony Hillerman
Jonathon King

David Lindsey
Michael McGarrity
Boston Teran

Dan Fesperman
US   Adventure/Thriller

www.danfesperman.com   ⚑ Vladko Petric - Bosnia

CWA 2003

Michael Dibdin	Joseph Kanon
Karin Fossum	Martin Cruz Smith
Robert Harris	Robert Wilson

Jasper Fforde
1961-   Wales   Crime: Humour

www.jasperfforde.com   ⚑ Thursday Next, Literary detective - Swindon

Douglas Adams	Christopher Fowler	Malcolm Pryce
Robert Asprin	Tom Holt	Robert Rankin
Marius Brill	Terry Pratchett	Connie Willis

Katie Fforde
1952-   Aga saga

www.katiefforde.com

Clare Chambers	Nina Dufort	Elizabeth Palmer
Lucy Clare	Kate Fenton	Ann Swinfen
Victoria Clayton	Julia Hamilton	Alan Titchmarsh

Helen Fielding
1958-   Chick Lit

www.fantasticfiction.co.uk/authors/Helen_Fielding.htm

Sherry Ashworth	Amy Jenkins	Yvonne Roberts
Victoria Corby	Serena Mackesy	Stephanie Theobald
Veronica Henry	Alexandra Potter	Lynne Truss

F

Joy Fielding
1945-   Can   Crime: Psychological

www.joyfielding.com

Mark Billingham	Faye Kellerman	Margaret Murphy
Mary Higgins Clark	Judith Kelman	Christina Schwarz
John Connolly	Gloria Murphy	

Kate Fielding
1949-   Aga saga

also writes as **Jenny Oldfield**   Ravensdale Series - Yorkshire

Nina Dufort	Hazel Hucker	Elizabeth Pewsey
Patricia Fawcett	Erica James	Rebecca Shaw
Rebecca Gregson	Jan Karon	

Joseph Finder
1958-   US   Adventure/Thriller

www.josephfinder.com

David Baldacci	Robert Ludlum
Vince Flynn	Gareth O'Callaghan

Anne Fine 1947- General

www.annefine.co.uk

Rachel Billington
Rachel Cusk
Anabel Donald
Lucy Ellman
Catherine Feeny
Angela Green
Zoë Heller
Joan Lingard
Liz Rigbey

Patricia Finney Crime: Historical - C16th

also writes as P F Chisholm
www.patricia-finney.co.uk

David Becket & Simon Ames
Elizabethan England

Higham 1977

Michael Clynes
Judith Cook
Philip Gooden
C C Humphreys
Edward Marston
John Pilkington
C J Sansom
Martin Stephen
Peter Tonkin

Tibor Fischer 1959- General

www.contemporarywriters.com/authors/?p=auth35

Louis de Bernières
Joseph Heller
John Irving
Ian McEwan

F

Jude Fisher Fantasy: Epic

also writes as Gabriel King; *is* Jane Johnson
www.judefisher.com

James Barclay
Joanne Bertin
Steven Erikson
Robin Hobb
Ian Irvine
Juliet E McKenna
Sean Russell
J R R Tolkien

F Scott Fitzgerald 1896-1940 US General

www.sc.edu/fitzgerald

Ethan Canin
E L Doctorow
E M Forster
Ernest Hemingway
Craig Holden
Carson McCullers
John Steinbeck

Penelope Fitzgerald 1916-2000 General

www.fantasticfiction.co.uk/authors/Penelope_Fitzgerald.htm

Booker 1979

Jane Austen
Beryl Bainbridge
Rachel Billington
Anita Brookner
A S Byatt
Penelope Lively
Emma Tennant
Salley Vickers
Edith Wharton

Bill Fitzhugh   US   Crime: Humour

www.billfitzhugh.com

Dave Barry	Christopher Brookmyre	Carl Hiaasen
Anthony Bourdain	Christopher Buckley	Joe R Lansdale
Gene Brewer	Tim Dorsey	Laurence Shames

Fannie Flagg   1941-   US   General

is Patricia Neal
www.randomhouse.com/features/fannieflagg

Elizabeth Berg	Laurie Graham	Annie Proulx
Jenny Crusie	Jan Karon	Adriana Trigiani
Louise Erdrich	Haven Kimmel	Rebecca Wells

Sean Flannery   US   Adventure/Thriller

is David Hagberg
www.fantasticfiction.co.uk/authors/Sean_Flannery.htm

Dan Brown	Robert Ludlum	A J Quinnell
Daniel Easterman	Gareth O'Callaghan	Mark T Sullivan
David Hagberg	Douglas Preston	

Ian Fleming   1908-64   Adventure/Thriller

www.ianflemingcentre.com   ⚇ James Bond   **F**

Eric Ambler	Barry Eisler	John Gardner
Raymond Benson	James Follett	Gavin Lyall
John Buchan	Brian Freemantle	Daniel Silva

Cy Flood   Lad Lit

Dougie Brimson	Mike Gayle	John King
Paul Burke	Alex George	Kevin Sampson
Colin Butts		

David Flusfeder   1960-   US   General

www.contemporarywriters.com/authors/?p=auth01J16O2702126 20187

Martin Amis	Sue Gee	Encore 1997
Jenny Diski	Graham Greene	
Helen Dunmore	Glenn Patterson	

Go to back for lists of:
Authors by Genre
Characters and Series
Prize Winners
Further Reading

Katie Flynn   1936-   Saga

also writes as Judith Saxton; *is* Judy Turner   🏃 Lilac Larkin - Liverpool
www.katieflynn.com

Anne Baker	Ruth Hamilton	Marie Joseph
Josephine Cox	Audrey Howard	Elizabeth Murphy
Helen Forrester	Anna Jacobs	Lynda Page

Vince Flynn   US   Adventure/Thriller

www.vinceflynn.com   🏃 Mitch Rapp - CIA Washington

Suzanne Brockmann	Joseph Finder	Brian Haig
Dan Brown	David Hagberg	Mark T Sullivan
Stephen Coonts		

Giles Foden   1967-   General

www.fantasticfiction.co.uk/authors/Giles_Foden.htm

William Boyd	Sebastian Faulks	Whitbread 1998
James Clavell	Pamela Jooste	Holtby 1998
Robert Edric	Paul Theroux	S Maugham 1999

James Follett   1939-   Adventure/Thriller

www.fantasticfiction.co.uk/authors/James_Follett.htm

James Adams	Ian Fleming	Justin Scott
Desmond Bagley	Alistair MacLean	Craig Thomas
Raymond Benson	Matthew Reilly	Glover Wright

Ken Follett   1949-   Adventure/Thriller

www.ken-follett.com

Desmond Bagley	Nelson DeMille	John Lawton
Nicholas Coleridge	Clare Francis	Robert Littell
John Gordon Davis	Humphrey Hawksley	Michael Shea

Alan Folsom   US   Adventure/Thriller

David Baldacci	Conor Cregan	Thomas Kelly
Tom Bradby	Pete Hamill	Robert Ludlum
Dan Brown	Greg Iles	

Colin Forbes   1923-   Adventure/Thriller

is Raymond Harold Sawkins   🏃 Tweed & Newman
www.fantasticfiction.co.uk/authors/Colin_Forbes.htm   SIS

Ted Allbeury	Campbell Armstrong	Clive Egleton
Evelyn Anthony	Jon Cleary	Frederick Forsyth

Leslie Forbes   Can   Adventure/Thriller: Psychological

www.fantasticfiction.co.uk/authors/Leslie_Forbes.htm

Michael Dibdin	Joanna Hines	Donna Leon
Michael Frayn	Peter Hoeg	Barbara Nadel
Carol Goodman	H R F Keating	Arturo Pérez-Reverte

G M Ford   1945-   US   Crime: Hardboiled
⚐ Frank Corso, Journalist - Seattle

Ace Atkins	Robert Crais	J A Jance
Caroline Carver	James Hall	Jim Kelly
Harlan Coben	Denise Hamilton	Dennis Lehane
Michael Connelly	Steve Hamilton	Liza Marklund

Michael Curtis Ford   US   Historical
Ancient Greece

www.fantasticfiction.co.uk/authors/Michael_Curtis_Ford.htm

Robert Graves	Mary Renault
Steven Pressfield	Simon Scarrow

Richard Ford   1944-   US   General

www.fantasticfiction.co.uk/authors/Richard_Ford.htm

Robert Olen Butler	Jim Harrison	Pulitzer 1996
Raymond Carver	Tama Janowitz	
Michael Cunningham	Garrison Keillor	
Pete Dexter	Alice Munro	Walker Percy
Andre Dubus	Tim O'Brien	Tobias Wolff

F

C S Forester   1899-1966   Sea: Historical
⚐ Horatio Hornblower
C18th/19th England

www.fantasticfiction.co.uk/authors/C_S_Forester.htm

David Donachie	James L Nelson	Dudley Pope
Alexander Kent	Patrick O'Brian	Julian Stockwin
Jonathan Lunn	Marcus Palliser	Showell Styles
Jan Needle	Dan Parkinson	Victor Suthren

Helen Forrester   1919-   Saga
Liverpool

www.helenforrester.com

Anne Baker	Audrey Howard	Maureen Lee
Katie Flynn	Joan Jonker	Mary Mackie
June Francis	Marie Joseph	Elizabeth Murphy

Go to back for lists of:
Authors by Genre • Characters and Series • Prize Winners • Further Reading

E M Forster   1879-1970   General

F Scott Fitzgerald	Anthony Powell	H G Wells
Henry James	Paul Scott	Edith Wharton
Ruth Prawer Jhabvala	Carolyn Slaughter	Virginia Woolf

Margaret Forster   1938-   General
www.fantasticfiction.co.uk/authors/Margaret_Forster.htm

Kate Atkinson	Sue Gee	Mary Morrissy
Kate Bingham	Linda Grant	Anna Quindlen
Maureen Duffy	Charlotte Mendelson	Elizabeth Tettmar

Frederick Forsyth   1938-   Adventure/Thriller
www.fantasticfiction.co.uk/authors/Frederick_Forsyth.htm

Clive Egleton	James Long	Kyle Mills
Colin Forbes	Mike Lunnon-Wood	Daniel Silva
Paul Henke	Glenn Meade	James Thayer

Karin Fossum   1954-   Nor   Crime: Police work - Norway
www.fantasticfiction.co.uk/authors/Karin_Fossum.htm   🏃 Insp Konrad Sejer & Jacob Skarre
Oslo

Karin Alvtegen	Donna Leon	Ruth Rendell
Roger Jon Ellory	Pierre Magnan	Pernille Rygg
Dan Fesperman	Henning Mankell	Maj Sjöwall and
Jean-Christophe Grangé	Liza Marklund	Per Wahlöö
John Harvey		

Alan Dean Foster   1946-   US   Science Fiction: Space opera
www.alandeanfoster.com

Piers Anthony	Orson Scott Card	Colin Greenland
Robert Asprin	C J Cherryh	Elizabeth Haydon
David Brin	Simon R Green	

Christopher Fowler   1953-   Horror
www.christopherfowler.co.uk

Clive Barker	Graham Joyce	British Fantasy 2004
David Bowker	Graham Masterton	
Ramsey Campbell	Kim Newman	
Jonathan Carroll	Malcolm Pryce	Michael Marshall Smith

Go to back for lists of:
Authors by Genre • Characters and Series • Prize Winners • Further Reading

F

Christopher Fowler 1953-   Crime: Humour

www.christopherfowler.co.uk   🏃 Arthur Bryant & John May, Policemen - London

Peter Ackroyd   Jasper Fforde   Iain Sinclair
Christopher Brookmyre   Malcolm Pryce

Connie May Fowler 1958- US   General

www.conniemayfowler.com

William Faulkner   Carson McCullers
J Robert Lennon   Joyce Carol Oates

Karen Joy Fowler 1950- US   General

www.sfwa.org/members/Fowler

Patricia Gaffney   Jodi Picoult   Anne Tyler
William Kowalski   Anne Rivers Siddons   Rebecca Wells
Elinor Lipman

John Fowles 1926-   General

www.fowlesbooks.com

Peter Ackroyd   William Golding   Robert Nye
Bruce Chatwin   Alasdair Gray   Graham Swift
Maggie Gee   Thomas Hardy   Rupert Thomson

F

Catherine Fox 1961-   General

Catherine Dunne   Julia Hamilton   Susan Howatch
Eileen Goudge   Elizabeth Jane Howard   Barbara Trapido

Janet Frame 1924-2004 NZ   General

www.fantasticfiction.co.uk/authors/Janet_Frame.htm

Elizabeth Jolley   Paul Sayer   Commonwealth 1989
Doris Lessing   Fay Weldon

Ronald Frame 1953- Sco   General

Robert Goddard   Bernard MacLaverty   Paul Micou
Kazuo Ishiguro   Allan Massie   William Trevor

Clare Francis 1946-   Adventure/Thriller

www.fantasticfiction.co.uk/authors/Clare_Francis.htm

Evelyn Anthony   Paula Gosling   Hilary Norman
Lisa Appignanesi   Gloria Murphy   Christina Schwarz
Ken Follett

87

Dick Francis   1920-   Wales

Crime: Amateur sleuth
Sid Halley & Kit Fielding
Horse racing
CWA 1979

John Francome
Gavin Lyall
Jenny Pitman
Richard Pitman
Lyndon Stacey

June Francis

Saga
Liverpool

Lyn Andrews
Julia Bryant
Jean Chapman
Helen Forrester
Lena Kennedy
Gwen Madoc
Sheila Newberry
June Tate
Margaret Thornton

John Francome   1952-

Crime: Amateur sleuth
Horse racing

www.authorpages.hoddersystems.com/johnfrancome

Dick Francis
Gavin Lyall
Jenny Pitman
Richard Pitman
Lyndon Stacey

Jonathan Franzen   1959-   US

General

www.jonathanfranzen.com

Ethan Canin
Michael Cunningham
Don Delillo
Jeffrey Eugenides
A M Homes
Richard Powers
Annie Proulx   Black 2002
Donna Tartt
John Updike

Anthea Fraser   1930-

Crime: Police work - UK
DCI David Webb & DS Ken Jackson
'Broadshire', Home Counties, England
Rhona Parish

also writes as **Vanessa Graham**
www.fantasticfiction.co.uk/authors/Anthea_Fraser.htm

Marian Babson
Elizabeth Ferrars
Ann Granger
June Thomson

Caro Fraser   Sco

General

www.fantasticfiction.co.uk/authors/Caro_Fraser.htm

Nina Bawden
John Mortimer
Mary Ryan
Joanna Trollope

Christine Marion Fraser   1945-2003   Sco

Saga
Rhanna Series • Kings Series •
Noble Series - Scotland

www.fantasticfiction.co.ukauthors/Christine_Marion_Fraser.htm

Emma Blair
Margaret Thomson Davis
Nora Kay
Gwen Kirkwood
Isobel Neill
Pamela Oldfield
Jessica Stirling
Kirsty White
Mary Withall

F

George Macdonald Fraser 1925- Sco — Humour

www.fantasticfiction.co.uk/authors/George_MacDonald_Fraser.htm

Boris Akunin
Joseph Heller
Tom Holt
Tom Sharpe
Leslie Thomas
P G Wodehouse

Sara Fraser 1937- — Saga

also writes as Roy Clews

⚲ Tildy Crawford - Midlands

Catrin Collier
Josephine Cox
Patricia Grey
Meg Hutchinson
Annie Murray
Lynda Page
Alison Stuart
Janet Tanner

Michael Frayn 1933- — Humour

www.fantasticfiction.co.uk/authors/Michael_Frayn.htm

Kingsley Amis
Malcolm Bradbury
Leslie Forbes
Howard Jacobson
David Lodge
Simon Mawer

Whitbread 2002

Margaret Frazer US — Crime: Historical - Medieval

also writes as Mary Monica Parker
is Gail Frazer
www.margaret-frazer.com

⚲ Sister Frevisse
C15th England

Alys Clare
Judith Cook
Philip Gooden
Michael Jecks
Ellis Peters
Candace Robb
Kate Sedley
Peter Tremayne

F

Charles Frazier 1950- US — General

www.fantasticfiction.co.uk/authors/Charles_Frazier.htm

Thomas Eidson
Leif Enger
Nicholas Evans
David Guterson
Thomas Keneally
Cormac McCarthy
Larry McMurtry
Tim O'Brien
Stewart O'Nan

Brian Freemantle 1936- — Adventure/Thriller

also writes as John Maxwell
www.fantasticfiction.co.uk/authors/Brian_Freemantle.htm

⚲ Charlie Muffin - MI6

Ted Allbeury
Ian Fleming
John Gardner
John Le Carré
Anthony Price

Go to back for lists of:
Authors by Genre
Characters and Series
Prize Winners
Further Reading

Nicci French 1958-　　Adventure/Thriller: Psychological

is Nicci Gerrard & Sean French　　　　　　　🤸 Dr Samantha Laschen
www.fantasticfiction.co.uk/authors/Nicci_French.htm

Lisa Appignanesi	Gay Longworth	Gemma O'Connor
Jeremy Dronfield	Phil Lovesey	Patrick Redmond
Frances Hegarty	Elizabeth McGregor	Chris Simms
Alice Hoffman	J Wallis Martin	

Esther Freud 1963-　　　　　　　　General

www.contemporarywriters.com/authors/?p=auth38

Sophie Cooke	Alex Garland	Polly Samson
Rachel Cusk	Terry McMillan	Meera Syal
Suzannah Dunn	Gwendoline Riley	Emma Tennant

Kinky Friedman 1944-　US　　　　Crime: Humour

www.kinkyfriedman.com　　🤸 Kinky Friedman, Country & Western singer
New York

Anthony Bourdain	Dashiell Hammett	Susan Isaacs
Charlotte Carter	James Hawes	Elmore Leonard
Tim Dorsey	Sparkle Hayter	Robert B Parker

F Stephen Fry 1957-　　　　　　　　Humour

www.fantasticfiction.co.uk/authors/Stephen_Fry.htm

Roddy Doyle	Tim Lott	Mark Wallington
Ben Elton	Geoff Nicholson	Nigel Williams
Charles Higson	Alexei Sayle	P G Wodehouse

Carlos Fuentes 1928-　Mex　　　　General

www.kirjasto.sci.fi/fuentes.htm

Isabel Allende	Tomas Eloy Martinez
Gabriel Garcia Márquez	Mario Vargas Llosa

Alexander Fullerton 1924-　　　Adventure/Thriller

www.fantasticfiction.co.uk/authors/Alexander_Fullerton.htm

Brian Callison	Hammond Innes	James Pattinson
Duncan Harding	Philip McCutchan	Richard Woodman

John Fullerton 　　　　　　Adventure/Thriller

www.johnfullerton.com

Michael Asher	Alan Judd	John Nichol
Mark Burnell	Andy McNab	Gerald Seymour

Maggie Furey   1955-   Fantasy: Epic
www.fantasticfiction.co.uk/authors/Maggie_Furey.htm

Terry Brooks	Raymond E Feist	J V Jones
Chris Bunch	Terry Goodkind	Paul Kearney
Kate Elliott	Julia Gray	George R R Martin

Alan Furst   1941-   US   Adventure/Thriller
www.alanfurst.net

Evelyn Anthony	John Gordon Davis	Robert Littell
Nicholas Coleridge	Joseph R Garber	Robert Ryan
Conor Cregan	Jean-Christophe Grangé	Robert Wilson

Frances Fyfield   1948-   Crime: Amateur sleuth
is Frances Hegarty   ⚕ Helen West, Lawyer, &
www.fantasticfiction.co.uk/authors/Frances_Fyfield.htm   DS Geoffrey Bailey - London
                                              ⚕ Sarah Fortune, Lawyer

Jane Adams	Joanna Hines	CWA 1990 & 1991
Natasha Cooper	M R D Meek	
Jonathan Davies	Margaret Murphy	
Elizabeth George	Robert K Tanenbaum	

Jostein Gaarder   1952-   Nor   General
www.fantasticfiction.co.uk/authors/Jostein_Gaarder.htm

| Umberto Eco | Mark Haddon | Iris Murdoch |
| Gabriel Garcia Márquez | Peter Hoeg | |

Diana Gabaldon   1952-   US   Historical
www.cco.caltech.edu/~gatti/gabaldon/gabaldon.html   Outlander Series

Jean M Auel	Julie Garwood	Reay Tannahill
Inga Dunbar	Judith Lennox	Patricia Wendorf
Dorothy Dunnett	James Long	

Reg Gadney   1941-   Crime: PI
www.fantasticfiction.co.uk/authors/Reg_Gadney.htm   ⚕ Alan Rosslyn

| Harry Bingham | John McLaren | Michael Ridpath |
| Paul Kilduff | Sara Paretsky | |

Patricia Gaffney   US   General
www.sff.net/people/PGaffney

Elizabeth Berg	Sue Miller	Libby Purves
Karen Joy Fowler	Maggie O'Farrell	Adriana Trigiani
Barbara Kingsolver	Jodi Picoult	

Neil Gaiman   1960-   Fantasy: Contemporary
www.neilgaiman.com

Douglas Adams   Charles de Lint   Philip Pullman
Clive Barker   Tim Powers   Martin Scott
John Crowley

Patrick Gale   1962-   General
www.galewarning.org

Alan Hollinghurst   Paul Micou
Armistead Maupin   Edmund White

Stephen Gallagher   1954-   Horror
www.stephengallagher.com

Chaz Brenchley   James Herbert   Graham Masterton
John Farris   Peter James   Mark Morris
Muriel Gray   Dean R Koontz   T M Wright

Janice Galloway   1956-   Sco   General
www.galloway.1to1.org

Regi Claire   Andrew O'Hagan   Alan Spence
Amanda Craig   Agnes Owens   Zoë Strachan
A L Kennedy   Ali Smith

G John Galsworthy   1867-1933   General
www.fantasticfiction.co.uk/authors/John_Galsworthy.htm

R F Delderfield   J B Priestley
D H Lawrence   Anthony Trollope

Joseph R Garber   1943-   US   Adventure/Thriller
also writes as **Edgar Still**
www.josephgarber.com

Alan Furst   Alan Judd   Chris Ryan
Paul Henke   Andy McNab

Gabriel Garcia Márquez   1928-   Col   General
www.fantasticfiction.co.uk/authors/Gabriel_Garcia_Marquez.htm

Isabel Allende   Paulo Coelho   David Grossman
T Coraghessan Boyle   Laura Esquivel   Tomas Eloy Martinez
Anthony Burgess   Carlos Fuentes   Ben Okri
Peter Carey   Jostein Gaarder   Mario Vargas Llosa

Luiz Alfredo Garcia-Roza 1936- Braz Crime: Police work - Brazil

www.garcia-roza.com   🚶 Insp Espinosa - Rio de Janeiro

Andrea Camilleri	José Latour	Manuel Vázquez Montalbán
Michael Dibdin	Donna Leon	Barbara Nadel
Juan Goytisolo	Patricia Melo	Qiu Xiaolong

Jane Gardam 1928- General

www.contemporarywriters.com/authors/?p=auth40

Hilary Bailey	Joan Lingard	Higham 1975
Nina Bawden	Jane Rogers	Whitbread 1991
Amanda Craig	Jill Paton Walsh	
Susan Hill	Teresa Waugh	

Meg Gardiner US Crime: PI

www.meggardiner.com   🚶 Evan Delaney - Santa Barbara, California

Linda Barnes	Laurie King	Marcia Muller
Jan Burke	Laura Lippman	Carol O'Connell
Lynn Hightower	Theresa Monsour	Dana Stabenow

Craig Shaw Gardner 1949- US Fantasy: Humour

also writes as **Peter Garrison**
www.fantasticfiction.co.uk/authors/Craig_Shaw_Gardner.htm

Piers Anthony	Andrew Harman	Terry Pratchett
Robert Asprin	Tom Holt	

John Gardner 1926- Adventure/Thriller

www.john-gardner.com   🚶 Big Herbie Kruger

Eric Ambler	Ian Fleming	Gavin Lyall
Desmond Bagley	Brian Freemantle	Julian Rathbone
Raymond Benson	Jack Higgins	

John Gardner 1926- Crime: Police work - UK

www.john-gardner.com   🚶 DS Suzie Mountford - 1940s London

Martha Grimes	Sally Spencer	Josephine Tey
Michael Innes	Andrew Taylor	

Lisa Gardner US Adventure/Thriller

www.lisagardner.com   🚶 Pierre Quincy - FBI Special Agent

Max Allan Collins	Iris Johansen	Erica Spindler
Linda Fairstein	Karin Slaughter	

G

Alex Garland   1970-   General

www.thaistudents.com/thebeach/alexgarland.html

Matthew Branton
Douglas Coupland
Esther Freud
William Golding

James Hamilton-Paterson
Jack Kerouac
Tim Lott
Timothy Mo

Betty Trask 1997

William Sutcliffe

Julie Garwood   1946   US   Historical

also writes as **Emily Chase**
www.juliegarwood.com

Joy Chambers
Catherine Coulter

Margaret Elphinstone
Diana Gabaldon

Amanda Quick

Jonathan Gash   1933-   Crime: Amateur sleuth

also writes as **Jonathan Grant**; is John Grant
www.fantasticfiction.co.uk/authors/Jonathan_Gash.htm

🏃 Lovejoy, Antique dealer - London
Dr Clare Burtonall

Robert Barnard
Simon Brett
Sarah Caudwell
Gerald Hammond

Philip Hook
Alison Joseph
John Malcolm
Charles Spencer

CWA 1977

David Williams

Mike Gayle   1970-   Lad Lit

www.mikegayle.co.uk

Mark Barrowcliffe
Matthew Beaumont
Nick Earls

Cy Flood
Alex George

Tony Parsons
Matt Whyman

G

Pauline Gedge   1945-   NZ   Historical

www.fantasticfiction.co.uk/authors/Pauline_Gedge.htm
Lord of the Two Lands Trilogy

Jean M Auel
Christian Jacq

Simon Scarrow
Wilbur Smith

Maggie Gee   1948-   General

www.contemporarywriters.com/authors/?p=auth41

Peter Ackroyd
Trezza Azzopardi
Tracy Chevalier

Jenny Diski
John Fowles
Rachel Seiffert

Graham Swift
Rose Tremain

Go to back for lists of:
Authors by Genre
Characters and Series
Prize Winners
Further Reading

Sue Gee 1947-   General

Kate Bingham   Joan Lingard
David Flusfeder   Charlotte Mendelson
Margaret Forster   Deborah Moggach
Charlotte Lamb   Elizabeth Russell Taylor

David Gemmell 1948-   Fantasy: Epic

also writes as **Ross Harding**
www.geocities.com/Area51/shadowlands/5025/gemmell.html

James Barclay   Simon R Green   Stan Nicholls
Terry Brooks   J V Jones   Adam Nichols
Steven Erikson   Paul Kearney   Michael Scott Rohan
Julia Gray   Valery Leith   Jane Welch

Nikki Gemmell Aus   General

www.nikkigemmell.com

Helen Dunmore   Sue Miller   Anita Shreve
Zoë Heller   Maggie O'Farrell

Mary Gentle 1956-   Fantasy: Epic

www.fantasticfiction.co.uk/authors/Mary_Gentle.htm

Storm Constantine   China Miéville   BSFA 2000
Colin Greenland   Michael Moorcock
Gwyneth Jones   Tim Powers
Ursula K Le Guin   Philip Pullman   Sheri S Tepper

G

Alex George 1970-   Lad Lit

www.alexgeorge.net

Mark Barrowcliffe   Cy Flood   Nick Hornby
Matthew Beaumont   Mike Gayle   Tony Parsons

Elizabeth George 1949- US   Crime: Police work - UK
www.elizabethgeorgeonline.com   ⚘ DCI Thomas Lynley & DS Barbara Havers - London

Deborah Crombie   Martha Grimes   Barry Maitland
Marjorie Eccles   P D James   Maureen O'Brien
Frances Fyfield   Alison Joseph

Margaret George 1943- US   Historical
www.margaretgeorge.com

Will Davenport   Rosalind Miles   Wilbur Smith
Christian Jacq   Edith Pargeter   Gore Vidal
Colleen McCullough

Adèle Geras 1944- Aga saga

www.adelegeras.com

Maeve Binchy	Audrey Howard	Eileen Ramsay
Anne Christie	Sarah MacDonald	Mary Wesley
Patricia Fawcett	Rosamunde Pilcher	Marcia Willett

Sylvie Germain Fr Fantasy: Myth

www.fantasticfiction.co.uk/authors/Sylvie_Germain.htm

Alice Borchardt	Katharine Kerr
C J Cherryh	T H White

Nicci Gerrard 1958- General

is Nicci French

www.figuressdestyle.com/french/us_web/gerrard1.htm

Lesley Glaister	Shirley Hazzard	Julie Myerson
Angela Green	Siri Hustvedt	Liz Rigbey
Jules Hardy		

Tess Gerritsen 1953- US Crime: Medical

www.tessgerritsen.com

Paul Carson	Alex Kava	Jenny Siler
Max Allan Collins	Ken McClure	Karin Slaughter
Mo Hayder	Michael Palmer	Stephen White
Tami Hoag	Leah Ruth Robinson	

G

Lury Gibson Adventure/Thriller

www.fantasticfiction.co.uk/authors/lury.gibson.htm

John Case	Bill Napier
Michael Cordy	Douglas Preston

Maggie Gibson Ire Humour

www.fantasticfiction.co.uk/authors/Maggie_Gibson.htm

Faith Bleasdale	Sue Limb	Pauline McLynn
Sparkle Hayter	L McCrossan	Allison Pearson

William Gibson 1948- US Science Fiction: Near future

www.williamgibsonbooks.com

Steve Aylett	Alastair Reynolds	Lucius Shepard
Eric Brown	Justina Robson	Michael Marshall Smith
Michael Crichton	Nick Sagan	Kurt Vonnegut
		Connie Willis

Bartholomew Gill
1943-2002   US   Crime: Police work - Ireland

was **Mark McGarrity**
www.fantasticfiction.co.uk/authors/Bartholomew_Gill.htm

🚶 Insp Peter McGarr
Dublin

Ruth Dudley Edwards	Jim Lusby
John Harvey	Ian Rankin

Elizabeth Gill
1950-   Saga

also writes as **Elizabeth Hankin**

Irene Carr	Sheila Jansen	Elvi Rhodes
Jean Chapman	Freda Lightfoot	Janet MacLeod Trotter
Una Horne	Mary McCarthy	

John Gilstrap
1957-   US   Adventure/Thriller

www.johngilstrap.com

Alice Blanchard	Jefferson Parker	Scott Smith
Lee Child	Paullina Simons	Stuart Woods

Lesley Glaister
1956-   General

www.contemporarywriters.com/authors/?p=auth183

Lisa Appignanesi	Angela Green	S Maugham 1991
Carol Birch	Jules Hardy	
Jenny Diski	Shirley Hazzard	
Louise Doughty	Joanna Hines	Alice Sebold
Nicci Gerrard	Catherine Merriman	Gillian White

G

Janet Gleeson
Crime: Historical - C18th

www.fantasticfiction.co.uk/authors/Janet_Gleeson.htm

C18th England

Bruce Alexander	Deryn Lake	Edward Marston
Gwendoline Butler	Janet Laurence	Fidelis Morgan
John Maclachlan Gray	David Liss	Iain Pears
Jane Jakeman	Hannah March	Derek Wilson

Robert Goddard
1954-   Adventure/Thriller

www.fantasticfiction.co.uk/authors/Robert_Goddard.htm

Lisa Appignanesi	Susanna Kearsley	TGR 1992
Hilary Bonner	J Robert Lennon	
John Buchan	Patrick Redmond	
Ronald Frame	Charles Todd	
Gregory Hall		

Go to back for lists of:
Authors by Genre • Characters and Series • Prize Winners • Further Reading

Rumer Godden 1907-98 General
www.fantasticfiction.co.uk/authors/Rumer_Godden.htm

Fred D'Aguiar
Ruth Prawer Jhabvala
Elizabeth Jolley
John Masters
R K Narayan
Vikram Seth

Arthur Golden 1957- US General
www.fantasticfiction.co.uk/authors/Arthur_Golden.htm

Michelle de Kretser
Kazuo Ishiguro
Catherine Lim
Timothy Mo
Amy Tan

William Golding 1911-93 General
www.william-golding.co.uk

Anthony Burgess
Fred D'Aguiar
Patricia Duncker
Umberto Eco
John Fowles
Alex Garland
Thomas Hardy
Anthony Trollope
Marianne Wiggins

Booker 1980

Olivia Goldsmith 1954-2004 US Glitz & Glamour

Louise Bagshawe
Sandra Brown
Elizabeth Buchan
Candace Bushnell
Alexandra Campbell
Judith Michael
Anne Rivers Siddons
Robyn Sisman
Penny Vincenzi

Philip Gooden Crime: Historical - C16th
www.fantasticfiction.co.uk/authors/Philip_Gooden.htm

🏃 Nick Revill, Shakespearean actor
C16th England

Michael Clynes
Judith Cook
Patricia Finney
Margaret Frazer
C C Humphreys
Edward Marston
Fidelis Morgan
Iain Pears
John Pilkington
C J Sansom
Martin Stephen
Peter Tonkin

G

Terry Goodkind 1948- US Fantasy: Epic
www.terrygoodkind.com

🏃 Richard Cypher

Mark Anthony
Carol Berg
Trudi Canavan
Mark Chadbourn
David A Drake
Maggie Furey
Julia Gray
Ian Irvine
Robert Newcomb
Stan Nicholls
Mickey Zucker Reichert
Jane Welch

Go to back for lists of:
Authors by Genre
Characters and Series
Prize Winners
Further Reading

Carol Goodman US Crime: Psychological

www.fantasticfiction.co.uk/authors/Carol_Goodman.htm

Mary Higgins Clark
Leslie Forbes
Joanna Hines
Iris Johansen
Judith Kelman
Pierre Magnan
Fiona Mountain
Gloria Murphy
Donna Tartt
Minette Walters
Gillian White
Laura Wilson

Nadine Gordimer 1923- SA General

Booker 1974

Margaret Atwood
Lynne Reid Banks
André Brink
J M Coetzee
Christopher Hope
Pamela Jooste
Doris Lessing
Paul Scott
Patrick White

Paula Gosling 1939- US Crime: Police work - US

also writes as Ainslie Skinner
www.fantasticfiction.co.uk/authors/Paula_Gosling.htm

Sheriff Matt Gabriel, Lt Jack Stryker & Prof Kate Trevorne - 'Blackwater Bay', Michigan

CWA 1978 & 1985

Lilian Jackson Braun
Deborah Crombie
Clare Francis
Martha Grimes
Laurie King
Jill McGown
Archer Mayor

Eileen Goudge 1950- US General

www.eileengoudge.com

Elizabeth Buchan
Catherine Fox
Elizabeth Jane Howard
Joan Lingard

Judith Gould 1952- US Glitz & Glamour

also writes as W R Gallaher; *is* Nicholas Bienes
www.fantasticfiction.co.uk/authors/Judith_Gould.htm

Joan Collins
Jilly Cooper
Judith Krantz
Jayne Ann Krentz
Susan Lewis
Judith McNaught
Judith Michael
Madge Swindells
Caroline Upcher

Iris Gower 1939- Wales Saga

www.fantasticfiction.co.uk/authors/Iris_Gower.htm

Cordwainer Series - South Wales
Sweet Rosie Series • Firebird Series

Jessica Blair
Catrin Collier
Gloria Cook
Catrin Morgan
Joan O'Neill
Cynthia S Roberts
Grace Thompson
Barbara Whitnell
Barbara Wood

Juan Goytisolo   1931-   Spain   Crime: Police work - Spain

Andrea Camilleri   Luiz Alfredo Garcia-Roza   Rebecca Pawel
Michael Dibdin   Manuel Vázquez Montalbán

Sue Grafton   1940-   US   Crime: PI
www.suegrafton.com   ⚐ Kinsey Millhone - 'Santa Teresa', California

Cara Black   Carol Higgins Clark   Zoë Sharp
Edna Buchanan   Steve Hamilton   Dana Stabenow
Alafair Burke   Laura Lippman   Sarah Strohmeyer
Jan Burke   Carol O'Connell

Caroline Graham   1931-   Crime: Police work - UK
www.fantasticfiction.co.uk/authors/Caroline_Graham.htm   ⚐ DCI Tom Barnaby & DS Troy -
                                                             'Midsomer Worthy'

Clare Curzon   Geraldine Evans   Ann Purser
Freda Davies   J M Gregson   Nicholas Rhea
Eileen Dewhurst   Roy Hart   Dorothy Simpson
Margaret Duffy   Veronica Heley   Sally Spencer

Janice Graham   General

Robert Edric   Alice Hoffman   Nancy Thayer
Alison Fell   Barbara Kingsolver   Robert James Waller

Laurie Graham   1947-   General
www.lauriegraham.com

Elizabeth Berg   Sue Limb   Yvonne Roberts
Amanda Craig   Elinor Lipman   Sue Townsend
Fannie Flagg   Ben Richards   Arabella Weir

Margaret Graham   1945-   Saga

Tessa Barclay   Maggie Craig   Denise Robertson
Jessica Blair   Meg Henderson   Sally Spencer
Brenda Clarke   Margaret Kaine   Sally Stewart

Winston Graham   1909-2003   General
www.fantasticfiction.co.uk/authors/Winston_Graham.htm

Pat Conroy   Joanna Hines   Claire Rayner
R F Delderfield   Malcolm Macdonald   Jean Stubbs
Howard Fast

Winston Graham 1909-2003 — Historical

www.fantasticfiction.co.uk/authors/Winston_Graham.htm

Rosemary Aitken
Anita Burgh
Gloria Cook
June Drummond
Elizabeth Hawksley
Joanna Hines
Jane Aiken Hodge
Malcolm Ross
Nigel Tranter
Kate Tremayne

Jean-Christophe Grangé 1961- Fr — Adventure/Thriller

Pierre Niemans & Abdouf

John Case
Karin Fossum
Alan Furst
Paul Henke
Henry Porter
Wilbur Smith

Ann Granger 1939- — Crime: Police work - UK

also writes as Ann Hulme
www.fantasticfiction.co.uk/authors/Ann_Granger.htm

Div Supt Alan Markby & Meredith Mitchell - Cotswolds, England
Fran Varady, PI - London

Janie Bolitho
Freda Davies
Eileen Dewhurst
Geraldine Evans
Anthea Fraser
J M Gregson
Roy Hart
Hazel Holt
Ann Purser
Betty Rowlands
Sally Spencer
Rebecca Tope

Linda Grant 1951- — General

www.lindagrant.co.uk

Higham 1996
Orange 2000

Beryl Bainbridge
Pat Barker
Margaret Forster
Mary Morrissy
Anna Quindlen
Teresa Waugh

G

Rob Grant — Science Fiction: Humour

also writes as Grant Naylor (with Doug Naylor)
www.fantasticfiction.co.uk/authors/Rob_Grant.htm

Douglas Adams
David Baddiel
Harry Harrison
Tom Holt
Terry Pratchett
Robert Rankin

Robert Graves 1895-1985 — General

www.robertgraves.org

Howard Fast
Michael Curtis Ford
Conn Iggulden
Colleen McCullough
Valerio Massimo Manfredi
Allan Massie
Steven Pressfield
Erich Maria Remarque
Mary Renault
Gore Vidal

Go to back for lists of:
Authors by Genre • Characters and Series • Prize Winners • Further Reading

Alasdair Gray   1934-   Sco   General

www.alasdairgray.co.uk

Michel Faber   A L Kennedy   Guardian 1992
John Fowles   Agnes Owens   Whitbread 1992
James Kelman   Iain Sinclair

Alex Gray   Sco   Crime: Police work - UK

www.fantasticfiction.co.uk/authors/Alex_Gray.htm   ☝ DCI Lorrimer - Glasgow

Quintin Jardine   Denise Mina
Frederic Lindsay   Ian Rankin

John Maclachlan Gray   Can   Crime: Historical - C19th

                              ☝ Edmund Whitty, Journalist - Victorian London

Janet Gleeson   Andrew Martin   Arturo Perez-Reverte
Jane Jakeman   Iain Pears   Gerard Williams
Peter Lovesey

Julia Gray   Fantasy: Epic

also writes as Jonathan Wylie
is Mark & Julia Smith
www.fantasticfiction.co.uk/authors/Julia_Gray.htm

Sara Douglass   Terry Goodkind   Guy Gavriel Kay
Maggie Furey   Ian Irvine   Adam Nichols
David Gemmell   Kate Jacoby   Jane Welch

G

Muriel Gray   1959-   Sco   Horror

www.fantasticfiction.co.uk/authors/Muriel_Gray.htm

Richard Bachman   Stephen Gallagher   Mark Morris
Simon Clark   Bentley Little

Richard Grayson   1922-   Sco   Crime: Historical - C19th

is Richard Grindal   ☝ Insp Jean-Paul Gauthier
www.fantasticfiction.co.uk/authors/Richard_Grayson.htm   Belle Epoque, Paris

Laurie King   Deryn Lake   Amy Myers
Alanna Knight   Gillian Linscott

Sarah Grazebrook   General

Diana Appleyard   Julia Lisle   Mary Sheepshanks
Faith Bleasdale   Juliette Mead   Judith Summers
Karen Hayes   Karen Nelson   M J Trow

Angela Green General

Anne Fine
Nicci Gerrard
Lesley Glaister

Jules Hardy
Zoë Heller

Joan Lingard
Liz Rigbey

Jane Green Chick Lit

www.fantasticfiction.co.uk/authors/Jane_Green.htm

Lisa Armstrong
Melissa Bank
Mavis Cheek

Lisa Jewell
Louise Kean
Sharon Mulrooney

Allison Pearson
Linda Taylor
Lynne Truss

Jonathan Green Fantasy: Dark

www.fantasticfiction.co.uk/authors/Jonathan_Green.htm

Dan Abnett
Ben Counter

Tanith Lee
Freda Warrington

Simon R Green   1955- Fantasy: Epic

www.fantasticfiction.co.uk/authors/Simon_R_Green.htm

Kevin J Anderson
Alan Dean Foster
David Gemmell

Holly Lisle
L E Modesitt Jr
Adam Nichols

Terry Pratchett
Martin Scott
Jane Welch

Graham Greene   1904-91 General

www.fantasticfiction.co.uk/authors/Graham_Greene.htm

G

Elizabeth Bowen
Justin Cartwright
Glen Duncan
Patricia Duncker

David Flusfeder
Pauline Melville
Brian Moore
George Orwell

Anthony Powell
Piers Paul Read
Nicholas Shakespeare
Morris West

Colin Greenland   1954- Science Fiction: Space opera

www.infinityplus.co.uk/misc/cg.htm

John Brosnan
Lois McMaster Bujold
C J Cherryh
Alan Dean Foster

Mary Gentle
Peter F Hamilton
Harry Harrison
Brian Stableford

> BSFA 1990
> Arthur C Clarke 1991

Andrew Sean Greer   1970- US General

www.andrewgreer.com

Jeffrey Eugenides
Kazuo Ishiguro

Jhumpa Lahiri
Vladimir Nabokov

Darin Strauss

Philippa Gregory 1954-   Historical
www.fantasticfiction.co.uk/authors/Philippa_Gregory.htm   Wideacre Trilogy

Zoë Fairbairns   Edward Rutherfurd   Romantic 2002
Caroline Harvey   Kate Saunders
Joanna Hines   Reay Tannahill
Robin Maxwell   Sarah Waters
Julian Rathbone

Susanna Gregory 1958-   Crime: Historical - Medieval
also writes as **Simon Beaufort**   ⚘ Matthew Bartholomew
is **Elizabeth Cruwys**   C14th England
www.matthewbartholomew.co.uk

Paul Doherty   Viviane Moore   Candace Robb
Michael Jecks   Ellis Peters   Kate Sedley
Bernard Knight

J M Gregson   Crime: Police work - UK
also writes as **Jim Gregson**   ⚘ DI Percy Peach - East Lancashire
www.fantasticfiction.co.uk/authors/J_M_Gregson.htm   Det John Lambert & Det Bert Hook

Jeffrey Ashford   Geraldine Evans   Nicholas Rhea
Meg Elizabeth Atkins   Caroline Graham   Sally Spencer
Janie Bolitho   Ann Granger

Rebecca Gregson   Aga saga

Judy Astley   Kate Fielding   Kate Long
G Sarah Challis   Julia Hamilton   Ann Swinfen
Elizabeth Falconer   Julie Highmore   Marcia Willett

Andrew Greig 1951- Sco   General
www.contemporarywriters.com/authors/?p=auth02D9L380712627427

Francis Cottam   Simon Mawer   Robert Radcliffe
Sebastian Faulks   Andrew O'Hagan   Alan Spence
Robin Jenkins

Kate Grenville 1950- Aus   General
www.users.bigpond.com/kgrenville

Suzanne Berne   Jacquelyn Mitchard   Orange 2001
Candida Crewe   Imogen Parker
Barbara Kingsolver   Jane Smiley
Juliette Mead

Patricia Grey
is **Liz Evans**

Saga
London

Anne Bennett	Sara Fraser	Alice Taylor
Philip Boast	Anna King	Elizabeth Waite
Harry Cole	Elizabeth Lord	Jeanne Whitmee

W E B Griffin   1929-   US

War: Modern
Corps Series
Badge of Honour Series
Brotherhood of War Series

also writes as **Alex Baldwin**
is **William E Butterworth III**
www.webgriffin.com

Harold Coyle	Matthew Reilly	Terence Strong
Graham Hurley	David L Robbins	James Webb
Robert Jackson	Derek Robinson	

W E B Griffin   1929-   US

Crime: Police work - US
Philadelphia

also writes as **Alex Baldwin**
is **William E Butterworth III**
www.webgriffin.com

Donald Harstad	Margaret Maron	Joseph Wambaugh
Ed McBain	Ridley Pearson	

Niall Griffiths   1966-

General

www.fantasticfiction.co.uk/authors/Niall_Griffiths.htm

Anthony Burgess	Sean Hughes
Roddy Doyle	Irvine Welsh

Martha Grimes   1931-   US

Crime: Police work - UK
🏃 DCI Richard Jury - London

www.marthagrimes.com

Barbara Cleverly	Elizabeth George	Maureen O'Brien
Deborah Crombie	Paula Gosling	Dorothy L Sayers
John Gardner	Graham Ison	Charles Todd

Jon Courtenay Grimwood

Science Fiction: Near future
🏃 Ashraf Bey

www.j-cg.co.uk

BSFA 2003

Pat Cadigan	Jeff Noon	
Greg Egan	Justina Robson	
Ian McDonald	Lucius Shepard	Tad Williams
John Meaney	Neal Stephenson	David Wingrove

G

Go to back for lists of:
Authors by Genre • Characters and Series • Prize Winners • Further Reading

James Grippando   US   Crime: Legal/financial

www.jamesgrippando.com   ♘ Jack Swyteck, Lawyer - Miami

Jeff Abbott
William Bernhardt
D W Buffa
John T Lescroart

Steve Martini
Richard North Patterson
Robert K Tanenbaum

Scott Turow
Sabin Willett
Stuart Woods

John Grisham   1955-   US   Crime: Legal/financial

www.jgrisham.com

William Bernhardt
D W Buffa
Linda Davies
Craig Holden

John T Lescroart
John McLaren
David Michie
Christopher Reich

Lisa Scottoline
Susan R Sloan
Scott Turow
Sabin Willett

David Grossman   1954-   Isr   General

Gabriel Garcia Márquez
Amos Oz

Salman Rushdie
Isaac Bashevis Singer

Wingate 2004

Sandra Gulland   1944-   US   Historical

www.sandragulland.com

Cynthia Harrod-Eagles
Anne Haverty
Jane Aiken Hodge

Ross King
Rosalind Laker

Robin Maxwell
Anya Seton

G Jeff Gulvin   1962-   Adventure/Thriller

www.fantasticfiction.co.uk/authors/Jeff_Gulvin.htm

Jake Arnott
Lorenzo Carcaterra
Pete Hamill

Quintin Jardine
Thomas Kelly
Jenny Maxwell

R D Wingfield
Glover Wright

Alan Gurganus   1947-   US   General

William Boyd
Michael Carson

Jay McInerney
Paul Micou

Tom Wolfe

Abdulrazak Gurnah   1948-   Zan   General

www.contemporarywriters.com/authors/?p=auth46

Monica Ali
Joseph Conrad

Ruth Prawer Jhabvala
Rohinton Mistry

V S Naipaul
Paul Theroux

Go to back for lists of:
Authors by Genre • Characters and Series • Prize Winners • Further Reading

David Guterson 1956- US General

www.fantasticfiction.co.uk/authors/David_Guterson.htm

Robert Olen Butler	Stuart M Kaminsky	Alistair MacLeod
Pete Dexter	Michael Kimball	Jacquelyn Mitchard
Charles Frazier	William Kowalski	Amy Tan
Peter Hoeg	Cormac McCarthy	Jane Urquhart

Peter Guttridge 1951- Crime: Humour

www.peterguttridge.com ⚐ Nick Madrid, Journalist

Colin Bateman	Claire McNab	Laurence Shames
Marc Blake	Chris Niles	Charles Spencer
Carl Hiaasen	Zane Radcliffe	

Sue Haasler Chick Lit

www.suehaasler.com

Sarah Ball	Amanda Lees	Laura Wolf
Louise Harwood	Carmen Reid	Stephanie Zia

Mark Haddon 1962- General

www.fantasticfiction.co.uk/authors/Mark_Haddon.htm

Paulo Coelho	Steve Martin	McKitterick 2004
Jostein Gaarder	Alice Sebold	Whitbread 2003
Yann Martel		

David Hagberg US Adventure/Thriller

also writes as **Sean Flannery**
www.fantasticfiction.co.uk/authors/David_Hagberg.htm

Suzanne Brockmann	Clive Cussler	Gordon Kent
Dan Brown	Sean Flannery	Robert Ludlum
Tom Clancy	Vince Flynn	Stanley Pottinger
Stephen Coonts		

Brian Haig US Adventure/Thriller

www.brianhaig.com

Tom Clancy	Robert Ludlum	Mark T Sullivan
Vince Flynn	Douglas Preston	

Joe Haldeman 1943- US Science Fiction: Space opera

http://home.earthlink.net/~haldeman

Brian W Aldiss	David Feintuch	Lucius Shepard
J G Ballard	Harry Harrison	Robert Silverberg
Orson Scott Card	Robert A Heinlein	Dan Simmons
Harlan Ellison		

Georgie Hale
Crime: Police work - UK

www.georgiehale.com   🚶 DI Ray Whitelaw & DI Dave Shenfield - 'Blackport'

Meg Elizabeth Atkins	Patricia Hall	Graham Hurley
Ann Cleeves	Reginald Hill	Stuart Pawson
Freda Davies	Lesley Horton	Peter Robinson

Daniel Hall
War: Historical

Bernard Cornwell	Alexander Kent
Richard Howard	Allan Mallinson

Gregory Hall   1948-
Crime: Psychological

www.fantasticfiction.co.uk/authors/Gregory_Hall.htm

Hilary Bonner	Juliet Hebden	Morag Joss
Robert Goddard	Mark Hebden	Andrew Taylor

James Hall   1947-   US
Crime: PI

www.jameswhall.com   🚶 Thorn • Alexandra Rafferty, Police photographer
Florida

Edna Buchanan	Robert Ferrigno	Elmore Leonard
James Lee Burke	G M Ford	John D Macdonald
Lee Child	Jonathon King	Laurence Shames

Patricia Hall   1940-
Crime: Police work - UK

is Maureen O'Connor   🚶 DCI Michael Thackeray & Laura Ackroyd, Journalist
www.patriciahall.co.uk   'Bradfield', Yorkshire

Robert Barnard	Paul Charles	Georgie Hale
Pauline Bell	Ann Cleeves	Lesley Horton
Ken Bruen	John Connor	Graham Hurley
Mark Burnell	Marjorie Eccles	Stuart Pawson

Sarah Hall   1974-
General

www.fantasticfiction.co.uk/authors/Sarah_Hall.htm

Melvyn Bragg	Thomas Hardy
Neil Cross	D H Lawrence

Barbara Hambly   1951-   US
Fantasy

www.barbarahambly.com

Marion Zimmer Bradley	Mercedes Lackey	Elizabeth Moon
C J Cherryh	Anne McCaffrey	Tim Powers
Louise Cooper	Julian May	Melanie Rawn
Michael P Kube-McDowell		

Pete Hamill   1935-   US   Adventure/Thriller

www.petehamill.com

Alan Folsom   Greg Iles   Jenny Maxwell
Jeff Gulvin   Thomas Kelly   Glover Wright

Denise Hamilton   US   Crime: Amateur sleuth

www.denisehamilton.com   ⚲ Eve Diamond, Journalist - Los Angeles

Edna Buchanan   Caroline Carver   Liza Marklund
Jan Burke   G M Ford

Jane Hamilton   1957-   US   General

Lynn Coady   Barbara Kingsolver   Ann Patchett
Andre Dubus   Mary Lawson   Mona Simpson
Catherine Dunne   Alice Munro   Jane Smiley

Julia Hamilton   1956-   Aga saga

Jane Asher   Catherine Fox   Hazel Hucker
Anne Doughty   Rebecca Gregson   Catherine Merriman
Katie Fforde

Laurell K Hamilton   1963-   US   Horror

is Laurell Kaye Klin Klein   ⚲ Anita Blake, Necromancer & crime investigator
www.laurellkhamilton.org

Kelley Armstrong   Tanya Huff   Kim Newman
Nancy Collins   Jeanne Kalogridis   Anne Rice
Charlaine Harris   Holly Lisle   Steven Spruill

Peter F Hamilton   1960-   Science Fiction: Space opera **H**

www.peterfhamilton.com

Kevin J Anderson   Lois McMaster Bujold Robert Reed
Neal Asher   C J Cherryh   Dan Simmons
Iain M Banks   Colin Greenland   Charles Stross

Ruth Hamilton   Saga

www.ruthhamilton.co.uk   Liverpool & Lancashire

Lyn Andrews   Catherine Cookson   Meg Henderson
Rita Bradshaw   Emma Dally   Maureen Lee
Alexandra Connor   Katie Flynn   Freda Lightfoot

Go to back for lists of:
Authors by Genre • Characters and Series • Prize Winners • Further Reading

Steve Hamilton 1961- US Crime: PI
www.authorstevehamilton.com ⚐ Alex McKnight - 'Paradise', Michigan

Giles Blunt	Sue Grafton	Walter Mosley
C J Box	Jonathon King	Dana Stabenow
Loren D Estleman	Elmore Leonard	Robert K Tanenbaum
G M Ford	Michael McGarrity	Jess Walter

Sylvian Hamilton Crime: Historical - C13th
⚐ Sir Richard Straccan, Pedlar in relics - C13th England

Simon Beaufort	Edward Marston	Ellis Peters
Alys Clare	Viviane Moore	Joan Wolf
Michael Jecks		

James Hamilton-Paterson 1941- General
www.fantasticfiction.co.uk/authors/James_Hamilton-Paterson.htm

John Banville	Alex Garland	Whitbread 1989
Joseph Conrad	Timothy Mo	
Louis de Bernières	William Rivière	Nicholas Shakespeare

Dashiell Hammett 1894-1961 US Crime: PI
www.kirjasto.sci.fi/dhammett.htm ⚐ The Continental Op • Sam Spade - San Francisco

Lawrence Block	Kinky Friedman	Michael Malone
James Hadley Chase	Stuart M Kaminsky	Walter Mosley
Loren D Estleman	Ross Macdonald	

Gerald Hammond 1926- Sco Crime: Amateur sleuth
also writes as **Arthur Douglas, Dalby Holden** ⚐ Keith Calder, Gunsmith
www.fantasticfiction.co.uk/authors/Gerald_Hammond.htm John Cunningham, Kennel owner
Scottish Borders

M C Beaton	Joyce Holms	Margaret Yorke
Jonathan Gash	Bill Knox	

Maeve Haran 1950- General
www.fantasticfiction.co.uk/authors/Maeve_Haran.htm

Charlotte Bingham	Josephine Hart	Charlotte Lamb
Claire Calman	Helen Humphreys	Kathleen Rowntree
Sarah Harrison		

Duncan Harding 1926- Sea: Modern
also writes as **Leo Kessler**; *is* **Charles Whiting**
www.fantasticfiction.co.uk/authors/Duncan_Harding.htm

James Cobb	Alexander Fullerton	Terence Strong
	Nicholas Monsarrat	Peter Tonkin

H

John Harding — Lad Lit: Humour

Tim Lott
John O'Farrell

Tony Parsons
Willy Russell

Matt Whyman

Jules Hardy — General

www.fantasticfiction.co.uk/authors/Jules_Hardy.htm

Nicci Gerrard
Lesley Glaister

Angela Green
Julie Myerson

Thomas Hardy 1840-1928 — General

Melvyn Bragg
John Fowles
William Golding

Sarah Hall
D H Lawrence

Adam Thorpe
Edith Wharton

Andrew Harman 1964- — Fantasy: Humour

www.fantasticfiction.co.uk/authors/Andrew_Harman.htm

Robert Asprin
Craig Shaw Gardner

Tom Holt
Terry Pratchett

Robert Rankin
Martin Scott

Charlaine Harris 1951- US — Horror

www.charlaineharris.com

⚐ Sookie Stackhouse, Vampire

Laurell K Hamilton
Tanya Huff

Elizabeth Pewsey
Robert Rankin

Joanne Harris 1964- — General

www.joanne-harris.co.uk

Emma Donoghue
Lucy Ellman
Sarah Kate Lynch

Michèle Roberts
Polly Samson
Barbara Trapido

Salley Vickers
Barbara Wood

H

Robert Harris 1957- — Adventure/Thriller

www.fantasticfiction.co.uk/authors/Robert_Harris.htm

Paul Adam
Brendan Dubois
Dan Fesperman
Donald James

Joseph Kanon
Robert Littell
Glenn Meade
Rebecca Pawel

Henry Porter
Michael Shea
Guy Walters
James Webb

TGR 1993

Go to back for lists of:
Authors by Genre • Characters and Series • Prize Winners • Further Reading

Thomas Harris　　1940-　US　　Adventure/Thriller: Modern

www.randomhouse.com/features/thomasharris/hannibal.html　　🏃 Dr Hannibal Lecter, Serial Killer
Clarice Starling, FBI

Keith Russell Ablow	Andrew Klavan	Steven Spruill
Thomas H Cook	Michael Marshall	Boston Teran
John Katzenbach	Jonathan Nasaw	Tim Willocks

Colin Harrison　　1960-　US　　Adventure/Thriller

www.fantasticfiction.co.uk/authors/Colin_Harrison.htm

Jeffrey Archer	Phillip Margolin	Scott Turow
Paul Kilduff	Lawrence Sanders	Tom Wolfe
Michael Kimball		

Harry Harrison　　1925-　US　　Science Fiction: Humour

also writes as **Felix Boyd, Frank Dempsey**
www.harryharrison.com

Rob Grant	Robert A Heinlein	Robert Rankin
Colin Greenland	Tom Holt	Martin Scott
Joe Haldeman	Larry Niven	

Janis Harrison　　US　　Crime: Amateur sleuth

www.fantasticfiction.co.uk/authors/Janis_Harrison.htm　　🏃 Bretta Solomon, Florist
'River City', Missouri

M C Beaton	Carolyn G Hart	Charlotte MacLeod
Lilian Jackson Braun	Sharyn McCrumb	Margaret Maron

Jim Harrison　　1937-　US　　General

www.fantasticfiction.co.uk/authors/Jim_Harrison.htm

Jim Crace	Nicholas Evans	Cormac McCarthy
Pete Dexter	Richard Ford	Larry McMurtry

H

Ray Harrison　　1928-　　Crime: Historical - C19th

www.fantasticfiction.co.uk/authors/Ray_Harrison.htm　　🏃 Sgt Bragg & PC Morton
C19th London

Alanna Knight	Peter Lovesey	Roberta Rogow
Deryn Lake	Andrew Martin	Norman Russell
Gillian Linscott	Amy Myers	M J Trow
Joan Lock	Anne Perry	Gerard Williams

Go to back for lists of:
Authors by Genre
Characters and Series
Prize Winners
Further Reading

Sarah Harrison 1946- General

www.sarah-harrison.net

Charlotte Bingham	Susan Howatch	Wendy Perriam
Rose Boucheron	Susan Isaacs	Diana Saville
Maeve Haran	Imogen Parker	Grace Wynne-Jones

Stuart Harrison Adventure/Thriller

www.stuartharrison.com

Alice Blanchard	Nicholas Evans	Stuart Woods
Harlan Coben	Cormac McCarthy	

Cynthia Harrod-Eagles 1948- Historical

also writes as **Elizabeth Bennett, Emma Woodhouse**
www.cynthiaharrodeagles.com

⚐ Morland Dynasty

June Drummond	Victoria Holt	Romantic 1993
Sandra Gulland	Rosalind Laker	E V Thompson
Joanna Hines	Reay Tannahill	Patricia Wendorf

Cynthia Harrod-Eagles 1948- Crime: Police work - UK

www.cynthiaharrodeagles.com

⚐ DI Bill Slider - London

Gwendoline Butler	Graham Ison
Deborah Crombie	Barry Maitland

Eric L Harry 1958- US War: Modern

www.eharry.com

Tom Clancy	Robert Jackson	James Webb
James Cobb	David L Robbins	
Johnny 'Two Combs' Howard		

H

Lilian Harry 1939- Saga

also writes as **Donna Baker**
www.fantasticfiction.co.uk/authors/Lilian_Harry.htm

Lyons Corner House Series
Portsmouth

Helen Carey	Audrey Howard	Mary Minton
Elizabeth Daish	Beryl Matthews	Victor Pemberton
Margaret Dickinson	Margaret Mayhew	June Tate

Donald Harstad US Crime: Police work - US

www.donaldharstad.com

⚐ Dep Sheriff Carl Houseman - Nation County, Iowa

Giles Blunt	J A Jance	Deon Meyer
C J Box	Ed McBain	Ridley Pearson
W E B Griffin	Michael McGarrity	Scott Smith
Tony Hillerman	Archer Mayor	Dana Stabenow

113

Carolyn G Hart   1936-   US

www.carolynhart.com

Crime: Amateur sleuth

🏃 Annie Darling and Max Darling, Bookseller
'Chastain', S Carolina

M C Beaton	Janis Harrison	Charlotte MacLeod
Lilian Jackson Braun	Sharyn McCrumb	Margaret Maron
Simon Brett	Marianne MacDonald	

Josephine Hart   1942-   Ire

General

Lisa Appignanesi	Maeve Haran	Hilary Norman
Candida Clark	Helen Humphreys	Rosie Thomas

Roy Hart

www.fantasticfiction.co.uk/authors/Roy_Hart.htm

Crime: Police work - UK

🏃 CI Douglas Roper - Dorset

Meg Elizabeth Atkins	Freda Davies	Caroline Graham
Janie Bolitho	Kate Ellis	Ann Granger
W J Burley		

Caroline Harvey   1943-

is Joanna Trollope
www.fantasticfiction.co.uk/authors/Caroline_Harvey.htm

Historical

Philippa Gregory	Judith Lennox	Anya Seton
Victoria Holt	Diana Norman	Patricia Wendorf

Jack Harvey   1960-   Sco

also writes as Ian Rankin

Adventure/Thriller

Christopher Brookmyre	Frank Lean	David L Robbins
Graham Hurley	David Martin	Terence Strong

H John Harvey   1938-

also writes as Terry Lennox, James Mann
www.mellotone.co.uk

Crime: Police work - UK

🏃 DI Charlie Resnick - Nottingham
DI Elder, Retired policeman

Robert Barnard	Simon Kernick	Higham 1979
Karin Fossum	Jim Lusby	CWA 2004
Bartholomew Gill	Iain McDowall	Maj Sjöwall and
Reginald Hill	Chris Paling	Per Wahlöö
Graham Hurley	Nicholas Royle	Sally Spencer

Sarah Harvey

Chick Lit

Jessica Adams	Victoria Colby	Cathy Kelly
Catherine Alliott	Christina Jones	Victoria Routledge
Anita Anderson		

Louise Harwood
Chick Lit

Trisha Ashley
Sue Haasler

Laura Lockington
Marissa Mackle

Sarah Mason
Claudia Pattison

Ben Hatch
Lad Lit: Humour

Simon Armitage
David Baddiel
James Delingpole

Christina Jones
L McCrossan
Mil Millington

Damien Owens
Paul Reizin

Kate Hatfield 1951-
General

is Daphne Wright

Zoë Fairbairns
Charlotte Lamb

Angela Lambert
Hilary Norman

Kate Saunders
Mary Wesley

Anne Haverty 1959- Ire
Historical

Tracy Chevalier
Emma Donoghue
Sandra Gulland

Helen Hollick
Sheri Holman

Sarah Waters
Patricia Wendorf

James Hawes 1960- Wales
Humour

Christopher Brookmyre
Jeremy Cameron
Ben Elton

Kinky Friedman
Charles Higson
John McCabe

Zane Radcliffe
Tom Sharpe
Louisa Young

Elizabeth Hawksley
Historical

Pamela Evans
Winston Graham

Georgette Heyer
Jane Aiken Hodge

Helen Hollick
Rosalind Miles

H

Humphrey Hawksley 1964-
Adventure/Thriller

www.hhawksley.co.uk

James Clavell
Ken Follett

Alan Judd
Tim Sebastian

Donna Hay
Chick Lit

Anita Anderson
Zoë Barnes
Melissa Hill

Christina Jones
Dorothy Koomson
Laura Lockington

L McCrossan
Sarah Mason
Sarah Webb

Mo Hayder

Crime: Psychological

www.mohayder.net/welcome.html

🏃 DI Jack Caffery - London

TGR 2002

Mark Billingham	Daniel Hecht	
Ingrid Black	Jonathan Kellerman	
John Connolly	Peter Lovesey	
Jeffery Deaver	Michael Palmer	Jenny Siler
Tess Gerritsen	James Patterson	Boris Starling

Elizabeth Haydon   US

Fantasy: Epic

www.elizabethhaydon.com

Steven Brust	Alan Dean Foster	Juliet E McKenna
David Eddings	Anne McCaffrey	

Karen Hayes

General

also writes as **Karen Nelson**

Marika Cobbold	Stevie Morgan	Mary Sheepshanks
Sarah Grazebrook	Karen Nelson	Joanna Trollope
Helen Humphreys	Rebecca Shaw	

Sparkle Hayter   1958-   Can

Crime: Humour

www.sparklehayter.com

🏃 Robin Hudson, TV journalist - New York

Edna Buchanan	Kinky Friedman	Pauline McLynn
Stella Duffy	Maggie Gibson	Sarah Strohmeyer
Janet Evanovich	Lauren Henderson	Scarlett Thomas
Liz Evans	Susan Isaacs	Valerie Wilson Wesley

Shirley Hazzard   1931-   US

General

www.fantasticfiction.co.uk/authors/Shirley_Hazzard.htm

Suzanne Berne	Lesley Glaister	Thomas Keneally
Jill Dawson	Siri Hustvedt	Anita Shreve
Nicci Gerrard	Elizabeth Jolley	Gillian White

Tara Heavey   Ire

Chick Lit

Colette Caddle	Amy Jenkins	Monica McInerney
Jenny Eclair	Cathy Kelly	Jennifer Weiner
Melissa Hill		

Juliet Hebden

Crime: Police work - France

is daughter of Mark Hebden

🏃 Insp Evariste Pel - Burgundy

www.fantasticfiction.co.uk/authors/Juliet_Hebden.htm

Gregory Hall	J Robert Janes	Magdalen Nabb
Mark Hebden	Roderic Jeffries	Louis Sanders
	H R F Keating	Georges Simenon

H

Mark Hebden   1916-91   Crime: Police work - France
also wrote as **Max Hennessy**; *was* **John Harris**   ⚲ Insp Evariste Pel - Burgundy
www.fantasticfiction.co.uk/authors/Mark_Hebden.htm

Gregory Hall	Roderic Jeffries	Louis Sanders
Juliet Hebden	H R F Keating	Georges Simenon
J Robert Janes	Magdalen Nabb	

Daniel Hecht   US   Crime: Psychological
www.danielhecht.com   ⚲ Lucrezia 'Cree' Black, Parapsychologist

Mo Hayder	Sharyn McCrumb	James Patterson
Christiane Heggan	Val McDermid	Erica Spindler
Alex Kava	Jonathan Nasaw	Stephen White
Jonathan Kellerman	Meg O'Brien	Derek Wilson

William Heffernan   US   Crime: Police work - US
www.williamheffernan.com   ⚲ Det Paul Devlin

James Lee Burke	Thomas Laird	Carol O'Connell
Michael Connelly	Dennis Lehane	Jess Walter
David Cray	Reggie Nadelson	

Frances Hegarty   1949-   Crime: Psychological
also writes as **Frances Fyfield**
www.fantasticfiction.co.uk/authors/Frances_Fyfield.htm

Jenny Diski	Judith Kelman	Barbara Vine
Nicci French	Gloria Murphy	

Christiane Heggan   Fr   Crime: Psychological
www.christianeheggan.com

Daniel Hecht	Meg O'Brien
Tami Hoag	Erica Spindler

H

Robert A Heinlein   1907-88   US   Science Fiction: Space and time
also writes as **Anson MacDonald**
www.nitrosyncretic.com/rah

Brian W Aldiss	Philip K Dick	Jules Verne
Isaac Asimov	Joe Haldeman	John Wyndham
Ray Bradbury	Harry Harrison	

Veronica Heley   1933-   Crime: Amateur sleuth
www.fantasticfiction.co.uk/authors/Veronica_Heley.htm   ⚲ Ellie Quicke

Simon Brett	Marianne Macdonald	Betty Rowlands
Clare Curzon	Ann Purser	Alexander McCall Smith
Caroline Graham		

Joseph Heller   1923-99   US   General
www.fantasticfiction.co.uk/authors/Joseph_Heller.htm

Saul Bellow	John Irving	Tom Robbins
Tibor Fischer	Norman Mailer	Philip Roth
George Macdonald Fraser	Tim O'Brien	Leslie Thomas

Mandasue Heller   Crime: Hardboiled
www.fantasticfiction.co.uk/authors/Mandasue_Heller.htm   Manchester

Martina Cole	Frank Lean	Cath Staincliffe
Lynda La Plante	Val McDermid	

Zoë Heller   1965-   General
www.fantasticfiction.co.uk/authors/Zoe_Heller.htm

Jill Dawson	Angela Green	Julie Myerson
Anne Fine	Joan Lingard	Alice Sebold
Nikki Gemmell	Valerie Martin	

Ernest Hemingway   1898-1961   US   General
www.hemingway.org

Raymond Carver	Norman Mailer	William Styron
Joseph Conrad	Nevil Shute	Paul Theroux
F Scott Fitzgerald	John Steinbeck	Paul Watkins

Lauren Henderson   1966-   Crime: Amateur sleuth
www.tartcity.com   ☂ Sam Jones, Sculptress - London

Linda Barnes	Sparkle Hayter	Gillian Slovo
Tim Cockey	Pauline McLynn	Scarlett Thomas
Stella Duffy	Zoë Sharp	Stella Whitelaw

H

Meg Henderson   1948-   Sco   Saga

Maggie Craig	Ruth Hamilton	Mary McCarthy
Margaret Thomson Davis	Evelyn Hood	Gilda O'Neill
Margaret Graham	Meg Hutchinson	Frances Paige

Vicki Hendricks   1951-   US   Crime: Hardboiled
www.vickihendricks.com   Miami

Anthony Bourdain	Tim Dorsey
James Hadley Chase	Jason Starr

Go to back for lists of:
Authors by Genre • Characters and Series • Prize Winners • Further Reading

Paul Henke · Wales · Adventure/Thriller

www.henke.co.uk

Tom Clancy
Clive Cussler
Duncan Falconer

Frederick Forsyth
Joseph R Garber
Jean-Christophe Grangé

Gerald Seymour
Wilbur Smith
Terence Strong

Veronica Henry · General

www.veronicahenry.co.uk

Victoria Colby
Joan Collins

Jilly Cooper
Helen Fielding

Philip Hensher · General

www.fantasticfiction.co.uk/authors/Philip_Hensher.htm

Jeffrey Archer
William Boyd
Raymond Carver
Michael Dobbs

John Lanchester
Peter Rawlinson
James Robertson
Tom Sharpe

S Maugham 1997

Brian Herbert · 1947- · US · Science Fiction: Space opera

www.dunenovels.com

Brian W Aldiss
David Brin

Frank Herbert
Kristine Kathryn Rusch

Charles Stross

Frank Herbert · 1920-86 · US · Science Fiction: Space opera

www.dunenovels.com/bios/frank.html

Brian W Aldiss
Kevin J Anderson
J G Ballard

David Brin
Brian Herbert
Ursula K Le Guin

Larry Niven
Adam Roberts
Sheri S Tepper

H

James Herbert · 1943- · Horror

www.james-herbert.co.uk

Richard Bachman
Stephen Gallagher
Peter James

Stephen Laws
Bentley Little

Phil Rickman
Steven Spruill

Richard Herman · 1939- · US · Adventure/Thriller

www.fantasticfiction.co.uk/authors/Richard_Herman.htm

Dale Brown
James Cobb
Stephen Coonts

Graham Hurley
John Nichol

Justin Scott
James Thayer

David Hewson   1953-   Crime: Police work - Italy

www.davidhewson.com

🏃 Det Nic Costa - Rome

Andrea Camilleri	Donna Leon	Barbara Nadel
Michael Dibdin	Magdalen Nabb	

Georgette Heyer   1902-74   Historical

www.fantasticfiction.co.uk/authors/Georgette_Heyer.htm

Elizabeth Aston	Marion Chesney	Jane Aiken Hodge
Jane Austen	Howard Fast	Diana Norman
Elizabeth Chadwick	Elizabeth Hawksley	Amanda Quick

Carl Hiaasen   1953-   US   Crime: Humour

www.carlhiaasen.com

Florida

CWA 1992

Dave Barry	Bill Fitzhugh	
Marc Blake	Peter Guttridge	
Marius Brill	Douglas Lindsay	
Christopher Brookmyre	Shane Maloney	Donald E Westlake
Christopher Buckley	Zane Radcliffe	Don Winslow

George V Higgins   1939-99   US   Crime: Hardboiled

www.kirjasto.sci.fi/higg.htm

🏃 Jerry Kennedy, Attorney - Boston

Lorenzo Carcaterra	Michael Malone	John B Spencer
Jerome Charyn	Mario Puzo	Jim Thompson
Elmore Leonard		

Jack Higgins   1929-   Adventure/Thriller

also writes as **Martin Fallon**; *is* **Harry Patterson**

🏃 Sean Dillon

www.fantasticfiction.co.uk/authors/Jack_Higgins.htm

H

Desmond Bagley	Stephen Leather	James Webb
Harold Coyle	James Thayer	Glover Wright
John Gardner	Craig Thomas	

Suzanne Higgins   Ire   Chick Lit

www.suzannehiggins.com

Jaye Carroll	Tara Manning	Marian Murphy
Clare Dowling	Anna Maxted	Carmen Reid

Julie Highmore   Aga saga

Raffaella Barker	Rebecca Gregson	Elizabeth Noble
Susie Boyt	Sophie Kinsella	Marcia Willett
Sarah Challis	Chris Manby	

Patricia Highsmith   1921-95   US   Crime: Psychological

also wrote as **Clare Morgan**   ☺ Tom Ripley - London
www.kirjasto.sci.fi/highsm.htm

Karin Alvtegen	Gay Longworth	Josephine Tey
Douglas Kennedy	Simon Shaw	Stuart Woods

Lynn Hightower   1956-   US   Crime: Police work - US

also writes as **Lynn S Hightower**   ☺ Det Sonora Blair - Cincinnati
www.lynnhightower.com

Patricia D Cornwell	Meg Gardiner	Theresa Monsour
David Cray	Tami Hoag	Kathy Reichs

Charles Higson   1958-   Humour

www.fantasticfiction.co.uk/authors/Charles_Higson.htm

Joseph Connolly	James Hawes	John McCabe
Ben Elton	Sean Hughes	Alexei Sayle
Stephen Fry	Robert Llewellyn	

Elizabeth Ann Hill   Saga

Rosemary Aitken	Connie Monk	Eileen Stafford
Gloria Cook	Sheila Newberry	E V Thompson
Elizabeth Jeffrey	Malcolm Ross	Nicola Thorne

Melissa Hill   Chick Lit

www.fantasticfiction.co.uk/authors/Melissa_Hill.htm

Clare Dowling	Tara Heavey	Anita Notaro
Imogen Edwards-Jones	Monica McInerney	Geraldine O'Neill
Donna Hay	Sharon Mulrooney	Morag Prunty

H

Reginald Hill   1936-   Crime: Police work - UK

also writes as **Dick Morland, Patrick Ruell,
Charles Underhill**   ☺ DS Pascoe & DI Dalziel - Yorkshire
www.randomhouse.com/features/reghill   Joe Sixsmith, PI - Luton

John Baker	Georgie Hale	Bill James	CWA 1990
Robert Barnard	John Harvey	Bill Knox	
Colin Dexter	Lesley Horton	Frank Lean	
Geraldine Evans	Graham Hurley	Iain McDowall	

Go to back for lists of:

Susan Hill 1942- General

www.susan-hill.com

Virginia Andrews	Jennifer Johnston	
Sara Donati	Penelope Lively	Mail 1972
Daphne Du Maurier	Ann Patchett	Whitbread 1972
Jane Gardam	William Trevor	Teresa Waugh

Tobias Hill 1970- Adventure/Thriller

www.fantasticfiction.co.uk/authors/Tobias_Hill.htm

Martin Amis	Peter Carey	Ian Rankin
J G Ballard	Stewart Home	Will Self
Dan Brown	Tim Lott	

Tony Hillerman 1925- US Crime: Police work - US

www.tonyhillermanbooks.com

Jim Chee & Joe Leaphorn - Navajo Reservation, Arizona

C J Box	J A Jance	Deon Meyer
James Lee Burke	Sharyn McCrumb	Eliot Pattison
Robert Ferrigno	Michael McGarrity	Alexander McCall Smith
Donald Harstad	Michael Malone	Christopher West

Joanna Hines 1949- Adventure/Thriller: Psychological

www.joannahines.co.uk

Leslie Forbes	Lesley Glaister	Minette Walters
Frances Fyfield	Carol Goodman	Gillian White

Joanna Hines 1949- Historical

www.joannahines.co.uk

H

Daphne Du Maurier	Cynthia Harrod-Eagles	Susanna Kearsley
Winston Graham	Jane Aiken Hodge	Ross King
Philippa Gregory		

Tami Hoag 1959- US Crime: Psychological

www.randomhouse.com/bantamdell/tamihoag

Patricia D Cornwell	Iris Johansen	Jenny Siler
Tess Gerritsen	Alex Kava	Karin Slaughter
Christiane Heggan	Meg O'Brien	Erica Spindler
Lynn Hightower	James Patterson	Stephen White

Robin Hobb 1952- US Fantasy: Epic

is Megan Lindholm
www.robinhobb.com

Sarah Ash	Jude Fisher	Robert Newcomb
Carol Berg	Guy Gavriel Kay	Kristine Kathryn Rusch
James Clemens	Juliet Marillier	Sean Russell
Cecilia Dart-Thornton	Caiseal Mor	Tad Williams

Jane Aiken Hodge 1917- Historical

June Drummond	Elizabeth Hawksley	Victoria Holt
Winston Graham	Georgette Heyer	Robin Maxwell
Sandra Gulland	Joanna Hines	Barbara Michaels

Peter Hoeg 1957- Den General

Leslie Forbes	Henning Mankell	CWA 1994
Jostein Gaarder	Haruki Murakami	
David Guterson	Annie Proulx	
Stuart M Kaminsky	Jane Smiley	Jane Urquhart

Alice Hoffman 1952- US General

www.alicehoffman.com

Michael Collins	Janice Graham	Alice McDermott
Candida Crewe	A M Homes	Jacquelyn Mitchard
Alison Fell	Janette Turner Hospital	Anna Quindlen
Nicci French	William Kowalski	Mona Simpson

Craig Holden US Crime: Legal/financial

www.craigholden.com

David Baldacci	F Scott Fitzgerald	Lisa Scottoline
E L Doctorow	John Grisham	Scott Turow

H

Wendy Holden 1965- Chick Lit

www.fantasticfiction.co.uk/authors/Wendy_Holden.htm

Lisa Armstrong	Francesca Clementis	Yvonne Roberts
Melissa Bank	Amy Jenkins	Daisy Waugh
Faith Bleasdale	L McCrossan	Isabel Wolff

Go to back for lists of:
Authors by Genre
Characters and Series
Prize Winners
Further Reading

Robert Holdstock 1948-   Fantasy: Literary

also writes as **Robert Black, Ken Blake, Chris Carlsen, Robert Faulcon, Richard Kirk**
http://robertholdstock.com

Marion Zimmer Bradley	Guy Gavriel Kay	BSFA 1984 & 1988
Charles de Lint	Tim Powers	
Graham Joyce	Jan Siegel	Gene Wolfe

Tom Holland 1947-   Horror

www.fantasticfiction.co.uk/authors/Tom_Holland.htm

Poppy Z Brite	Kim Newman	Iain Sinclair
Nancy Collins	Anne Rice	S P Somtow
Brian Lumley		

Helen Hollick 1953-   Historical

www.fantasticfiction.co.uk/authors/Helen_Hollick.htm 　 ✇ Arthurian Trilogy

Marion Zimmer Bradley	Elizabeth Hawksley	Sharon Penman
Barbara Erskine	Stephen R Lawhead	Mary Stewart
Anne Haverty	Rosalind Miles	

Alan Hollinghurst 1954-   General

www.fantasticfiction.co.uk/authors/Alan_Hollinghurst.htm

Michael Carson	Armistead Maupin	S Maugham 1989
Patrick Gale	Edmund White	Black 1994
		Man Booker 2004

Sheri Holman 1966- US   Historical

Charles Dickens	Anne Haverty	Ann Patchett
Sara Donati	Ross King	Rose Tremain
Emma Donoghue	Matthew Kneale	Sarah Waters

Joyce Holms Sco   Crime: Amateur sleuth

www.joyceholms.com 　 ✇ Fizz Fitzgerald & Tam Buchanan, Legal student & Lawyer
Edinburgh

M C Beaton	Hazel Holt	Betty Rowlands
Natasha Cooper	Quintin Jardine	Scarlett Thomas
Liz Evans	Bill Knox	Rebecca Tope
Gerald Hammond	M R D Meek	Stella Whitelaw

Go to back for lists of:
Authors by Genre • Characters and Series • Prize Winners • Further Reading

H

Hazel Holt   1928-   Crime: Amateur sleuth
www.hazelholt.co.uk   ⚑ Sheila Malory - 'Taviscombe'

Caroline Carver	Joyce Holms	Betty Rowlands
Sarah Caudwell	Alison Joseph	Dorothy L Sayers
Freda Davies	Marianne Macdonald	Dorothy Simpson
Ann Granger	Ann Purser	Rebecca Tope

Tom Holt   1961-   Humour
www.edlin.org/holt

Jasper Fforde	David Nobbs	Sue Townsend
Garrison Keillor	Tom Sharpe	P G Wodehouse
Robert Llewellyn		

Tom Holt   1961-   Fantasy: Humour
www.edlin.org/holt

Douglas Adams	Rob Grant	Terry Pratchett
Robert Asprin	Andrew Harman	Robert Rankin
George Macdonald Fraser	Harry Harrison	Martin Scott
Craig Shaw Gardner		

Victoria Holt   1906-93   Historical
also wrote as **Philippa Carr, Jean Plaidy**; *was* **Eleanor Alice Hibbert**
www.fantasticfiction.co.uk/authors/Victoria_Holt.htm

Catherine Coulter	Caroline Harvey	Sara Hylton
Sara Donati	Jane Aiken Hodge	Claire Lorrimer
Cynthia Harrod-Eagles	Harriet Hudson	Anya Seton

Stewart Home   General

J G Ballard	Tobias Hill
Bret Easton Ellis	Alan Warner

H

A M Homes   US   General
is Amy Michael Homes

Jonathan Franzen	Hilary Mantel	Ali Smith
Alice Hoffman	Alice Sebold	

Evelyn Hood   1936-   Sco   Saga
www.evelynhood.co.uk   Scotland

Maggie Bennett	Meg Henderson	Linda Sole
Maggie Craig	Gwen Kirkwood	Mary Withall
Inga Dunbar	Malcolm Ross	Valerie Wood

Philip Hook
www.fantasticfiction.co.uk/authors/Philip_Hook.htm

Adventure/Thriller
Art world

Jonathan Gash
Graham Hurley
John Malcolm
Iain Pears

Christopher Hope   1944-   SA
www.fantasticfiction.co.uk/authors/Christopher_Hope.htm

General

William Boyd
André Brink
Justin Cartwright
J M Coetzee
Nadine Gordimer
Pamela Jooste
Amos Oz
Richard Powers

Higham 1981
Whitbread 1984

Shifra Horn   Isr
www.shifra-horn.com

General

Isabel Allende
Laura Esquivel
Rohinton Mistry
Salman Rushdie

Nick Hornby   1957-
www.fantasticfiction.co.uk/authors/Nick_Hornby.htm

Lad Lit

Robert Chalmers
James Delingpole
Alex George
John McCabe
Mil Millington
David Nicholls
John O'Farrell
Ben Richards
Willy Russell
Polly Samson
Sean Thomas
Matt Whyman

WHSmith 2001

Una Horne

Saga
NE England

Rita Bradshaw
Irene Carr
Jean Chapman
Catherine Cookson
Elizabeth Gill
Sheila Jansen
Brenda McBryde
Wendy Robertson
Janet MacLeod Trotter

H

Lesley Horton
www.lesleyhorton.co.uk

Crime: Police work - UK
DI Handford & DS Khalid Ali - Bradford, Yorkshire

Ann Cleeves
John Connor
Georgie Hale
Patricia Hall
Reginald Hill
Graham Hurley
Iain McDowall
Nick Oldham
Peter Robinson

Janette Turner Hospital   1942-   Aus
www.fantasticfiction.co.uk/authors/Janette_Turner_Hospital.htm

General

Alice Hoffman
Elizabeth Jolley
Thomas Keneally
David Malouf
Toni Morrison
Michèle Roberts
Salman Rushdie

Audrey Howard   1929-   Saga
www.fantasticfiction.co.uk/authors/Audrey_Howard.htm   Liverpool & Lancashire

Anne Baker   Adèle Geras   Romantic 1988
Catherine Cookson   Lilian Harry
Katie Flynn   Marie Joseph
Helen Forrester   Sue Sully   Valerie Wood

Elizabeth Jane Howard   1923-   General
www.fantasticfiction.co.uk/authors/Elizabeth_Jane_Howard.htm

Jane Asher   Victoria Clayton   Charlotte Moore
Margaret Bacon   Catherine Fox   Anna Quindlen
Rachel Billington   Eileen Goudge   Ann Swinfen
Rose Boucheron   Angela Lambert   Elizabeth Tettmar

Johnny 'Two Combs' Howard   1960-   War: Modern
www.fantasticfiction.co.uk/authors/Johnny_Two_Combs_Howard.htm

Murray Davies   David Mason   Chris Ryan
Eric L Harry   John Nichol   James Webb
Robert Jackson

Richard Howard   War: Historical
                          ⚔ Sgt Alain Lausard - C18th French Dragoon
                                                    Bonaparte Series

Bernard Cornwell   Philip McCutchan   Patrick O'Brian
Garry Douglas   Allan Mallinson   Patrick Rambaud
Daniel Hall

Susan Howatch   1940-   Saga
www.fantasticfiction.co.uk/authors/Susan_Howatch.htm   Church of England Series
                                                        St Benet's Trilogy   **H**

Daphne Du Maurier   Sarah Harrison   Sue Sully
Zoë Fairbairns   Susanna Kearsley   Kate Tremayne
Catherine Fox   Jean Stubbs   Anthony Trollope

Hazel Hucker   1937-   Aga saga

Anne Atkins   Julia Hamilton   Rebecca Shaw
Lucy Clare   Erica James   Mary Sheepshanks
Kate Fielding   Julia Lisle   Madeleine Wickham

Go to back for lists of:
Authors by Genre • Characters and Series • Prize Winners • Further Reading

Harriet Hudson   1938-   Saga

is **Amy Myers**
www.amymyers.net

Betty Burton   Sara Hylton   Patricia Wendorf
Elizabeth Daish   Margaret Pemberton   Audrey Willsher
Victoria Holt   Caroline Stickland   Sally Worboyes

Tanya Huff   1957-   Can   Horror

www.fantasticfiction.co.uk/authors/Tanya_Huff.htm   ⚲ Henry Fitzroy & Vicki Nelson, PI

Kelley Armstrong   Charlaine Harris   Holly Lisle
Poppy Z Brite   Jeanne Kalogridis   Steven Spruill
Laurell K Hamilton

Sean Hughes   1965-   Ire   Humour

www.fantasticfiction.co.uk/authors/Sean_Hughes.htm

Martin Amis   James Kelman   Will Self
Niall Griffiths   Patrick McCabe   Irvine Welsh
Charles Higson   Alexei Sayle

C C Humphreys   Can   Historical

www.cchumphreys.com   ⚲ Jack Absolute - C18th
                                        Jean Rombaud, Executioner - C16th England

Judith Cook   Philip Gooden   Martin Stephen
Bernard Cornwell   John Pilkington   Peter Tonkin
Patricia Finney   C J Sansom

Helen Humphreys   1961-   Can   General

Charlotte Bingham   Karen Hayes   Margaret Mayhew
Maeve Haran   Angela Huth   Titia Sutherland
Josephine Hart

Gwen Hunter   1956-   US   Adventure/Thriller

also writes as **Gary Hunter**
www.gwenhunter.com

Virginia Andrews   Peter Rawlinson
Stephen Hunter   Paullina Simons

Stephen Hunter   1946-   US   Adventure/Thriller

www.fantasticfiction.co.uk/authors/Stephen_Hunter.htm

Gwen Hunter   Chris Ryan   Paullina Simons
John R Maxim   John Sandford

Graham Hurley 1946- Crime: Police work - UK

www.grahamhurley.co.uk

⚿ DI Joe Faraday - Portsmouth

Paul Charles	John Harvey	Iain McDowall
Robert Edric	Reginald Hill	Ian Rankin
Georgie Hale	Lesley Horton	Peter Robinson
Patricia Hall	Quintin Jardine	Michelle Spring

Graham Hurley 1946- Adventure/Thriller

www.grahamhurley.co.uk

Geoffrey Archer	W E B Griffin	Philip Hook
Dale Brown	Jack Harvey	Chris Ryan
Lee Child	Richard Herman	

Siri Hustvedt 1955- US General

Jeffrey Eugenides	Shirley Hazzard
Nicci Gerrard	Anita Shreve

Meg Hutchinson 1933- Saga

also writes as **Margaret Astbury** Birmingham
www.fantasticfiction.co.uk/authors/Meg_Hutchinson.htm

Donna Baker	Sara Fraser	Annie Murray
Maggie Bennett	Meg Henderson	Jessica Stirling
Rita Bradshaw	Gwen Madoc	Audrey Willsher

Angela Huth 1938- General

Elizabeth Buchan	Angela Lambert	Deborah Moggach
Elizabeth Darrell	Shena Mackay	Elizabeth Tettmar
Helen Humphreys	Margaret Mayhew	

Shaun Hutson 1958- Horror

www.shaunhutson.com

Simon Clark	Graham Masterton	Phil Rickman
Richard Laymon	Mark Morris	John Saul
Bentley Little	Christopher Pike	Whitley Strieber

Aldous Huxley 1894-1963 General

www.fantasticfiction.co.uk/authors/Aldous_Huxley.htm

Margaret Atwood	D H Lawrence	Anthony Powell
Ray Bradbury	George Orwell	

H

Sara Hylton — Saga

Louise Brindley
Teresa Crane
Victoria Holt

Harriet Hudson
Marie Joseph
Claire Lorrimer

Margaret Pemberton
Judith Saxton
Elizabeth Walker

Conn Iggulden 1971- — Historical

www.conniggulden.com

Lindsey Davis
Robert Graves
Christian Jacq

Valerio Massimo Manfredi
Allan Massie
Steven Pressfield

Mary Renault
Simon Scarrow
Manda Scott

Greg Iles US — Adventure/Thriller

www.gregiles.com

Conor Cregan
Alan Folsom
Pete Hamill

Donald James
Alan Judd
Robert Ludlum

Glenn Meade
Kyle Mills

Hammond Innes 1913-1998 — Adventure/Thriller

www.fantasticfiction.co.uk/authors/Hammond_Innes.htm

Desmond Bagley
Jon Cleary
Clive Cussler

Alexander Fullerton
Alistair MacLean
Nicholas Monsarrat

James Pattinson
Douglas Reeman
Nevil Shute

Michael Innes 1906-94 Sco — Crime: Police work - UK

was John Innes Mackintosh Stewart
www.fantasticfiction.co.uk/authors/Michael_Innes.htm

🚶 DI John Appleby
London

Margery Allingham
John Gardner

Gladys Mitchell
Dorothy L Sayers

Josephine Tey
Patricia Wentworth

H
I

Ian Irvine 1950- Aus — Fantasy: Epic

www.ian-irvine.com

Stephen Donaldson
David A Drake
David Eddings

Jude Fisher
Terry Goodkind
Julia Gray

Robert Jordan
Juliet E McKenna
Freda Warrington

John Irving 1942- US — General

www.fantasticfiction.co.uk/authors/John_Irving.htm

Jonathan Coe
Tibor Fischer
Joseph Heller
William Kowalski

Terry McMillan
Larry McMurtry
Rick Moody
Tim O'Brien

Thomas Pynchon
Tom Robbins
John Updike
Tobias Wolff

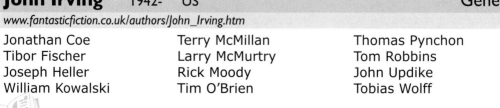

Susan Isaacs 1943- US General
www.susanisaacs.com

Anabel Donald	Sparkle Hayter	Sarah Strohmeyer
Kinky Friedman	Pauline McLynn	Jennifer Weiner
Sarah Harrison	Anna Quindlen	

Kazuo Ishiguro 1954- Ja General
www.fantasticfiction.co.uk/authors/Kazuo_Ishiguro.htm

Michelle de Kretser	Timothy Mo	Holtby 1982
Ronald Frame	Haruki Murakami	Whitbread 1986
Arthur Golden	Michael Ondaatje	Booker 1989
Andrew Sean Greer	Darin Strauss	
		Adam Thorpe

Alan Isler 1934- US General
www.fantasticfiction.co.uk/authors/Alan_Isler.htm

William Boyd	Philip Roth	Wingate 1996
Howard Jacobson	Bernhard Schlink	
Amos Oz	Tom Sharpe	Isaac Bashevis Singer

Graham Ison Crime: Police work - UK
www.grahamison.co.uk

🏃 DI Brock & DS Poole ⎱ London
DI Hardcastle & DS Charles Marriott - WWI ⎰

Paul Charles	Cynthia Harrod-Eagles	Michael Pearce
Barbara Cleverly	Maureen O'Brien	Anne Perry
Martha Grimes		

Jon A Jackson 1938- US Crime: Hardboiled
www.jonajackson.com

🏃 Sgt 'Fang' Mulheisen - Detroit
Joe Service, Hitman

Loren D Estleman	Joe R Lansdale	Ed McBain
Danny King	Dennis Lehane	Ridley Pearson

I
J

Robert Jackson 1941- War: Modern
www.fantasticfiction.co.uk/authors/Robert_Jackson.htm

W E B Griffin	Derek Robinson
Eric L Harry	Julian Jay Savarin
Johnny 'Two Combs' Howard	James Webb

Go to back for lists of:
Authors by Genre
Characters and Series
Prize Winners
Further Reading

Anna Jacobs   Aus   Saga

also writes as **Sherry-Anne Jacobs, Shannah Jay**   ⚘ Annie Gibson - Lancashire
www.annajacobs.com   Kershaw Sisters

Julia Bryant	Elizabeth Elgin	Marie Joseph
Irene Carr	Katie Flynn	Maureen Lee
Alexandra Connor	Penny Jordan	Mary Minton

Howard Jacobson   1942-   General

www.fantasticfiction.co.uk/authors/Howard_Jacobson.htm

Edward Docx	Amos Oz	Wingate 1999
Michael Frayn	Frederic Raphael	
Alan Isler	Philip Roth	
Rod Liddle	Tom Sharpe	Adam Thirlwell

Kate Jacoby   Aus   Fantasy: Epic

www.katejacoby.com

James Barclay	Julia Gray	K J Parker
Sara Douglass	Juliet E McKenna	Freda Warrington
David Farland		

Christian Jacq   1947-   Fr   Historical

also writes as **J B Livingstone**   Queen of Freedom Trilogy
www.fantasticfiction.co.uk/authors/Christian_Jacq.htm   Stone of Light Trilogy

Jean M Auel	Conn Iggulden	Steven Pressfield
Pauline Gedge	Colleen McCullough	Manda Scott
Margaret George	Valerio Massimo Manfredi	Wilbur Smith

Jane Jakeman   Crime: Historical - C19th

http://malfine.tripod.com   ⚘ Lord Ambrose Malfine & Belos, Servant
                                        Early C19th France

David Dickinson	Deryn Lake	Hannah March
Janet Gleeson	David Liss	Andrew Martin
John Maclachlan Gray		

J

Bill James   1929-   Wales   Crime: Hardboiled

also writes as **David Craig, Judith James**   ⚘ Ch Supt Colin Harpur & ACC Desmond Iles
is **James Tucker**   Simon Abelard, Intelligence Officer
www.fantasticfiction.co.uk/authors/Bill_James.htm   Wales

Jeffrey Ashford	Reginald Hill	Robert T Price
Ken Bruen	Simon Kernick	Mark Timlin
Martin Edwards	David Peace	David Williams

Donald James 1931-   Adventure/Thriller

www.fantasticfiction.co.uk/authors/Donald_James.htm   ☀ Inspector Vadim - Moscow

Lee Child	Robert Harris	Glenn Meade
Conor Cregan	Greg Iles	Reggie Nadelson
Len Deighton	Joseph Kanon	

Erica James 1960-   General

www.fantasticfiction.co.uk/authors/Erica_James.htm

Amanda Brookfield	Hazel Hucker	Melissa Nathan
Lucy Clare	Jan Karon	Ann Purser
Kate Fielding	Julia Lisle	Rebecca Shaw

Henry James 1843-1916   US   General

www.fantasticfiction.co.uk/authors/Henry_James.htm

Hilary Bailey	E M Forster	Edith Wharton
Ethan Canin	W Somerset Maugham	Patrick White
Joseph Conrad		

Judi James   Glitz & Glamour

Sally Beauman	Jenn Crowell	Judith Michael
Sandra Brown	Julie Ellis	Una-Mary Parker
Joan Collins	Susan Lewis	Harold Robbins

P D James 1920-   Crime: Police work - UK

www.randomhouse.com/features/pdjames   ☀ Supt Adam Dalgleish ⎱ London
Cordelia Gray, PI ⎰

CWA 1971, 1975 & 1986

Jane Adams	Elizabeth George	
Vivien Armstrong	Morag Joss	
Brian Cooper	Jim Kelly	
Kate Ellis	M R D Meek	

Peter James 1948-   Horror

J

www.peterjames.com

David Ambrose	Stephen Gallagher	Stephen King
Richard Bachman	James Herbert	Tim Wilson

Russell James 1942-   Crime: Hardboiled

www.russelljames.co.uk   London

Mark Billingham	Paul Charles	John B Spencer
Ken Bruen	Julian Rathbone	Jim Thompson

Sian James   Wales   General

Candida Clark	Julia Lisle	Joanna Trollope
Suzannah Dunn	Libby Purves	Louise Voss
Charlotte Lamb	Titia Sutherland	

J A Jance   1944-   US   Crime: Police work - US

www.jajance.com

🏃 Det J P Beaumont - Seattle
Sheriff Joanna Brady - Bisbee, Arizona

Michael Connelly	Tony Hillerman	Michael McGarrity
G M Ford	Ed McBain	Claire McNab
Donald Harstad	John D Macdonald	Robert B Parker

J Robert Janes   1935-   Can   Crime: Historical - C20th

www.fantasticfiction.co.uk/authors/J_Robert_Janes.htm

🏃 Jean-Louis St-Cyr & Hermann Kohler
Occupied France

Juliet Hebden	Philip Kerr	Georges Simenon
Mark Hebden	Rebecca Pawel	

Tama Janowitz   US   General

Richard Ford	Armistead Maupin
Jay McInerney	Tom Wolfe

Sheila Jansen   Saga

Newcastle, NE England

Irene Carr	Una Horne	Wendy Robertson
Catherine Cookson	Brenda McBryde	Sally Stewart
Elizabeth Gill	Denise Robertson	Janet MacLeod Trotter

Quintin Jardine   1945-   Sco   Crime: Police work - UK

also writes as **Matthew Reid**
www.quintinjardine.com

🏃 DCI Bob Skinner - Edinburgh
Oz Blackstone & Primavera Phillips

Alex Gray	Paul Johnston	Denise Mina
Jeff Gulvin	Bill Knox	Ian Rankin
Joyce Holms	Frederic Lindsay	Nicholas Royle
Graham Hurley	Jim Lusby	Peter Turnbull

Michael Jecks   1960-   Crime: Historical - Medieval

www.michaeljecks.co.uk

🏃 Sir Baldwin Furnshill & Simon Puttock, Bailiff - C14th Devon

Simon Beaufort	Susanna Gregory	Ellis Peters
Alys Clare	Sylvian Hamilton	Kate Sedley
Paul Doherty	Bernard Knight	Peter Tonkin
Margaret Frazer	Edward Marston	Joan Wolf

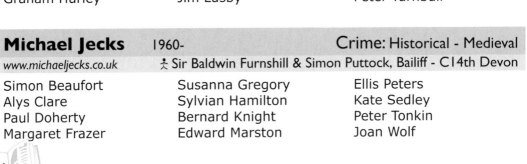

J

Elizabeth Jeffrey · Historical

is Olive Whaley

Margaret Dickinson
Elizabeth Ann Hill
Lena Kennedy

Beryl Kingston
Mary Mackie

Robin Maxwell
Sarah Shears

Roderic Jeffries · 1926- · Crime: Police work - Spain

also writes as Peter Alding, Jeffrey Ashford,
Roderic Graeme, Graham Hastings
www.fantasticfiction.co.uk/authors/Roderic_Jeffries.htm

⚥ DI Enrique Alvarez
Mallorca

Juliet Hebden
Mark Hebden

Manuel Vázquez Montalbán
Magdalen Nabb

Michael Pearce
Christopher West

Amy Jenkins · 1963- · Chick Lit

Anne Dunlop
Helen Fielding
Tara Heavey

Wendy Holden
Dorothy Koomson
Sheila Norton

Stephanie Theobald
Jennifer Weiner
Isabel Wolff

Robin Jenkins · 1912- · Sco · General

Andrew Greig
Andrew O'Hagan

James Robertson
Alan Spence

K W Jeter · 1950- · US · Science Fiction: Technical

www.fantasticfiction.co.uk/authors/K_W_Jeter.htm

Eric Brown
Pat Cadigan

Philip K Dick
Gwyneth Jones

Ian McDonald

Lisa Jewell · 1968- · Chick Lit

www.lisa-jewell.co.uk

Susannah Bates
Rebecca Campbell
Jane Green

Amanda Lees
Marissa Mackle
Claire Naylor

Daisy Waugh
Liz Young
Laura Zigman

J

Ruth Prawer Jhabvala · 1927- · US · General

www.fantasticfiction.co.uk/authors/Ruth_Prawer_Jhabvala.htm

Anita Desai
E M Forster
Rumer Godden
Abdulrazak Gurnah

Lee Langley
John Masters
V S Naipaul
Paul Scott

Booker 1975

Carolyn Slaughter

Laurent Joffrin   1952-   Fr   Adventure/Thriller

www.fantasticfiction.co.uk/authors/Laurent_Joffrin.htm

Sebastian Faulks	Philip Kerr
Douglas Kennedy	Michael Taylor

Iris Johansen   US   Crime: Forensic

www.irisjohansen.com

🏃 Eve Duncan, Forensic sculptor
Sarah Patrick & Monty, Search & rescue worker & dog

Max Allan Collins	Carol Goodman	Keith McCarthy
Patricia D Cornwell	Tami Hoag	Gloria Murphy
Lisa Gardner	Judith Kelman	Erica Spindler

Jennifer Johnston   1930-   Ire   General

www.fantasticfiction.co.uk/authors/Jennifer_Johnston.htm

Elizabeth Bowen	Valerie Martin	Authors 1973
Susan Hill	Edna O'Brien	Whitbread 1979
Joan Lingard	Colm Toibin	
Shena Mackay	William Trevor	Niall Williams

Paul Johnston   1957-   Sco   Crime: PI

www.paul-johnston.co.uk

🏃 Quintilian Dalrymple - C21st Edinburgh
Alex Mavros, PI - Greece

Nicholas Blincoe	Quintin Jardine	CWA 1997
Eric Brown	Douglas Lindsay	
Jeremy Cameron	Paul J McAuley	J D Robb

Elizabeth Jolley   1923-   Aus   General

Janet Frame	Janette Turner Hospital	Alice Munro
Rumer Godden	David Malouf	V S Naipaul
Shirley Hazzard	Hilary Mantel	

Christina Jones   1948-   Chick Lit

www.christinajones.co.uk

Louise Bagshawe	Sarah Harvey	Kathy Lette
Claire Calman	Ben Hatch	Laura Lockington
Jilly Cooper	Donna Hay	Sheila Norton

> *Go to back for lists of:*
> Authors by Genre
> Characters and Series
> Prize Winners
> Further Reading

Gwyneth Jones 1952-   Science Fiction: Near future

also writes as **Ann Halam**
http://homepage.ntlworld.com/gwynethann

Steve Aylett
Sara Douglass
Mary Gentle
K W Jeter

Ian McDonald
Neal Stephenson
Sheri S Tepper
Ian Watson

Arthur C Clarke 2002

David Wingrove

J V Jones 1963-   Fantasy: Epic

www.jvj.com

Kate Elliott
David Farland
Maggie Furey

David Gemmell
Katherine Kurtz
Valery Leith

Megan Lindholm
Kristine Kathryn Rusch
Freda Warrington

Joan Jonker   Saga
www.fantasticfiction.co.uk/authors/Joan_Jonker.htm   Liverpool

Lyn Andrews
Benita Brown
Alexandra Connor

Elizabeth Daish
Helen Forrester
Penny Jordan

Maureen Lee
Margaret Mayhew
Sharon Owens

Pamela Jooste SA   General

J M Coetzee
Giles Foden

Nadine Gordimer
Christopher Hope

Doris Lessing
Paul Scott

Penny Jordan 1946-   Saga
www.fantasticfiction.co.uk/authors/Penny_Jordan.htm

Barbara Delinsky
Anna Jacobs
Joan Jonker

Margaret Kaine
Jayne Ann Krentz
Judith McNaught

Mary Minton
Una-Mary Parker

Robert Jordan 1948- US   Fantasy: Epic

also writes as **Chang Lung, Regan O'Neal,
Jackson O'Reilly, Regan O'Reilly**
is James Oliver Rigney, Jr
www.sffworld.com/author/286.html

J

Mark Anthony
Ashok K Banker
Chris Bunch
Louise Cooper

David Eddings
David Farland
Ian Irvine
John Marco

Robert Newcomb
Stan Nicholls
Sean Russell
J R R Tolkien

Alison Joseph   1958-   Crime: Amateur sleuth

www.fantasticfiction.co.uk/authors/Alison_Joseph.htm

Sister Agnes Bourdillon, Nun

Marian Babson
Elizabeth Ferrars
Jonathan Gash

Elizabeth George
Hazel Holt

Morag Joss
Marianne Macdonald

Marie Joseph   Saga

www.fantasticfiction.co.uk/authors/Marie_Joseph.htm

Lancashire

Romantic 1987

Donna Baker
Margaret Thomson Davis
Katie Flynn
Helen Forrester

Audrey Howard
Sara Hylton
Anna Jacobs
Lena Kennedy

Mary Minton

Morag Joss   Crime: Psychological

www.fantasticfiction.co.uk/authors/Morag_Joss.htm

Sara Selkirk, Cellist - Bath

CWA 2003

Hilary Bonner
Gregory Hall
P D James
Alison Joseph

Marianne Macdonald
Fiona Mountain
Gemma O'Connor
Sarah Rayne

Ruth Rendell

Graham Joyce   1954-   Horror

www.grahamjoyce.net

Jonathan Aycliffe
Jonathan Carroll
Christopher Fowler
Robert Holdstock

David Martin
Mark Morris
Phil Rickman
Scott Nicholson

British Fantasy 1993, 1996,
1997 & 2000

James Joyce   1882-1941   Ire   General

www.jamesjoyce.ie/home

Martin Amis
William Faulkner

D H Lawrence
John McGahern

Vladimir Nabokov
Virginia Woolf

J Alan Judd   1946-   Adventure/Thriller

www.fantasticfiction.co.uk/authors/Alan_Judd.htm

Charles Thoroughgood

Guardian 1991
Holtby 1992

James Buchan
John Fullerton
Joseph R Garber
Humphrey Hawksley

Greg Iles
John Le Carré
Andy McNab
Daniel Silva

Go to back for lists of:
Authors by Genre • Characters and Series • Prize Winners • Further Reading

Margaret Kaine

Saga

www.margaretkaine.com

1950s Staffordshire potteries

Benita Brown	Claire Lorrimer
Margaret Graham	Gwen Madoc
Penny Jordan	Elizabeth Murphy
Freda Lightfoot	Sharon Owens

Jeanne Kalogridis   1954-   US

Horror

www.fantasticfiction.co.uk/authors/Jeanne_Kalogridis.htm

🏃 Family Dracul, Vampire

Laurell K Hamilton	Anne Rice	S P Somtow
Tanya Huff	Dan Simmons	Steven Spruill

Stuart M Kaminsky   1934-   US

Crime: Historical - C20th

www.stuartkaminsky.com

🏃 Toby Peters - 1940s Hollywood
Insp Porfiry Rostnikov, Police - Moscow

Raymond Chandler	David Guterson	Peter Hoeg
James Hadley Chase	Dashiell Hammett	Philip Kerr
James Ellroy		

Joseph Kanon   1946-   US

Adventure/Thriller

www.josephkanon.com

Eric Ambler	Donald James	John Le Carré
Dan Fesperman	John Lawton	Robert Ryan
Robert Harris		

Manju Kapur   Ind

General

Kavita Daswani	Cauvery Madhavan	Anita Nair
Sharon Maas	Nisha Minhas	Preethi Nair

Jan Karon   1937-   US

General

www.mitfordbooks.com

Mitford Series - USA

Kate Fielding	Garrison Keillor	Rebecca Shaw
Fannie Flagg	Ann Purser	Adriana Trigiani
Erica James	Miss Read	

John Katzenbach   US

Adventure/Thriller   **K**

www.johnkatzenbach.com

Russell Andrews	Jeffery Deaver	Dean R Koontz
Harlan Coben	Thomas Harris	Stephen White
Michael Connelly		

Alex Kava   US   Crime: Psychological
www.alexkava.com   ⚐ Maggie O'Dell, FBI Agent

Tess Gerritsen	Jonathan Nasaw	Karin Slaughter
Daniel Hecht	Meg O'Brien	Susan R Sloan
Tami Hoag	James Patterson	Erica Spindler
Jonathan Kellerman	Jenny Siler	Stephen White

Guy Gavriel Kay   1954-   Can   Fantasy: Epic
www.brightweavings.com

Mark Anthony	Robin Hobb	Stephen R Lawhead
Mark Chadbourn	Robert Holdstock	Michael Scott Rohan
Charles de Lint	Katharine Kerr	J R R Tolkien
Julia Gray	Greg Keyes	Jane Welch

Nora Kay   Saga
Scotland

Emma Blair	Isobel Neill	Jessica Stirling
Doris Davidson	Frances Paige	Anne Vivis
Christine Marion Fraser	Eileen Ramsay	Mary Withall

Erin Kaye   Ire   Saga

Maeve Binchy	Geraldine O'Neill	Grace Thompson
Josephine Cox	Sharon Owens	Valerie Wood
Claire Lorrimer	Liz Ryan	

M M Kaye   1908-2004   General
www.fantasticfiction.co.uk/authors/M_M_Kaye.htm

Thalassa Ali	John Masters	Paul Scott
Lee Langley	Gita Mehta	Mary Stewart

Louise Kean   Chick Lit

Dawn Cairns	Marian Keyes	Sharon Mulrooney
Jane Green	L McCrossan	Kate Thompson

K
Paul Kearney   1967-   Ire   Fantasy: Epic
www.paulkearneyonline.com

Stephen Donaldson	Maggie Furey	Valery Leith
Kate Elliott	David Gemmell	Harry Turtledove
Raymond E Feist	Stephen R Lawhead	Jonathan Wylie

Susanna Kearsley   1966-   Can   General

Daphne Du Maurier	Joanna Hines	Ross King
Robert Goddard	Susan Howatch	Mary Stewart

H R F Keating   1926-   Crime: Police work - UK

also writes as **Evelyn Hervey**   ☆ Insp Ghote - Bombay
www.fantasticfiction.co.uk/authors/H_R_F_Keating.htm   DCI Harriet Martens -
'Greater Birchester'

Leslie Forbes	Priscilla Masters	CWA 1980
Juliet Hebden	Magdalen Nabb	
Mark Hebden	Michael Pearce	
Lynda La Plante	Daniel Pennac	Georges Simenon

Garrison Keillor   1942-   US   Humour

is **Gary Edward Keillor**

Ethan Canin	Tom Holt	William Kennedy
Richard Ford	Jan Karon	

Faye Kellerman   1952-   US   Crime: Police work - US

www.bookreporter.com/authors/au-kellerman-faye.asp   ☆ Lt Pete Decker, Officer Cindy Decker &
Rina Lazarus - Los Angeles
DS Romulus Poe - Las Vegas

Jan Burke	Jenny Maxwell	Jefferson Parker
Joy Fielding	Carol O'Connell	Ridley Pearson
Ed McBain		

Jonathan Kellerman   1949-   US   Crime: Police work - US

www.randomhouse.com/features/kellerman   ☆ Det Milo Sturgis & Alex Delaware,
Psychologist - Los Angeles
Det Petra O'Connor - Hollywood

Keith Russell Ablow	Daniel Hecht	James Patterson
Harlan Coben	Alex Kava	Ridley Pearson
John Connolly	Jonathan Nasaw	Erica Spindler
Mo Hayder	Jefferson Parker	Stephen White

Cathy Kelly   Ire   Chick Lit

www.cathy-kelly.com

Claudine Cullimore	Marian Murphy	Romantic 2001
Sarah Harvey	Geraldine O'Neill	
Tara Heavey	Kate O'Riordan	
Josie Lloyd & Emlyn Rees	Linda Taylor	Kate Thompson

K

Jim Kelly

Crime: Amateur sleuth

www.fantasticfiction.co.uk/authors/Jim_Kelly.htm

⚐ Philip Dryden, Journalist
Ely, Cambridgeshire

Martin Edwards	P D James	Peter Robinson
Roger Jon Ellory	Ed O'Connor	Chris Simms
G M Ford	Ruth Rendell	Michelle Spring

Sheelagh Kelly

Saga

⚐ Feeney Family ⎱ Yorkshire
Prince Family ⎰

Helen Cannam	D M Purcell	Patricia Shaw
Mary A Larkin	Elvi Rhodes	Anne Worboys
Genevieve Lyons	Liz Ryan	

Susan B Kelly   1955-

Crime: Police work - UK

also writes as **Susan Kelly**
www.fantasticfiction.co.uk/authors/Susan_B_Kelly.htm

⚐ DCI Nick Trevellyan & Alison Hope
Supt Gregory Summers - Thames Valley

Vivien Armstrong	Natasha Cooper	Veronica Stallwood
Paul Charles	Colin Dexter	

Thomas Kelly   US

Adventure/Thriller

Jake Arnott	Jeff Gulvin	Jenny Maxwell
Lorenzo Carcaterra	Pete Hamill	David Michie
Alan Folsom		

James Kelman   1946-   Sco

General

www.contemporarywriters.com/authors/?p=auth55

Des Dillon	Sean Hughes	Black 1989
Michel Faber	A L Kennedy	Booker 1994
Alasdair Gray	Agnes Owens	Irvine Welsh

Judith Kelman   1945-   US

Adventure/Thriller

www.jkelman.com

Virginia Andrews	Frances Hegarty	Fiona Mountain
Joy Fielding	Iris Johansen	Hilary Norman
Carol Goodman	Barbara Michaels	

K

Go to back for lists of:
Authors by Genre
Characters and Series
Prize Winners
Further Reading

Thomas Keneally　1935-　Aus　　　　　　　General

also writes as **William Coyle**
www.fantasticfiction.co.uk/authors/Thomas_Keneally.htm

Peter Carey	Janette Turner Hospital	Booker 1982
E L Doctorow	David Malouf	
Robert Drewe	Brian Moore	
Charles Frazier	Julian Rathbone	Patrick White
Shirley Hazzard	Adam Thorpe	Tim Winton

A L Kennedy　1965-　Sco　　　　　　　General

www.alkennedy.co.uk

Ron Butlin	Janice Galloway	S Maugham 1994
Amanda Craig	Alasdair Gray	Encore 1996
Glen Duncan	James Kelman	
Michel Faber	Andrew O'Hagan	Ali Smith

Douglas Kennedy　1955-　US　　　Adventure/Thriller

www.fantasticfiction.co.uk/authors/Douglas_Kennedy.htm

Francis Cottam	Andrew Klavan	TGR 1998
Patricia Highsmith	Richard North Patterson	Paul Watkins
Laurent Joffrin	Michael Taylor	Stuart Woods

Lena Kennedy　1913- 1986　　　　　　　Saga
　　　　　　　　　　　　　　　　　　　　　　London

www.fantasticfiction.co.uk/authors/Lena_Kennedy.htm

Philip Boast	Marie Joseph	Sally Worboyes
June Francis	Beryl Kingston	Anne Worboys
Elizabeth Jeffrey	Genevieve Lyons	

William Kennedy　1928-　US　　　　　General
　　　　　　　　　　　　　　　　　　　Albany Series

www.fantasticfiction.co.uk/authors/William_Kennedy.htm

Pete Dexter	Garrison Keillor	Pulitzer 1984
E L Doctorow	John Steinbeck	

Alexander Kent　1924-　　　　　Sea: Historical

is **Douglas Reeman**　　　　　⚇ Richard Bolitho • Adam Bolitho
www.bolithomaritimeproductions.com

Tom Connery	Daniel Hall	Jan Needle
David Donachie	Jonathan Lunn	Marcus Palliser
C S Forester	Philip McCutchan	Julian Stockwin

K

143

Gordon Kent US   Adventure/Thriller

is Ken & Christian Cameron   ☃ Alan Craik - US Naval Intelligence
www.navnov.com/about.htm   Mike Dukas

Dale Brown   David Hagberg   John J Nance
Tom Clancy   Charles McCarry

Simon Kernick 1966-   Crime: Hardboiled

www.simonkernick.com   ☃ DI John Gallan & DS Tina Boyd - London

Jake Arnott   Robert Edric   Stuart Pawson
Mark Billingham   John Harvey   David Peace
Anthony Bourdain   Bill James   John B Spencer
Ken Bruen   Barry Maitland   Mark Timlin

Jack Kerouac 1922-69 US   General

www.jackkerouac.com/index.php

Alex Garland   Larry McMurtry
Jay McInerney   John Steinbeck

Katharine Kerr 1944- US   Fantasy: Myth

www.deverry.com

Alice Borchardt   Guy Gavriel Kay   Anne McCaffrey
Mark Chadbourn   Greg Keyes   Caiseal Mor
Sylvie Germain   Stephen R Lawhead   Judith Tarr

Philip Kerr 1956- Sco   Adventure/Thriller

www.fantasticfiction.co.uk/authors/Philip_Kerr.htm

Geoffrey Archer   Laurent Joffrin   Martin Cruz Smith
Michael Crichton   Stuart M Kaminsky   Nigel West
J Robert Janes   Rebecca Pawel   Robert Wilson

Leo Kessler 1926-   War: Modern

also writes as Duncan Harding, John Kerrigan; *is* Charles Whiting
www.fantasticfiction.co.uk/authors/Leo_Kessler.htm

Harold Coyle   Derek Robinson
David L Robbins   Alan Savage

K

Greg Keyes 1963- US   Fantasy: Epic

www.gregkeyes.com

James Barclay   Katharine Kerr   Sean Russell
Steven Erikson   Stephen R Lawhead   H G Wells
Guy Gavriel Kay   George R R Martin   Tad Williams

144

Marian Keyes   1963-   Ire   Chick Lit

www.mariankeyes.com

Melissa Bank	Kate O'Riordan	Kate Thompson
Clare Dowling	Judith Summers	Grace Wynne-Jones
Louise Kean	Linda Taylor	Laura Zigman

Paul Kilduff   1965-   Ire   Crime: Legal/financial

www.paulkilduff.com

David Baldacci	Reg Gadney	Brad Meltzer
Harry Bingham	Colin Harrison	Scott Turow
Po Bronson	John McLaren	

Michael Kimball   US   Adventure/Thriller

www.michaelkimball.com

David Guterson	Stephen King	John Sandford
Colin Harrison	Lawrence Sanders	

Haven Kimmel   US   General

www.havenkimmel.com

Leif Enger	Mary Lawson	Anne Tyler
Fannie Flagg	Adriana Trigiani	

Anna King   1948-   Saga
London

Harry Bowling	Patricia Grey	Jenny Oldfield
Helen Carey	Elizabeth Lord	Elizabeth Waite
Harry Cole	Anne Melville	Sally Worboyes

Danny King   1969-   Crime: Humour

www.dannykingbooks.com

Richard Asplin	Anthony Bourdain	Joe R Lansdale
Mark Barrowcliffe	Jeremy Cameron	Douglas Lindsay
Dave Barry	Nick Earls	Malcolm Pryce
Colin Bateman	Jon A Jackson	Mike Ripley

John King   1960-   Lad Lit   **K**

www.fantasticfiction.co.uk/authors/John_King.htm

Dougie Brimson	Colin Butts	Kevin Sampson
Paul Burke	Cy Flood	

Jonathon King   US   Crime: Amateur sleuth

www.jonathonking.com   🏃 Max Freeman, Retired policeman - Florida

Ace Atkins	Robert Ferrigno	Steve Hamilton
James Lee Burke	James Hall	Michael Malone

Laurie King   1952-   US   Crime: Historical - C20th

also writes as Laurie R King   🏃 Sherlock Holmes & Mary Russell - C20th London
www.laurierking.com   Det Kate Martinelli & Det Al Hawkin - San Francisco
Anne Waverley

Jan Burke	Paula Gosling	Anne Perry
Barbara Cleverly	Richard Grayson	Roberta Rogow
Arthur Conan Doyle	Gillian Linscott	Charles Todd
Meg Gardiner	Claire McNab	Gerard Williams

Ross King   Historical

Umberto Eco	Joanna Hines	Susanna Kearsley
Sandra Gulland	Sheri Holman	

Stephen King   1947-   US   Horror

also writes as Richard Bachman   The Dark Tower Series
www.stephenking.com

Douglas Clegg	Stephen Laws	British Fantasy 1999
John Crowley	Michael Marshall	
John Farris	Andrew Pyper	
Peter James	Phil Rickman	Dan Simmons
Michael Kimball	John Saul	T M Wright

Barbara Kingsolver   1955-   US   General

www.kingsolver.com/home/index.asp

Gail Anderson-Dargatz	Janice Graham	Anne-Marie MacDonald
Louise Erdrich	Kate Grenville	Jacquelyn Mitchard
Patricia Gaffney	Jane Hamilton	Amy Tan

Beryl Kingston   1931-   Saga

www.fantasticfiction.co.uk/authors/Beryl_Kingston.htm   Easter Empire - London

K

Philip Boast	Anne Melville	Claire Rayner
Rose Boucheron	Sheila Newberry	Malcolm Ross
Elizabeth Jeffrey	Gilda O'Neill	June Tate
Lena Kennedy		

Go to back for lists of:
Authors by Genre • Characters and Series • Prize Winners • Further Reading

Sophie Kinsella   1969-   Chick Lit
is Madeleine Wickham
www.randomhouse.com/bantamdell/kinsella

Melissa Bank	Jenny Eclair	Louise Marley
Susannah Bates	Julie Highmore	Alexandra Potter
Jenny Crusie	Laura Lockington	Laura Zigman

Gwen Kirkwood   Saga
www.gwenkirkwood.co.uk   'Fiarlyden' Series - Scotland

Doris Davidson	Elisabeth McNeill	Kirsty White
Christine Marion Fraser	Eileen Ramsay	Mary Withall
Evelyn Hood		

Andrew Klavan   1954-   US   Adventure/Thriller: Psychological
also writes as Keith Peterson
www.andrewklavan.com

Chaz Brenchley	Sharyn McCrumb	TGR 1996
Thomas Harris	Scott Smith	
Douglas Kennedy	Tim Willocks	Stuart Woods

Matthew Kneale   Historical
www.fantasticfiction.co.uk/authors/Matthew_Kneale.htm

William Boyd	Christopher Peachment	Mail 1992
Will Davenport	Julian Rathbone	Whitbread 2000
Margaret Elphinstone	James Robertson	
Sheri Holman	Jane Stevenson	Evelyn Waugh

Alanna Knight   1923-   Sco   Crime: Historical - C19th
www.alannaknight.com   ⅄ DI Jeremy Faro • Rose McQuinn - C19th Edinburgh
                                        Tam Eildor - Jacobean Scotland

Arthur Conan Doyle	Joan Lock	David Pirie
Richard Grayson	Peter Lovesey	Roberta Rogow
Ray Harrison	Amy Myers	Norman Russell
Gillian Linscott	Anne Perry	Martin Stephen

Bernard Knight   1931-   Wales   Crime: Historical - Medieval
www.fantasticfiction.co.uk/authors/Bernard_Knight.htm   ⅄ Sir John de Wolfe, 'Crowner John'
                                                         C12th Devon

K

Alys Clare	Michael Jecks	Candace Robb
Paul Doherty	Edward Marston	Kate Sedley
Susanna Gregory	Viviane Moore	

India Knight 1965- General

www.fantasticfiction.co.uk/authors/India_Knight.htm

Raffaella Barker	Anna Maxted	Sue Townsend
Emily Barr	Claire Naylor	Daisy Waugh
Victoria Corby	Adele Parks	Isabel Wolff

Bill Knox 1928-1999 Sco Crime: Police work - UK

also wrote as **Michael Kirk,**   ⚐ DCI Colin Thane & DI Phil Moss - Glasgow
Robert MacLeod, Noah Webster   Webb Garrick, Scottish Fisheries Inspector
www.fantasticfiction.co.uk/authors/Bill_Knox.htm

Jeffrey Ashford	Reginald Hill	CWA 1986
M C Beaton	Joyce Holms	
Margaret Duffy	Quintin Jardine	
Gerald Hammond	Jim Lusby	Ian Rankin

Elizabeth Knox 1959 NZ General

Ian McEwan	Haruki Murakami	Elizabeth Russell Taylor
Andrew Miller	Lawrence Norfolk	Salley Vickers
David Mitchell		

Dorothy Koomson Chick Lit

www.dorothykoomson.co.uk

Trisha Ashley	Amy Jenkins	Alexandra Potter
Victoria Colby	Jacinta McDevitt	Kate Thompson
Donna Hay	Melissa Nathan	

Dean R Koontz 1945- US Horror

also writes as **Brian Coffey, Deanne Dwyer, K R Dwyer,
Leigh Nicols, Owen West, Aaron Wolfe**
www.randomhouse.com/bantamdell/koontz

Richard Bachman	Robert McCammon	Peter Straub
Stephen Gallagher	Richard Matheson	Whitley Strieber
John Katzenbach	John Saul	Tim Willocks
Richard Laymon		

William Kowalski 1973- US General

www.williamkowalski.com

K

Karen Joy Fowler	Alice Hoffman	Anne Tyler
David Guterson	John Irving	

Judith Krantz   1928-   US   Glitz & Glamour

www.fantasticfiction.co.uk/authors/Judith_Krantz.htm

Lisa Appignanesi	Jilly Cooper	Roberta Latow
Jackie Collins	Julie Ellis	Johanna Lindsey
Joan Collins	Judith Gould	Madge Swindells

Jayne Ann Krentz   1948-   US   Glitz & Glamour

also writes as **Jayne Castle, Amanda Quick**
www.jayneannkrentz.com

Sandra Brown	Judith Gould	Lynne Pemberton
Candace Bushnell	Penny Jordan	Madge Swindells
Janet Dailey	Judith McNaught	

Michael P Kube-McDowell   1954-   US   Science Fiction: Space opera

also writes as **Michael Hudson**
www.sff.net/people/k-mac/default.htm

Kevin J Anderson	Arthur C Clarke	Kristine Kathryn Rusch
Orson Scott Card	Barbara Hambly	

Hanif Kureishi   1954-   General

www.hanifkureishi.com

Monica Ali	Caryl Phillips	Whitbread 1990
Bernardine Evaristo	Zadie Smith	
Armistead Maupin	Meera Syal	
Gita Mehta	Louisa Young	

Katherine Kurtz   1944-   US   Fantasy: Epic

www.deryni.net

J V Jones	Valery Leith
Mercedes Lackey	Melanie Rawn

Lynda La Plante   1946-   Crime: Police work

www.laplanteproductions.com

◿ DCI Jane Tennison • Supt Mike Walker
Lorraine Page, PI - Los Angeles

John Baker	Mandasue Heller	Gay Longworth
Martina Cole	H R F Keating	Sara Paretsky
John Connor		

K
L

Go to back for lists of:
Authors by Genre
Characters and Series
Prize Winners
Further Reading

149

Mercedes Lackey 1950- US Fantasy: Epic

www.mercedeslackey.com

Carol Berg	Holly Lisle	Melanie Rawn
Barbara Hambly	Anne McCaffrey	Mickey Zucker Reichert
Katherine Kurtz	L E Modesitt Jr	R A Salvatore
Tanith Lee	Elizabeth Moon	

Jhumpa Lahiri 1967- General

www.fantasticfiction.co.uk/authors/Jhumpa_Lahiri.htm

Anita Rau Badami	Andrew Sean Greer	Anita Nair
Kavita Daswani	Anne-Marie MacDonald	Preethi Nair
Chitra Banerjee Divakaruni	Cauvery Madhavan	Zadie Smith

Thomas Laird Crime: Police work - US

🏃 Det Jimmy Parisi - Chicago

Jerome Charyn	William Heffernan	George P Pelecanos
Michael Connelly	Dennis Lehane	Jess Walter
David Cray	Carol O'Connell	

Deryn Lake 1937- Crime: Historical - C18th

is Dinah Lampitt

🏃 John Rawlings, Apothecary

C18th London

www.fantasticfiction.co.uk/authors/Deryn_Lake.htm

Bruce Alexander	Richard Grayson	Janet Laurence
Gwendoline Butler	Ray Harrison	David Liss
Janet Gleeson	Jane Jakeman	Hannah March

Rosalind Laker 1925- Historical

also writes as Barbara Paul; is Barbara Douglas

www.fantasticfiction.co.uk/authors/Rosalind_Laker.htm

Elizabeth Chadwick	Cynthia Harrod-Eagles	Maureen Peters
Jean Chapman	Judith Lennox	Cynthia S Roberts
Sandra Gulland	Edith Pargeter	

Charlotte Lamb 1937-2000 General

also wrote as Sheila Coastes, Laura Hardy, Sheila Holland,
Sheila Lancaster, Victoria Woolf

www.fantasticfiction.co.uk/authors/Charlotte_Lamb.htm

Daphne Du Maurier	Kate Hatfield	Claire Rayner
Sue Gee	Sian James	Lindsay Townsend
Maeve Haran	Imogen Parker	

Angela Lambert 1940- General

Hilary Bailey
Kate Hatfield
Elizabeth Jane Howard
Angela Huth

Hilary Mantel
Edna O'Brien
Kate Saunders
Elizabeth Tettmar

Romantic 1998 **L**

John Lanchester 1962- General

www.contemporarywriters.com/authors/?p=auth59

Jonathan Coe
Philip Hensher
David Nicholls

Mark Wallington
Nigel Williams

Betty Trask 1996
Hawthornden 1997

Lee Langley 1932- US General

www.contemporarywriters.com/authors/?p=auth196

Anita Desai
Ruth Prawer Jhabvala
M M Kaye

Penelope Lively
Paul Scott

Vikram Seth
Reay Tannahill

Joe R Lansdale 1951- US Crime: Humour

www.joerlansdale.com

🏃 Hap Collins & Leonard Pine ⎫
Constable Sunset Jones - 1930s ⎬ Texas

Anthony Bourdain
Robert Crais
Bill Fitzhugh

Jon A Jackson
Danny King

David Lindsey
Laurence Shames

Mary A Larkin 1935- Ire Saga

is Mary A McNulty
www.marylarkin.co.uk

Northern Ireland

Elaine Crowley
Frank Delaney
Rose Doyle

Sheelagh Kelly
Genevieve Lyons
Mary McCarthy

Catrin Morgan
Geraldine O'Neill
Sharon Owens

José Latour 1940- Cuba Crime: Police work - Cuba

🏃 Capt Trujillo - Havana

Anthony Bourdain
Luiz Alfredo Garcia-Roza
Elmore Leonard

Laurence Shames
Martin Cruz Smith

Donald E Westlake
Don Winslow

Go to back for lists of:
Authors by Genre
Characters and Series
Prize Winners
Further Reading

Roberta Latow US — Glitz & Glamour

www.fantasticfiction.co.uk/authors/Roberta_Latow.htm

Maria Barrett	Jenn Crowell	Frankie McGowan
Sandra Brown	Judith Krantz	Fern Michaels
Jackie Collins	Johanna Lindsey	Penny Vincenzi

Janet Laurence 1937- — Crime: Amateur sleuth

also writes as Julia Lisle
𐍈 Darina Lisle, Cook
www.fantasticfiction.co.uk/authors/Janet_Laurence.htm
Canaletto, Artist - C18th London

Bruce Alexander	Deryn Lake	Hannah March
Gwendoline Butler	Roy Lewis	Amy Myers
Janet Gleeson	David Liss	David Williams

Stephen R Lawhead 1950- US — Fantasy: Myth

www.stephenlawhead.com

C J Cherryh	Katharine Kerr	Caiseal Mor
Helen Hollick	Greg Keyes	Adam Nichols
Guy Gavriel Kay	Valery Leith	Michael Scott Rohan
Paul Kearney	Morgan Llywelyn	Jane Welch

D H Lawrence 1885-1930 — General

also wrote as Lawrence H Davison, Jessie Chambers
www.nottingham.ac.uk/mss/online/dhlawrence

John Galsworthy	Thomas Hardy	James Joyce
Sarah Hall	Aldous Huxley	Alan Sillitoe

Stephen Laws 1952- — Horror

www.stephenlaws.com

Jonathan Aycliffe	Stephen King	Phil Rickman
Ramsey Campbell	Richard Matheson	Peter Straub
James Herbert	Christopher Pike	Tim Wilson

Mary Lawson Can — General

McKitterick 2003

Lynn Coady	Alistair MacLeod
Jane Hamilton	David Park
Haven Kimmel	Carol Shields
Alice McDermott	Adriana Trigiani
Anne-Marie MacDonald	

Go to back for lists of:
Authors by Genre • Characters and Series • Prize Winners • Further Reading

John Lawton
www.fantasticfiction.co.uk/authors/John_Lawton.htm

Adventure/Thriller

♟ Frederick Troy **L**

James Adams	Jon Cleary	Ken Follett
Ted Allbeury	Len Deighton	Joseph Kanon
Stephen J Cannell		

Richard Laymon   1947-2001   US

Horror

also wrote as **Richard Kelly**
www.fantasticfiction.co.uk/authors/Richard_Laymon.htm

Clive Barker	Dean R Koontz	Christopher Pike
John Farris	Bentley Little	Peter Straub
Shaun Hutson	Scott Nicholson	T M Wright

John Le Carré   1931-

Adventure/Thriller

♟ George Smiley, Spy

is **David Cornwell**
www.johnlecarre.com

William Bernhardt	Joseph Kanon	CWA 1977
James Buchan	Charles McCarry	
John Burdett	Kyle Mills	
Brian Freemantle	Henry Porter	Daniel Silva
Alan Judd	Anthony Price	Robin White

Ursula K Le Guin   1929-   US

Fantasy: Epic

www.ursulakleguin.com

Trudi Canavan	C S Lewis	T H White
Mary Gentle	Judith Tarr	Gene Wolfe
Frank Herbert	Sheri S Tepper	Sarah Zettel

Frank Lean   1942-

Crime: PI

♟ Dave Cunane
Manchester

is **Frank Leneghan**
www.fantasticfiction.co.uk/authors/Frank_Lean.htm

John Baker	Alan Dunn	Cath Staincliffe
Adam Baron	Jack Harvey	Mark Timlin
Cara Black	Mandasue Heller	Peter Turnbull
Stella Duffy	Reginald Hill	Martyn Waites

Stephen Leather

Adventure/Thriller

www.stephenleather.com

Geoffrey Archer	Jack Higgins	Tim Sebastian
Tom Bradby	James Long	Gerald Seymour
Harold Coyle	David Mason	

Harper Lee   1926-   US   General

is Nelle Harper Lee
www.kirjasto.sci.fi/harperle.htm

Suzanne Berne	Stewart O'Nan	*Pulitzer 1961*
Pat Conroy	J D Salinger	
Carson McCullers	John Steinbeck	
Toni Morrison	Meera Syal	Alice Walker

Maureen Lee   Saga

www.maureenlee.co.uk   ⚲ Pearl Street - Liverpool

Lyn Andrews	Anna Jacobs	*Romantic 2000*
Anne Baker	Joan Jonker	
Helen Forrester	Margaret Mayhew	
Ruth Hamilton	Elizabeth Murphy	Lynda Page

Tanith Lee   1947-   Fantasy: Dark

also writes as Esther Garber   Venus (Venice)
is Tanith Lee Kaiine
www.tanithlee.com

Dan Abnett	Ben Counter	Holly Lisle
Marion Zimmer Bradley	Jonathan Green	Freda Warrington
C J Cherryh	Mercedes Lackey	

Amanda Lees   Chick Lit

Sarah Ball	Sue Haasler	Marissa Mackle
Lynne Barrett-Lee	Lisa Jewell	

Gordon Legge   1961-   Sco   General

Iain Banks	Anne Donovan	Alan Spence
Des Dillon	Duncan McLean	Alan Warner

Dennis Lehane   1966-   US   Crime: Police work - US

www.fantasticfiction.co.uk/authors/Dennis_Lehane.htm   ⚲ Patrick Kenzie & Angie Gennaro
Boston, Mass.

Jerome Charyn	William Heffernan	James Patterson
John Connolly	Jon A Jackson	Andrew Pyper
David Cray	Thomas Laird	John Shannon
G M Ford	Reggie Nadelson	Boston Teran

Valery Leith   1968-

Fantasy: Epic

is Tricia Sullivan

Everien

David Gemmell   Paul Kearney   Stephen R Lawhead
J V Jones   Katherine Kurtz

J Robert Lennon

General

www.jrobertlennon.com

Andre Dubus   Robert Goddard
Connie May Fowler   Anita Shreve

Judith Lennox   1953-

Saga

www.fantasticfiction.co.uk/authors/Judith_Lennox.htm

Diana Gabaldon   Sybil Marshall   Mary Stewart
Caroline Harvey   Imogen Parker   Margaret Thornton
Rosalind Laker   Rosamunde Pilcher

Donna Leon   1942-   US

Crime: Police work - Italy

www.groveatlantic.com/leon/author.htm   ⚬ Commissario Guido Brunetti - Venice

Andrea Camilleri   Luiz Alfredo Garcia-Roza   Barbara Nadel
Michael Dibdin   David Hewson   Eliot Pattison
Leslie Forbes   Henning Mankell   Fred Vargas
Karin Fossum   Magdalen Nabb   Qiu Xiaolong

Elmore Leonard   1925-   US

Crime: Hardboiled

www.elmoreleonard.com

Lawrence Block   Steve Hamilton   Patricia Melo
Tim Cockey   George V Higgins   Scott Phillips
Kinky Friedman   José Latour   Donald E Westlake
James Hall   Shane Maloney   Don Winslow

John T Lescroart   1948-   US

Crime: Legal/financial

www.johnlescroart.com   ⚬ Dismas Hardy, Attorney ⎱ San Francisco
                                 Abe Glitsky, Policeman ⎰

William Bernhardt   James Grippando   Nancy Taylor Rosenberg
Harry Bingham   John Grisham   Lisa Scottoline
Linda Fairstein   Steve Martini

Go to back for lists of:
Authors by Genre
Characters and Series
Prize Winners
Further Reading

Doris Lessing   1919-   General

also writes as **Jane Somers**
is **Doris Tayler**
http://lessing.redmood.com

J M Coetzee	Pamela Jooste	Iris Murdoch
Janet Frame	Candia McWilliam	Joyce Carol Oates
Nadine Gordimer	Anne Michaels	Muriel Spark

Kathy Lette   1958-   Aus   Chick Lit

www.kathylette.com

Sherry Ashworth	Christina Jones	Alexandra Potter
Jenny Eclair	Josie Lloyd & Emlyn Rees	Sue Townsend
Catherine Feeny	Tyne O'Connell	Laura Zigman

Andrea Levy   1956-   General

www.andrealevy.co.uk

Monica Ali	Caryl Phillips	Orange 2004
Ian McEwan	Zadie Smith	Whitbread 2004
Pauline Melville	Meera Syal	Commonwealth 2005

C S Lewis   1898-1963   Fantasy: Literary

www.cslewis.com

Ursula K Le Guin	J R R Tolkien	T H White
H P Lovecraft	Jules Verne	Sarah Zettel
Philip Pullman		

Roy Lewis   1933-   Wales   Crime: Amateur sleuth

also writes as **J R Lewis, David Springfield**   ⚐ Arnold Landon, Archaeologist - Newcastle
www.fantasticfiction.co.uk/authors/Roy_Lewis.htm   Eric Ward, Solicitor - Tyneside
                                                          DI John Crow, Northumberland police

Paul Adam	Janet Laurence	David Williams
Jeffrey Ashford	John Malcolm	Derek Wilson
Kate Ellis	M R D Meek	

Susan Lewis   Glitz & Glamour

www.susanlewis.com

Louise Bagshawe	Judith Gould	Freya North
Maria Barrett	Judi James	Imogen Parker
Sally Beauman	Frankie McGowan	Danielle Steel

Go to back for lists of:
Authors by Genre • Characters and Series • Prize Winners • Further Reading

Rod Liddle   1960-   General

Edward Docx   Philip Roth
Howard Jacobson   Adam Thirlwell

Freda Lightfoot   Saga

also writes as **Marion Carr**   Manchester
www.fredalightfoot.co.uk

Rita Bradshaw   Elizabeth Gill   Claire Lorrimer
Betty Burton   Ruth Hamilton   Mary McCarthy
Alexandra Connor   Margaret Kaine   Beryl Matthews

Catherine Lim   1942- Sing   General

Regi Claire   Timothy Mo
Arthur Golden   Amy Tan

Sue Limb   1946-   Humour

www.suelimb.com

Faith Bleasdale   Maggie Gibson   Sue Townsend
Mavis Cheek   Laurie Graham   Arabella Weir
Kate Fenton   Allison Pearson   Louise Wener

Megan Lindholm   1952- US   Fantasy: Epic

also writes as **Robin Hobb**
www.meganlindholm.com

Alice Borchardt   Sara Douglass   Sheri S Tepper
C J Cherryh   J V Jones

Douglas Lindsay   1964- Sco   Crime: Humour

www.barney-thomson.com   ⚲ Barney Thomson, Barber
                                                         Scotland

Dave Barry   Tim Dorsey   Paul Johnston
Colin Bateman   Carl Hiaasen   Danny King
Christopher Brookmyre

Frederic Lindsay   1933- Sco   Crime: Police work - UK

www.fantasticfiction.co.uk/authors/Frederic_Lindsay.htm   ⚲ DI Jim Meldrum
                                                         Scotland

Alex Gray   Denise Mina   Peter Turnbull
Quintin Jardine   Ian Rankin

157

David Lindsey 1944- US Adventure/Thriller: Police work - US
www.davidlindsey.com ☆ Det Stuart Haydon, Homicide police intelligence
Houston, Texas

Thomas H Cook	Michael Malone	John Sandford
Robert Ferrigno	Theresa Monsour	Tim Willocks
Joe R Lansdale	Richard North Patterson	Stuart Woods

Johanna Lindsey 1952- US Glitz & Glamour
www.fantasticfiction.co.uk/authors/Johanna_Lindsey.htm

Jenn Crowell	Judith Krantz	Jean Saunders
Jude Deveraux	Roberta Latow	Madge Swindells
Lucinda Edmonds	Fern Michaels	

Joan Lingard 1932- Sco General
www.joanlingard.co.uk

Anne Fine	Eileen Goudge	Jennifer Johnston
Jane Gardam	Angela Green	Bernard MacLaverty
Sue Gee	Zoë Heller	Deborah Moggach

Gillian Linscott 1944- Crime: Historical - C20th
www.gillianlinscott.co.uk ☆ Nell Bray, Suffragette

Barbara Cleverly	Alanna Knight	CWA 2000
Clare Curzon	Joan Lock	
Richard Grayson	Peter Lovesey	
Ray Harrison	Gwen Moffat	Charles Todd
Laurie King	Elizabeth Peters	Gerard Williams

Elinor Lipman 1950- US General

Karen Joy Fowler	Adriana Trigiani	Rebecca Wells
Laurie Graham	Anne Tyler	Mary Wesley
Carol Shields		

Laura Lippman 1959- US Crime: PI
www.lauralippman.com ☆ Tess Monaghan - Baltimore

Edna Buchanan	Meg Gardiner	Marcia Muller
Jan Burke	Sue Grafton	Sara Paretsky
Carol Higgins Clark	Margaret Maron	Susan R Sloan
Tim Cockey	Theresa Monsour	Valerie Wilson Wesley

Go to back for lists of:
Authors by Genre • Characters and Series • Prize Winners • Further Reading

Holly Lisle   1960-   US   Fantasy: Epic

www.hollylisle.com

Alice Borchardt	Simon R Green	Mercedes Lackey
Marion Zimmer Bradley	Laurell K Hamilton	Tanith Lee
Kate Elliott	Tanya Huff	

Julia Lisle   1937-   General

also writes as **Janet Laurence**

Sarah Grazebrook	Sian James	Louise Voss
Hazel Hucker	Karen Nelson	Marcia Willett
Erica James	Libby Purves	

David Liss   1966-   US   Crime: Historical - C18th

www.davidliss.com

Bruce Alexander	Jane Jakeman	Hannah March
Gwendoline Butler	Deryn Lake	Fidelis Morgan
Janet Gleeson	Janet Laurence	

Toby Litt   1968-   General

www.tobylitt.com

Jake Arnott	Ian McEwan	Tim Parks
Colin Bateman	Alistair MacLeod	

Robert Littell   1935-   US   Adventure/Thriller

Eric Ambler	Ken Follett	CWA 1973
Stephen J Cannell	Alan Furst	
Nelson DeMille	Robert Harris	Glenn Meade

Bentley Little   1960-   US   Horror

also writes as **Phillip Emmons**
www.fantasticfiction.co.uk/authors/Bentley_Little.htm

Clive Barker	James Herbert	Mark Morris
Simon Clark	Shaun Hutson	Scott Nicholson
Muriel Gray	Richard Laymon	Dan Simmons

Penelope Lively   1933-   General

www.penelopelively.net

Lynne Reid Banks	Penelope Fitzgerald	Booker 1987
Nina Bawden	Susan Hill	
Rachel Billington	Lee Langley	
Elizabeth Bowen	Charlotte Mendelson	Louise Voss
A S Byatt	Libby Purves	Meg Wolitzer

Robert Llewellyn   1956-   Humour
www.llew.co.uk

Ben Elton	Tom Holt	Tony Parsons
Charles Higson	Geoff Nicholson	

Sam Llewellyn   1948-   Adventure/Thriller
www.fantasticfiction.co.uk/authors/Sam_Llewellyn.htm

Bernard Cornwell	Philip McCutchan
Mike Lunnon-Wood	Antony Trew

Josie Lloyd & Emlyn Rees   Chick Lit
www.fantasticfiction.co.uk/authors/Josie_Lloyd.html &
www.fantasticfiction.co.uk/authors/Emlyn_Rees.html

Rebecca Campbell	Serena Mackesy	Tyne O'Connell
Cathy Kelly	Chris Manby	Isabel Wolff
Kathy Lette	Sue Margolis	

Morgan Llywelyn   1947-   Ire   Historical
also writes as **Shannon Lewis**
http://celt.net/Boru/boru1.html

Marion Zimmer Bradley	Diana Norman	Sharon Penman
Stephen R Lawhead	Edith Pargeter	

Joan Lock   Crime: Historical - C19th
www.joanlock.co.uk   ⚗ DI Ernest Best - Victorian London

Ray Harrison	Peter Lovesey	Norman Russell
Alanna Knight	Anne Perry	M J Trow
Gillian Linscott		

Laura Lockington   Chick Lit

Francesca Clementis	Donna Hay	Sophie Kinsella
Louise Harwood	Christina Jones	Jacinta McDevitt

David Lodge   1935-   General
www.contemporarywriters.com/authors/?p=auth62

Kingsley Amis	John Mortimer	Hawthornden 1975
Tim Binding	Alan Sillitoe	Whitbread 1980
Michael Frayn	Leslie Thomas	
Stanley Middleton	Keith Waterhouse	Evelyn Waugh

James Long
also writes as **Will Davenport**
www.fantasticfiction.co.uk/authors/James_D_Long.htm

Adventure/Thriller

L

James Adams	Frederick Forsyth	Stephen Leather
Stephen J Cannell	Diana Gabaldon	

Kate Long
Aga saga
www.fantasticfiction.co.uk/author s/Kate_Long.htm

Amanda Brookfield	Rebecca Gregson	Joanna Trollope
Marika Cobbold	Sarah MacDonald	Marcia Willett
Anne Doughty	Robin Pilcher	

Gay Longworth
Crime: Psychological
www.fantasticfiction.co.uk/authors/Gay_Longworth.htm
⋏ DI Jessie Driver - London

Ann Cleeves	Patricia Highsmith	Ed O'Connor
John Connor	Lynda La Plante	Ian Rankin
Nicci French	Barry Maitland	Alison Taylor

Elizabeth Lord
Saga
London

Harry Bowling	Anna King	Elizabeth Waite
Pamela Evans	Mary Jane Staples	Jeanne Whitmee
Patricia Grey	Alison Stuart	

Claire Lorrimer   1921-
Saga
⋏ Rochford Family
also writes as **Beatrice Coogan, Patricia Robins**
www.fantasticfiction.co.uk/authors/Claire_Lorrimer.htm

Victoria Holt	Erin Kaye	Barbara Whitnell
Sara Hylton	Freda Lightfoot	Janet Woods
Margaret Kaine		

Tim Lott   1956-
Lad Lit
www.contemporarywriters.com/authors/?p=auth241

Whitbread 1999

Simon Armitage	Alex Garland	
Matthew Beaumont	John Harding	
Neil Cross	Tobias Hill	
Stephen Fry	John McCabe	Sean Thomas

Go to back for lists of:
Authors by Genre • Characters and Series • Prize Winners • Further Reading

H P Lovecraft   1890-1937   US   Horror
www.hplovecraft.com

Ray Bradbury	C S Lewis	S P Somtow
Ramsey Campbell	Brian Lumley	Peter Straub
John Farris		

James Lovegrove   1965-   Science Fiction: Near future
www.jameslovegrove.com

J G Ballard	John Meaney	Neal Stephenson
Eric Brown	Michael Marshall Smith	Bruce Sterling
Pat Cadigan		

Peter Lovesey   1936-   Crime: Historical - C19th & Police - UK
also writes as **Peter Lear**

🏃 Sgt Cribb & PC Thackeray - C19th England
Peter Diamond, Police - C20th Bath

Arthur Conan Doyle	Gillian Linscott	CWA 1978, 1982, 1995, 1996 & 2000
John Maclachlan Gray	Joan Lock	
Ray Harrison	Andrew Martin	
Mo Hayder	Amy Myers	
Alanna Knight	Norman Russell	M J Trow

Phil Lovesey   1963-   Crime: Psychological
www.fantasticfiction.co.uk/authors/Phil_Lovesey.htm

Carol Anne Davis	Patrick Redmond	Tony Strong
Nicci French	Boris Starling	Laura Wilson
Val McDermid		

Shari Low   1968-   Chick Lit
www.fantasticfiction.co.uk/authors/Shari_Low.htm

Anita Anderson	Clare Dowling	Kathy Rodgers
Dawn Cairns	Sabine Durrant	Andrea Semple
Rebecca Campbell	Sharon Mulrooney	Sarah Webb

Robert Ludlum   1927-2001   US   Adventure/Thriller
also wrote as **Jonathan Ryder, Michael Shepherd**   Covert-One Series
www.robertludlumbooks.com

Tom Bradby	Joseph Finder	Brian Haig
John Burdett	Sean Flannery	Greg Iles
Conor Cregan	Alan Folsom	Kyle Mills
Brendan Dubois	David Hagberg	Kenneth Royce

Brian Lumley   1937-   Horror
www.brianlumley.com   ⚐ Harry Keogh   **L**

Poppy Z Brite   H P Lovecraft   T M Wright
Tom Holland   Anne Rice

Jonathan Lunn   Sea: Historical
is Daniel Hall   ⚐ Kit Killigrew - C19th
www.fantasticfiction.co.uk/authors/Jonathan_Lunn.htm

C S Forester   James L Nelson   Dudley Pope
Alexander Kent   Patrick O'Brian   Julian Stockwin
Philip McCutchan   Marcus Palliser   Richard Woodman

Mike Lunnon-Wood   War: Modern

Geoffrey Archer   Andy McNab   Craig Thomas
Frederick Forsyth   John Nichol   Peter Tonkin
Sam Llewellyn

Alison Lurie   1926-   US   General
http://people.cornell.edu/pages/al28

Jane Austen   Lorrie Moore   Pulitzer 1985
Nina Bawden   Jane Rogers
Rachel Billington   Teresa Waugh
Louise Erdrich   Edith Wharton   Meg Wolitzer

Jim Lusby   1951-   Ire   Crime: Police work - Ireland
also writes as James Kennedy   ⚐ DI Cal McCadden
www.fantasticfiction.co.uk/authors/Jim_Lusby.htm   Waterford

Bartholomew Gill   Quintin Jardine
John Harvey   Bill Knox

Eric Lustbader   1946-   US   Adventure/Thriller
also writes as Eric Van Lustbader   ⚐ Nicholas Linnear
www.ericvanlustbaderbooks.com

Bryce Courtenay   David Morrell   Alan Savage
Colin Falconer   Christopher Nicole   Justin Scott

> *Go to back for lists of:*
> Authors by Genre
> Characters and Series
> Prize Winners
> Further Reading

Gavin Lyall 1932-2003 Adventure/Thriller

www.fantasticfiction.co.uk/authors/Gavin_Lyall.htm

🏃 Harry Maxim, Spy
Captain Matthew Ranklin, Spy

Jon Cleary	John Francome	A J Quinnell
Len Deighton	John Gardner	Robert Radcliffe
Ian Fleming	Alistair MacLean	Derek Robinson
Dick Francis	Richard Pitman	Michael Shea

Sarah Kate Lynch 1962- NZ General

www.bookcouncil.org.nz/writers/lynchsarah.html

Emma Donoghue	Joanne Harris
Lucy Ellman	Michèle Roberts

Genevieve Lyons Ire Historical

Catherine Coulter	Sheelagh Kelly	Elisabeth McNeill
Teresa Crane	Lena Kennedy	Anne Melville
Elaine Crowley	Mary A Larkin	Mary Minton

Amin Maalouf 1949- Leb Adventure/Thriller

www.kirjasto.sci.fi/maalouf

James Clavell	Daniel Easterman	Julian Rathbone
Bryce Courtenay	Lawrence Norfolk	Alan Savage

Sharon Maas 1951- Guy General

www.sharonmaas.com

Anita Rau Badami	Manju Kapur	Nisha Minhas
Kavita Daswani	Cauvery Madhavan	Preethi Nair

Paul J McAuley 1955- Science Fiction: Technical

www.omegacom.demon.co.uk

Gregory Benford	Linda Nagata	Arthur C Clarke 1996
Paul Johnston	Richard Powers	
Jack McDevitt	Ian Watson	
Ian McDonald	David Wingrove	
John Meaney		

Go to back for lists of:
Authors by Genre
Characters and Series
Prize Winners
Further Reading

Ed McBain   1926-   US   Crime: Police work - US

also writes as **Curt Cannon, Hunt Collins, Evan Hunter, Richard Marsten**; *is* **Salvatore Lombino**
www.edmcbain.com

Ⅳ Det Steve Carella
87th Precinct,
'Isola' Police Department

David Cray	Jon A Jackson	Deon Meyer
William Diehl	J A Jance	Robert B Parker
W E B Griffin	Faye Kellerman	J D Robb
Donald Harstad	Michael Malone	Joseph Wambaugh

Brenda McBryde   Saga

NE England

Irene Carr	Wendy Robertson	Janet MacLeod Trotter
Una Horne	Sarah Shears	Dee Williams
Sheila Jansen		

John McCabe   1967-   Humour

www.fantasticfiction.co.uk/authors/John_McCabe.htm

Douglas Coupland	James Hawes	Nick Hornby
Ben Elton	Charles Higson	Tim Lott

Patrick McCabe   1955-   Ire   General

www.contemporarywriters.com/authors/?p=auth69

Dermot Bolger	Sean Hughes	Patrick McGrath
Bruce Chatwin	Colum McCann	Joseph O'Connor
Roddy Doyle	John McGahern	Glenn Patterson

Anne McCaffrey   1926-   US   Science Fiction: Space and time

http://mccaffrey.srellim.org/default.htm

Sarah Ash	Barbara Hambly	Julian May
Joanne Bertin	Elizabeth Haydon	Robert Newcomb
Lois McMaster Bujold	Katharine Kerr	Ricardo Pinto
James Clemens	Mercedes Lackey	

Robert McCammon   1952-   US   Horror

www.robertmccammon.com

John Farris	Anne Rice	Peter Straub
Dean R Koontz	John Saul	Whitley Strieber
Graham Masterton	Steven Spruill	T M Wright

Colum McCann   1965-   Ire   General

Dermot Bolger	Brian Moore
Patrick McCabe	Joseph O'Connor

Charles McCarry   US   Adventure/Thriller

www.fantasticfiction.co.uk/authors/Charles_McCarry.htm   ⚐ Paul Christopher, FBI agent

Eric Ambler	John Le Carré	Gerald Seymour
Gordon Kent	John J Nance	Nigel West

M   Cormac McCarthy   1933-   US   General

www.cormacmccarthy.com   South-west USA

Thomas Eidson	David Guterson	Carson McCullers
William Faulkner	Jim Harrison	Stewart O'Nan
Charles Frazier	Stuart Harrison	J D Salinger

Keith McCarthy   Crime: Forensic

www.fantasticfiction.co.uk/authors/Keith_McCarthy.htm   ⚐ Helena Flemming, Solicitor, & John Eisenmenger, Pathologist

Max Allan Collins	Iris Johansen	Kathy Reichs
Patricia D Cornwell	Nigel McCrery	Karin Slaughter

Mary McCarthy   Ire   Saga

www.kirjasto.sci.fi/marymcc.htm

Benita Brown	Mary A Larkin	Sharon Owens
Elizabeth Gill	Freda Lightfoot	Valerie Wood
Meg Henderson		

Wil McCarthy   1966-   US   Science Fiction: Technical

www.wilmccarthy.com

Stephen Baxter	Michael Moorcock	Robert Charles Wilson
Greg Bear	Linda Nagata	David Wingrove
Gregory Benford		

Ken McClure   Sco   Crime: Medical

also writes as **Ken Begg**   ⚐ Steven Dunbar

www.kenmcclure.freeuk.com

Paul Adam	Robin Cook	Tess Gerritsen
Colin Andrews	Michael Crichton	Leah Ruth Robinson
Paul Carson		

Nigel McCrery   1953-   Crime: Forensic

www.fantasticfiction.co.uk/authors/Nigel_McCrery.htm   ⚐ Sam Ryan, Pathologist - Cambridge

Max Allan Collins	Keith McCarthy	Kathy Reichs
Patricia D Cornwell	Val McDermid	Karin Slaughter

L McCrossan
Chick Lit

Lynne Barrett-Lee
Claudine Cullimore
Isla Dewar

Maggie Gibson
Ben Hatch
Donna Hay

Wendy Holden
Louise Kean

M

Sharyn McCrumb   1948-   US
Crime: Psychological

www.sharynmccrumb.com

⚘ Elizabeth McPherson, Anthropologist -
Appalachians, East Tennessee
Sheriff Spenser Arrowood

Janis Harrison
Carolyn G Hart
Daniel Hecht

Tony Hillerman
Andrew Klavan
Margaret Maron

Carol O'Connell
Ruth Rendell

Carson McCullers   1917 - 67   US
General
Southern USA

www.carson-mccullers.com

William Faulkner
F Scott Fitzgerald
Connie May Fowler

Harper Lee
Cormac McCarthy

J D Salinger
Anne Rivers Siddons

Colleen McCullough   1938-   Aus
Historical

www.fantasticfiction.co.uk/authors/Colleen_McCullough.htm

Margaret George
Robert Graves
Christian Jacq
Lynne Pemberton

Alice Randall
Mary Renault
Rosemary Rowe
Edward Rutherfurd

Simon Scarrow
Patricia Shaw
Wilbur Smith
Nancy Thayer

Philip McCutchan   1920-1996
Sea: Historical & Modern

also wrote as Duncan MacNeil
www.fantasticfiction.co.uk/authors/Philip_McCutchan.htm

⚘ Donald Cameron ⎫ Royal Navy
St Vincent Halfhyde ⎭
Commodore Kemp, Merchant Marine
Capt James Ogilvie, Queens Own Royal Strathspeys

Alexander Fullerton
Richard Howard
Alexander Kent

Sam Llewellyn
Jonathan Lunn
Dudley Pope

Peter Tonkin
Antony Trew
Richard Woodman

Go to back for lists of:
Authors by Genre
Characters and Series
Prize Winners
Further Reading

Val McDermid 1955- Sco Crime: Psychological

www.valmcdermid.com

⚐ DCI Carol Jordan & Dr Tony Hill, Psychologist
Kate Brannigan, PI - Manchester • Lindsay Gordon, Journalist - Glasgow
Fiona Cameron, Academic psychologist

Mark Billingham	Denise Mina	CWA 1995
Daniel Hecht	Gemma O'Connor	
Mandasue Heller	Danuta Reah	
Phil Lovesey	Patrick Redmond	Boris Starling
Nigel McCrery	Zoë Sharp	Stephen White

M

Alice McDermott 1953- US General

www.fantasticfiction.co.uk/authors/Alice_McDermott.htm

Lynn Coady	Mary Lawson	Anita Shreve
Sebastian Faulks	Anne-Marie MacDonald	Adriana Trigiani
Alice Hoffman	Carol Shields	

Jacinta McDevitt Ire Chick Lit

Susannah Bates	Sabine Durrant	Laura Lockington
Jaye Carroll	Dorothy Koomson	Patricia Scanlan

Jack McDevitt 1935- US Science Fiction: Space and time

www.sfwa.org/members/mcdevitt

Poul Anderson	Arthur C Clarke	Ken MacLeod
Stephen Baxter	Paul J McAuley	Alastair Reynolds

Anne-Marie MacDonald 1958- Can General

Kate Atkinson	Barbara Kingsolver	Alice McDermott
Pat Barker	Jhumpa Lahiri	Carol Shields
Lynn Coady	Mary Lawson	Jane Urquhart

Ian McDonald 1960- Science Fiction: Space and time

www.lysator.liu.se/~unicorn/mcdonald

Stephen Baxter	K W Jeter	BSFA 2004
Pat Cadigan	Gwyneth Jones	
Greg Egan	Paul J McAuley	
Jon Courtenay Grimwood	Linda Nagata	Brian Stableford

John D MacDonald 1916-86 US Crime: PI

www.fantasticfiction.co.uk/authors/John_D_MacDonald.htm

⚐ Travis McGee - Florida

Lawrence Block	James Hadley Chase	J A Jance
Raymond Chandler	James Hall	Lawrence Sanders
		Donald E Westlake

Malcolm Macdonald   1932-   Saga

also writes as M R O'Donnell, Malcolm Ross   🏃 Stevenson Family Series

Gloria Cook   Caroline Stickland   T R Wilson
R F Delderfield   Janet Tanner   Janet Woods
Winston Graham

Marianne MacDonald   1934-   Can   Crime: Amateur sleuth

www.fantasticfiction.co.uk/authors/Marianne_MacDonald.htm   🏃 Dido Hoare,
                                              Antiquarian bookseller - London

Natasha Cooper   Hazel Holt   Fiona Mountain
Carolyn G Hart   Alison Joseph   Ann Purser
Veronica Heley   Morag Joss   Veronica Stallwood

Ross Macdonald   1915-83   US   Crime: PI

also wrote as John Macdonald, John Ross Macdonald   🏃 Lew Archer
was Kenneth Millar   California
www.kirjasto.sci.fi/rossmacd.htm

Lawrence Block   James Crumley   George P Pelecanos
Raymond Chandler   Dashiell Hammett   James Sallis
James Hadley Chase

Sarah MacDonald   Aga saga

Sarah Challis   Adèle Geras   Robin Pilcher
Anne Christie   Kate Long   Rosamunde Pilcher
Nina Dufort   Charlotte Moore   Marcia Willett

Iain McDowall   Sco   Crime: Police work - UK

www.crowby.co.uk   🏃 DCI Jacobson & DS Kerr
                                                  'Crowby', Midlands

John Baker   Ann Cleeves   Reginald Hill
Hilary Bonner   John Connor   Lesley Horton
Stephen Booth   John Harvey   Graham Hurley

Ian McEwan   1948-   General

www.ianmcewan.com
                                                   Whitbread 1987
Iain Banks   Toby Litt   Booker 1998
Jeremy Dronfield   Patrick McGrath   WHSmith 2002
Tibor Fischer   Alistair MacLeod
Elizabeth Knox   Simon Mawer   Tim Parks
Andrea Levy   Julie Myerson   Elizabeth Russell Taylor

John McGahern   1934-   Ire   General

www.fantasticfiction.co.uk/authors/John_McGahern.htm

John Banville	Brian Moore	Colm Toibin
James Joyce	David Park	William Trevor
Patrick McCabe		

M

Michael McGarrity   US   Crime: Police work - US

www.michaelmcgarrity.net   ♟ Kevin Kearney - New Mexico

Ace Atkins	Steve Hamilton	J A Jance
C J Box	Donald Harstad	Archer Mayor
Robert Ferrigno	Tony Hillerman	

Frankie McGowan   Glitz & Glamour

Barbara Taylor Bradford	Susan Lewis	Harold Robbins
Joan Collins	Fern Michaels	Penny Vincenzi
Roberta Latow		

Jill McGown   1947-   Sco   Crime: Police work - UK

www.jillmcgown.com   ♟ DCI Lloyd & DI Judy Hill - 'Stansfield'

Jo Bannister	Geraldine Evans	Priscilla Masters
Stephen Booth	Paula Gosling	Rebecca Tope
Linda Davies		

Patrick McGrath   1950-   General

www.fantasticfiction.co.uk/authors/Patrick_McGrath.htm

Bruce Chatwin	Ian McEwan	
Patrick McCabe	Tobias Wolff	

Elizabeth McGregor   Crime: Psychological

also writes as **Holly Fox**

Nicci French	Carol Smith	
J Wallis Martin	Barbara Vine	

Jay McInerney   1955-   US   General

T Coraghessan Boyle	Jack Kerouac	J D Salinger
Alan Gurganus	Armistead Maupin	Matt Thorne
Tama Janowitz	Philip Roth	

Go to back for lists of:
Authors by Genre • Characters and Series • Prize Winners • Further Reading

Monica McInerney   Aus   Chick Lit

www.monicamcinerney.com

Colette Caddle   Tara Heavey   Morag Prunty
Clare Dowling   Melissa Hill   Tina Reilly
Anne Dunlop   Sheila O'Flanagan   Jane Wenham-Jones

M

Shena Mackay   1944- Sco   General

www.contemporarywriters.com/authors/?p=auth64

Jane Asher   Jennifer Johnston   Marge Piercy
Mavis Cheek   Candia McWilliam   Gwendoline Riley
Angela Huth   Valerie Martin   Muriel Spark

Juliet E McKenna   1965-   Fantasy: Epic

www.dspace.dial.pipex.com/juliet.e.mckenna

James Barclay   Elizabeth Haydon   George R R Martin
David Farland   Ian Irvine   K J Parker
Jude Fisher   Kate Jacoby   Freda Warrington

Serena Mackesy   Chick Lit

www.fantasticfiction.co.uk/authors/Serena_Mackesy.htm

Jessica Adams   Josie Lloyd & Emlyn Rees   Sue Margolis
Zoë Barnes   Chris Manby   Tyne O'Connell
Helen Fielding

Mary Mackie   Saga

also writes as **Alex Andrews, Caroline Charles,**   Lincolnshire
Cathy Christopher, Mary Christopher, Susan Stevens   Norfolk

Margaret Dickinson   Connie Monk   Sue Sully
Helen Forrester   Elizabeth Murphy   T R Wilson
Elizabeth Jeffrey   Judith Saxton

Marissa Mackle   1973- Ire   Chick Lit

Sarah Ball   Sabine Durrant   Amanda Lees
Dawn Cairns   Louise Harwood   Jill Mansell
Jenny Colgan   Lisa Jewell   Claudia Pattison

John McLaren   1951- Sco   Crime: Legal/financial

www.fantasticfiction.co.uk/authors/John_McLaren.htm

Harry Bingham   John Grisham   Brad Meltzer
Jonathan Davies   Paul Kilduff   Scott Turow
Reg Gadney

Bernard MacLaverty 1942- Ire General
www.bernardmaclaverty.com

Ronald Frame	Joseph O'Connor	Piers Paul Read
Joan Lingard	David Park	Adam Thorpe
Allan Massie	Julian Rathbone	Niall Williams

Alistair MacLean 1922-87 Sco Adventure/Thriller
also writes as **Ian Stuart**
www.kirjasto.sci.fi/maclean.htm

Desmond Bagley	Gavin Lyall	A J Quinnell
James Follett	Andy McNab	Peter Tonkin
Hammond Innes	Nicholas Monsarrat	

Duncan McLean 1964- Sco General

Iain Banks	Ruaridh Nicoll	S Maugham 1993
Ron Butlin	Andrew O'Hagan	
Des Dillon	Paul Sayer	
Gordon Legge	Alan Spence	Alan Warner

Alistair MacLeod 1936- Can General

William Boyd	Mary Lawson	Michael Ondaatje
Jim Crace	Toby Litt	David Park
David Guterson	Ian McEwan	Carol Shields

Charlotte MacLeod 1922- Can Crime: Amateur sleuth
also writes as **Ailsa Craig**
www.fantasticfiction.co.uk/authors/Charlotte_MacLeod.htm

⚲ Prof Peter Shandy
Max Bittersohn & Sarah Kelling
New England

Marian Babson	Carolyn G Hart	Gwen Moffat
Lilian Jackson Braun	Margaret Maron	David Williams
Janis Harrison		

Ken MacLeod 1954- Sco Science Fiction: Space and time
www.fantasticfiction.co.uk/authors/Ken_MacLeod.htm

Steve Aylett	Jack McDevitt	BSFA 1999
Iain M Banks	John Meaney	
Ray Bradbury	China Miéville	
Greg Egan	Richard Morgan	Adam Roberts

Pauline McLynn   Ire

Crime: Humour

www.fantasticfiction.co.uk/authors/Pauline_McLynn.htm

🚶 Leo Street, PI - Dublin

Janet Evanovich
Liz Evans
Maggie Gibson

Sparkle Hayter
Lauren Henderson

Susan Isaacs
Sarah Strohmeyer

M

Terry McMillan   1951-   US

General

http://voices.cla.umn.edu/newsite/authors/McMillanTerry.html

Esther Freud
John Irving

Toni Morrison
Alice Walker

Valerie Wilson Wesley

Larry McMurtry   1936-   US

General

www.bookreporter.com/authors/au-mcmurtry-larry.asp

Pat Conroy
Nicholas Evans
Charles Frazier
Jim Harrison

John Irving
Jack Kerouac
James A Michener
Walker Percy

Pulitzer 1986

Scott Phillips

Andy McNab   1960-

War: Modern

www.fantasticfiction.co.uk/authors/Andy_McNab.htm

🚶 Nick Stone, SIS

Shaun Clarke
Murray Davies
Duncan Falconer

John Fullerton
Joseph R Garber
Alan Judd

Mike Lunnon-Wood
Alistair MacLean
John Nichol

Claire McNab   1940-   Aus

Crime: Police work - Australia

also writes as **Clare Carmichael**
www.fantasticfiction.co.uk/authors/Claire_McNab.htm

🚶 DI Carol Ashton - Sydney
Denise Cleever, Intelligence agent -
Australia

Jan Burke
Jon Cleary
Stella Duffy

Peter Guttridge
J A Jance
Laurie King

Chris Niles
Carol O'Connell

Judith McNaught   1944-   US

General

www.fantasticfiction.co.uk/authors/Judith_McNaught.htm

Catherine Coulter
Barbara Delinsky
Judith Gould

Penny Jordan
Jayne Ann Krentz
Amanda Quick

LaVyrle Spencer
Danielle Steel

Go to back for lists of:
Authors by Genre • Characters and Series • Prize Winners • Further Reading

Elisabeth McNeill 1931- Sco

Saga
Scotland

Emma Blair	Gwen Kirkwood	Elvi Rhodes
Teresa Crane	Genevieve Lyons	Sarah Shears
Doris Davidson	Anne Melville	Kirsty White

M

Candia McWilliam 1955- Sco

General

www.contemporarywriters.com/authors/?p=auth65

Nicola Barker	Shena Mackay	Guardian 1994
Elizabeth Bowen	Allan Massie	
A S Byatt	Iris Murdoch	Muriel Spark
Doris Lessing	Jane Rogers	Jill Paton Walsh

Cauvery Madhavan 1962 Ind

General

www.cauverymadhavan.com

Anita Rau Badami	Jhumpa Lahiri	Nisha Minhas
Manju Kapur	Sharon Maas	Anita Nair

Gwen Madoc Wales

Saga
Swansea

June Francis	Beryl Matthews	Mary Jane Staples
Meg Hutchinson	Sharon Owens	Dee Williams
Margaret Kaine		

Pierre Magnan 1922- Fr

Crime: Psychological
♟ Seraphin Monge - Provence

www.fantasticfiction.co.uk/authors/Pierre_Magnan.htm

Karin Fossum	Arturo Perez-Reverte
Carol Goodman	Louis Sanders

Norman Mailer 1923- US

General

Don Delillo	John Steinbeck	Gore Vidal — Pulitzer 1980
Joseph Heller	William Styron	Tom Wolfe
Ernest Hemingway	John Updike	

Barry Maitland 1941- Sco

Crime: Police work - UK
♟ DCI David Brock & DS Kathy Kolla
London

www.barrymaitland.com

Jo Bannister	Stephen Booth	Simon Kernick
Mark Billingham	Elizabeth George	Gay Longworth
Giles Blunt	Cynthia Harrod-Eagles	Ed O'Connor

John Malcolm   1936-

www.fantasticfiction.co.uk/authors/John_Malcolm.htm

Crime: Amateur sleuth

🏃 Tim Simpson, Art investment advisor

Jonathan Gash
Philip Hook

Roy Lewis
Iain Pears

Derek Wilson

Amulya Malladi   1974-   Ind

www.amulyamalladi.com

General M

Anita Rau Badami
Anita Desai

Rohinton Mistry
Bharati Mukherjee

Allan Mallinson

www.fantasticfiction.co.uk/authors/Allan_Mallinson.htm

War: Historical

🏃 Matthew Hervey, Captain
C19th Light Dragoons

Tom Connery
Bernard Cornwell
Garry Douglas

Daniel Hall
Richard Howard
Christopher Nicole

Patrick O'Brian
Dan Parkinson
Patrick Rambaud

Michael Malone   US

www.fantasticfiction.co.uk/authors/Michael_Malone.htm

Crime: Police work - US

🏃 Chief Cuddy Mangum &
Det Justin Savile
'Hillston', North Carolina

James Lee Burke
Thomas H Cook
Dashiell Hammett
George V Higgins

Tony Hillerman
Jonathon King
David Lindsey
Ed McBain

Jefferson Parker
George P Pelecanos
John Sandford
Stuart Woods

Shane Maloney   Aus

www.shanemaloney.com

Crime: Amateur sleuth

🏃 Murray Whelan, Political adviser
Melbourne

Carl Hiaasen
Elmore Leonard

Laurence Shames
Don Winslow

David Malouf   1934-   Aus

www.middlemiss.org/lit/authors/maloufd/maloufd.html

General

Peter Carey
James Clavell
Robert Drewe
Janette Turner Hospital

Elizabeth Jolley
Thomas Keneally
Ben Okri
Morris West

Commonwealth 1991
IMPAC 1996

Patrick White

Go to back for lists of:
Authors by Genre • Characters and Series • Prize Winners • Further Reading

Chris Manby 1972- Chick Lit
www.fantasticfiction.co.uk/authors/Chris_Manby.htm

Jessica Adams	Jenny Eclair	Serena Mackesy
Faith Bleasdale	Julie Highmore	Sue Margolis
Jenny Crusie	Josie Lloyd & Emlyn Rees	Linda Taylor

Valerio Massimo Manfredi 1943- It Historical
www.fantasticfiction.co.uk/authors/Valerio_Massimo_Manfredi.htm   🏃 Alexander the Great

Robert Graves	Allan Massie	Steven Saylor
Conn Iggulden	Steven Pressfield	Manda Scott
Christian Jacq	Mary Renault	Wilbur Smith

Henning Mankell 1948- Swe Crime: Police work - Sweden
www.henningmankell.com   🏃 Insp Kurt Wallander - Ystad

Karin Alvtegen	Donna Leon	CWA 2001
Giles Blunt	Liza Marklund	
Colin Dexter	Archer Mayor	
Karin Fossum	Barbara Nadel	Maj Sjöwall and Per Wahlöö
Peter Hoeg	Pernille Rygg	Fred Vargas

Tara Manning Ire Chick Lit

Lynne Barrett-Lee	Amanda Murphy	Tina Reilly
Suzanne Higgins	Carmen Reid	Jane Wenham-Jones

Jill Mansell Chick Lit
http://authorpages.hoddersystems.com/jillmansell

Cecelia Ahern	Francesca Clementis	Marissa Mackle
Trisha Ashley	Jenny Crusie	Penny Vincenzi
Jaye Carroll	Jenny Eclair	Liz Young

Hilary Mantel 1952- General
www.contemporarywriters.com/authors/?p=auth67

Hilary Bailey	Elizabeth Jolley	Holtby 1990
Candida Crewe	Angela Lambert	Hawthornden 1996
Rachel Cusk	Julie Myerson	
A M Homes	Jane Rogers	Alice Sebold

Hannah March 1962- Crime: Historical - C18th
also writes as T R Wilson, Tim Wilson   🏃 Robert Fairfax - C18th England

Bruce Alexander	Jane Jakeman	David Liss
Gwendoline Butler	Deryn Lake	Fidelis Morgan
Janet Gleeson	Janet Laurence	Derek Wilson

John Marco US Fantasy: Epic

James Barclay
Terry Brooks

Chris Bunch
Steven Erikson

Raymond E Feist
Robert Jordan

Phillip Margolin 1944- US Crime: Legal/financial

also writes as **Phillip M Margolin**
www.phillipmargolin.com

William Bernhardt
D W Buffa
William Diehl

Colin Harrison
Steve Martini
Richard North Patterson

Nancy Taylor Rosenberg
John Sandford
Lisa Scottoline

Sue Margolis Chick Lit

www.fantasticfiction.co.uk/authors/Sue_Margolis.htm

Cecelia Ahern
Catherine Alliott
Josie Lloyd & Emlyn Rees

Serena Mackesy
Chris Manby
Amanda Murphy

Sheila O'Flanagan
Isabel Wolff

Juliet Marillier NZ Fantasy: Myth

www.julietmarillier.com

Sarah Ash
Ashok K Banker
Alice Borchardt
Marion Zimmer Bradley

Trudi Canavan
Storm Constantine
Cecilia Dart-Thornton
Charles de Lint

Robin Hobb
Caiseal Mor
Catrin Morgan
Jan Siegel

Liza Marklund 1962- Swe Crime: Amateur sleuth

www.lizamarklund.net   ⚐ Annika Bengtzon, Journalist - Stockholm

Edna Buchanan
Jan Burke
G M Ford

Karin Fossum
Denise Hamilton
Henning Mankell

Pernille Rygg
Maj Sjöwall and Per Wahlöö

Louise Marley Ire Chick Lit

www.louisemarley.co.uk

Anne Dunlop
Sabine Durrant

Imogen Edwards-Jones
Sophie Kinsella

Arabella Weir

Margaret Maron 1959- US Crime: Amateur sleuth

www.margaretmaron.com   ⚐ Deborah Knott, Judge - North Carolina
Sigrid Harald - New York Police

Lilian Jackson Braun
Jan Burke
Carol Higgins Clark

W E B Griffin
Janis Harrison
Carolyn G Hart

Laura Lippman
Sharyn McCrumb
Charlotte MacLeod

Ngaio Marsh 1895-1982 NZ Crime: Police work - UK

www.fantasticfiction.co.uk/authors/Ngaio_Marsh.htm ⚐ DI Roderick Alleyn

Margery Allingham	Elizabeth Ferrars	Dorothy Simpson
Agatha Christie	David Roberts	Josephine Tey
Barbara Cleverly	Dorothy L Sayers	Patricia Wentworth

M

Michael Marshall 1965- Adventure/Thriller

also writes as **Michael Marshall-Smith** ⚐ Ward Hopkins, ex-CIA
www.michaelmarshallsmith.com

Lee Child	Stephen King	Jeff Noon
Jeffery Deaver	Richard Morgan	James Patterson
Thomas Harris		

Sybil Marshall 1913- General

'Old Swithinford'

Margaret Dickinson	Pamela Oldfield	Miss Read
Judith Lennox	Mary E Pearce	Pam Rhodes
Nora Naish	Ann Purser	Ann Widdecombe

Edward Marston 1940- Wales Crime: Historical - Medieval

also writes as A E Marston, Kenneth Miles, ⚐ Nicholas Bracewell, Theatre - C16th England
Christopher Mountjoy Ralph Delchard & Gervase Bret - C11th England
is Keith Miles Christopher Redmayne & Jonathan Bale - C17th England
www.edwardmarston.com Insp Robert Colbeck - C19th London

Simon Beaufort	Janet Gleeson	Bernard Knight
Judith Cook	Philip Gooden	John Pilkington
Paul Doherty	Sylvian Hamilton	C J Sansom
Patricia Finney	Michael Jecks	Martin Stephen

Yann Martel 1963- Can General

www.fantasticfiction.co.uk/authors/Yann_Martel.htm

Jim Crace	David Mitchell	Man Booker 2002
Louis de Bernières	V S Naipaul	
Mark Haddon	D B C Pierre	
Steve Martin	Salman Rushdie	Paul Theroux

Andrew Martin Crime: Historical - C19th

www.fantasticfiction.co.uk/authors/Andrew_Martin.htm ⚐ Jim Stringer, Railwayman

John Maclachlan Gray	Jane Jakeman	Anne Perry
Ray Harrison	Peter Lovesey	

Go to back for lists of:
Authors by Genre • Characters and Series • Prize Winners • Further Reading

David Martin   1946-   US   Horror
www.fantasticfiction.co.uk/authors/David_Martin.htm

Chaz Brenchley	Graham Masterton	Kim Newman
Jack Harvey	Richard Matheson	Whitley Strieber
Graham Joyce		

M

George R R Martin   1948-   US   Fantasy: Epic
www.georgerrmartin.com

Ashok K Banker	Maggie Furey	Ricardo Pinto
James Barclay	Greg Keyes	Jan Siegel
C J Cherryh	Juliet E McKenna	Robert Silverberg
David A Drake	Stan Nicholls	Harry Turtledove

J Wallis Martin   Adventure/Thriller: Psychological
is Julia Wallis Martin
www.fantasticfiction.co.uk/authors/Julia_Wallis_Martin.htm

| Nicci French | Maureen O'Brien | Minette Walters |
| Elizabeth McGregor | Ruth Rendell | Robert Wilson |

Steve Martin   1945-   US   General
www.stevemartin.com

| Paulo Coelho | Yann Martel | Alice Sebold |
| Mark Haddon | D B C Pierre | |

Valerie Martin   1948-   US   General
www.fantasticfiction.co.uk/authors/Valerie_Martin.htm

Margaret Atwood	Jennifer Johnston	Orange 2003
Pat Barker	Shena Mackay	Julie Myerson
Zoë Heller	Toni Morrison	Ann Patchett

Tomas Eloy Martinez   1934-   Arg   General

| Isabel Allende | Gabriel Garcia Márquez | Mario Vargas Llosa |
| Carlos Fuentes | Armistead Maupin | |

Steve Martini   1946-   US   Crime: Legal/financial
www.stevemartini.com   ⚘ Paul Madriani, Lawyer - San Diego

Harry Bingham	John T Lescroart	Nancy Taylor Rosenberg
Alafair Burke	Phillip Margolin	Lisa Scottoline
Linda Fairstein	Brad Meltzer	Susan R Sloan
James Grippando	Richard North Patterson	Robert K Tanenbaum

David Mason 1951- US Adventure/Thriller

Jeffrey Archer	Johnny 'Two Combs'	John Nichol
Stephen J Cannell	Howard	Chris Ryan
Conor Cregan	Stephen Leather	

M

Sarah Mason Chick Lit

www.fantasticfiction.co.uk/authors/Sarah_J_Mason.htm

Trisha Ashley	Donna Hay	Romantic 2003
Claire Calman	Melissa Nathan	
Louise Harwood	Jennifer Weiner	Arabella Weir

Allan Massie 1938- Sco General

www.fantasticfiction.co.uk/authors/Allan_Massie.htm

Ronald Frame	Candia McWilliam	Piers Paul Read
Bernard MacLaverty	Frederic Raphael	William Rivière

Allan Massie 1938- Sco Historical

www.fantasticfiction.co.uk/authors/Allan_Massie.htm

Robert Graves	Robert Nye	Simon Scarrow
Conn Iggulden	Rosemary Rowe	Marilyn Todd
Valerio Massimo Manfredi	Steven Saylor	David Wishart

John Masters 1914-83 US General

Amit Chaudhuri	M M Kaye	V S Naipaul
Rumer Godden	James A Michener	R K Narayan
Ruth Prawer Jhabvala	Nicholas Monsarrat	Morris West

Priscilla Masters 1952- Crime: Police work - UK

www.joannapiercy.com   ⅄ DI Joanna Piercy & DS Mike Korpanski
'Moorlands', Staffordshire

Jo Bannister	Deborah Crombie	Marjorie Eccles
Stephen Booth	Judith Cutler	H R F Keating
John Connor	Margaret Duffy	Jill McGown

Graham Masterton 1946- Sco Horror

www.grahammasterton.co.uk

John Farris	Shaun Hutson	Kim Newman
Christopher Fowler	Robert McCammon	John Saul
Stephen Gallagher	David Martin	Whitley Strieber

Richard Matheson   1926-   US   Horror

also writes as **Logan Swanson**
www.fantasticfiction.co.uk/authors/Richard_Matheson.htm

Jonathan Aycliffe
Dean R Koontz

Stephen Laws
David Martin

Peter Straub

M

Beryl Matthews   Saga
♀ Webster Family

Benita Brown
Catherine Cookson
Elizabeth Elgin

Lilian Harry
Freda Lightfoot
Gwen Madoc

Judith Saxton
Mary Jane Staples
June Tate

Carole Matthews   Chick Lit

www.carolematthews.co.uk

Jessica Adams
Catherine Alliott
Zoë Barnes

Francesca Clementis
Isla Dewar

Julie Ellis
Arabella Weir

W Somerset Maugham   1874-1965   General

www.fantasticfiction.co.uk/authors/W_Somerset_Maugham.htm

Joseph Conrad
Charles Dickens

Michel Faber
Henry James

J B Priestley
Morris West

Armistead Maupin   1944-   US   General

www.armisteadmaupin.com

Patrick Gale
Alan Hollinghurst
Tama Janowitz

Hanif Kureishi
Jay McInerney

Tomas Eloy Martinez
Edmund White

Simon Mawer   1948-   General

www.simonmawer.com

William Boyd
Sebastian Faulks
Michael Frayn

Andrew Greig
Ian McEwan
Iris Murdoch

Andrew O'Hagan
Niall Williams

John R Maxim   US   Adventure/Thriller
♀ Paul Bannerman, US Intelligence
Connecticut

www.geocities.com/john_r_maxim

Raymond Benson
Stephen Coonts

Daniel Easterman
Stephen Hunter

Anna Maxted

Chick Lit

www.annamaxted.com

Elizabeth Buchan
Martina Devlin
Isla Dewar

Sabine Durrant
Suzanne Higgins
India Knight

Claire Naylor
Adele Parks

M

Jenny Maxwell

Sco

Adventure/Thriller

www.fantasticfiction.co.uk/authors/Jenny_Maxwell.htm

Louise Doughty
Jeff Gulvin

Pete Hamill
Faye Kellerman

Thomas Kelly
Carol Smith

Robin Maxwell

US

Historical

Philippa Gregory
Sandra Gulland
Jane Aiken Hodge

Elizabeth Jeffrey
Rosalind Miles
Edith Pargeter

Maureen Peters
Anya Seton

Julian May

1931-   US

Fantasy: Epic

also writes as Lee N Falconer, Ian Thorne
www.fantasticfiction.co.uk/authors/Julian_May.htm

Marion Zimmer Bradley
Stephen Donaldson
Barbara Hambly

Anne McCaffrey
Michael Moorcock
William Sarabande

Robert Silverberg
Gene Wolfe

Peter May

1951-   Sco

Crime: Police work - China

www.petermay.co.uk

🏃 Det Li Yan & Margaret Campbell, Pathologist
China

Martin Booth
Martina Cole
Patricia D Cornwell

Kathy Reichs
Lisa See
Martin Cruz Smith

Christopher West
Qiu Xiaolong

Margaret Mayhew

Saga

www.fantasticfiction.co.uk/authors/Margaret_Mayhew.htm

Anne Baker
Helen Carey
Elizabeth Elgin

Lilian Harry
Helen Humphreys
Angela Huth

Joan Jonker
Maureen Lee
Victor Pemberton

Archer Mayor

US

Crime: Police work - US

www.archermayor.com

🏃 Lt Joe Gunther - Brattleboro, Vermont

Giles Blunt
Paula Gosling

Donald Harstad
Michael McGarrity

Henning Mankell
Theresa Monsour

Juliette Mead   1960-   General

Elizabeth Buchan
Joy Chambers
Elizabeth Darrell

Sebastian Faulks
Sarah Grazebrook

Kate Grenville
Hilary Norman

Glenn Meade   1957-   Ire   Adventure/Thriller

www.fantasticfiction.co.uk/authors/Glenn_Meade.htm

Campbell Armstrong
Frederick Forsyth

Robert Harris
Greg Iles

Donald James
Robert Littell

John Meaney   Science Fiction: Technical

http://johnmeaney.tripod.com

Iain M Banks
Greg Bear
Gene Brewer
Jon Courtenay Grimwood

James Lovegrove
Paul J McAuley
Ken MacLeod

Robert Reed
Alastair Reynolds
Adam Roberts

M R D Meek   1918-   Sco   Crime: Amateur sleuth

⚘ Lennox Kemp, Solicitor
London

Colin Dexter
Martin Edwards
Frances Fyfield

Joyce Holms
P D James

Roy Lewis
R D Wingfield

Gita Mehta   1943-   Ind   General

Amit Chaudhuri
Anita Desai
Chitra Banerjee Divakaruni

M M Kaye
Hanif Kureishi
Bharati Mukherjee

R K Narayan
Michael Ondaatje
Salman Rushdie

Patricia Melo   Braz   Adventure/Thriller

Brazil

Luiz Alfredo Garcia-Roza
Elmore Leonard

Walter Mosley
James Sallis

Brad Meltzer   1970-   US   Adventure/Thriller: Legal/financial

www.bradmeltzer.com

David Baldacci
Po Bronson
Paul Kilduff

John McLaren
Steve Martini

Christopher Reich
Michael Ridpath

Anne Melville 1926-1998 Saga

🚶 Lorimer Family • Hardie Family

Anna King
Beryl Kingston
Genevieve Lyons

Elisabeth McNeill
Mary Minton
Pamela Oldfield

Claire Rayner
Sarah Shears
Anne Worboys

Pauline Melville 1948- Guy General

www.contemporarywriters.com/authors/?p=auth72

Fred D'Aguiar
Patricia Duncker
Lucy Ellman
Graham Greene

Andrea Levy
Bernice Rubens
Evelyn Waugh

Guardian 1990
Whitbread 1997

Charlotte Mendelson 1972- General

www.fantasticfiction.co.uk/authors/Charlotte_Mendelson.htm

Kate Atkinson
Anita Brookner
Margaret Forster

Sue Gee
Penelope Lively
Maggie O'Farrell

Mail 2003
S Maugham 2004

Catherine Merriman 1949- Wales General

Carol Birch
Melvyn Bragg

Helen Dunmore
Lesley Glaister

Julia Hamilton

Deon Meyer 1958- SA Crime

www.deonmeyer.com

🚶 Zatopek "Zed" van Heerden, Retired policeman
South Africa

Donald Harstad
Tony Hillerman

Ed McBain
Joseph Wambaugh

Judith Michael 1934- US Glitz & Glamour

is Judith Barnard and Michael Fain
www.fantasticfiction.co.uk/authors/Judith_Michael.htm

Sally Beauman
Celia Brayfield
Jackie Collins

Lucinda Edmonds
Julie Ellis
Olivia Goldsmith

Judith Gould
Judi James
Caroline Upcher

Anne Michaels 1958- Can General

www.fantasticfiction.co.uk/authors/Anne_Michaels.htm

Doris Lessing
Caryl Phillips
Michèle Roberts

Bernhard Schlink
Rachel Seiffert
Carol Shields
Jane Urquhart

Guardian 1997
Orange 1997
Wingate 1997

Barbara Michaels   1927-   US   General

also writes as **Elizabeth Peters**; *is* **Barbara Mertz**
www.mpmbooks.com

June Drummond
Jane Aiken Hodge

Judith Kelman
Mary Stewart

Madge Swindells

Fern Michaels   1933-   US   Glitz & Glamour

is **Mary Kuczkir**
www.fernmichaels.com

Jackie Collins
Jude Deveraux
Lucinda Edmonds

Julie Ellis
Roberta Latow
Johanna Lindsey

Frankie McGowan
LaVyrle Spencer

James A Michener   1907-1997   US   General

www.jamesmichener.com

Howard Fast
Larry McMurtry

John Masters
Edward Rutherfurd

Leon Uris
Gore Vidal

David Michie   Zim   Adventure/Thriller

www.davidmichie.com

Jeff Abbott
David Baldacci

John Grisham
Thomas Kelly

Henry Porter
Christopher Reich

Paul Micou   1959-   US   General

T Coraghessan Boyle
Ronald Frame
Patrick Gale

Alan Gurganus
J D Salinger

Evelyn Waugh
Tom Wolfe

Stanley Middleton   1919-   General

www.fantasticfiction.co.uk/authors/Stanley_Middleton.htm

Kingsley Amis
Melvyn Bragg

David Lodge
Alan Sillitoe

Booker 1974

China Miéville   1972-   Science Fiction: Space and time

www.runagate-rampant.netfirms.com

Stephen Baxter
Mary Gentle
Ken MacLeod
Richard Morgan
Philip Pullman

Alastair Reynolds
Adam Roberts
Kim Stanley Robinson
Michael Marshall Smith

Arthur C Clarke 2001 & 2005
British Fantasy 2001 & 2003

Rosalind Miles

Historical

www.rosalind.net

Margaret George	Robin Maxwell	Anya Seton
Elizabeth Hawksley	Sharon Penman	Mary Stewart
Helen Hollick	Maureen Peters	Lindsay Townsend

Andrew Miller 1960-

Historical

www.andrewmiller-author.co.uk

Tracy Chevalier	Jane Stevenson	Black 1997
Elizabeth Knox	Rose Tremain	IMPAC 1999
Lawrence Norfolk	Barry Unsworth	
Julian Rathbone	Peter Watt	

Sue Miller 1943- US

General

www.fantasticfiction.co.uk/authors/Sue_Miller.htm

Ethan Canin	Lorrie Moore	Christina Schwarz
Patricia Gaffney	Maggie O'Farrell	Mona Simpson
Nikki Gemmell	Marge Piercy	Sarah Willis

Mil Millington

Lad Lit: Humour

www.fantasticfiction.co.uk/authors/Mil_Millington.htm

Richard Asplin	Ben Hatch	Paul Reizin
Paul Burke	Nick Hornby	Alexei Sayle
James Delingpole	Damien Owens	

Kyle Mills 1966- US

Adventure/Thriller

🏃 Mark Beamon - FBI

www.kylemills.com

Dale Brown	Frederick Forsyth	John Le Carré
Tom Clancy	Greg Iles	Robert Ludlum
Brendan Dubois		

Magnus Mills 1954-

Humour

www.fantasticfiction.co.uk/authors/Magnus_Mills.htm

Jonathan Coe	Graham Swift	McKitterick 1999
Roddy Doyle	Keith Waterhouse	
Michel Faber		

Go to back for lists of:
Authors by Genre
Characters and Series
Prize Winners
Further Reading

Denise Mina 1966- Sco

www.denisemina.co.uk

Crime: Amateur sleuth

⚐ Maureen O'Donnell - Glasgow
London

Andrea Badenoch
Alex Gray
Quintin Jardine

Frederic Lindsay
Val McDermid
Theresa Monsour

Ian Rankin
Chris Simms

CWA 1998

M

Nisha Minhas

General

Manju Kapur
Sharon Maas

Cauvery Madhavan
Preethi Nair

Mary Minton

Saga

Anne Bennett
Brenda Clarke
Lilian Harry

Anna Jacobs
Penny Jordan
Marie Joseph

Genevieve Lyons
Anne Melville
Alexandra Raife

Rohinton Mistry 1952- Can

General

www.contemporarywriters.com/authors/?p=auth73

Thalassa Ali
Amit Chaudhuri
Charles Dickens
Abdulrazak Gurnah
Shifra Horn

Amulya Malladi
V S Naipaul
R K Narayan
Paul Scott

Commonwealth 1992 & 1996
Holtby 1996

Jacquelyn Mitchard 1953- US

General

www.jacquelynmitchardbooks.com

Elizabeth Berg
Kate Grenville

David Guterson
Alice Hoffman

Barbara Kingsolver
Jane Smiley

David Mitchell 1969-

General

www.contemporarywriters.com/authors/?p=auth03A30M451712634910

Margaret Atwood
Jim Crace
Louis de Bernières
Elizabeth Knox

Yann Martel
Haruki Murakami
Elizabeth Russell Taylor

Mail 1999

Gladys Mitchell 1901-83

Crime: Amateur sleuth

also wrote as **Stephen Hockaby, Malcolm Torrie**
www.gladysmitchell.com

⚐ Mrs Beatrice Bradley, Psychiatrist

Catherine Aird
Agatha Christie

Michael Innes
Gwen Moffat

David Roberts
Patricia Wentworth

Timothy Mo 1953-   General
www.timothymo.com

Michelle de Kretser   Catherine Lim
Alex Garland   Caryl Phillips   Faber 1979
Arthur Golden   William Rivière   Hawthornden 1982
James Hamilton-Paterson   Amy Tan   Black 1999
Kazuo Ishiguro

M

L E Modesitt Jr 1943- US   Fantasy: Epic
www.travelinlibrarian.info/recluce   Erde

C J Cherryh   Simon R Green   R A Salvatore
Louise Cooper   Mercedes Lackey   Janny Wurts
David A Drake   Mickey Zucker Reichert   Jonathan Wylie

Gwen Moffat 1924-   Crime: Amateur sleuth
www.fantasticfiction.co.uk/authors/Gwen_Moffat.htm   ⚐ Melinda Pink, Travel writer

Gillian Linscott   Gladys Mitchell   Patricia Wentworth
Charlotte MacLeod   Betty Rowlands

Deborah Moggach 1948-   General
www.deborahmoggach.com

Jane Asher   Catherine Feeny   Christopher Peachment
Carol Birch   Sue Gee   Rose Tremain
Candida Crewe   Angela Huth   Susan Vreeland
Jill Dawson   Joan Lingard   Gillian White

Connie Monk   Saga
                                                         West Country

Brenda Clarke   Eileen Stafford   Dee Williams
Elizabeth Ann Hill   Janet Tanner   Janet Woods
Mary Mackie

Nicholas Monsarrat 1910-79   Sea: Modern
www.fantasticfiction.co.uk/authors/Nicholas_Monsarrat.htm

Duncan Harding   John Masters   Peter Tonkin
Hammond Innes   Justin Scott   Antony Trew
Alistair MacLean   Nevil Shute

Go to back for lists of:
Authors by Genre • Characters and Series • Prize Winners • Further Reading

Theresa Monsour

US

www.fantasticfiction.co.uk/authors/Theresa_Monsour.htm

Crime: Police work - US

♁ Det Paris Murphy - Minneapolis

Ingrid Black	David Lindsey	Carol O'Connell
Giles Blunt	Laura Lippman	J D Robb
Meg Gardiner	Archer Mayor	Dana Stabenow
Lynn Hightower	Denise Mina	Jess Walter

M

Manuel Vázquez Montalbán

1939-2003 Spain Crime: PI

www.vespito.net/mvm/indeng.htm

♁ Pepe Carvalho - Barcelona

Michael Dibdin	Roderic Jeffries	Daniel Pennac
Luiz Alfredo Garcia-Roza	Barbara Nadel	Arturo Pérez-Reverte
Juan Goytisolo	Rebecca Pawel	Fred Vargas

Santa Montefiore

1970- General

www.fantasticfiction.co.uk/authors/Santa_Montefiore.htm

Judy Astley	Sarah Challis	Susan Sallis
Amanda Brookfield	Marika Cobbold	Marcia Willett

Rick Moody

1961- US General

Jeffrey Eugenides	Lorrie Moore	John Updike
John Irving	Philip Roth	

Elizabeth Moon

1945- US Fantasy: Epic

www.sff.net/people/elizabeth.moon

Terry Brooks	Barbara Hambly	R A Salvatore
Lois McMaster Bujold	Mercedes Lackey	Margaret Weis
Kate Elliott	Mickey Zucker Reichert	Janny Wurts

Michael Moorcock

1939- Fantasy: Epic

also writes as Edward P Bradbury, James Colvin
www.multiverse.org

Jonathan Carroll	Wil McCarthy	Guardian 1977
Louise Cooper	Julian May	
Philip K Dick	Linda Nagata	
Mary Gentle	Christopher Priest	Kristine Kathryn Rusch

Brian Moore

1921-1999 Can General

www.fantasticfiction.co.uk/authors/Brian_Moore.htm

Dermot Bolger	Colum McCann	Colm Toibin
Graham Greene	John McGahern	Morris West
Thomas Keneally	Joseph O'Connor	Tim Winton

Charlotte Moore 1959-   Aga saga

also writes as **Charlotte McKay**

Judy Astley   Elizabeth Jane Howard   Stevie Morgan
Anne Atkins   Sarah MacDonald   Kathleen Rowntree
Patricia Fawcett

M

Lorrie Moore 1957- US   General

www.fantasticfiction.co.uk/authors/Lorrie_Moore.htm

Suzannah Dunn   Rick Moody   Irish Times 1999
Louise Erdrich   Anna Quindlen
Alison Lurie   Paul Sayer
Sue Miller   Meg Wolitzer

Viviane Moore 1960-   Crime: Historical - Medieval

www.fantasticfiction.co.uk/authors/Viviane_Moore.htm   ⚘ Chevalier Galeran de Lesnevan
                                                       C12th France

Alys Clare   Sylvian Hamilton   Candace Robb
Paul Doherty   Bernard Knight   Kate Sedley
Susanna Gregory   Ellis Peters   Joan Wolf

Caiseal Mor   Aus   Fantasy: Myth

www.home.aone.net.au/caismor/caiseal.html

Ashok K Banker   Cecilia Dart-Thornton   Katharine Kerr
James Barclay   Charles de Lint   Stephen R Lawhead
Marion Zimmer Bradley   Robin Hobb   Juliet Marillier

Catrin Morgan   Wales   Saga

                                                   Lily Walters - Wales

Catrin Collier   Mary A Larkin   Cynthia S Roberts
Margaret Dickinson   Juliet Marillier   Grace Thompson
Iris Gower

Fidelis Morgan 1952-   Crime: Historical - C17th

also writes as **Morgan Benedict**   ⚘ Countess Ashby-de-la-Zouche and Alpiew, Maid
www.fidelismorgan.com   C17th London

Bruce Alexander   Ruth Dudley Edwards   David Liss
Gwendoline Butler   Janet Gleeson   Hannah March
Judith Cook   Philip Gooden   Iain Pears

Go to back for lists of:
Authors by Genre • Characters and Series • Prize Winners • Further Reading

Richard Morgan   1966-   Science Fiction: Near future

www.fantasticfiction.co.uk/authors/Richard_Morgan.htm   🏃 Takeshi Kovacs

Neal Asher	China Miéville	Justina Robson
Michael Crichton	Alastair Reynolds	Nick Sagan
Ken MacLeod	J D Robb	Bruce Sterling
Michael Marshall		

M

Stevie Morgan   Aga saga

is Nicola Davies

Diana Appleyard	Karen Hayes	Diana Saville
Judy Astley	Charlotte Moore	Peta Tayler

David Morrell   1943-   Can   Adventure/Thriller

www.davidmorrell.net   🏃 Rambo

Campbell Armstrong	William Diehl	A J Quinnell
David Baldacci	Eric Lustbader	Alan Savage

Mark Morris   1963-   Horror

also writes as J M Morris
www.fantasticfiction.co.uk/authors/Mark_Morris.htm

Richard Bachman	Muriel Gray	Bentley Little
Simon Clark	Shaun Hutson	Kim Newman
Stephen Gallagher	Graham Joyce	Tim Wilson

Toni Morrison   1931-   US   General

is Chloe Anthony Wofford
www.kirjasto.sci.fi/tmorris.htm

William Faulkner	Terry McMillan	Pulitzer 1988
Janette Turner Hospital	Valerie Martin	Alice Walker
Harper Lee	Alice Randall	Amy Tan

Mary Morrissy   1957-   Ire   General

www.irishwriters-online.com/marymorrissy.html

Kate Atkinson	Pat Barker	Linda Grant
Beryl Bainbridge	Margaret Forster	Tim Parks

John Mortimer   1923-   Humour

www.fantasticfiction.co.uk/authors/John_Mortimer.htm   🏃 Horace Rumpole, Barrister - London
Leslie Titmus - 'Rapstone Valley'

Malcolm Bradbury	Frederic Raphael	Keith Waterhouse
Caro Fraser	Peter Rawlinson	P G Wodehouse
David Lodge		

Walter Mosley 1952- US Crime: Hardboiled

www.twbookmark.com/features/waltermosley ♒ Easy Rawlins • Socrates Fortlow • Paris Minton
Los Angeles

Stephen Donaldson
Steve Hamilton
Dashiell Hammett
Patricia Melo

Richard Price
James Sallis
Cath Staincliffe

CWA 1991

M

Fiona Mountain Crime: Amateur sleuth

www.fionamountain.com ♒ Natasha Blake, Genealogist

Mary Higgins Clark
Carol Goodman

Morag Joss
Judith Kelman

Marianne MacDonald

Bharati Mukherjee 1940- Ind General

Anita Rau Badami
Anita Desai

Chitra Banerjee Divakaruni
Amulya Malladi

Gita Mehta

Marcia Muller 1944- US Crime: PI

www.marciamuller.com ♒ Sharon McCone - San Francisco

Nicola Barker
Linda Barnes
Cara Black

Carol Higgins Clark
Stella Duffy
Meg Gardiner

Laura Lippman
John Shannon

Sharon Mulrooney Ire Chick Lit

Susannah Bates
Dawn Cairns
Jane Green

Melissa Hill
Louise Kean

Shari Low
Carmen Reid

Alice Munro 1931- Can General

www.fantasticfiction.co.uk/authors/Alice_Munro.htm

Gail Anderson-Dargatz
Raymond Carver
Lynn Coady
Richard Ford
Jane Hamilton

Elizabeth Jolley
Edna O'Brien
Mona Simpson
Amy Tan

WHSmith 1995

Haruki Murakami 1949- Ja General

www.randomhouse.com/features/murakami

Paul Auster
Raymond Carver
Michelle de Kretser

Don Delillo
Bret Easton Ellis
Peter Hoeg

Kazuo Ishiguro
Elizabeth Knox
David Mitchell

Iris Murdoch 1919-1999 General
www.irismurdoch.plus.com

Elizabeth Bowen	Muriel Spark	
Jostein Gaarder	Emma Tennant	
Doris Lessing	A N Wilson	
Candia McWilliam	Virginia Woolf	
Simon Mawer		

Whitbread 1974
Booker 1978

Amanda Murphy Ire Chick Lit

Catherine Alliott	Clare Dowling	Sue Margolis
Colette Caddle	Anne Dunlop	Tara Manning

Elizabeth Murphy Saga
🕴 Ward Family

Anne Baker	Helen Forrester	Mary Mackie
Benita Brown	Margaret Kaine	Alice Taylor
Katie Flynn	Maureen Lee	Margaret Thornton

Gloria Murphy US Horror
www.fantasticfiction.co.uk/authors/Gloria_Murphy.htm

Mary Higgins Clark	Carol Goodman	Iris Johansen
Joy Fielding	Frances Hegarty	Christina Schwarz
Clare Francis		

Margaret Murphy 1959- Crime: Psychological
www.margaretmurphy.co.uk

Ingrid Black	Ridley Pearson	Barbara Vine
Joy Fielding	Sarah Rayne	Laura Wilson
Frances Fyfield	Chris Simms	

Marian Murphy Ire Chick Lit
www.irishwriters-online.com/marianmurphy.html

Louise Bagshawe	Jenny Colgan	Cathy Kelly
Lynne Barrett-Lee	Suzanne Higgins	Sarah Webb

Annie Murray Saga
Birmingham
www.fantasticfiction.co.uk/authors/Annie_Murray.htm

Donna Baker	Alexandra Connor	Sheila Newberry
Rita Bradshaw	Sara Fraser	June Tate
Jean Chapman	Meg Hutchinson	

Amy Myers 1938- Crime: Historical - C19th

also writes as **Laura Daniels, Harriet Hudson**
www.amymyers.net

⚐ Auguste Didier, Chef
C19th Europe

Richard Grayson	Janet Laurence	Elizabeth Peters
Ray Harrison	Peter Lovesey	M J Trow
Alanna Knight		

Julie Myerson 1960- General

www.fantasticfiction.co.uk/authors/Julie_Myerson.htm

Nicci Gerrard	Ian McEwan	Valerie Martin
Jules Hardy	Hilary Mantel	Muriel Spark
Zoë Heller		

Magdalen Nabb 1947- Crime: Police work - Italy

www.fantasticfiction.co.uk/authors/Magdalen_Nabb.htm

⚐ Marshal Guarnaccia - Florence

Michael Dibdin	David Hewson	Donna Leon
Juliet Hebden	Roderic Jeffries	Georges Simenon
Mark Hebden	H R F Keating	

Vladimir Nabokov 1899-1977 Rus General

www.fantasticfiction.co.uk/authors/Vladimir_Nabokov.htm

Martin Amis	Andrew Sean Greer	Alexander Solzhenitsyn
John Banville	James Joyce	Darin Strauss
Anthony Burgess	Thomas Pynchon	John Updike

Barbara Nadel Crime: Police work - Turkey

www.fantasticfiction.co.uk/authors/Barbara_Nadel.htm

⚐ Cetin Ikmen - Istanbul

Michael Dibdin	Donna Leon	Michael Pearce
Leslie Forbes	Henning Mankell	Lisa See
Luiz Alfredo Garcia-Roza	Manuel Vázquez Montalbán	Christopher West
David Hewson	Eliot Pattison	Qiu Xiaolong

Reggie Nadelson US Crime: PI

www.fantasticfiction.co.uk/authors/Reggie_Nadelson.htm

⚐ Artie Cohen - New York

Lawrence Block	Robert Crais	William Heffernan
Raymond Chandler	David Cray	Donald James
Michael Connelly	Loren D Estleman	Dennis Lehane

Go to back for lists of:
Authors by Genre
Characters and Series
Prize Winners
Further Reading

Linda Nagata   1960-   US   Science Fiction: Technical

www.maui.net/~nagata

Paul J McAuley   Michael Moorcock   Robert Charles Wilson
Wil McCarthy   Kim Stanley Robinson   David Wingrove
Ian McDonald

V S Naipaul   1932-   Carib   General

www.kirjasto.sci.fi/vnaipaul.htm

Joseph Conrad   Elizabeth Jolley   Booker 1971
Chitra Banerjee Divakaruni   Yann Martel
Abdulrazak Gurnah   John Masters
Ruth Prawer Jhabvala   Rohinton Mistry   Patrick White

N

Anita Nair   Ind   General

www.anitanair.net

Anita Rau Badami   Jhumpa Lahiri
Manju Kapur   Cauvery Madhavan

Preethi Nair   Ind   General

www.fantasticfiction.co.uk/authors/Preethi_Nair.htm

Kavita Daswani   Jhumpa Lahiri   Nisha Minhas
Manju Kapur   Sharon Maas   Jane Yardley

Nora Naish   Aga saga

Sybil Marshall   Kathleen Rowntree   Peta Tayler
Elizabeth Palmer   Jean Saunders   Mary Wesley
Ann Purser   Mary Sheepshanks

John J Nance   US   Adventure/Thriller

♟ Kat Bronsky - Aviation

www.johnjnance.com

Dale Brown   Gordon Kent   John Nichol
Dan Brown   Charles McCarry   Craig Thomas
Tom Clancy

Bill Napier   1940-   Sco   Adventure/Thriller

http://star.arm.ac.uk/staff/billn.html

John Case   Michael Crichton   Douglas Preston
Michael Cordy   Lury Gibson

R K Narayan   1906-2001   Ind   General

www.fantasticfiction.co.uk/authors/R_K_Narayan.htm

Amit Chaudhuri	John Masters	Arundhati Roy
Anita Desai	Gita Mehta	Vikram Seth
Rumer Godden	Rohinton Mistry	

Jonathan Nasaw   US   Crime: Psychological

www.fantasticfiction.co.uk/authors/Jonathan_Nasaw.htm

N

🏃 Agent E L Pender - FBI

Giles Blunt	Daniel Hecht	James Patterson
Patricia D Cornwell	Alex Kava	Christopher Reich
Jeffery Deaver	Jonathan Kellerman	John Sandford
Thomas Harris	Meg O'Brien	Stephen White

Melissa Nathan   Chick Lit

www.fantasticfiction.co.uk/authors/Melissa_Nathan.htm

Maggie Alderson	Victoria Corby	Sarah Mason
Lisa Armstrong	Erica James	Freya North
Francesca Clementis	Dorothy Koomson	Victoria Routledge

Claire Naylor   Chick Lit

Martina Devlin	Anna Maxted	Adele Parks
Lisa Jewell	Sheila Norton	Daisy Waugh
India Knight	Anita Notaro	

Jan Needle   1943-   Sea: Historical

also writes as Frank Kippax
www.janneedle.com

🏃 William Bentley, Sea Officer
C18th British Navy

Tom Connery	Alexander Kent	Dudley Pope
David Donachie	Patrick O'Brian	Richard Woodman
C S Forester	Dan Parkinson	

Isobel Neill   Sco   Saga
Scotland

Emma Blair	Nora Kay	Jessica Stirling
Margaret Thomson Davis	Frances Paige	Kirsty White
Christine Marion Fraser	Eileen Ramsay	

Go to back for lists of:
Authors by Genre
Characters and Series
Prize Winners
Further Reading

James L Nelson   US   Sea: Historical

www.jameslnelson.com
⚑ Thomas Marlowe, ex Pirate - USA
Brethren of the Coast Trilogy • Revolution at Sea Saga

David Donachie   Patrick O'Brian   Julian Stockwin
C S Forester   Marcus Palliser   Showell Styles
Jonathan Lunn   Dan Parkinson

Karen Nelson   General

also writes as **Karen Hayes**

Amanda Brookfield   Karen Hayes   Joanna Trollope
Victoria Clayton   Julia Lisle   Mary Wesley
Sarah Grazebrook   Judith Summers   Marcia Willett

N

Sheila Newberry   Saga
WW2

Catherine Cookson   Beryl Kingston   June Tate
June Francis   Annie Murray   Dee Williams
Elizabeth Ann Hill   Gilda O'Neill

Robert Newcomb   US   Fantasy: Epic

www.robertnewcomb.com

Sarah Ash   James Clemens   Robin Hobb
Carol Berg   Stephen Donaldson   Robert Jordan
Joanne Bertin   Terry Goodkind   Anne McCaffrey

Kim Newman   1959-   Horror

also writes as **Jack Yeovil**
www.johnnyalucard.com
⚑ Anno Dracula Series

Jonathan Aycliffe   Laurell K Hamilton   Graham Masterton
Poppy Z Brite   Tom Holland   Mark Morris
Christopher Fowler   David Martin

John Nichol   1963-   Adventure/Thriller

www.johnnichol.com

Michael Asher   Richard Herman   Andy McNab
Shaun Clarke   Johnny 'Two Combs'   David Mason
Murray Davies   Howard   John J Nance
Duncan Falconer   Mike Lunnon-Wood   Chris Ryan
John Fullerton

David Nicholls

Lad Lit

www.fantasticfiction.co.uk/authors/David_Nicholls.htm

Jonathan Coe	John Lanchester	Matt Thorne
Nick Hornby	Geoff Nicholson	

Stan Nicholls

Fantasy: Epic

www.stannicholls.com

James Barclay	Raymond E Feist	Robert Jordan
Terry Brooks	David Gemmell	George R R Martin
David Eddings	Terry Goodkind	Tad Williams

Adam Nichols

Fantasy: Epic

⚐ Elinor Whiteblade

David Gemmell	Stephen R Lawhead	Jane Welch
Julia Gray	Michael Scott Rohan	Tad Williams
Simon R Green		

Geoff Nicholson   1953-

Humour

www.fantasticfiction.co.uk/authors/Geoff_Nicholson.htm

Jonathan Coe	Robert Llewellyn	Iain Sinclair
Joseph Connolly	David Nicholls	Leslie Thomas
Stephen Fry	Tom Sharpe	Nigel Williams

Scott Nicholson   US

Horror

www.hauntedcomputer.com

Douglas Clegg	Richard Laymon	Phil Rickman
Graham Joyce	Bentley Little	Tim Wilson

William Nicholson   1948

Fantasy: Epic

www.williamnicholson.co.uk

Trudi Canavan	Eoin Colfer	J K Rowling
Justin Cartwright	Garth Nix	

Christopher Nicole   1930-

Adventure/Thriller

also writes as **Caroline Gray, Mac Marlow, Alan Savage, Andrew York**
www.fantasticfiction.co.uk/authors/Christopher_Nicole.htm

James Clavell	Eric Lustbader
Colin Falconer	Allan Mallinson

Ruaridh Nicoll   1969-   Sco   General

Iain Banks   Duncan McLean   Alan Warner
Ron Butlin   Paul Sayer

Chris Niles   NZ   Crime: Amateur sleuth
www.fantasticfiction.co.uk/authors/Chris_Niles.htm   ☆ Sam Ridley, Radio journalist - Sydney

Marc Blake   Ron Ellis   Claire McNab
Jan Burke   Peter Guttridge

N

Larry Niven   1938-   US   Science Fiction: Space and time
www.larryniven.org

Kevin J Anderson   John Brosnan   Kim Stanley Robinson
Neal Asher   Harry Harrison   Ian Watson
Isaac Asimov   Frank Herbert   Roger Zelazny
Ben Bova

Garth Nix   1963-   Aus   Fantasy: Myth
http://members.ozemail.com.au/~garthnix/garthnix.html

Trudi Canavan   Tim Powers   J K Rowling
William Nicholson   Philip Pullman

David Nobbs   1935-   Humour
www.fantasticfiction.co.uk/authors/David_Nobbs.htm   ☆ Reginald Perrin

Kingsley Amis   Leslie Thomas   Nigel Williams
Roddy Doyle   Alan Titchmarsh   P G Wodehouse
Tom Holt   Mark Wallington

Elizabeth Noble   Aga saga
www.fantasticfiction.co.uk/authors/Elizabeth_Noble.htm

Cecelia Ahern   Julie Highmore   Amanda Eyre Ward
Zoë Barnes   Pam Rhodes   Madeleine Wickham
Marika Cobbold   Kate Saunders   Jane Yardley

Jeff Noon   1957-   Science Fiction: Near future
www.fantasticfiction.co.uk/authors/Jeff_Noon.htm

Steve Aylett   Michael Marshall   Arthur C Clarke 1994
Gene Brewer   Michael Marshall Smith
Pat Cadigan   Neal Stephenson
Jon Courtenay Grimwood Kurt Vonnegut

Lawrence Norfolk   1963-   General
www.contemporarywriters.com/authors/?p=auth81   ⅋ John Lempriere - C17th London

Umberto Eco	Amin Maalouf	Graham Swift
Elizabeth Knox	Andrew Miller	Adam Thorpe

Diana Norman   1935-   Historical

Caroline Harvey	Morgan Llywelyn	Anya Seton
Georgette Heyer	Maureen Peters	Connie Willis

N

Hilary Norman   General

also writes as **Alexandra Henry**
www.fantasticfiction.co.uk/authors/Hilary_Norman.htm

Sally Beauman	Josephine Hart	Juliette Mead
Celia Brayfield	Kate Hatfield	Lesley Pearse

Hilary Norman   Adventure/Thriller

also writes as **Alexandra Henry**
www.fantasticfiction.co.uk/authors/Hilary_Norman.htm

Mary Higgins Clark	Clare Francis
Martina Cole	Judith Kelman

Freya North   1968-   Chick Lit

www.freyanorth.co.uk

Maggie Alderson	Jenn Crowell	Daisy Waugh
Jaye Carroll	Susan Lewis	Deborah Wright
Victoria Colby	Melissa Nathan	Laura Zigman

Sheila Norton   Chick Lit

www.fantasticfiction.co.uk/authors/Sheila_Norton.htm

Lynne Barrett-Lee	Amy Jenkins	Claire Naylor
Claire Calman	Christina Jones	Liz Young
Victoria Colby		

Anita Notaro   Chick Lit

Colette Caddle	Melissa Hill	Tyne O'Connell
Claudine Cullimore	Claire Naylor	Alexandra Potter

Go to back for lists of:
Authors by Genre • Characters and Series • Prize Winners • Further Reading

Robert Nye   1939-   General
www.fantasticfiction.co.uk/authors/Robert_Nye.htm

Peter Ackroyd	Julian Rathbone	Guardian 1976
Bruce Chatwin	Iain Sinclair	Hawthornden 1976
John Fowles	Jane Stevenson	
Allan Massie	Rose Tremain	Barry Unsworth

Patrick O'Brian   1914-2000   Sea: Historical
was Richard Patrick Russ   ⚘ Jack Aubrey & Stephen Maturin
www.wwnorton.com/pob   C18th/19th

Tom Connery	Jonathan Lunn	Marcus Palliser
David Donachie	Allan Mallinson	Dan Parkinson
C S Forester	Jan Needle	Showell Styles
Richard Howard	James L Nelson	Victor Suthren

Edna O'Brien   1932-   Ire   General
www.kirjasto.sci.fi/eobrien.htm

Lynne Reid Banks	Angela Lambert	J D Salinger
Clare Boylan	Alice Munro	Fay Weldon
Jennifer Johnston	Joyce Carol Oates	Niall Williams

Maureen O'Brien   Crime: Police work - UK
www.fantasticfiction.co.uk/authors/Maureen_OBrien.htm   ⚘ DI John Bright - London

Paul Charles	Martha Grimes	J Wallis Martin
Elizabeth Ferrars	Graham Ison	Ruth Rendell
Elizabeth George		

Meg O'Brien   US   Crime: Psychological
www.megobrien.com

Daniel Hecht	Alex Kava	Erica Spindler
Christiane Heggan	Jonathan Nasaw	Stephen White
Tami Hoag	James Patterson	

Tim O'Brien   1946-   US   General
www.illyria.com/tobhp.html

Michael Collins	Richard Ford	Joseph Heller
Michael Cunningham	Charles Frazier	John Irving

Gareth O'Callaghan   Ire   Adventure/Thriller

John Case	Joseph Finder	Mark T Sullivan
Lee Child	Sean Flannery	

Carol O'Connell 1947- US Crime: Police work - US

www.fantasticfiction.co.uk/authors/Carol_OConnell.htm 🚶 Sgt Kathleen Mallory - New York

Jerome Charyn	William Heffernan	Claire McNab
Linda Davies	Faye Kellerman	Theresa Monsour
Meg Gardiner	Thomas Laird	Kathy Reichs
Sue Grafton	Sharyn McCrumb	J D Robb

Tyne O'Connell Aus Chick Lit

www.tyneoconnell.com

Zoë Barnes	Josie Lloyd & Emlyn Rees	Anita Notaro
Claire Calman	Serena Mackesy	Yvonne Roberts
Kathy Lette		

O Ed O'Connor Crime: Psychological

🚶 DI Alison Dexter & DI John Underwood
'New Bolden', Cambridgeshire

Jane Adams	Jim Kelly	Danuta Reah
Stephen Booth	Gay Longworth	Chris Simms
John Connor	Barry Maitland	Alison Taylor

Gemma O'Connor Ire Crime: Psychological

www.gemmaoconnor.com

Andrea Badenoch	Morag Joss	Carol Smith
Sarah Diamond	Val McDermid	Laura Wilson
Nicci French		

Joseph O'Connor 1963- Ire Humour

www.fantasticfiction.co.uk/authors/Joseph_OConnor.htm

Dermot Bolger	Colum McCann	Glenn Patterson
Roddy Doyle	Bernard MacLaverty	Niall Williams
Patrick McCabe	Brian Moore	

John O'Farrell 1962- Lad Lit: Humour

www.fantasticfiction.co.uk/authors/John_OFarrell.htm

John Harding	Tony Parsons
Nick Hornby	Willy Russell

Maggie O'Farrell 1972- Ire General

www.fantasticfiction.co.uk/authors/Maggie_OFarrell.htm

Sophie Cooke	Nikki Gemmell	Nora Roberts
Helen Dunmore	Charlotte Mendelson	Anita Shreve
Patricia Gaffney	Sue Miller	Sarah Willis

Sheila O'Flanagan 1962- Ire Chick Lit

www.sheilaoflanagan.net

Dawn Cairns
Jenn Crowell
Claudine Cullimore

Martina Devlin
Clare Dowling
Monica McInerney

Sue Margolis
Geraldine O'Neill
Lesley Pearse

Andrew O'Hagan 1968- Sco General

www.fantasticfiction.co.uk/authors/Andrew_OHagan.htm

Melvyn Bragg
Janice Galloway
Andrew Greig
Robin Jenkins
A L Kennedy

Duncan McLean
Simon Mawer
Tim Pears
Alan Spence

Holtby 1999
Black 2003

O

Stewart O'Nan US General

www.stewart-onan.com

Thomas Eidson
Louise Erdrich

Charles Frazier
Harper Lee

Cormac McCarthy

Geraldine O'Neill Ire Saga

www.fantasticfiction.co.uk/authors/Geraldine_ONeill.htm

Maeve Binchy
Melissa Hill
Erin Kaye

Cathy Kelly
Mary A Larkin
Sheila O'Flanagan

D M Purcell
Liz Ryan

Gilda O'Neill Saga
East End of London

www.fantasticfiction.co.uk/authors/Gilda_ONeill.htm

Emma Dally
Meg Henderson
Beryl Kingston

Sheila Newberry
Pamela Oldfield
Sally Spencer

Alison Stuart
June Tate
Jeanne Whitmee

Joan O'Neill Ire Saga
Ireland

www.fantasticfiction.co.uk/authors/Joan_ONeill.htm

Josephine Cox
Elaine Crowley
Frank Delaney

Rose Doyle
Catherine Dunne
Iris Gower

Liz Ryan
Mary Ryan
Nicola Thorne

Kate O'Riordan Ire Humour

www.irishwriters-online.com/kateoriordan.html

Sherry Ashworth
Colette Caddle

Martina Devlin
Cathy Kelly

Marian Keyes

Perri O'Shaughnessy US

Crime: Legal/financial

is Pamela & Mary O'Shaughnessy
www.perrio.com

⚐ Nina Reilly, Attorney
Lake Tahoe, California

D W Buffa
Alafair Burke
Linda Fairstein

Nancy Taylor Rosenberg
Lisa Scottoline

Susan R Sloan
Robert K Tanenbaum

Joyce Carol Oates 1938- US

General

also writes as **Rosamond Smith**
www.fantasticfiction.co.uk/authors/Joyce_Carol_Oates.htm

Raymond Carver
Jenny Diski
William Faulkner

Connie May Fowler
Doris Lessing
Edna O'Brien

John Steinbeck
Edith Wharton

Ben Okri 1959- Nigeria

General

www.kirjasto.sci.fi/okri.htm

Angela Carter
Gabriel Garcia Márquez

David Malouf
Caryl Phillips

Booker 1991

Jenny Oldfield 1949-

Saga

also writes as **Kate Fielding**

⚐ Parsons Family - London

Anna King
Victor Pemberton

Sally Spencer
Sally Stewart

Jeanne Whitmee
Sally Worboyes

Pamela Oldfield 1931-

Saga

Heron Saga - Kent • Foxearth Trilogy

Tessa Barclay
Betty Burton
Christine Marion Fraser

Sybil Marshall
Anne Melville
Gilda O'Neill

Jeanne Whitmee
Sarah Woodhouse
Janet Woods

Nick Oldham 1956-

Crime: Police work - UK

www.fantasticfiction.co.uk/authors/Nick_Oldham.htm

⚐ DI Henry Christie - Blackpool

Nicholas Blincoe
Judith Cutler

Lesley Horton
Leslie Thomas

Mark Timlin
Stuart Pawson

Michael Ondaatje 1943- Sri Lan

General

www.fantasticfiction.co.uk/authors/Michael_Ondaatje.htm

Kazuo Ishiguro
Alistair MacLeod
Gita Mehta
David Park

William Rivière
Salman Rushdie
Colin Thubron
Paul Watkins

Irish Times 1991
Booker 1992

Marianne Wiggins

George Orwell 1903-50 General
was Eric Blair

Margaret Atwood	Anthony Burgess	Aldous Huxley
Ray Bradbury	Graham Greene	

Agnes Owens 1926- Sco General

Isla Dewar	Janice Galloway	James Kelman
Anne Donovan	Alasdair Gray	Alan Spence

Damien Owens 1971- Ire Lad Lit: Humour

Richard Asplin	Ben Hatch	Paul Reizin
Mark Barrowcliffe	Mil Millington	

O P

Sharon Owens 1968- Ire Saga
www.fantasticfiction.co.uk/authors/Sharon_Owens.htm

Margaret Dickinson	Erin Kaye	Mary McCarthy
Joan Jonker	Mary A Larkin	Gwen Madoc
Margaret Kaine		

Amos Oz 1939- Isr General

Saul Bellow	Christopher Hope	Isaac Bashevis Singer
William Faulkner	Alan Isler	Alexander Solzhenitsyn
David Grossman	Howard Jacobson	

Lynda Page 1950- Saga
Leicester
www.leicesterandleicestershire.com/Market_Place1.htm

Lyn Andrews	Josephine Cox	Maureen Lee
Anne Baker	Katie Flynn	Margaret Thornton
Rita Bradshaw	Sara Fraser	Audrey Willsher

Frances Paige Sco Saga

🏃 MacKintosh Sisters • McGrath Family
Scotland

Tessa Barclay	Inga Dunbar	Isobel Neill
Maggie Bennett	Meg Henderson	Anne Vivis
Doris Davidson	Nora Kay	Kirsty White

Go to back for lists of:
Authors by Genre • Characters and Series • Prize Winners • Further Reading

Chuck Palahniuk   1961-   US   Crime: Hardboiled

www.chuckpalahniuk.net

Anthony Bourdain   Don DeLillo   James Ellroy
Douglas Coupland   Bret Easton Ellis   Richard Price

Chris Paling   1956-   Adventure/Thriller

www.fantasticfiction.co.uk/authors/Chris_Paling.htm

Robert Edric   John Harvey   Nicholas Royle
Sebastian Faulks   Ian Rankin   Martyn Waites

Marcus Palliser   1949-2002   US   Sea: Historical
✞ Matthew Loftus

C S Forester   James L Nelson   Julian Stockwin
Alexander Kent   Patrick O'Brian   Showell Styles
Jonathan Lunn   Dan Parkinson

P ## Elizabeth Palmer   1942-   Aga saga

Amanda Brookfield   Libby Purves   Peta Tayler
Katie Fforde   Titia Sutherland   Sarah Woodhouse
Nora Naish   Ann Swinfen

Michael Palmer   US   Adventure/Thriller: Medical

www.michaelpalmerbooks.com

Colin Andrews   Robin Cook   Mo Hayder
Paul Carson   Tess Gerritsen   Leah Ruth Robinson

Sara Paretsky   1947-   US   Crime: PI

www.saraparetsky.com   ✞ V I Warshawski - Chicago

Linda Barnes   Reg Gadney   CWA 1988, 2002 & 2004
Cara Black   Lynda La Plante
Edna Buchanan   Laura Lippman
Charlotte Carter   John Shannon   Gillian Slovo
Carol Higgins Clark   Zoë Sharp   Dana Stabenow

Edith Pargeter   1913-95   Historical

also wrote as **Ellis Peters**
www.fantasticfiction.co.uk/authors/Edith_Pargeter.htm

Margaret George   Morgan Llywelyn   Sharon Penman
Rosalind Laker   Robin Maxwell   Nigel Tranter

David Park   1954-   Ire   General

www.bloomsbury.com/authors/microsite.asp?id=138

Mary Lawson   Alistair MacLeod   Colm Toibin
John McGahern   Michael Ondaatje   William Trevor
Bernard MacLaverty   Glenn Patterson

Imogen Parker   1958-   General

Maeve Binchy   Sarah Harrison   Judith Lennox
Victoria Clayton   Charlotte Lamb   Susan Lewis
Kate Grenville

Jefferson Parker   US   Crime: Police work - US
                                                            California
also writes as T Jefferson Parker
www.tjeffersonparker.com

Mark Burnell   Faye Kellerman   John Shannon
John Connolly   Jonathan Kellerman   Martin Cruz Smith
Barry Eisler   Michael Malone   Joseph Wambaugh
John Gilstrap   Ridley Pearson   Stuart Woods

K J Parker   Fantasy: Epic

www.fantasticfiction.co.uk/authors/K_J_Parker.htm

Chaz Brenchley   Juliet E McKenna   Freda Warrington
Kate Jacoby   Tim Powers   Jane Welch

Robert B Parker   1932-   US   Crime: PI

www.linkingpage.com/spenser
                   ☆ Spenser, PI • Sunny Randall, PI - Boston, Mass
                            Chief Jesse Stone - 'Paradise', Mass

Lawrence Block   Kinky Friedman   John Shannon
James Hadley Chase   J A Jance   Donald E Westlake
Harlan Coben   Ed McBain

Una-Mary Parker   1930-   Glitz & Glamour

Maria Barrett   Barbara Delinsky   Penny Jordan
Sally Beauman   Julie Ellis   LaVyrle Spencer
Barbara Taylor Bradford   Judi James   Danielle Steel

Dan Parkinson   1935-   Sea: Historical
                                                      ☆ Patrick Dalton
www.fantasticfiction.co.uk/authors/Dan_Parkinson.htm

Tom Connery   Allan Mallinson   Patrick O'Brian
David Donachie   Jan Needle   Marcus Palliser
C S Forester   James L Nelson   Julian Stockwin

P

Adele Parks

Chick Lit

Trisha Ashley
Emily Barr
Jaye Carroll

Victoria Corby
Martina Devlin
India Knight

Anna Maxted
Claire Naylor
Jennifer Weiner

Tim Parks   1954-

General

Julian Barnes
William Boyd
Bret Easton Ellis
Toby Litt

Ian McEwan
Mary Morrissy
Amanda Prantera
Barbara Trapido

S Maugham 1986
Betty Trask 1986

Julie Parsons   1951-   Ire

Adventure/Thriller: Psychological

Andrea Badenoch
Neil Cross
Sarah Diamond

Ruth Rendell
Liz Rigbey
Louis Sanders

Barbara Vine
Margaret Yorke

P

Tony Parsons   1955-

Lad Lit

Neil Cross
Mike Gayle
Alex George

John Harding
Robert Llewellyn
John O'Farrell

Ben Richards
Sean Thomas
Matt Whyman

Ann Patchett   1963-   US

General

Trezza Azzopardi
Jane Hamilton
Susan Hill
Sheri Holman

Valerie Martin
Alice Sebold
Jane Urquhart
Susan Vreeland

Orange 2002

Glenn Patterson   1961-   Ire

General

Dermot Bolger
David Flusfeder

Patrick McCabe
Joseph O'Connor

David Park
Colm Toibin

Go to back for lists of:
Authors by Genre
Characters and Series
Prize Winners
Further Reading

James Patterson 1947- US Crime: Psychological

www.jamespatterson.com

Det Alex Cross - Washington DC
'Women's Murder Club' - San Francisco
Hugh de Lac - Medieval France

Jeffery Deaver	Alex Kava	Jonathan Nasaw
Mo Hayder	Jonathan Kellerman	Meg O'Brien
Daniel Hecht	Dennis Lehane	James Siegel
Tami Hoag	Michael Marshall	Boris Starling

Richard North Patterson 1947- US Crime: Legal/financial

www.fantasticfiction.co.uk/authors/Richard_North_Patterson.htm

Christopher Paget, Attorney
San Francisco

D W Buffa	Douglas Kennedy	Steve Martini
William Diehl	David Lindsey	Michael Ridpath
James Grippando	Phillip Margolin	Nancy Taylor Rosenberg

James Pattinson Adventure/Thriller

www.fantasticfiction.co.uk/authors/James_Pattinson.htm

P

Brian Callison	Clive Cussler	Hammond Innes
James Cobb	Alexander Fullerton	Douglas Reeman

Claudia Pattison Chick Lit

Sarah Ball	Marissa Mackle	Tina Reilly
Louise Harwood	Alexandra Potter	Laura Zigman

Eliot Pattison 1971- Sco Crime: PI

www.eliotpattison.com

Insp Shan Tao Yun, Former policeman
China

Michael Dibdin	Barbara Nadel	Christopher West
Tony Hillerman	Lisa See	Qiu Xiaolong
Donna Leon	Martin Cruz Smith	

Rebecca Pawel US Crime: Historical - C20th

www.rebeccapawel.com

Carlos Tejada
Civil War Spain

Juan Goytisolo	Philip Kerr	David Roberts
Robert Harris	Manuel Vázquez Montalbán	Guy Walters
J Robert Janes	Arturo Perez-Reverte	

Stuart Pawson 1940- Crime: Police work - UK
www.meanstreets.co.uk ⚘ DI Charlie Priest - Yorkshire

John Baker	Georgie Hale	Nick Oldham
Robert Barnard	Patricia Hall	Nicholas Rhea
Pauline Bell	Simon Kernick	Peter Turnbull

David Peace 1967- Crime: Hardboiled
www.contemporarywriters.com/authors/?p=auth03B5O3314I2634980 Red Riding Quartet
Yorkshire

Jake Arnott	Bill James	Ian Rankin
Ken Bruen	Simon Kernick	Danuta Reah

Christopher Peachment Historical

Tracy Chevalier	Matthew Kneale	James Runcie
Will Davenport	Deborah Moggach	Susan Vreeland

P Mary E Pearce 1932- Saga
Appletree Saga • Wayman Family - Worcestershire

Margaret Dickinson	Miss Read	Caroline Stickland
Sybil Marshall	Sarah Shears	Anne Worboys

Michael Pearce 1933- Crime: Historical - C20th
www.fantasticfiction.co.uk/authors/Michael_Pearce.htm ⚘ The Mamur Zapt (Gareth Owen),
Secret police - early C20th Egypt
Dmitri Kameron, Lawyer - Tsarist Russia
Seymour, Special Branch

Boris Akunin	Roderic Jeffries	CWA 1993
Barbara Cleverly	H R F Keating	
David Dickinson	Barbara Nadel	
Graham Ison	Elizabeth Peters	Laura Joh Rowland

Iain Pears 1955- Crime: Amateur sleuth
www.fantasticfiction.co.uk/authors/Iain_Pears.htm ⚘ Jonathan Argyll, Art historian

Gwendoline Butler	John Maclachlan Gray	Fidelis Morgan
Janet Gleeson	Philip Hook	Arturo Pérez-Reverte
Philip Gooden	John Malcolm	Derek Wilson

Tim Pears 1956- General
www.contemporarywriters.com/authors/?p=auth245

Tim Binding	Robert Edric	Hawthornden 1994
Jonathan Coe	Andrew O'Hagan	
Glen Duncan	J B Priestley	Paul Sayer

Lesley Pearse   1945-   General
www.lesleypearse.co.uk

Zoë Barnes   Hilary Norman   Claire Rayner
Susie Boyt   Sheila O'Flanagan   Michael Taylor
Jilly Cooper

Allison Pearson   Humour
www.fantasticfiction.co.uk/authors/Allison_Pearson.htm

Amanda Craig   Jane Green   Libby Purves
Maggie Gibson   Sue Limb   Louise Wener

Ridley Pearson   1953-   US   Crime: Police work - US
also writes as Wendell McCall, Joyce Reardon   ⚕ Sgt Lou Boldt & Daphne Matthews,
www.ridleypearson.com   Forensic psychologist - Seattle

Giles Blunt   Jon A Jackson   Jefferson Parker
Jeffery Deaver   Faye Kellerman   John Sandford
W E B Griffin   Jonathan Kellerman   P J Tracy
Donald Harstad   Margaret Murphy   Jess Walter

George P Pelecanos   1957-   US   Crime: Hardboiled
www.georgepelecanos.com   ⚕ Nick Stefanos • Derek Strange & Terry Quinn
                                                            Washington DC

Jeff Abbott   David Cray   Ross Macdonald
James Lee Burke   James Crumley   Michael Malone
Raymond Chandler   Roger Jon Ellory   Richard Price
Jerome Charyn   Thomas Laird   Jim Thompson

Lynne Pemberton   General

Maria Barrett   Colleen McCullough   LaVyrle Spencer
Sally Beauman   Belva Plain   Judith Summers
Jayne Ann Krentz   Nora Roberts   Rosie Thomas

Margaret Pemberton   1943-   Historical
also writes as Maggie Hudson   London Sequence
www.fantasticfiction.co.uk/authors/Margaret_Pemberton.htm

Harry Bowling   Sara Hylton   Danielle Steel
Emma Dally   Judith Saxton   Nicola Thorne
Harriet Hudson   Patricia Shaw

P

Go to back for lists of:
Authors by Genre • Characters and Series • Prize Winners • Further Reading

Victor Pemberton

Saga
London

Philip Boast
Harry Bowling
Pamela Evans

Lilian Harry
Margaret Mayhew
Jenny Oldfield

Sally Spencer
Mary Jane Staples
Sally Worboyes

Sharon Penman   US

Historical

www.sharonkaypenman.com

Elizabeth Chadwick
Will Davenport
Dorothy Dunnett

Helen Hollick
Morgan Llywelyn
Rosalind Miles

Edith Pargeter
Mary Stewart
Nigel Tranter

Daniel Pennac   1944-   Fr

Crime: Humour

www.fantasticfiction.co.uk/authors/Daniel_Pennac.htm   ☆ Benjamin Malaussène - Paris, France

Michael Dibdin
H R F Keating

Manuel Vázquez Montalbán
Georges Simenon

P

Walker Percy   1916-1990   US

General

www.fantasticfiction.co.uk/authors/Walker_Percy.htm

Richard Ford
Larry McMurtry

Richard Powers
John Updike

Arturo Pérez-Reverte   Spain   Adventure/Thriller: Historical

www.perez-reverte.com   ☆ Captain Alatriste - C17th Spain

Andrea Camilleri
Umberto Eco
Leslie Forbes

John Maclachlan Gray
Pierre Magnan
Manuel Vázquez Montalbán

Rebecca Pawel
Iain Pears

Wendy Perriam   1940-

General

www.perriam.demon.co.uk

Clare Boylan
Sarah Harrison

Gwendoline Riley
Emma Tennant

Fay Weldon

Anne Perry   1938-   NZ   Crime: Historical - C19th

www.anneperry.net   ☆ Insp Thomas Pitt & Charlotte Pitt
Insp William Monk & Hester Monk
C19th England

David Dickinson
Arthur Conan Doyle
Ray Harrison
Graham Ison

Laurie King
Alanna Knight
Joan Lock
Andrew Martin

Roberta Rogow
Norman Russell
M J Trow
Gerard Williams

Elizabeth Peters   1927-   US

also writes as **Barbara Michaels**; *is* **Barbara Mertz**
www.mpmbooks.com

Crime: Historical - C19th

🏃 Amelia Peabody, Egyptologist

Barbara Cleverly	David Dickinson	Amy Myers
Clare Curzon	Gillian Linscott	Michael Pearce

Ellis Peters   1913-95

was **Edith Pargeter**
www.fantasticfiction.co.uk/authors/Ellis_Peters.htm

Crime: Historical - Medieval

🏃 Brother Cadfael - C13th Shropshire
CI George Felse, Police UK

CWA 1980

Simon Beaufort	Sylvian Hamilton	
Alys Clare	Michael Jecks	
Paul Doherty	Viviane Moore	
Margaret Frazer	Candace Robb	Peter Tremayne
Susanna Gregory	Kate Sedley	Joan Wolf

Maureen Peters   1935-   Wales

also writes as **Veronica Black, Catherine Darby, Elizabeth Law**
www.fantasticfiction.co.uk/authors/Maureen_Peters.htm

Historical

P

Tracy Chevalier	Robin Maxwell	Diana Norman
Rosalind Laker	Rosalind Miles	Jean Stubbs

Elizabeth Pewsey   1948-

also writes as **Elizabeth Aston**

General

Nina Bawden	Jill Dawson	Kate Fielding
Amanda Brookfield	Elizabeth Falconer	Charlaine Harris
Clare Chambers	Catherine Feeny	Sophia Watson

Caryl Phillips   1958-   Carib

www.carylphillips.com

General

Fred D'Aguiar	Anne Michaels	Sunday Times 1992
Hanif Kureishi	Timothy Mo	Black 1993
Andrea Levy	Ben Okri	Commonwealth 2004

Scott Phillips   US

http://scottphillipsauthor.com

Crime: Humour

Tim Dorsey	Elmore Leonard	Jim Thompson
Thomas Eidson	Larry McMurtry	

Jodi Picoult   1967-   US

www.jodipicoult.com

General

Karen Joy Fowler	Anita Shreve	Rebecca Wells
Patricia Gaffney	Anne Tyler	

213

Marge Piercy 1936- US General

http://archer-books.com/Piercy

Maureen Duffy	Mona Simpson	Arthur C Clarke 1993
Shena Mackay	Jane Smiley	
Sue Miller	Caroline Stickland	

D B C Pierre 1961- US General

is Peter Finlay
www.fantasticfiction.co.uk/authors/D_B_C_Pierre.htm

Martin Amis	Steve Martin	Man Booker 2003
Paul Auster	J D Salinger	Whitbread 2003
Yann Martel		

Christopher Pike 1954- US Horror

is Kevin McFadden
www.fantasticfiction.co.uk/authors/Christopher_Pike.htm

Shaun Hutson   Richard Laymon
Stephen Laws   John Saul

Robin Pilcher 1950- Sco Aga saga

www.robinpilcher.co.uk

Margaret Bacon	Rosamunde Pilcher	Diana Saville
Kate Long	Alexandra Raife	Ann Swinfen
Sarah MacDonald	Jean Saunders	

Rosamunde Pilcher 1924- Aga saga

also writes as Jane Fraser
www.fantasticfiction.co.uk/authors/Rosamunde_Pilcher.htm

Margaret Bacon	Sarah MacDonald	Romantic 1996
Sarah Challis	Robin Pilcher	
Victoria Clayton	Jean Saunders	
Adèle Geras	Sally Stewart	Nancy Thayer
Judith Lennox	Ann Swinfen	Marcia Willett

John Pilkington Crime: Historical - C16th

⚔Thomas the Falconer
Elizabethan London

Michael Clynes	Philip Gooden	C J Sansom
Judith Cook	C C Humphreys	Martin Stephen
Patricia Finney	Edward Marston	Peter Tonkin

Ricardo Pinto 1961- Sco   Fantasy: Myth
www.ricardopinto.com

James Clemens   Steven Erikson   Anne McCaffrey
David Eddings   Raymond E Feist   George R R Martin

David Pirie 1946- Sco   Crime: Historical - C19th
www.fantasticfiction.co.uk/authors/David_Pirie.htm   ☃ Arthur Conan Doyle & Dr Joseph Bell
                                                                        Edinburgh

Gwendoline Butler   Alanna Knight   M J Trow
David Dickinson   Barrie Roberts   Gerard Williams
Arthur Conan Doyle   Roberta Rogow

Jenny Pitman 1946-   Crime: Amateur sleuth
www.fantasticfiction.co.uk/authors/Jenny_Pitman.htm   Horse racing

Dick Francis   Richard Pitman
John Francome   Lyndon Stacey

Richard Pitman   Crime: Amateur sleuth
www.fantasticfiction.co.uk/authors/Richard_Pitman.htm   Horse racing

Dick Francis   Gavin Lyall   Lyndon Stacey
John Francome   Jenny Pitman

Belva Plain 1919- US   Saga
www.fantasticfiction.co.uk/authors/Belva_Plain.htm   ☃ Werner Family - USA

Teresa Crane   Jude Deveraux   LaVyrle Spencer
Janet Dailey   Lynne Pemberton   Sue Sully
Barbara Delinsky   Anne Rivers Siddons   Rosie Thomas

Dudley Pope 1925-1997   Sea: Historical & Modern
www.fantasticfiction.co.uk/authors/Dudley_Pope.htm

Tom Connery   Jonathan Lunn   Showell Styles
David Donachie   Philip McCutchan   Richard Woodman
C S Forester   Jan Needle

Henry Porter   Adventure/Thriller
www.fantasticfiction.co.uk/authors/Henry_Porter.htm   ☃ Robert Harland

Jean-Christophe Grangé   John Le Carré   Gerald Seymour
Robert Harris   David Michie   Robert Wilson

P

215

Alexandra Potter   1972-   Chick Lit

Jessica Adams   Dorothy Koomson   Claudia Pattison
Helen Fielding   Kathy Lette   Fiona Walker
Sophie Kinsella   Anita Notaro

Stanley Pottinger   US   Adventure/Thriller
www.fantasticfiction.co.uk/authors/Stanley_Pottinger.htm

Russell Andrews   Nelson DeMille
Suzanne Brockmann   David Hagberg

Anthony Powell   1905-2000   General
www.anthonypowell.org.uk

E M Forster   Aldous Huxley   Evelyn Waugh
Graham Greene   J B Priestley   A N Wilson

P Richard Powers   1957-   US   Science Fiction: Near future

Jeffrey Eugenides   Walker Percy   Bruce Sterling
Jonathan Franzen   Lucius Shepard   Tobias Wolff
Paul J McAuley   Neal Stephenson

Richard Powers   1957-   US   General

William Boyd   Christopher Hope
Don DeLillo   Thomas Pynchon

Tim Powers   1952-   US   Fantasy: Contemporary
http://pw2.netcom.com/~cbranch/powers.html

Philip K Dick   Robert Holdstock   Michael Scott Rohan
Neil Gaiman   Garth Nix   H G Wells
Mary Gentle   K J Parker   Connie Willis
Barbara Hambly   Philip Pullman   Gene Wolfe

Amanda Prantera   1942-   General
www.fantasticfiction.co.uk/authors/Amanda_Prantera.htm

J M Coetzee   Elizabeth Falconer   Barbara Trapido
Amanda Craig   Tim Parks   Barry Unsworth
Maureen Duffy   Rupert Thomson   Peter Watt

Terry Pratchett 1948- Fantasy: Humour

www.terrypratchettbooks.com

Douglas Adams
Piers Anthony
Robert Asprin
Eoin Colfer
Jasper Fforde

Craig Shaw Gardner
Rob Grant
Simon R Green
Andrew Harman
Tom Holt

Robert Rankin
Martin Scott

BSFA 1989

Steven Pressfield 1943- US Historical
Ancient Greece

www.stevenpressfield.com

Bernard Cornwell
Michael Curtis Ford
Robert Graves

Conn Iggulden
Christian Jacq

Valerio Massimo Manfredi
Mary Renault

Douglas Preston 1956- US Adventure/Thriller

also writes jointly with **Lincoln Child**
www.prestonchild.com

Dan Brown
John Case
Lincoln Child

Michael Cordy
Sean Flannery
Lury Gibson

Brian Haig
Bill Napier
A J Quinnell

P

Anthony Price 1928- Adventure/Thriller
⚐ Dr David Audley

www.fantasticfiction.co.uk/authors/Anthony_Price.htm

Len Deighton
Clive Egleton
Brian Freemantle

John Le Carré
A J Quinnell
Julian Rathbone

CWA 1970 & 1974

Richard Price 1949- US Crime: Hardboiled

www.fantasticfiction.co.uk/authors/Richard_Price.htm

Bret Easton Ellis
James Ellroy

Walter Mosley
Chuck Palahniuk

George P Pelecanos

Robert T Price Sco Crime: Hardboiled
⚐ Kenny Madigan, Former car thief
Stratford-upon-Avon

www.fantasticfiction.co.uk/authors/Robert_M_Price.htm

Ron Ellis
Bill James

Mike Ripley
Mark Timlin

Go to back for lists of:
Authors by Genre • Characters and Series • Prize Winners • Further Reading

Christopher Priest   1943-   Science Fiction: Space and time

www.christopher-priest.co.uk

J G Ballard
Philip K Dick
Michael Moorcock

Robert Silverberg
H G Wells
Connie Willis

BSFA 1998 & 2002
Arthur C Clarke 2003

J B Priestley   1894-1984   General

www.jbpriestley.co.uk

R F Delderfield
John Galsworthy

W Somerset Maugham
Tim Pears

Anthony Powell
Angus Wilson

Annie Proulx   1935-   US   General

also wrote previously as **E Annie Proulx**
www.fantasticfiction.co.uk/authors/Annie_Proulx.htm

Margaret Atwood
Suzanne Berne
Thomas Eidson
Louise Erdrich

Fannie Flagg
Jonathan Franzen
Peter Hoeg
Donna Tartt

Irish Times 1993
Pulitzer 1994

Morag Prunty   1964-   Sco   Chick Lit

Cecelia Ahern
Colette Caddle

Claudine Cullimore
Melissa Hill

Monica McInerney
Jennifer Weiner

Malcolm Pryce   1960-   Crime: Humour

www.malcolmpryce.com   ⚐ Louie Knight - Aberystwyth

Colin Bateman
Marius Brill
Christopher Brookmyre

Christopher Buckley
Jasper Fforde

Christopher Fowler
Danny King

Philip Pullman   1946-   Fantasy

www.randomhouse.com/features/pullman/philippullman

Eoin Colfer
Neil Gaiman
Mary Gentle
C S Lewis

China Miéville
Garth Nix
Tim Powers
Michael Scott Rohan

J K Rowling

Whitbread 2002

D M Purcell   Saga

also wrote previously as **Deirdre Purcell**   Ireland
www.fantasticfiction.co.uk/authors/Deirdre_Purcell.htm

Elaine Crowley
Frank Delaney
Rose Doyle

Sheelagh Kelly
Geraldine O'Neill
Liz Ryan

Mary Ryan
Susan Sallis
Patricia Scanlan

P

Ann Purser
General

http://myweb.tiscali.co.uk/annpurser/index.html
'Round Ringford'

Anne Atkins	Jan Karon	Nora Naish
Marika Cobbold	Sybil Marshall	Miss Read
Erica James		

Ann Purser
Crime: Amateur sleuth

http://myweb.tiscali.co.uk/annpurser/index.html
🏃 Lois Meade, Cleaner - 'Long Farnden'

Caroline Graham	Veronica Heley	Marianne MacDonald
Ann Granger	Hazel Holt	Betty Rowlands

Libby Purves 1950-
General

www.fantasticfiction.co.uk/authors/Libby_Purves.htm

Lynne Reid Banks	Julia Lisle	Joanna Trollope
Candida Clark	Penelope Lively	Louise Voss
Patricia Gaffney	Elizabeth Palmer	Louise Wener
Sian James	Allison Pearson	Meg Wolitzer

P
Q

Mario Puzo 1920-1999 US
General

www.mariopuzo.com
🏃 The Godfather

Lorenzo Carcaterra	Harold Robbins
George V Higgins	Joseph Wambaugh

Thomas Pynchon 1937- US
General

www.fantasticfiction.co.uk/authors/Thomas_Pynchon.htm

Paul Auster	Vladimir Nabokov	Tom Robbins
Don Delillo	Richard Powers	Tom Wolfe
John Irving		

Andrew Pyper 1968- Can
Crime: Psychological

www.andrewpyper.com

Stephen King	Pernille Rygg	Erica Spindler
Dennis Lehane	John Saul	Stephen White

Amanda Quick 1948- US
Historical

also writes as Jayne Castle
is Jayne Ann Krentz
www.krentz-quick.com

Marion Chesney	Julie Garwood	Judith McNaught
Catherine Coulter	Georgette Heyer	Patricia Shaw

Anna Quindlen   1953-   US   General
www.fantasticfiction.co.uk/authors/Anna_Quindlen.htm

Elizabeth Berg   Alice Hoffman   Lorrie Moore
Margaret Forster   Elizabeth Jane Howard   Jane Smiley
Linda Grant   Susan Isaacs

A J Quinnell   1939-   Adventure/Thriller
www.fantasticfiction.co.uk/authors/A_J_Quinnell.htm   ⚑ Creasy, Ex-mercenary

Tom Bradby   Sean Flannery   Douglas Preston
Dan Brown   Gavin Lyall   Anthony Price
Lincoln Child   Alistair MacLean   Michael Shea
Michael Cordy   David Morrell   Mark T Sullivan

Robert Radcliffe   War: Modern

Andrew Greig   Derek Robinson
Gavin Lyall   Paul Watkins

Zane Radcliffe   1969-   Ire   Crime: Humour
www.fantasticfiction.co.uk/authors/Zane_Radcliffe.htm

Q Dave Barry   Christopher Brookmyre   James Hawes
R Colin Bateman   Christopher Buckley   Carl Hiaasen
       Marc Blake   Peter Guttridge

Alexandra Raife   Saga
www.fantasticfiction.co.uk/authors/Alexandra_Raife.htm   Scotland

Sophie Cooke   Mary Minton   Liz Ryan
Margaret Thomson Davis Robin Pilcher   Adriana Trigiani
Elizabeth Falconer   Elvi Rhodes   Anne Vivis

Patrick Rambaud   1946-   Fr   War: Historical
www.fantasticfiction.co.uk/authors/Patrick_Rambaud.htm   Napoleonic wars

Bernard Cornwell   Richard Howard
Garry Douglas   Allan Mallinson

Eileen Ramsay   Sco   Saga
www.eileenramsay.co.uk   Scotland

Emma Blair   Doris Davidson   Gwen Kirkwood
Jessica Blair   Adèle Geras   Isobel Neill
Maggie Craig   Nora Kay   Mary Withall

Alice Randall US General

www.alicerandall.com

Colleen McCullough
Toni Morrison
Alice Walker
Tom Wolfe

Ian Rankin 1960- Sco Crime: Police work - UK

also writes as **Jack Harvey**
www.ianrankin.net

✝ DI John Rebus & DC Siobhan Clarke
Edinburgh

CWA 1997

Bartholomew Gill
Alex Gray
Tobias Hill
Graham Hurley
Quintin Jardine
Bill Knox
Frederic Lindsay
Gay Longworth
Denise Mina
Chris Paling
David Peace
Nicholas Royle

Robert Rankin 1949- Science Fiction: Humour

www.fantasticfiction.co.uk/authors/Robert_Rankin.htm

Douglas Adams
Jasper Fforde
Rob Grant
Andrew Harman
Charlaine Harris
Harry Harrison
Tom Holt
Terry Pratchett
Martin Scott

Frederic Raphael 1931- US General

Saul Bellow
Howard Jacobson
Allan Massie
John Mortimer
Piers Paul Read

Julian Rathbone 1935- Adventure/Thriller R

www.fantasticfiction.co.uk/authors/Julian_Rathbone.htm

✝ Comm Jan Argand

John Gardner
Russell James
Amin Maalouf
Bernard MacLaverty
Anthony Price
Craig Thomas

Julian Rathbone 1935- Historical

www.fantasticfiction.co.uk/authors/Julian_Rathbone.htm

Philippa Gregory
Thomas Keneally
Matthew Kneale
Andrew Miller
Robert Nye
James Robertson
Barry Unsworth

Peter Rawlinson 1919- General

www.fantasticfiction.co.uk/authors/Peter_Rawlinson.htm

Jeffrey Archer
Michael Dobbs
Philip Hensher
Gwen Hunter
John Mortimer
Michael Shea
Nigel West

221

Melanie Rawn 1954- US   Fantasy: Epic
also writes as **Ellen Randolph**
www.melanierawn.com

Sarah Ash	Louise Cooper	Mercedes Lackey
Carol Berg	Barbara Hambly	Jan Siegel
Marion Zimmer Bradley	Katherine Kurtz	Margaret Weis

Sarah Rayne   Crime: Psychological
also writes as **Frances Gordon, Bridget Wood**; *is* **Bridget Wood**
www.sarahrayne.co.uk

| Hilary Bonner | Sarah Diamond | Margaret Murphy |
| Caroline Carver | Morag Joss | Minette Walters |

Claire Rayner 1931-   Saga
www.twbooks.co.uk/authors/crayner.html   ⚘ Tilly Quentin • Performers Series
                                                                      Poppy Chronicles

Anita Burgh	Charlotte Lamb	Judith Saxton
Winston Graham	Anne Melville	Alice Taylor
Beryl Kingston	Lesley Pearse	

Miss Read 1913-   Saga
is **Mrs Dora Saint**   Fairacre • Thrush Green
www.fantasticfiction.co.uk/authors/Miss_Read.htm

Jan Karon	Ann Purser	Sarah Shears
Sybil Marshall	Pam Rhodes	Anne Worboys
Mary E Pearce	Rebecca Shaw	

Piers Paul Read 1941-   General
www.contemporarywriters.com/authors/?p=auth213

Graham Greene	Paul Theroux	Hawthornden 1970
Bernard MacLaverty	Colin Thubron	Black 1988
Allan Massie	Angus Wilson	
Frederic Raphael		

Danuta Reah   Crime: Psychological
www.danutareah.co.uk

Jane Adams	John Connor	David Peace
Andrea Badenoch	Val McDermid	Alison Taylor
Stephen Booth	Ed O'Connor	Margaret Yorke

Patrick Redmond 1966-   Crime: Psychological

www.fantasticfiction.co.uk/authors/Patrick_Redmond.htm

Nicci French
Robert Goddard
Phil Lovesey

Val McDermid
Boris Starling

Tony Strong
Barbara Vine

Robert Reed 1956- US   Science Fiction: Space opera

www.starbaseandromeda.com/reed.html

Stephen Baxter
David Brin
John Brosnan

Arthur C Clarke
Greg Egan
Peter F Hamilton

John Meaney
Alastair Reynolds

Douglas Reeman 1924-   Sea: Modern

also writes as **Alexander Kent**   🏃 Mike Blackwood
www.bolithomaritimeproductions.com

Brian Callison
James Cobb

Hammond Innes
James Pattinson

Patrick Robinson
Antony Trew

Christopher Reich 1961- US   Crime: Legal/financial

www.fantasticfiction.co.uk/authors/Christopher_Reich.htm

Harry Bingham
John Grisham

Brad Meltzer
David Michie

Jonathan Nasaw
Sabin Willett

Mickey Zucker Reichert 1962- US   Fantasy: Epic

R

www.mickeyzuckerreichert.com

Terry Brooks
David Eddings
Raymond E Feist
Terry Goodkind

Mercedes Lackey
L E Modesitt Jr
Elizabeth Moon

R A Salvatore
Margaret Weis
Janny Wurts

Kathy Reichs 1950- US   Crime: Forensic

http://literati.net/Reichs   🏃 Dr Temperance Brennan, Pathologist
Montreal, North Carolina

Giles Blunt
Max Allan Collins
Patricia D Cornwell
Jeffery Deaver

Linda Fairstein
Lynn Hightower
Keith McCarthy
Nigel McCrery

Peter May
Carol O'Connell
Karin Slaughter
P J Tracy

> Go to back for lists of:
> Authors by Genre
> Characters and Series
> Prize Winners
> Further Reading

Carmen Reid   Sco   Chick Lit

www.fantasticfiction.co.uk/authors/Carmen_Reid.htm

Sarah Ball	Sue Haasler	Sharon Mulrooney
Jaye Carroll	Suzanne Higgins	Stephanie Zia
Anne Dunlop	Tara Manning	

Matthew Reilly   1974-   Aus   Adventure/Thriller

www.matthewreilly.com   ⚹ Capt Shane Schofield - US Marine Corps

Stephen Coonts	James Follett	David L Robbins
Harold Coyle	W E B Griffin	Craig Thomas
Clive Cussler		

Tina Reilly   Ire   Chick Lit

Jenny Colgan	Monica McInerney	Stephanie Theobald
Sabine Durrant	Tara Manning	Daisy Waugh
Imogen Edwards-Jones	Claudia Pattison	Laura Zigman

Paul Reizin   Lad Lit: Humour

Richard Asplin	Ben Hatch	Damien Owens
James Delingpole	Mil Millington	Alexei Sayle

Erich Maria Remarque   1898-1970   Ger   General

Pat Barker	Robert Graves
Sebastian Faulks	Paul Watkins

Mary Renault   1905-83   Historical

www.fantasticfiction.co.uk/authors/Mary_Renault.htm

Dorothy Dunnett	Conn Iggulden	Simon Scarrow
Howard Fast	Colleen McCullough	Manda Scott
Michael Curtis Ford	Valerio Massimo Manfredi	Wilbur Smith
Robert Graves	Steven Pressfield	Gore Vidal

Ruth Rendell   1930-   Crime: Police work - UK

also writes as **Barbara Vine**   ⚹ DCI George Wexford
www.fantasticfiction.co.uk/authors/Ruth_Rendell.htm   'Kingsmarkham'

Karin Fossum	Maureen O'Brien	CWA 1976, 1984 & 1986
Morag Joss	Julie Parsons	
Jim Kelly	Nicholas Rhea	
Sharyn McCrumb	Peter Robinson	June Thomson
J Wallis Martin	Dorothy Simpson	Laura Wilson

R

Alastair Reynolds   1966-   Wales   Science Fiction: Space opera

www.fantasticfiction.co.uk/authors/Alastair_Reynolds.htm

Kevin J Anderson
Neal Asher
William Gibson
Jack McDevitt

John Meaney
China Miéville
Richard Morgan
Robert Reed

BSFA 2001

Adam Roberts
Kim Stanley Robinson

Nicholas Rhea   1936-   Crime: Police work - UK

also writes as **Andrew Arncliffe**,
Christopher Coram, James Ferguson, Tom Ferris
is **Peter Norman Walker**
www.nicholasrhea.co.uk

⚡ PC Nick Parish -
'Adensfield', Yorkshire
DS Mark Pemberton
DI Montague Pluke

Robert Barnard
Caroline Graham
J M Gregson

Stuart Pawson
Ruth Rendell

Leslie Thomas
M J Trow

Elvi Rhodes   c1930-   Saga
Yorkshire

www.elvirhodes.com

Helen Cannam
Inga Dunbar
Elizabeth Gill

Sheelagh Kelly
Elisabeth McNeill
Alexandra Raife

Susan Sallis
Linda Sole
Anne Worboys

Pam Rhodes   Saga

Anne Atkins
Sybil Marshall
Elizabeth Noble

Miss Read
Kathleen Rowntree

Joanna Trollope
Ann Widdecombe

R

Anne Rice   1941-   US   Horror
Vampire Chronicles

also writes as **Anne Rampling**
www.annerice.com

Jonathan Aycliffe
Poppy Z Brite
Nancy Collins

Storm Constantine
Laurell K Hamilton
Tom Holland

Jeanne Kalogridis
Brian Lumley
Robert McCammon

Ben Richards   1964-   General

www.fantasticfiction.co.uk/authors/Ben_Richards.htm

Mavis Cheek
Douglas Coupland

Laurie Graham
Nick Hornby

Tony Parsons
Will Self

Go to back for lists of:
Authors by Genre • Characters and Series • Prize Winners • Further Reading

225

Phil Rickman　　　　　　　　　　　　　　　　　　Horror

also writes as Will Kingdom
www.philrickman.co.uk

Kelley Armstrong	Shaun Hutson	Stephen Laws
David Bowker	Graham Joyce	Scott Nicholson
James Herbert	Stephen King	Tim Wilson

Michael Ridpath　　1961-　　Adventure/Thriller: Legal/financial

www.michaelridpath.com

Harry Bingham	Linda Davies	Brad Meltzer
Po Bronson	Reg Gadney	Richard North Patterson
Jonathan Davies		

Liz Rigbey　　　　　　　　　　　　　　　　Crime: Psychological

Mary Higgins Clark	Nicci Gerrard	Julie Parsons
Anne Fine	Angela Green	

Gwendoline Riley　　1979-　　　　　　　　　　General

Anita Brookner	Wendy Perriam	Muriel Spark
Esther Freud	Ali Smith	Emma Tennant
Shena Mackay		

R

Mike Ripley　　1952-　　　　　　Crime: Amateur sleuth

www.fantasticfiction.co.uk/authors/Mike_Ripley.htm　　🏃 Fitzroy Maclean Angel, Taxi driver
London

Colin Bateman	Robert T Price	CWA 1989 & 1991
Alan Dunn	Mark Timlin	
Danny King		

William Rivière　　1954-　　　　　　　　　　General

www.fantasticfiction.co.uk/authors/William_Riviere.htm

Martin Booth	Allan Massie	Michael Ondaatje
James Hamilton-Paterson	Timothy Mo	

Candace Robb　　1950-　　US　　Crime: Historical - Medieval

www.candacerobb.com　　🏃 Owen Archer - C14th York
Margaret Kerr - C13th Scotland

Simon Beaufort	Susanna Gregory	Ellis Peters
Alys Clare	Bernard Knight	Kate Sedley
Margaret Frazer	Viviane Moore	

J D Robb   1950-   US   Crime: Police work - US

also writes as **Elly Wilder**
is **Nora Roberts**
www.noraroberts.com

       🏃 Eve Dallas
       Future New York

Pat Cadigan	Theresa Monsour	Carol O'Connell
Paul Johnston	Richard Morgan	Bruce Sterling
Ed McBain		

David L Robbins   US   War: Modern

www.davidlrobbins.com

W E B Griffin	Jack Harvey	Matthew Reilly
Eric L Harry	Leo Kessler	Terence Strong

Harold Robbins   1912-1997   US   Glitz & Glamour

www.fantasticfiction.co.uk/authors/Harold_Robbins.htm

Sandra Brown	Judi James	Mario Puzo
Jackie Collins	Frankie McGowan	Sidney Sheldon
Joan Collins		

Tom Robbins   1936-   US   General

www.fantasticfiction.co.uk/authors/Tom_Robbins.htm

Joseph Heller	Thomas Pynchon
John Irving	Tobias Wolff

Adam Roberts   1965-   Science Fiction: Space opera   **R**

www.adamroberts.com

Gene Brewer	Ken MacLeod	Alastair Reynolds
Eric Brown	John Meaney	Nick Sagan
Frank Herbert	China Miéville	Gene Wolfe

Barrie Roberts   1939-   Crime: Historical - C19th

www.barrieroberts.com

       🏃 Sherlock Holmes - C19th England
       Chris Tyroll, Lawyer - West Midlands

Boris Akunin	Arthur Conan Doyle	Roberta Rogow
Judith Cutler	Martin Edwards	M J Trow
David Dickinson	David Pirie	Gerard Williams

Cynthia S Roberts   Historical

Catrin Collier	Rosalind Laker	Grace Thompson
Gloria Cook	Catrin Morgan	Barbara Whitnell
Iris Gower	Patricia Shaw	Sarah Woodhouse

David Roberts

www.fantasticfiction.co.uk/authors/David_Roberts.htm

Crime: Historical - C20th

♣ Lord Edward Corinth & Verity Browne,
Journalist - 1930s England

Agatha Christie	Gladys Mitchell	Charles Todd
Barbara Cleverly	Rebecca Pawel	Stella Whitelaw
Ngaio Marsh	Dorothy L Sayers	

Michèle Roberts   1949-   Fr

General

www.contemporarywriters.com/authors/?p=auth109

Angela Carter	Sarah Kate Lynch	WHSmith 1993
Emma Donoghue	Anne Michaels	
Joanne Harris	Jeanette Winterson	
Janette Turner Hospital	Virginia Woolf	

Nora Roberts   1950-   US

General

also writes as J D Robb; *is* Elly Wilder

Three Sisters Island Trilogy

www.noraroberts.com

♣ Quinn Family

Virginia Andrews	Catherine Coulter	Maggie O'Farrell
Sandra Brown	Janet Dailey	Lynne Pemberton
Candace Bushnell	Jude Deveraux	Nicholas Sparks

Yvonne Roberts

General

Helen Fielding	Wendy Holden	Arundhati Roy
Laurie Graham	Tyne O'Connell	

R

Denise Robertson

Saga

♣ Beloved People Trilogy - NE England

Irene Carr	Margaret Graham	Eileen Stafford
Jean Chapman	Sheila Jansen	Janet MacLeod Trotter
Catherine Cookson		

James Robertson   Sco

Historical

William Boyd	Philip Hensher	Matthew Kneale
Margaret Elphinstone	Robin Jenkins	Julian Rathbone

Wendy Robertson

Saga

'Priorton', NE England

www.wendyrobertson.com

Irene Carr	Elizabeth Elgin	Brenda McBryde
Jean Chapman	Una Horne	Janet MacLeod Trotter
Josephine Cox	Sheila Jansen	Valerie Wood

Derek Robinson 1932- War: Modern

Francis Cottam
W E B Griffin
Robert Jackson

Leo Kessler
Gavin Lyall

Robert Radcliffe
Paul Watkins

Kim Stanley Robinson 1952- US Science Fiction: Near future

www.fantasticfiction.co.uk/authors/Kim_Stanley_Robinson.htm

BSFA 1992

Greg Bear
Ben Bova
China Miéville
Linda Nagata

Larry Niven
Alastair Reynolds
Brian Stableford
Sheri S Tepper

Leah Ruth Robinson US Crime: Medical

is Leah Robinson Rousmaniere
http://leahruthrobinson.com/index_flash.htm

🏃 Dr Evelyn Sutcliffe
New York

Paul Adam
Paul Carson

Robin Cook
Tess Gerritsen

Ken McClure
Michael Palmer

Patrick Robinson Ire Sea: Modern

www.patrickrobinson.com

Dale Brown
James Cobb
Douglas Reeman

Justin Scott
Peter Tonkin

Antony Trew
Robin White

Peter Robinson 1950- Crime: Police work - UK **R**

www.inspectorbanks.com

🏃 CI Alan Banks - Yorkshire

Rennie Airth
Robert Barnard
Pauline Bell
Janie Bolitho

Colin Dexter
Georgie Hale
Lesley Horton
Graham Hurley

Jim Kelly
Ruth Rendell
Dorothy Simpson
R D Wingfield

Justina Robson Science Fiction: Near future

www.justinarobson.co.uk

Eric Brown
William Gibson

Jon Courtenay Grimwood
Richard Morgan

Bruce Sterling

Kathy Rodgers Ire Chick Lit

Susannah Bates
Dawn Cairns

Jaye Carroll
Anne Dunlop

Sabine Durrant
Shari Low

Jane Rogers 1952- General

www.contemporarywriters.com/authors/?p=auth217

Margaret Atwood
Jane Gardam
Alison Lurie

Candia McWilliam
Hilary Mantel

S Maugham 1985

Roberta Rogow 1942- US Crime: Historical - C19th

www.fantasticfiction.co.uk/authors/Roberta_Rogow.htm

✦ Arthur Conan Doyle, Doctor
Victorian England

Arthur Conan Doyle
Ray Harrison
Laurie King

Alanna Knight
Anne Perry
David Pirie

Barrie Roberts
Norman Russell

Michael Scott Rohan 1951- Sco Fantasy

www.users.zetnet.co.uk/mike.scott.rohan

David Gemmell
Guy Gavriel Kay
Stephen R Lawhead

Adam Nichols
Tim Powers
Philip Pullman

J R R Tolkien
Tad Williams
Jonathan Wylie

Nancy Taylor Rosenberg 1946- US Crime: Legal/financial

www.nancytrosenberg.com

✦ Lily Forrester, DA - California

Alafair Burke
Carol Higgins Clark
Linda Fairstein

John T Lescroart
Phillip Margolin
Steve Martini

Perri O'Shaughnessy
Richard North Patterson
Susan R Sloan

R

Malcolm Ross 1932- Saga

also writes as Malcolm MacDonald, M R O'Donnell

Cornwall

Rosemary Aitken
Gloria Cook
Winston Graham

Elizabeth Ann Hill
Evelyn Hood
Beryl Kingston

Sue Sully
Barbara Whitnell

Philip Roth 1933- US General

www.kirjasto.sci.fi/proth.htm

Saul Bellow
Edward Docx
Joseph Heller
Alan Isler

Howard Jacobson
Rod Liddle
Jay McInerney
Rick Moody

Pulitzer 1998
WHSmith 2001 & 2004

Adam Thirlwell

Victoria Routledge 1975- Chick Lit

Trisha Ashley
Celia Brayfield

Victoria Colby
Sarah Harvey
Melissa Nathan

Robyn Sisman
Linda Taylor
Deborah Wright

Rosemary Rowe 1942-   Crime: Historical - Ancient

is Rosemary Aitken
www.raitken.wyenet.co.uk

⚐ Libertus, Mosaicist
Roman Britain

Lindsey Davis
Margaret Doody
Colleen McCullough

Allan Massie
Steven Saylor

Marilyn Todd
David Wishart

Laura Joh Rowland 1954- US   Crime: Historical - C17th

www.fantasticfiction.co.uk/authors/Laura_Joh_Rowland.htm

⚐ Sano Ichiro, Samurai
C17th Japan

James Clavell
Lindsey Davis

Michael Pearce
Christopher West

Betty Rowlands   Crime: Amateur sleuth

www.bettyrowlands.com

⚐ Melissa Craig, Writer - Cotswolds
Sukey Reynolds, Scene of crime officer

Janie Bolitho
Natasha Cooper
Marjorie Eccles

Ann Granger
Veronica Heley
Joyce Holms

Hazel Holt
Gwen Moffat
Ann Purser

J K Rowling 1965-   Fantasy: Epic

www.jkrowling.com

⚐ Harry Potter

Eoin Colfer
William Nicholson

Garth Nix
Philip Pullman

R

Kathleen Rowntree   Aga saga

Maeve Haran
Charlotte Moore
Nora Naish

Pam Rhodes
Jean Saunders
Ann Swinfen

Amanda Eyre Ward
Mary Wesley
Ann Widdecombe

Arundhati Roy 1961- Ind   General

www.fantasticfiction.co.uk/authors/Arundhati_Roy.htm

Monica Ali
Amit Chaudhuri

Bernardine Evaristo
R K Narayan

Yvonne Roberts
Vikram Seth

Kenneth Royce 1920-1997   Adventure/Thriller

also wrote as Oliver Jacks; *was* Kenneth Royce Gandley
www.fantasticfiction.co.uk/authors/Kenneth_Royce.htm

Clive Egleton
Robert Ludlum

Lawrence Sanders
Glover Wright

Nicholas Royle 1963- General
www.fantasticfiction.co.uk/authors/Nicholas_Royle.htm
🏃 Frank Warner, Journalist

John Harvey	Chris Paling	Martyn Waites
Quintin Jardine	Ian Rankin	

Bernice Rubens 1928-2004 General
www.fantasticfiction.co.uk/authors/Bernice_Rubens.htm

Barbara Anderson	Margaret Drabble	Booker 1970
Beryl Bainbridge	Pauline Melville	A N Wilson
Anita Brookner	Carolyn Slaughter	Jeanette Winterson

James Runcie Historical

Tracy Chevalier	Salley Vickers
Christopher Peachment	Susan Vreeland

Kristine Kathryn Rusch 1960- US Science Fiction: Space and time
also writes as **Kristine Grayson, Kris Nelscott, Sandy Schofield**
www.kristinekathrynrusch.com

Brian Herbert	J V Jones	Michael Moorcock
Robin Hobb	Michael P Kube-McDowell	R A Salvatore

Salman Rushdie 1947- General
www.kirjasto.sci.fi/rushdie.htm

R

Monica Ali	Shifra Horn	Black 1981
Anthony Burgess	Janette Turner Hospital	Booker 1981
Amit Chaudhuri	Yann Martel	Whitbread 1988 & 1995
Anita Desai	Gita Mehta	Vikram Seth
David Grossman	Michael Ondaatje	Marianne Wiggins

Norman Russell Crime: Historical - C19th
www.fantasticfiction.co.uk/authors/Norman_Russell.htm
🏃 DI Saul Jackson & Sgt Bottomley
Warwickshire, England

Arthur Conan Doyle	Joan Lock	Roberta Rogow
Ray Harrison	Peter Lovesey	M J Trow
Alanna Knight	Anne Perry	

Sean Russell 1952- Can Fantasy: Epic
www.sfsite.com/seanrussell

Stephen Donaldson	Jude Fisher	Robert Jordan
Steven Erikson	Robin Hobb	Greg Keyes

Willy Russell 1947- Lad Lit: Humour

www.fantasticfiction.co.uk/authors/Willy_Russell.htm

Simon Armitage	John Harding	John O'Farrell
Robert Chalmers	Nick Hornby	Matt Whyman

Edward Rutherfurd 1948- Historical

is Francis E Wintle

Jean M Auel	Philippa Gregory	Manda Scott
Bernard Cornwell	Colleen McCullough	Leon Uris
Dorothy Dunnett	James A Michener	

Chris Ryan 1961- Adventure/Thriller

www.fantasticfiction.co.uk/authors/Chris_Ryan.htm

Geoffrey Archer	Murray Davies	Stephen Hunter
Michael Asher	Duncan Falconer	Graham Hurley
Shaun Clarke	Joseph R Garber	David Mason
Conor Cregan	Johnny 'Two Combs' Howard	John Nichol

Liz Ryan Saga Ireland

www.irishwriters-online.com/lizryan.html

Maeve Binchy	Erin Kaye	Joan O'Neill
Elaine Crowley	Sheelagh Kelly	D M Purcell
Frank Delaney	Geraldine O'Neill	Alexandra Raife

R

Mary Ryan 1945 Ire General

Maeve Binchy	Frank Delaney	D M Purcell
Clare Boylan	Caro Fraser	Patricia Scanlan
Elaine Crowley	Joan O'Neill	

Robert Ryan Adventure/Thriller

www.robert-ryan.net

Francis Cottam	Joseph Kanon
Alan Furst	Guy Walters

Pernille Rygg 1963- Nor Crime: Psychological

Karin Alvtegen	Liza Marklund
Karin Fossum	Andrew Pyper
Henning Mankell	Maj Sjöwall and Per Wahlöö

Nick Sagan US Science Fiction: Near future

www.nicksagan.com

Greg Egan
William Gibson
Richard Morgan

Adam Roberts
Neal Stephenson

Bruce Sterling
Tad Williams

J D Salinger 1919- US General

www.kirjasto.sci.fi/salinger.htm

Nicola Barker
Harper Lee
Cormac McCarthy

Carson McCullers
Jay McInerney
Paul Micou

Edna O'Brien
D B C Pierre

James Sallis 1944- US Crime: Hardboiled

www.grasslimb.com/sallis

♣ Lew Griffin, Academic
New Orleans

Ace Atkins
James Lee Burke
Charlotte Carter

Raymond Chandler
Ross Macdonald
Patricia Melo

Walter Mosley
Cath Staincliffe

Susan Sallis 1929- Saga

also writes as **Susan Meadmore**

♣ Rising Family
West Country

www.fantasticfiction.co.uk/authors/Susan_Sallis.htm

Rosemary Aitken
Donna Baker
Louise Brindley

Gloria Cook
Elizabeth Elgin
Santa Montefiore

D M Purcell
Elvi Rhodes
Sally Stewart

R A Salvatore 1959- US Fantasy: Epic

www.rasalvatore.com

David A Drake
Mercedes Lackey
L E Modesitt Jr

Elizabeth Moon
Mickey Zucker Reichert
Kristine Kathryn Rusch

J R R Tolkien
Margaret Weis

Kevin Sampson Lad Lit

www.fantasticfiction.co.uk/authors/Kevin_Sampson.htm

Liverpool

Nicholas Blincoe
Dougie Brimson
Christopher Brookmyre
Paul Burke

Colin Butts
Cy Flood
John King

William Sutcliffe
Matt Thorne
Irvine Welsh

Go to back for lists of:
Authors by Genre • Characters and Series • Prize Winners • Further Reading

Polly Samson 1962- General

www.red-umbrella.co.uk

Raffaella Barker	Joanne Harris	Mona Simpson
Esther Freud	Nick Hornby	Barbara Trapido

Lawrence Sanders 1920-1998 US Adventure/Thriller

also writes as **Vincent Lardo** 🏃 Archie McNally
www.fantasticfiction.co.uk/authors/Lawrence_Sanders.htm

Jeffrey Archer	Michael Kimball	Sidney Sheldon
Brendan Dubois	John D Macdonald	Fred Vargas
Colin Harrison	Kenneth Royce	

Louis Sanders 1964- Fr Crime: Psychological
Dordogne, France
www.fantasticfiction.co.uk/authors/Louis_Sanders.htm

Juliet Hebden	Pierre Magnan	Margaret Yorke
Mark Hebden	Julie Parsons	

John Sandford 1944- US Crime: Police work - US

is **John R Camp** 🏃 Lucas Davenport - Minneapolis
www.johnsandford.org Kidd & LuEllen, Con artist & computer hacker - Mississippi

Alafair Burke	Stephen Hunter	Phillip Margolin
James Lee Burke	Michael Kimball	Jonathan Nasaw
Michael Connelly	David Lindsey	Ridley Pearson
Thomas H Cook	Michael Malone	James Siegel

C J Sansom Crime: Historical - C16th

🏃 Dr Matthew Shardlake
Henrician London
www.fantasticfiction.co.uk/authors/C_J_Sansom.htm

Michael Clynes	Philip Gooden	John Pilkington
Judith Cook	C C Humphreys	Martin Stephen
Patricia Finney	Edward Marston	Peter Tonkin

S

William Sarabande US Fantasy: Myth

www.fantasticfiction.co.uk/authors/William_Sarabande.htm

Piers Anthony	Julian May	T H White
Jean M Auel	Judith Tarr	

John Saul 1942- US Horror

www.johnsaul.com

Douglas Clegg	Dean R Koontz	Christopher Pike
Shaun Hutson	Robert McCammon	Andrew Pyper
Stephen King	Graham Masterton	

235

Jean Saunders 1932-

Aga saga

also writes as **Sally Blake, Jean Innes, Rachel Moore, Jodie Nicol, Rowena Summers**
http://hometown.aol.co.uk/jeanrowena/myhomepage/aboutme.html

Johanna Lindsey	Robin Pilcher	Kathleen Rowntree
Nora Naish	Rosamunde Pilcher	Madeleine Wickham

Kate Saunders

Aga saga

www.fantasticfiction.co.uk/authors/Kate_Saunders.htm

Claire Calman	Kate Hatfield	Robyn Sisman
Zoë Fairbairns	Angela Lambert	Mary Wesley
Philippa Gregory	Elizabeth Noble	

Alan Savage 1930-

War: Modern

is **Christopher Nicole**
www.fantasticfiction.co.uk/authors/Alan_Savage.htm

James Clavell	Eric Lustbader	David Morrell
Leo Kessler	Amin Maalouf	

Julian Jay Savarin

Adventure/Thriller

www.fantasticfiction.co.uk/authors/Julian_Jay_Savarin.htm

Geoffrey Archer	Stephen Coonts	Wilbur Smith
Campbell Armstrong	Clive Cussler	Craig Thomas
Dale Brown	Robert Jackson	

Diana Saville 1943-

Aga saga

Anne Atkins	Stevie Morgan	Peta Tayler
Clare Boylan	Robin Pilcher	Mary Wesley
Sarah Harrison		

S

Judith Saxton 1936-

Saga

also writes as **Kate Flynn**; *is* **Judy Turner**
www.fantasticfiction.co.uk/authors/Judith_Saxton.htm

⚘ Neyler Family

Teresa Crane	Mary Mackie	Claire Rayner
Janet Dailey	Beryl Matthews	Janet Tanner
Sara Hylton	Margaret Pemberton	Nicola Thorne

Paul Sayer 1955-

General

www.fantasticfiction.co.uk/authors/Paul_Sayer.htm

Ron Butlin	Duncan McLean	Ruaridh Nicoll
Janet Frame	Lorrie Moore	Tim Pears
		Alan Warner

Dorothy L Sayers 1893-1957 Crime: Amateur sleuth

www.sayers.org.uk

Margery Allingham
Agatha Christie
Martha Grimes

Hazel Holt
Michael Innes
Ngaio Marsh

David Roberts
Patricia Wentworth

Alexei Sayle 1952- Humour

www.fantasticfiction.co.uk/authors/Alexei_Sayle.htm

Stephen Fry
Charles Higson
Sean Hughes

Mil Millington
Paul Reizin

Will Self
Matt Thorne

Steven Saylor 1956- US Crime: Historical - Ancient
Gordianus the Finder
Ancient Rome

www.stevensaylor.com

Lindsey Davis
Margaret Doody
Valerio Massimo Manfredi

Allan Massie
Rosemary Rowe

Marilyn Todd
David Wishart

Patricia Scanlan Ire Chick Lit

www.fantasticfiction.co.uk/authors/Patricia_Scanlan.htm

Clare Boylan
Dawn Cairns
Martina Devlin

Jacinta McDevitt
D M Purcell
Mary Ryan

Robyn Sisman
Alice Taylor

Simon Scarrow Historical
Quintus Licinius Cato
C1st AD, Roman Europe

www.scarrow.fsnet.co.uk/author.htm

Lindsey Davis
Michael Curtis Ford
Pauline Gedge

Conn Iggulden
Colleen McCullough

Allan Massie
Mary Renault

Bernhard Schlink 1944- Ger General

Pat Barker
Alan Isler

Anne Michaels
Rachel Seiffert

William Styron

Christina Schwarz US Adventure/Thriller: Psychological

Mary Higgins Clark
Joy Fielding

Clare Francis
Sue Miller

Gloria Murphy
Susan R Sloan

S

Justin Scott 1944- US

www.fantasticfiction.co.uk/authors/Justin_Scott.htm

Sea: Modern
🏃 Ben Abbott

Brian Callison	James Follett	Nicholas Monsarrat
James Cobb	Richard Herman	Patrick Robinson
Clive Cussler	Eric Lustbader	Antony Trew

Manda Scott Sco

www.mandascott.co.uk

Historical
Roman Britain

Jean M Auel	Valerio Massimo Manfredi	Edward Rutherfurd
Conn Iggulden	Mary Renault	Leon Uris
Christian Jacq		

Martin Scott

is Martin Millar
www.martinmillar.com

Fantasy: Humour

Robert Asprin	Andrew Harman	Terry Pratchett
Neil Gaiman	Harry Harrison	Robert Rankin
Simon R Green	Tom Holt	

Paul Scott 1920-78

www.fantasticfiction.co.uk/authors/Paul_Scott.htm

General

Thalassa Ali	Pamela Jooste	Booker 1977
E M Forster	M M Kaye	
Nadine Gordimer	Lee Langley	
Ruth Prawer Jhabvala	Rohinton Mistry	Vikram Seth

Lisa Scottoline 1955- US

www.scottoline.com

Crime: Legal/financial
🏃 Rosato & Associates
Philadelphia

William Bernhardt	Craig Holden	Perri O'Shaughnessy
D W Buffa	John T Lescroart	Susan R Sloan
Linda Fairstein	Phillip Margolin	Erica Spindler
John Grisham	Steve Martini	Robert K Tanenbaum

Tim Sebastian 1952-

www.fantasticfiction.co.uk/authors/Tim_Sebastian.htm

Adventure/Thriller

Geoffrey Archer	Humphrey Hawksley	Gerald Seymour
Campbell Armstrong	Stephen Leather	Nigel West
Tom Bradby		

S

Alice Sebold   1963-   US   General

www.fantasticfiction.co.uk/authors/Alice_Sebold.htm

Kate Atkinson
Anita Diamant
Lesley Glaister

Mark Haddon
Zoë Heller
A M Homes

Hilary Mantel
Steve Martin
Ann Patchett

Kate Sedley   1926-   Crime: Historical - Medieval

is Brenda Clarke   ⚐ Roger the Chapman
www.fantasticfiction.co.uk/authors/Kate_Sedley.htm   C15th England

Alys Clare
Judith Cook
Margaret Frazer

Susanna Gregory
Michael Jecks
Bernard Knight

Viviane Moore
Ellis Peters
Candace Robb

Lisa See   US   Crime: Police work - China

www.lisasee.com   ⚐ David Stark, Attorney, & Insp Liu Hulan

Peter May
Barbara Nadel

Eliot Pattison
Christopher West

Qiu Xiaolong

Rachel Seiffert   1971-   General

www.fantasticfiction.co.uk/authors/Rachel_Seiffert.htm

Margaret Atwood
Trezza Azzopardi
Julian Barnes

Maggie Gee
Anne Michaels

Bernhard Schlink
Rose Tremain

Will Self   1961-   General

www.fantasticfiction.co.uk/authors/Will_Self.htm

J G Ballard
Glen Duncan
Bret Easton Ellis

Tobias Hill
Sean Hughes
Ben Richards

Faber 1993

Alexei Sayle
Matt Thorne

S

Andrea Semple   1976-   Chick Lit

www.andreasemple.com

Lynne Barrett-Lee
Victoria Corby
Shari Low

Stephanie Theobald
Sarah Webb

Laura Wolf
Stephanie Zia

Go to back for lists of:
Authors by Genre
Characters and Series
Prize Winners
Further Reading

Vikram Seth 1952- Ind General

www.contemporarywriters.com/authors/?p=auth89

Amit Chaudhuri
Bernardine Evaristo
Rumer Godden
Lee Langley

R K Narayan
Arundhati Roy
Salman Rushdie
Paul Scott

Commonwealth 1994
WHSmith 1994

Anya Seton 1916-90 Historical

www.fantasticfiction.co.uk/authors/Anya_Seton.htm

Sara Donati
Daphne Du Maurier
Sandra Gulland

Caroline Harvey
Victoria Holt
Robin Maxwell

Rosalind Miles
Diana Norman
Jean Stubbs

Gerald Seymour 1941- Adventure/Thriller

www.fantasticfiction.co.uk/authors/Gerald_Seymour.htm

Tom Bradby
James Buchan
John Burdett
John Fullerton

Paul Henke
Stephen Leather
Charles McCarry
Henry Porter

Tim Sebastian
James Siegel
Daniel Silva
Nigel West

Nicholas Shakespeare 1957- General

www.contemporarywriters.com/authors/?p=auth238

Malcolm Bradbury
Louis de Bernières
Graham Greene

James Hamilton-Paterson
Mario Vargas Llosa

S Maugham 1990

Laurence Shames 1951- US Crime: Humour

www.fantasticfiction.co.uk/authors/Laurence_Shames.htm

⚐ Peter Amsterdam, PI
Key West, Florida

S

Dave Barry
Anthony Bourdain
Bill Fitzhugh
Peter Guttridge

James Hall
Joe R Lansdale
José Latour
Shane Maloney

CWA 1995

John Shannon 1943- US Crime: PI

www.fantasticfiction.co.uk/authors/John_Shannon.htm

⚐ Jack Liffey - Los Angeles

Raymond Chandler
Michael Connelly
Robert Crais

Dennis Lehane
Marcia Muller
Sara Paretsky

Jefferson Parker
Robert B Parker

Zoë Sharp
www.zoesharp.com

Crime: Amateur sleuth
♕ Charlie Fox, Self-defence expert

Cara Black	Liz Evans	Val McDermid
Denise Danks	Sue Grafton	Sara Paretsky
Janet Evanovich	Lauren Henderson	Cath Staincliffe

Tom Sharpe   1928-
www.fantasticfiction.co.uk/authors/Tom_Sharpe.htm

Humour

Nicholson Baker	George Macdonald Fraser	Alan Isler
Joseph Connolly	James Hawes	Howard Jacobson
Roddy Doyle	Philip Hensher	Geoff Nicholson
Ruth Dudley Edwards	Tom Holt	Alan Titchmarsh

Patricia Shaw   1928-   Aus

Historical

Sheelagh Kelly	Amanda Quick	Eileen Townsend
Colleen McCullough	Cynthia S Roberts	Sarah Woodhouse
Margaret Pemberton	E V Thompson	

Rebecca Shaw
www.rebeccashaw.com

General
Barleybridge Series
Turnham Malpas Series

Anne Atkins	Karen Hayes	Jan Karon
Patricia Fawcett	Hazel Hucker	Miss Read
Kate Fielding	Erica James	Ann Widdecombe

Simon Shaw
www.fantasticfiction.co.uk/authors/Simon_Shaw.htm

Crime: Amateur sleuth
♕ Philip Fletcher - Theatre
Grace Cornish, PI - London

CWA 1990 & 1994

Marian Babson	Sarah Caudwell	
Robert Barnard	Denise Danks	
Simon Brett	Patricia Highsmith	Charles Spencer

S

Michael Shea   1938-   Sco
also writes as **Michael Sinclair**

General

Jeffrey Archer	Robert Harris	Peter Rawlinson
Michael Dobbs	Gavin Lyall	Nigel West
Ken Follett	A J Quinnell	

Go to back for lists of:
Authors by Genre • Characters and Series • Prize Winners • Further Reading

241

Sarah Shears

Saga

🚶 Annie Parsons • Franklin Family

Catrin Collier
Elizabeth Jeffrey
Brenda McBryde

Elisabeth McNeill
Anne Melville
Mary E Pearce

Miss Read
Alice Taylor
Barbara Whitnell

Mary Sheepshanks

General

Diana Appleyard
Cindy Blake
Lucy Clare

Kate Fenton
Sarah Grazebrook
Karen Hayes

Hazel Hucker
Nora Naish

Sidney Sheldon   1917-   US

Adventure/Thriller

www.sidneysheldon.com

Elizabeth Adler
Jeffrey Archer
Barbara Taylor Bradford

Lorenzo Carcaterra
Harold Robbins
Lawrence Sanders

Wilbur Smith
Danielle Steel

Lucius Shepard   1947-   US

Science Fiction: Near future

www.lucius-shepard.com

William Gibson
Jon Courtenay Grimwood
Joe Haldeman

Richard Powers
Dan Simmons
Bruce Sterling

Tad Williams
David Zindell

Carol Shields   1935-2003   Can

General

www.fantasticfiction.co.uk/authors/Carol_Shields.htm

Trezza Azzopardi
Joan Barfoot
Kate Bingham
Lynn Coady
Mary Lawson

Elinor Lipman
Alice McDermott
Anne-Marie MacDonald
Alistair MacLeod
Anne Michaels

Pulitzer 1995
Orange 1998

Donna Tartt
Marianne Wiggins

Anita Shreve   1946-   US

General

www.fantasticfiction.co.uk/authors/Anita_Shreve.htm

Elizabeth Berg
Suzanne Berne
Anita Diamant
Nikki Gemmell

Shirley Hazzard
Siri Hustvedt
J Robert Lennon
Alice McDermott

Maggie O'Farrell
Jodi Picoult
Nicholas Sparks
Robert James Waller

Go to back for lists of:
Authors by Genre • Characters and Series • Prize Winners • Further Reading

S

Nevil Shute 1899-1960   Adventure/Thriller

was Nevil Shute Norway
www.kirjasto.sci.fi/nshute.htm

Jon Cleary   Hammond Innes   Morris West
Ernest Hemingway   Nicholas Monsarrat

Anne Rivers Siddons 1936- US   Saga

www.anneriverssiddons.com

Pat Conroy   Olivia Goldsmith   Rosie Thomas
Janet Dailey   Carson McCullers   Adriana Trigiani
Karen Joy Fowler   Belva Plain   Rebecca Wells

James Siegel US   Adventure/Thriller

www.fantasticfiction.co.uk/authors/James_Siegel.htm

Dale Brown   John Sandford   Daniel Silva
Brendan Dubois   Gerald Seymour   Tony Strong
James Patterson

Jan Siegel   Fantasy: Epic

is Amanda Hemingway
www.fantasticfiction.co.uk/authors/Jan_Siegel.htm

Marion Zimmer Bradley   Robert Holdstock   Melanie Rawn
Mark Chadbourn   Juliet Marillier   Margaret Weis
Raymond E Feist   George R R Martin   Connie Willis

Jenny Siler US   Crime: Psychological

www.jennysiler.com

Tess Gerritsen   Tami Hoag   Karin Slaughter
Mo Hayder   Alex Kava   Jess Walter

S

Alan Sillitoe 1928-   General

www.kirjasto.sci.fi/sillitoe.htm

Kingsley Amis   David Lodge
D H Lawrence   Stanley Middleton

Daniel Silva US   Adventure/Thriller

www.danielsilvabooks.com   ⸙ Michael Osbourne - CIA

Brendan Dubois   Alan Judd   Gerald Seymour
Ian Fleming   John Le Carré   James Siegel
Frederick Forsyth

243

Robert Silverberg   1935-   US   Science Fiction: Space and time

also writes as Calvin M Knox, David Osborne, Robert Randall
www.majipoor.com

Arthur C Clarke	George R R Martin	Freda Warrington
David Eddings	Julian May	Roger Zelazny
Joe Haldeman	Christopher Priest	

Georges Simenon   1903-89   Belg   Crime: Police work - France

www.fantasticfiction.co.uk/authors/Georges_Simenon.htm   ⚘ Commissaire Jules Maigret - Paris

Andrea Camilleri	J Robert Janes	Daniel Pennac
Juliet Hebden	H R F Keating	Fred Vargas
Mark Hebden	Magdalen Nabb	

Dan Simmons   1948-   US   Science Fiction: Space opera

www.dansimmons.com

Kevin J Anderson	Arthur C Clarke	British Fantasy 1990
Neal Asher	Joe Haldeman	BSFA 1991
David Brin	Peter F Hamilton	
Orson Scott Card	Lucius Shepard	Charles Stross

Dan Simmons   1948-   US   Horror

www.dansimmons.com

Richard Bachman	Nancy Collins	Stephen King
Clive Barker	Jeanne Kalogridis	Bentley Little

Chris Simms   Crime: Psychological

www.fantasticfiction.co.uk/authors/Chris_Simms.htm

Mark Billingham	Denise Mina	Carol Smith
Nicci French	Margaret Murphy	Barbara Vine
Jim Kelly	Ed O'Connor	Laura Wilson

Paullina Simons   1963-   US   Adventure/Thriller

www.fantasticfiction.co.uk/authors/Paullina_Simons.htm

Alice Blanchard	John Gilstrap	Stephen Hunter
Pat Conroy	Gwen Hunter	Scott Smith
Jeffery Deaver		

Go to back for lists of:
Authors by Genre
Characters and Series
Prize Winners
Further Reading

S

Dorothy Simpson   1933-

www.fantasticfiction.co.uk/authors/Dorothy_Simpson.htm

Crime: Police work - UK

🏃 DI Luke Thanet & DS Lineham
'Sturrenden', Kent

CWA 1985

Meg Elizabeth Atkins	Hazel Holt	
Clare Curzon	Ngaio Marsh	
Caroline Graham	Ruth Rendell	Peter Robinson

Mona Simpson   1957-   US

www.fantasticfiction.co.uk/authors/Mona_Simpson.htm

General

Jane Hamilton	Alice Munro	Polly Samson
Alice Hoffman	Marge Piercy	Ann Widdecombe
Sue Miller		

Iain Sinclair   1943-

www.fantasticfiction.co.uk/authors/Iain_Sinclair.htm

General

Black 1991
Encore 1992

Peter Ackroyd	Alasdair Gray
Angela Carter	Tom Holland
Charles Dickens	Geoff Nicholson
Christopher Fowler	Robert Nye

Isaac Bashevis Singer   1904-1991   US

www.fantasticfiction.co.uk/authors/Isaac_Bashevis_Singer.htm

General

Saul Bellow	Alan Isler	Alexander Solzhenitsyn
David Grossman	Amos Oz	Leon Uris

Robyn Sisman   US

www.fantasticfiction.co.uk/authors/Robyn_Sisman.htm

General

Louise Bagshawe	Victoria Routledge	Patricia Scanlan
Olivia Goldsmith	Kate Saunders	

Maj Sjöwall and Per Wahlöö   1935-   Swe

www.kirjasto.sci.fi/sjowall.htm

Crime: Police work - Sweden

🏃 Martin Beck - Stockholm

Karin Alvtegen	John Harvey	Liza Marklund
Karin Fossum	Henning Mankell	Pernille Rygg

Carolyn Slaughter

General

Faber 1977

Thalassa Ali	Ruth Prawer Jhabvala
E M Forster	Bernice Rubens

S

Karin Slaughter US
www.karinslaughter.com

Crime: Forensic

🚶 Sara Linton, Medical examiner
'Heartsdale', Georgia

Max Allan Collins	Tess Gerritsen	Nigel McCrery
Patricia D Cornwell	Tami Hoag	Kathy Reichs
Linda Fairstein	Alex Kava	Jenny Siler
Lisa Gardner	Keith McCarthy	Erica Spindler

Susan R Sloan US
www.sloanbooks.com

Crime: Legal/financial

D W Buffa	Laura Lippman	Nancy Taylor Rosenberg
Linda Fairstein	Steve Martini	Christina Schwarz
John Grisham	Perri O'Shaughnessy	Lisa Scottoline
Alex Kava		

Gillian Slovo 1952- SA
www.contemporarywriters.com/authors/?p=auth235

General

Martin Edwards	Sara Paretsky
Lauren Henderson	Michelle Spring

Jane Smiley 1949- US
www.randomhouse.com/features/smiley

General

Thomas Eidson	Jacquelyn Mitchard	Pulitzer 1992
Kate Grenville	Marge Piercy	
Jane Hamilton	Anna Quindlen	
Peter Hoeg	Robert James Waller	Meg Wolitzer

S

Alexander McCall Smith 1948- Sco
www.randomhouse.com/features/mccallsmith/no1.html

Crime: PI

🚶 Precious Ramotswe - Botswana
Isabel Dalhousie - Edinburgh

Charlotte Carter	Tony Hillerman	Saga for Wit 2003
Veronica Heley	Valerie Wilson Wesley	

Ali Smith 1962- Sco
www.contemporarywriters.com/authors/?p=auth91

General

Kate Atkinson	A M Homes	Encore 2002
Ron Butlin	A L Kennedy	
Janice Galloway	Gwendoline Riley	Zoë Strachan

Carol Smith   Crime: Psychological

www.fantasticfiction.co.uk/authors/Carol_Smith.htm

Andrea Badenoch	Jenny Maxwell	Alison Taylor
Sarah Diamond	Gemma O'Connor	Minette Walters
Elizabeth McGregor	Chris Simms	Laura Wilson

Martin Cruz Smith   1942-   US   Crime: Police work - Russia

also writes as **Martin Quinn, Simon Quinn**   ⚇ Insp Arkady Renko - USSR
http://literati.net/MCSmith

CWA 1981

Stephen J Cannell	José Latour	
Dan Fesperman	Peter May	Eliot Pattison
Philip Kerr	Jefferson Parker	Joseph Wambaugh

Michael Marshall Smith   1965-   Science Fiction: Near future

also writes as **Michael Marshall**
www.michaelmarshallsmith.com

British Fantasy 1995

Gene Brewer	James Lovegrove	
John Crowley	China Miéville	
Christopher Fowler	Jeff Noon	
William Gibson	Neal Stephenson	

Scott Smith   1965-   US   Adventure/Thriller

Alice Blanchard	Donald Harstad	Paullina Simons
John Gilstrap	Andrew Klavan	

Wilbur Smith   1933-   Zam   Adventure/Thriller

www.wilbursmithbooks.com

Michael Asher	Nelson DeMille	Paul Henke
Bryce Courtenay	June Drummond	Julian Jay Savarin
John Gordon Davis	Jean-Christophe Grangé	Sidney Sheldon

S

Wilbur Smith   1933-   Zam   Historical

www.wilbursmithbooks.com

Joy Chambers	Christian Jacq	Mary Renault
Pauline Gedge	Colleen McCullough	Peter Watt
Margaret George	Valerio Massimo Manfredi	

Go to back for lists of:
Authors by Genre
Characters and Series
Prize Winners
Further Reading

Zadie Smith   1975-   General

Monica Ali
Amit Chaudhuri
Hanif Kureishi
Jhumpa Lahiri
Andrea Levy
Meera Syal
Louisa Young

Black 2000	WHSmith 2000
Guardian 2000	Betty Trask 2001
Pulitzer 2000	Sunday Times 2001
Whitbread 2000	Wingate 2003

Linda Sole   Saga

also writes as **Lynn Granville, Anne Herries, Emma Quincey**   Rose Saga
www.lindasole.co.uk

Emma Dally   Elvi Rhodes   Kate Tremayne
Margaret Dickinson   E V Thompson   Anne Vivis
Evelyn Hood   Grace Thompson

Alexander Solzhenitsyn   1918-   Rus   General

www.kirjasto.sci.fi/alesol.htm

Vladimir Nabokov   Amos Oz   Isaac Bashevis Singer

S P Somtow   1952-   Thai   Horror

http://somtow.net/lit.html

Alice Borchardt   Nancy Collins   H P Lovecraft
Poppy Z Brite   Tom Holland   Steven Spruill
Ramsey Campbell   Jeanne Kalogridis

Muriel Spark   1918-   Sco   General

www.nls.uk/murielspark

S Lynne Reid Banks   Shena Mackay   Julie Myerson
Nina Bawden   Candia McWilliam   Gwendoline Riley
Doris Lessing   Iris Murdoch   William Trevor

Nicholas Sparks   1965-   US   General

www.nicholassparks.com

Nicholas Evans   Anita Shreve   Rosie Thomas
Nora Roberts   Nancy Thayer   Robert James Waller

Alan Spence   1947-   Sco   General

Des Dillon   Andrew Greig   Duncan McLean
Anne Donovan   Robin Jenkins   Andrew O'Hagan
Janice Galloway   Gordon Legge   Agnes Owens

Charles Spencer
1955-

Crime: Amateur sleuth

www.fantasticfiction.co.uk/authors/Charles_Spencer.htm

🏃 Will Benson, Showbiz writer

Marian Babson	Jonathan Gash	Simon Shaw
Simon Brett	Peter Guttridge	Donald E Westlake

John B Spencer
1947-2002

Crime: Hardboiled
London

www.johnbspencer.com

Jake Arnott	James Ellroy	Russell James
Colin Bateman	George V Higgins	Simon Kernick
Anthony Bourdain		

LaVyrle Spencer
1943- US

Saga

also writes as **Elizabeth Gage**
www.fantasticfiction.co.uk/authors/LaVyrle_Spencer.htm

Janet Dailey	Fern Michaels	Belva Plain
Barbara Delinsky	Una-Mary Parker	Danielle Steel
Judith McNaught	Lynne Pemberton	

Sally Spencer

Saga

also writes as **Alan Rustage, James Garcia Woods**
www.alanrustage.com

🏃 Becky Worrell - London
Taylor Family - Midlands

Donna Baker	Pamela Evans	Gilda O'Neill
Charlotte Bingham	Margaret Graham	Victor Pemberton
Helen Carey	Jenny Oldfield	

Sally Spencer

Crime: Police work - UK

also writes as **Alan Rustage, James García Woods**
www.alanrustage.com

🏃 DCI Charlie Woodend -
Lancashire, England
Insp Sam Blackstone - C19th London

S

Meg Elizabeth Atkins	John Gardner	J M Gregson
Janie Bolitho	Caroline Graham	John Harvey
Colin Dexter	Ann Granger	June Thomson

Erica Spindler
US

Crime: Psychological

www.ericaspindler.com

Lisa Gardner	Iris Johansen	Andrew Pyper
Daniel Hecht	Alex Kava	Lisa Scottoline
Christiane Heggan	Jonathan Kellerman	Karin Slaughter
Tami Hoag	Meg O'Brien	Stephen White

Go to back for lists of:
Authors by Genre • Characters and Series • Prize Winners • Further Reading

Michelle Spring   Can   Crime: PI

www.lydmouth.demon.co.uk/us/michelle/spring.htm   🏃 Laura Principal - Cambridge

Judith Cutler	Graham Hurley	Gillian Slovo
Liz Evans	Jim Kelly	Veronica Stallwood

Steven Spruill   1946-   US   Horror

also writes as **Steven Harriman**
www.fantasticfiction.co.uk/authors/Steven_Spruill.htm

Laurell K Hamilton	Tanya Huff	Robert McCammon
Thomas Harris	Jeanne Kalogridis	S P Somtow
James Herbert		

Dana Stabenow   1952-   US   Crime: PI

www.stabenow.com   🏃 Kate Shugak • Sgt Liam Campbell
Alaska

Linda Barnes	Meg Gardiner	Donald Harstad
Giles Blunt	Sue Grafton	Theresa Monsour
C J Box	Steve Hamilton	Sara Paretsky

Brian Stableford   1948-   Science Fiction: Technical

also writes as **Francis Amery, Brian Craig**
http://freespace.virgin.net/diri.gini/brian.htm

Gregory Benford	Ian McDonald	Ian Watson
Colin Greenland	Kim Stanley Robinson	David Zindell

Lyndon Stacey   Adventure/Thriller: horse racing

www.fantasticfiction.co.uk/authors/Lyndon_Stacey.htm

Dick Francis	Jenny Pitman
John Francome	Richard Pitman

S

Eileen Stafford   Saga

Bristol

Brenda Clarke	Connie Monk	Sue Sully
Elizabeth Ann Hill	Denise Robertson	Janet Tanner

Cath Staincliffe   1956-   Crime: PI

www.fantasticfiction.co.uk/authors/Cath_Staincliffe.htm   🏃 Sal Kilkenny - Manchester

John Baker	Ron Ellis	James Sallis
Cara Black	Mandasue Heller	Zoë Sharp
John Connor	Frank Lean	Valerie Wilson Wesley
Denise Danks	Walter Mosley	Stella Whitelaw

Veronica Stallwood

www.veronicastallwood.com

Crime: Amateur sleuth

🏃 Kate Ivory, Writer - Oxford

Natasha Cooper	Anabel Donald	Marianne Macdonald
Colin Dexter	Susan B Kelly	Michelle Spring

Mary Jane Staples 1911-

Saga

also writes as **James Sinclair, Reginald Staples**
www.fantasticfiction.co.uk/authors/Mary_Jane_Staples.htm

🏃 Staples Family - London
Adams Family

Harry Bowling	Harry Cole	Beryl Matthews
Benita Brown	Elizabeth Lord	Victor Pemberton
Helen Carey	Gwen Madoc	Audrey Willsher

Boris Starling

www.borisstarling.com

Crime: Psychological

Mark Billingham	Phil Lovesey	Patrick Redmond
John Connolly	Val McDermid	Tony Strong
Mo Hayder	James Patterson	P J Tracy

Jason Starr 1966- US

Crime: Hardboiled

http://members.aol.com/JasonStarr/index.html

James Crumley	Vicki Hendricks	Jim Thompson
James Ellroy	Boston Teran	

Danielle Steel 1947- US

Saga

www.daniellesteel.com

Barbara Taylor Bradford	Susan Lewis	Margaret Pemberton
Barbara Delinsky	Judith McNaught	Sidney Sheldon
Jude Deveraux	Una-Mary Parker	LaVyrle Spencer

John Steinbeck 1902-68 US

General

www.steinbeck.org

F Scott Fitzgerald	Jack Kerouac	Joyce Carol Oates
Ernest Hemingway	Harper Lee	William Styron
William Kennedy	Norman Mailer	Leon Uris

Martin Stephen

www.fantasticfiction.co.uk/authors/Martin_Stephen.htm

Crime: Historical - C17th

🏃 Henry Gresham, Royal agent
C17th England

Judith Cook	C C Humphreys	John Pilkington
Patricia Finney	Alanna Knight	C J Sansom
Philip Gooden	Edward Marston	

S

Kay Stephens Saga

Stonemoor Series - Yorkshire

Aileen Armitage
Anne Bennett
Helen Cannam

Alexandra Connor
Inga Dunbar
Elizabeth Elgin

Kate Tremayne
Elizabeth Walker
Valerie Wood

Neal Stephenson   1959-   US   Science Fiction: Near future

also writes as **Stephen Bury**
www.well.com./user/neal

Steve Aylett
Eric Brown
Greg Egan
Jon Courtenay Grimwood

Gwyneth Jones
James Lovegrove
Jeff Noon
Richard Powers

Arthur C Clarke 2004

Nick Sagan
Michael Marshall Smith

Bruce Sterling   1954-   US   Science Fiction: Near future

www.fantasticfiction.co.uk/authors/Bruce_Sterling.htm

Steve Aylett
Eric Brown
James Lovegrove
Richard Morgan

Richard Powers
J D Robb
Justina Robson
Nick Sagan

Arthur C Clarke 2000

Lucius Shepard
Tad Williams

Jane Stevenson   1959-   Sco   Historical

Tracy Chevalier
Dorothy Dunnett
Matthew Kneale

Andrew Miller
Robert Nye

Rose Tremain
Sarah Waters

Mary Stewart   1916-   Sco   General

www.fantasticfiction.co.uk/authors/Mary_Stewart.htm

Helen Hollick
M M Kaye
Susanna Kearsley

Judith Lennox
Barbara Michaels
Rosalind Miles

Sharon Penman
Lindsay Townsend
Anne Worboys

S

Sally Stewart Saga

Betty Burton
Elizabeth Daish
Margaret Graham

Sheila Jansen
Jenny Oldfield
Rosamunde Pilcher

Susan Sallis
Judith Summers

Caroline Stickland   1955- Saga

Dorset

Brenda Clarke
Harriet Hudson

Malcolm Macdonald
Mary E Pearce
Marge Piercy

Janet Tanner
Patricia Wendorf
T R Wilson

Jessica Stirling 1935- Sco

also writes as **Caroline Crosby, Hugh C Rae**
www.fantasticfiction.co.uk/authors/Jessica_Stirling.htm

Saga

🏃 Clare Kelso
Nicholson Family • Patterson Family
Holly Beckman - Glasgow • Conway Family
Scotland

Emma Blair	Margaret Thomson Davis	Nora Kay
Maggie Craig	Christine Marion Fraser	Isobel Neill
Doris Davidson	Meg Hutchinson	Kirsty White

Julian Stockwin 1944-

www.julianstockwin.com

Sea: Historical

🏃 Thomas Paine Kydd
C18th/19th England

David Donachie	Jonathan Lunn	Dan Parkinson
C S Forester	James L Nelson	Showell Styles
Alexander Kent	Marcus Palliser	

Zoë Strachan 1975- Sco

www.fantasticfiction.co.uk/authors/Zoe_Strachan.htm

General

Isla Dewar	Janice Galloway
Anne Donovan	Ali Smith

Peter Straub 1943- US

www.peterstraub.net

Horror

Richard Bachman	Stephen Laws	Robert McCammon
Jonathan Carroll	Richard Laymon	Richard Matheson
John Farris	H P Lovecraft	T M Wright
Dean R Koontz		

Darin Strauss

www.darinstrauss.com

General

S

John Banville	Kazuo Ishiguro
Andrew Sean Greer	Vladimir Nabokov

Whitley Strieber 1945- US

www.fantasticfiction.co.uk/authors/Whitley_Strieber.htm

Horror

Ramsey Campbell	Dean R Koontz	David Martin
John Farris	Robert McCammon	Graham Masterton
Shaun Hutson		

Go to back for lists of:
Authors by Genre
Characters and Series
Prize winners
Further Reading

Sarah Strohmeyer   US   Crime: Humour

www.sarahstrohmeyer.com   ⵡ Bubbles Yablonsky, Journalist
                                                         Lehigh, Pennsylvania

Linda Barnes	Liz Evans	Susan Isaacs
Anthony Bourdain	Sue Grafton	Pauline McLynn
Janet Evanovich	Sparkle Hayter	Donald E Westlake

Terence Strong   1946-   War: Modern

www.fantasticfiction.co.uk/authors/Terence_Strong.htm

James Adams	Duncan Harding	Paul Henke
Brian Callison	Jack Harvey	David L Robbins
W E B Griffin		

Tony Strong   1962-   Crime: Psychological

www.fantasticfiction.co.uk/authors/Tony_Strong.htm   ⵡ Terry Williams

Mark Billingham	James Siegel	Scott Turow
Phil Lovesey	Boris Starling	Barbara Vine
Patrick Redmond	P J Tracy	Minette Walters

Charles Stross   1964-   Science Fiction: Space opera

www.fantasticfiction.co.uk/authors/Charles_Stross.htm

Poul Anderson	Orson Scott Card	Brian Herbert
Iain M Banks	Peter F Hamilton	Dan Simmons
Lois McMaster Bujold		

Alison Stuart   Saga
                                                              London

Betty Burton	Elizabeth Lord	Janet Tanner
Pamela Evans	Gilda O'Neill	Dee Williams
Sara Fraser	Jean Stubbs	Audrey Willsher

S

Jean Stubbs   1926-   Saga
                                                      Howarth Chronicles

Winston Graham	Anya Seton	Janet Tanner
Susan Howatch	Alison Stuart	Nicola Thorne
Maureen Peters	Reay Tannahill	

Showell Styles   1908-2005   Sea: Historical
                                                         ⵡ Mr Fitton

C S Forester	Patrick O'Brian	Julian Stockwin
James L Nelson	Marcus Palliser	Victor Suthren
	Dudley Pope	Richard Woodman

William Styron   1925-   US   General

www.fantasticfiction.co.uk/authors/William_Styron.htm

Saul Bellow	Ernest Hemingway	John Steinbeck
Pat Conroy	Norman Mailer	Alice Walker
William Faulkner	Bernhard Schlink	

Mark T Sullivan   US   Adventure/Thriller

www.marktsullivan.com

John Case	Vince Flynn	Gareth O'Callaghan
Sean Flannery	Brian Haig	A J Quinnell

Sue Sully   Saga
West Country

Donna Baker	Audrey Howard	Belva Plain
Anita Burgh	Susan Howatch	Malcolm Ross
Daphne Du Maurier	Mary Mackie	Eileen Stafford

Judith Summers   1953-   General

Sarah Grazebrook	Karen Nelson	Sally Stewart
Marian Keyes	Lynne Pemberton	Grace Wynne-Jones

William Sutcliffe   1971-   Humour

www.fantasticfiction.co.uk/authors/William_Sutcliffe.htm

Matthew Beaumont	Kevin Sampson	Matt Thorne
Matthew Branton	Sean Thomas	Evelyn Waugh
Alex Garland		

Titia Sutherland   General **S**

Louise Brindley	Helen Humphreys	Peta Tayler
Amanda Brookfield	Sian James	Louise Voss
Zoë Fairbairns	Elizabeth Palmer	

Victor Suthren   Can   Sea: Historical

Tom Connery	Patrick O'Brian	Antony Trew
C S Forester	Showell Styles	Richard Woodman

Go to back for lists of:
Authors by Genre
Characters and Series
Prize Winners
Further Reading

Graham Swift 1949-   General

www.contemporarywriters.co.uk/authors/?p=auth93

Julian Barnes   Lawrence Norfolk
Peter Benson   Rose Tremain
John Fowles   Gillian White
Maggie Gee   T R Wilson
Magnus Mills

Faber 1983
Guardian 1983
Holtby 1983
Black 1996
Booker 1996

Madge Swindells   Glitz & Glamour

www.fantasticfiction.co.uk/authors/Madge_Swindells.htm

Alexandra Campbell   Judith Krantz   Barbara Michaels
Jackie Collins   Jayne Ann Krentz   Caroline Upcher
Judith Gould   Johanna Lindsey

Ann Swinfen   Aga saga

Katie Fforde   Elizabeth Palmer   Kathleen Rowntree
Rebecca Gregson   Robin Pilcher   Amanda Eyre Ward
Elizabeth Jane Howard Rosamunde Pilcher   Jane Yardley

Meera Syal 1963-   General

www.contemporarywriters.co.uk/authors/?p=auth94

Monica Ali   Hanif Kureishi   Zadie Smith
Chitra Banerjee Divakaruni   Harper Lee   Louisa Young
Esther Freud   Andrea Levy

Amy Tan 1952- US   General

www.fantasticfiction.co.uk/authors/Amy_Tan.htm

Regi Claire   David Guterson   Timothy Mo
Anita Desai   Barbara Kingsolver   Toni Morrison
Arthur Golden   Catherine Lim   Alice Munro

Robert K Tanenbaum   US   Crime: Legal/financial

www.fantasticfiction.co.uk/authors/Robert_K_Tanenbaum.htm

⚲ Roger 'Butch' Karp,
Asst Chief DA - New York

D W Buffa   Frances Fyfield   Steve Martini
Loren D Estleman James Grippando   Perri O'Shaughnessy
Linda Fairstein   Steve Hamilton   Lisa Scottoline

Go to back for lists of:
Authors by Genre • Characters and Series • Prize Winners • Further Reading

Reay Tannahill
1929- Sco **Historical**

Inga Dunbar
Dorothy Dunnett
Barbara Erskine
Diana Gabaldon

Philippa Gregory
Cynthia Harrod-Eagles
Lee Langley
Jean Stubbs

Anne Vivis

Janet Tanner
Saga

🏃 Hillsbridge Family - Somerset

Sara Fraser
Malcolm Macdonald
Connie Monk

Judith Saxton
Eileen Stafford
Caroline Stickland

Jean Stubbs
Alison Stuart

Judith Tarr
US **Fantasy:** Myth

www.sff.net/people/judith-tarr/library.html

Storm Constantine
Katharine Kerr

Ursula K Le Guin
William Sarabande

T H White

Donna Tartt
1963- US **General**

www.donnatartt.co.uk

Margaret Atwood
Suzanne Berne
Edward Docx
Robert Edric

Jeffrey Eugenides
Jonathan Franzen
Carol Goodman
Annie Proulx

Carol Shields

June Tate
1930s **Saga**

WW2

Elizabeth Elgin
June Francis
Lilian Harry

Beryl Kingston
Beryl Matthews
Annie Murray

Sheila Newberry
Gilda O'Neill
Dee Williams

Peta Tayler
Aga saga

Clare Boylan
Sarah Challis
Lucy Clare

Patricia Fawcett
Stevie Morgan
Nora Naish

Elizabeth Palmer
Diana Saville
Titia Sutherland

T

Alice Taylor
Ire **Saga**

Maeve Binchy
Clare Boylan
Patricia Grey

Elizabeth Murphy
Claire Rayner
Patricia Scanlan

Sarah Shears
Margaret Thornton

257

Alison Taylor

Wales   **Crime: Psychological**

also writes as **Alison G Taylor**
www.alisontaylor.net

♟ DCI Michael McKenna
North Wales

Jane Adams	Stephen Booth	Danuta Reah
Janie Bolitho	Gay Longworth	Carol Smith
Hilary Bonner	Ed O'Connor	Margaret Yorke

Andrew Taylor

1951-   **Crime: Police work - UK**

also writes as **Andrew Saville, John Robert Taylor**
www.andrew-taylor.net

♟ Jill Francis & DI Richard Thornhill -
'Lydmouth', 1950s Welsh Borders
Roth Trilogy - North London

CWA 1982, 2001 & 2003

Ann Cleeves	David Williams
John Gardner	Laura Wilson
Gregory Hall	R D Wingfield

Elizabeth Russell Taylor

d.2001   **General**

Sue Gee	Ian McEwan
Elizabeth Knox	David Mitchell

Linda Taylor

Humour

www.fantasticfiction.co.uk/authors/Linda_Taylor.htm

Faith Bleasdale	Cathy Kelly	Chris Manby
Jane Green	Marian Keyes	Victoria Routledge

Michael Taylor

Saga

www.michaeltaylorauthor.com

R F Delderfield	Douglas Kennedy	E V Thompson
Laurent Joffrin	Lesley Pearse	Kate Tremayne

Emma Tennant

1937-   Sco   **General**

also writes as **Catherine Aydy**
www.fantasticfiction.co.uk/authors/Emma_Tennant.htm

Jane Austen	Esther Freud	Gwendoline Riley
Hilary Bailey	Iris Murdoch	Fay Weldon
Penelope Fitzgerald	Wendy Perriam	

Sheri S Tepper

1929-   US   **Fantasy: Epic**

also writes as **B J Oliphant, A J Orde**
www.fantasticfiction.co.uk/authors/Sheri_S_Tepper.htm

Marion Zimmer Bradley	Mary Gentle	Ursula K Le Guin
C J Cherryh	Frank Herbert	Megan Lindholm
	Gwyneth Jones	Kim Stanley Robinson

T

Boston Teran US

www.fantasticfiction.co.uk/authors/Boston_Teran.htm

Crime: Hardboiled

🏃 Sheriff John Victor Sully - California

CWA 2000

Alice Blanchard
James Crumley
James Ellroy
Robert Ferrigno
Thomas Harris
Dennis Lehane
Jason Starr

Elizabeth Tettmar General

Margaret Forster
Elizabeth Jane Howard
Angela Huth
Angela Lambert

Josephine Tey 1897-1952 Sco

was Elizabeth MacIntosh

www.fantasticfiction.co.uk/authors/Josephine_Tey.htm

Crime: Police work - UK

🏃 DI Alan Grant
London

Margery Allingham
John Gardner
Patricia Highsmith
Michael Innes
Ngaio Marsh

James Thayer US Adventure/Thriller

www.jamesthayer.com

Tom Clancy
Harold Coyle
Clive Cussler
Frederick Forsyth
Richard Herman
Jack Higgins

Nancy Thayer US General

www.nancythayer.com

Alison Fell
Janice Graham
Colleen McCullough
Rosamunde Pilcher
Nicholas Sparks
Robert James Waller

Stephanie Theobald Chick Lit

Jenny Colgan
Helen Fielding
Amy Jenkins
Tina Reilly
Andrea Semple
Kate Thompson
Stephanie Zia

T

Paul Theroux 1941- US General

www.fantasticfiction.co.uk/authors/Paul_Theroux.htm

Pat Conroy
Giles Foden
Abdulrazak Gurnah
Ernest Hemingway
Yann Martel
Piers Paul Read
Adam Thorpe
Colin Thubron

Whitbread 1978
Black 1981
S Maugham 2002

Go to back for lists of:
Authors by Genre • Characters and Series • Prize Winners • Further Reading

Adam Thirlwell 1978- General

www.contemporarywriters.com/authors/?p=auth03B5O533312634989

Edward Docx	Rod Liddle
Howard Jacobson	Philip Roth

Craig Thomas 1942- Adventure/Thriller

also writes as **David Grant**
www.fantasticfiction.co.uk/authors/Craig_Thomas.htm

Geoffrey Archer	Jack Higgins	Julian Rathbone
Harold Coyle	Mike Lunnon-Wood	Matthew Reilly
James Follett	John J Nance	Julian Jay Savarin

Leslie Thomas 1931- Wales General

www.fantasticfiction.co.uk/authors/Leslie_Thomas.htm

Wales

George Macdonald Fraser	Geoff Nicholson	Alan Titchmarsh
Joseph Heller	David Nobbs	Keith Waterhouse
David Lodge		

Leslie Thomas 1931- Wales Crime: Police work - UK

www.fantasticfiction.co.uk/authors/Leslie_Thomas.htm

ẋ 'Dangerous' Davies

Natasha Cooper	Nick Oldham
Anabel Donald	Nicholas Rhea

Rosie Thomas 1947- Wales Saga

also writes as **Jancy King**
www.fantasticfiction.co.uk/authors/Rosie_Thomas.htm

Barbara Taylor Bradford	Belva Plain	Romantic 1985
Candida Clark	Anne Rivers Siddons	
Josephine Hart	Nicholas Sparks	
Lynne Pemberton	Sophia Watson	

Scarlett Thomas 1973- Crime: Amateur sleuth

www.fantasticfiction.co.uk/authors/Scarlett_Thomas.htm

ẋ Lily Pascale - Devon

T

Judith Cutler	Sparkle Hayter	Rebecca Tope
Janet Evanovich	Lauren Henderson	Stella Whitelaw
Liz Evans	Joyce Holms	

Sean Thomas 1963- Lad Lit

David Baddiel	Nick Hornby	Tony Parsons
Colin Butts	Tim Lott	William Sutcliffe

E V Thompson 1931-   Historical

also writes as **James Munro**   ☆ Retallick Family
www.fantasticfiction.co.uk/authors/E_V_Thompson.htm

Gloria Cook   Elizabeth Ann Hill   Michael Taylor
R F Delderfield   Patricia Shaw   Kate Tremayne
Cynthia Harrod-Eagles   Linda Sole   Barbara Wood

Grace Thompson   Wales   Saga

also writes as **Kay Christopher**   Valley Series - Wales
                                              Pendragon Island Series

Catrin Collier   Erin Kaye   Cynthia S Roberts
Catherine Cookson   Catrin Morgan   Linda Sole
Iris Gower

Jim Thompson 1906-77   US   Crime: Hardboiled

www.kirjasto.sci.fi/jthompso.htm

Jerome Charyn   George V Higgins   Scott Phillips
James Crumley   Russell James   Jason Starr
James Ellroy   George P Pelecanos

Kate Thompson 1956-   Chick Lit

www.kate-thompson.com   Ireland

Colette Caddle   Cathy Kelly   Stephanie Theobald
Martina Devlin   Marian Keyes   Stephanie Zia
Louise Kean   Dorothy Koomson

June Thomson 1930-   Crime: Police work - UK

www.fantasticfiction.co.uk/authors/June_Thomson.htm   ☆ DCI Jack Finch - Essex

W J Burley   Elizabeth Ferrars   Ruth Rendell
Agatha Christie   Anthea Fraser   Sally Spencer
Arthur Conan Doyle

Rupert Thomson 1955-   General **T**

www.fantasticfiction.co.uk/authors/Rupert_Thomson.htm

David Ambrose   Jim Crace   John Fowles
Douglas Clegg   Michel Faber   Amanda Prantera
Douglas Coupland

Go to back for lists of:
Authors by Genre
Characters and Series
Prize Winners
Further Reading

Matt Thorne 1974-   Lad Lit

www.fantasticfiction.co.uk/authors/Matt_Thorne.htm

David Baddiel	David Nicholls	*Encore 2000*
Neil Cross	Kevin Sampson	Will Self
Jay McInerney	Alexei Sayle	William Sutcliffe

Nicola Thorne   Saga

also writes as **Katherine Yorke**; *is* **Rosemary Ellerbeck**   Champagne Series
www.nicolathorne.com   ⚘ Askham Family

Tessa Barclay	Joan O'Neill	Jean Stubbs
Barbara Taylor Bradford	Margaret Pemberton	Barbara Whitnell
Elizabeth Ann Hill	Judith Saxton	Barbara Wood

Margaret Thornton 1934-   Saga

www.fantasticfiction.co.uk/authors/Margaret_Thornton.htm   Blackpool

Lyn Andrews	Alexandra Connor	Elizabeth Murphy
Jessica Blair	June Francis	Lynda Page
Louise Brindley	Judith Lennox	Alice Taylor

Adam Thorpe 1956-   General

www.contemporarywriters.com/authors/?p=auth95

Paul Auster	Thomas Keneally	*Holtby 1993*
Thomas Hardy	Bernard MacLaverty	
Kazuo Ishiguro	Lawrence Norfolk	Paul Theroux

Colin Thubron 1939-   General

www.contemporarywriters.com/authors/?p=auth117

Michael Ondaatje	Paul Theroux
Piers Paul Read	Jeanette Winterson

Mark Timlin 1950-   Crime: PI

also writes as **Johnny Angelo, Jim Ballantyne, Tony Williams**   ⚘ Nick Sharman - London
www.nicksharman.co.uk

Jake Arnott	Bill James	Nick Oldham
Nicholas Blincoe	Simon Kernick	Robert T Price
Jeremy Cameron	Frank Lean	Mike Ripley

Alan Titchmarsh 1950-   Humour

www.alantitchmarsh.com

Katie Fforde	Tom Sharpe	Mark Wallington
David Nobbs	Leslie Thomas	Keith Waterhouse

T

Charles Todd

Crime: Historical - C20th

is Charles & Caroline Todd
www.charlestodd.com

☥ Insp Ian Rutledge
1920s England

Pat Barker	Martha Grimes	Gillian Linscott
Robert Goddard	Laurie King	David Roberts

Marilyn Todd 1958-

Crime: Historical - Ancient

www.fantasticfiction.co.uk/authors/Marilyn_Todd.htm

☥ Claudia Seferius - Ancient Rome

Lindsey Davis	Rosemary Rowe	Peter Tremayne
Margaret Doody	Steven Saylor	David Wishart
Allan Massie		

Colm Toibin 1955- Ire

General

www.colmtoibin.com

Peter Benson	Brian Moore	Encore 1993
Dermot Bolger	David Park	
Jennifer Johnston	Glenn Patterson	
John McGahern	William Trevor	Niall Williams

J R R Tolkien 1892-1973

Fantasy: Epic

www.tolkiensociety.org

Terry Brooks	Robert Jordan	R A Salvatore
Cecilia Dart-Thornton	Guy Gavriel Kay	T H White
David Eddings	C S Lewis	Tad Williams
Jude Fisher	Michael Scott Rohan	Sarah Zettel

Peter Tonkin 1950-

Sea: Modern
Mariner Series

www.fantasticfiction.co.uk/authors/Marilyn_Todd.htm

Duncan Harding	Philip McCutchan	Nicholas Monsarrat
C C Humphreys	Alistair MacLean	Patrick Robinson
Mike Lunnon-Wood		

Peter Tonkin 1950-

Crime: Historical - C16th **T**

www.fantasticfiction.co.uk/authors/Peter_Tonkin.htm

☥ Tom Musgrave, Master of Defence
C16th England

Michael Clynes	Philip Gooden	John Pilkington
Judith Cook	Michael Jecks	C J Sansom
Patricia Finney		

Go to back for lists of:
Authors by Genre
Characters and Series
Prize Winners
Further Reading

Rebecca Tope 1948- Crime: Amateur sleuth

www.rebeccatope.com

⚐ Drew Slocombe, Undertaker ⎫ Devon
PC Den Cooper ⎬

Tim Cockey	Joyce Holms	Scarlett Thomas
Liz Evans	Hazel Holt	Stella Whitelaw
Ann Granger	Jill McGown	

Eileen Townsend Sco Saga

Scotland

Jessica Blair	Teresa Crane	Elizabeth Walker
Helen Cannam	Patricia Shaw	

Lindsay Townsend 1960- General

www.lindsal.demon.co.uk/townsend/home.htm

Evelyn Anthony	Rosalind Miles
Charlotte Lamb	Mary Stewart

Sue Townsend 1946- Humour

www.leicesterandleicestershire.com/Sue_Townsend.htm

Clare Boylan	India Knight	Mark Wallington
Laurie Graham	Kathy Lette	Nigel Williams
Tom Holt	Sue Limb	

P J Tracy US Crime: Psychological

is P J & Traci Lambrecht
www.fantasticfiction.co.uk/authors/P_J_Tracy.htm

Russell Andrews	John Connolly	Kathy Reichs
Mark Billingham	Patricia D Cornwell	Boris Starling
Dan Brown	Ridley Pearson	Tony Strong

Nigel Tranter 1909-2000 Sco Historical

T

also wrote as Nye Tredgold
www.nigeltranter.co.uk

R F Delderfield	Howard Fast	Edith Pargeter
Dorothy Dunnett	Winston Graham	Sharon Penman

Barbara Trapido 1941- SA General

www.contemporarywriters.co.uk/authors/?p=auth02C22M1645l2627070

Jane Austen	Joanne Harris	Amanda Prantera
Amanda Craig	Tim Parks	Polly Samson
Catherine Fox		

Rose Tremain   1943-   General
www.contemporarywriters.co.uk/authors/?p=auth97

Geraldine Brooks	Deborah Moggach	
Maggie Gee	Robert Nye	Black 1992
Sheri Holman	Rachel Seiffert	Whitbread 1999
Andrew Miller	Jane Stevenson	Graham Swift

Kate Tremayne   Historical
is Pauline Bentley   ⚇ Loveday Series
www.katetremayne.com   Cornwall

Winston Graham	Linda Sole	Michael Taylor
Susan Howatch	Kay Stephens	E V Thompson

Peter Tremayne   1943-   Ire   Crime: Historical - Medieval
also writes as Peter Berresford Ellis   ⚇ Sister Fidelma
www.sisterfidelma.com   C7th Ireland

Alys Clare	Margaret Frazer	Marilyn Todd
Lindsey Davis	Ellis Peters	

William Trevor   1928-   Ire   General
www.contemporarywriters.co.uk/authors/?p=auth122

John Banville	Jennifer Johnston	Whitbread 1976, 1983 & 1994
Elizabeth Bowen	John McGahern	
Ronald Frame	David Park	
Susan Hill	Muriel Spark	Colm Toibin

Antony Trew   1906-1996   SA   Sea: Modern
www.fantasticfiction.co.uk/authors/Antony_Trew.htm

Brian Callison	Nicholas Monsarrat	Justin Scott
Sam Llewellyn	Douglas Reeman	Victor Suthren
Philip McCutchan	Patrick Robinson	

Adriana Trigiani   US   Saga **T**
www.randomhouse.com/features/trigiani

Elizabeth Berg	Patricia Gaffney	Elinor Lipman
Suzanne Berne	Jan Karon	Alice McDermott
Leif Enger	Haven Kimmel	Alexandra Raife
Fannie Flagg	Mary Lawson	Anne Rivers Siddons

Go to back for lists of:
Authors by Genre • Characters and Series • Prize Winners • Further Reading

Anthony Trollope   1815-82   General

www.fantasticfiction.co.uk/authors/Anthony_Trollope.htm

| Charles Dickens | William Golding | Tom Wolfe |
| John Galsworthy | Susan Howatch | |

Joanna Trollope   1943-   Aga saga

also writes as **Caroline Harvey**
www.joannatrollope.net

Diana Appleyard	Karen Hayes	Romantic 1980
Anne Doughty	Sian James	
Catherine Dunne	Kate Long	
Elizabeth Falconer	Karen Nelson	Pam Rhodes
Caro Fraser	Libby Purves	Sophia Watson

Janet MacLeod Trotter   1958-   Saga

www.janetmacleodtrotter.com   NE England

Irene Carr	Una Horne	Denise Robertson
Catherine Cookson	Sheila Jansen	Wendy Robertson
Elizabeth Gill	Brenda McBryde	

M J Trow   1949-   Wales   Crime: Amateur sleuth

is **Meirion James Trow**   ♁ Peter Maxwell, Teacher
www.fantasticfiction.co.uk/authors/M_J_Trow.htm   Det Supt Sholto Lestrade - C19th England

Arthur Conan Doyle	Peter Lovesey	Nicholas Rhea
Sarah Grazebrook	Amy Myers	Barrie Roberts
Ray Harrison	Anne Perry	Norman Russell
Joan Lock	David Pirie	Gerard Williams

Lynne Truss   Humour

Susie Boyt	Lucy Ellman	Arabella Weir
Mavis Cheek	Helen Fielding	Louise Wener
Isla Dewar	Jane Green	

T

Peter Turnbull   1950-   Crime: Police work - UK

www.fantasticfiction.co.uk/authors/Peter_Turnbull.htm   ♁ P Division - Glasgow
DCI Hennessy & DS Yellich - York

Meg Elizabeth Atkins	Pauline Bell	Frederic Lindsay
Jo Bannister	Quintin Jardine	Stuart Pawson
Robert Barnard	Frank Lean	

Go to back for lists of:
Authors by Genre • Characters and Series • Prize Winners • Further Reading

Scott Turow   1949-   US

www.scottturow.com

Crime: Legal/financial

D W Buffa
James Grippando
John Grisham

Colin Harrison
Craig Holden
Paul Kilduff

John McLaren   CWA 1987
Tony Strong
Sabin Willett

Harry Turtledove   1949-   US

Fantasy: Epic

also writes as Eric G Iverson, N H Turtletaub
www.sfsite.com/~silverag/turtledove.html

Chris Bunch
David Feintuch

Paul Kearney
George R R Martin

Guy Walters

Anne Tyler   1941-   US

General

www.kirjasto.sci.fi/atyler.htm

Gail Anderson-Dargatz
Joan Barfoot
Candida Crewe
Andre Dubus
Suzannah Dunn

Catherine Dunne
Karen Joy Fowler
Haven Kimmel
William Kowalski
Elinor Lipman

Pulitzer 1989

Jodi Picoult
Sarah Willis

Barry Unsworth   1930-

Historical

www.fantasticfiction.co.uk/authors/Barry_Unsworth.htm

John Banville
Bruce Chatwin
Jim Crace
Fred D'Aguiar
Andrew Miller

Robert Nye
Amanda Prantera
Julian Rathbone
Peter Watt

Booker 1992

Caroline Upcher   1946-

Glitz & Glamour

also writes as Carly McIntyre
www.carolineupcher.com

Sally Beauman
Alexandra Campbell
Jilly Cooper

Judith Gould
Judith Michael

Madge Swindells
Penny Vincenzi

**T
U**

John Updike   1932-   US

General

www.kirjasto.sci.fi/updike.htm

Saul Bellow
Ethan Canin
Justin Cartwright
E L Doctorow
Jeffrey Eugenides

Jonathan Franzen
John Irving
Norman Mailer
Rick Moody
Vladimir Nabokov

Pulitzer 1982 & 1991

Walker Percy
Tobias Wolff

Leon Uris 1924-2003 US General

www.fantasticfiction.co.uk/authors/Leon_Uris.htm

Howard Fast
James A Michener
Edward Rutherfurd

Manda Scott
Isaac Bashevis Singer

John Steinbeck
Morris West

Jane Urquhart 1949- Can General

Thomas Eidson
David Guterson

Peter Hoeg
Anne-Marie MacDonald

Anne Michaels
Ann Patchett

Fred Vargas 1957- Fr Crime: Police work - France
☆ Commissaire Adamsberg - Paris

www.fantasticfiction.co.uk/authors/Fred_Vargas.htm

Colin Dexter
Donna Leon

Henning Mankell
Manuel Vázquez
  Montalbán

Lawrence Sanders
Georges Simenon

Mario Vargas Llosa 1936- Peru General

www.kirjasto.sci.fi/vargas.htm

Isabel Allende
Louis de Bernières

Carlos Fuentes
Gabriel Garcia Márquez

Tomas Eloy Martinez
Nicholas Shakespeare

Jules Verne 1828-1905 Fr Science Fiction: Space and time

www.jules-verne.net

Robert A Heinlein
C S Lewis

Kurt Vonnegut
H G Wells

Salley Vickers General

www.salleyvickers.com

Anita Brookner
Tracy Chevalier
Stevie Davies

Anita Diamant
Penelope Fitzgerald
Joanne Harris

Elizabeth Knox
James Runcie
Susan Vreeland

Gore Vidal 1925- US General

also writes as **Edgar Box**
www.kirjasto.sci.fi/vidal.htm

U
V

Margaret George
Robert Graves

Norman Mailer
James A Michener

Mary Renault
Tom Wolfe

Penny Vincenzi   1939-   Glitz & Glamour

www.penny-vincenzi.com

Elizabeth Adler	Sandra Brown	Frankie McGowan
Susannah Bates	Olivia Goldsmith	Jill Mansell
Barbara Taylor Bradford	Roberta Latow	Caroline Upcher

Barbara Vine   1930-   Crime: Psychological

is Ruth Rendell
www.fantasticfiction.co.uk/authors/Barbara_Vine.htm

Karin Alvtegen	Frances Hegarty	CWA 1987 & 1991
Andrea Badenoch	Elizabeth McGregor	
Carol Anne Davis	Margaret Murphy	
Sarah Diamond	Julie Parsons	Chris Simms
Jeremy Dronfield	Patrick Redmond	Tony Strong

Anne Vivis   Sco   Saga
Strathannan Series - Scotland

Doris Davidson	Alexandra Raife	Kirsty White
Nora Kay	Linda Sole	Dee Williams
Frances Paige	Reay Tannahill	Mary Withall

Kurt Vonnegut   1922-   US   Science Fiction: Space and time

www.vonnegut.com

Brian W Aldiss	William Gibson	Jules Verne
J G Ballard	Jeff Noon	Roger Zelazny
Philip K Dick		

Louise Voss   General

www.fantasticfiction.co.uk/authors/Louise_Voss.htm

Candida Clark	Julia Lisle	Libby Purves
Sian James	Penelope Lively	Titia Sutherland

Susan Vreeland   1946-   US   Historical

www.svreeland.com

Tracy Chevalier	Ann Patchett	Salley Vickers
Anita Diamant	Christopher Peachment	Sarah Woodhouse
Deborah Moggach	James Runcie	

Go to back for lists of:
Authors by Genre
Characters and Series
Prize Winners
Further Reading

Elizabeth Waite

Saga
London

Philip Boast	Harry Cole	Anna King
Harry Bowling	Pamela Evans	Elizabeth Lord
Helen Carey	Patricia Grey	Audrey Willsher

W

Martyn Waites 1963-

Crime: Hardboiled

www.fantasticfiction.co.uk/authors/Martyn_Waites.htm

⚐ Stephen Larkin, Journalist
NE England

John Baker	Paul Charles	Frank Lean
Adam Baron	Alan Dunn	Chris Paling
Ken Bruen	Robert Edric	Nicholas Royle

Alice Walker 1944- US

General

Emma Donoghue	Toni Morrison	Pulitzer 1983
Harper Lee	Alice Randall	
Terry McMillan	William Styron	

Elizabeth Walker

is Elizabeth Neff Walker

Saga
Yorkshire

www.fantasticfiction.co.uk/authors/Elizabeth_Walker.htm

Aileen Armitage	Helen Cannam	Kay Stephens
Jessica Blair	Sara Hylton	Eileen Townsend
Barbara Taylor Bradford		

Fiona Walker 1969-

Chick Lit

www.fantasticfiction.co.uk/authors/Fiona_Walker.htm

Jessica Adams	Louise Bagshawe	Victoria Colby
Catherine Alliott	Emily Barr	Lucinda Edmonds
Anita Anderson	Susie Boyt	Alexandra Potter

Robert James Waller 1939- US

General

www.fantasticfiction.co.uk/authors/Robert_James_Waller.htm

Nicholas Evans	Anita Shreve	Nicholas Sparks
Janice Graham	Jane Smiley	Nancy Thayer

Mark Wallington 1953-

Humour

Stephen Fry	David Nobbs	Sue Townsend
John Lanchester	Alan Titchmarsh	Nigel Williams

Jill Paton Walsh 1937-   General

www.greenbay.co.uk/jpw.html

Peter Ackroyd   Jane Gardam
Umberto Eco   Candia McWilliam

Jess Walter   US   Crime: Police work - US **W**

www.jesswalter.com   🏃 Caroline Maybry - Spokane, Washington State

Giles Blunt   Steve Hamilton   Theresa Monsour
Jerome Charyn   William Heffernan   Ridley Pearson
David Cray   Thomas Laird   Jenny Siler

Guy Walters   War

www.guywalters.com

Robert Harris   Robert Ryan
Rebecca Pawel   Harry Turtledove

Minette Walters 1949-   Crime: Psychological

www.minettewalters.co.uk

Karin Alvtegen   Carol Anne Davis   CWA 1992, 1994 & 2003
Andrea Badenoch   Carol Goodman
Suzanne Berne   Joanna Hines
Ingrid Black   J Wallis Martin   Carol Smith
Stephen Booth   Sarah Rayne   Tony Strong

Joseph Wambaugh   1937-   US   Crime: Police work - US

www.fantasticfiction.co.uk/authors/Joseph_Wambaugh.htm   California

William Diehl   Ed McBain   Mario Puzo
James Ellroy   Deon Meyer   Martin Cruz Smith
W E B Griffin   Jefferson Parker   Stuart Woods

Amanda Eyre Ward   US   Aga saga

www.amandaward.com

Marika Cobbold   Ann Swinfen   Madeleine Wickham
Elizabeth Noble   Sophia Watson   Ann Widdecombe
Kathleen Rowntree   Mary Wesley   Jane Yardley

Alan Warner 1964-   Sco   General

www.contemporarywriters.com/authors/?p=auth02A14P105712626399

Iain Banks   Duncan McLean   S Maugham 1996
Ron Butlin   Ruaridh Nicoll   Encore 1998
Stewart Home   Paul Sayer
Gordon Legge   Irvine Welsh

271

Freda Warrington 1956- Fantasy: Epic

www.members.aol.com/fredamike

Robert Asprin	Jonathan Green	Tanith Lee
James Barclay	Ian Irvine	Juliet E McKenna
Storm Constantine	Kate Jacoby	K J Parker
Ben Counter	J V Jones	Robert Silverberg

Keith Waterhouse 1929- Humour

Kingsley Amis	Ben Elton	John Mortimer
Nicholson Baker	David Lodge	Leslie Thomas
Malcolm Bradbury	Magnus Mills	Alan Titchmarsh

Sarah Waters 1966- Wales General

www.sarahwaters.com

Stevie Davies	Sheri Holman	Sunday Times 2000
Philippa Gregory	Jane Stevenson	S Maugham 2000
Anne Haverty	Jeanette Winterson	CWA 2002

Paul Watkins 1964- Wales General

www.paulwatkins.com

Francis Cottam	Robert Radcliffe	Encore 1990
Ernest Hemingway	Erich Maria Remarque	Holtby 1995
Douglas Kennedy	Derek Robinson	
Michael Ondaatje		

Ian Watson 1943- Science Fiction: Space and time

www.ianwatson.info

J G Ballard	Gwyneth Jones	BSFA 1977
Iain M Banks	Paul J McAuley	
Stephen Baxter	Larry Niven	
Gregory Benford	Brian Stableford	Robert Charles Wilson

Sophia Watson 1962- Aga saga

Judy Astley	Rosie Thomas	Amanda Eyre Ward
Amanda Brookfield	Joanna Trollope	Jane Yardley
Elizabeth Pewsey		

Peter Watt Aus Historical

www.peterwatt.com

Bryce Courtenay	Andrew Miller	Wilbur Smith
Robert Drewe	Amanda Prantera	Barry Unsworth

Daisy Waugh 1967-   Chick Lit

www.fantasticfiction.co.uk/authors/Daisy_Waugh.htm

Cecelia Ahern   Lisa Jewell   Freya North
Victoria Corby   India Knight   Tina Reilly
Wendy Holden   Claire Naylor   Jennifer Weiner

Evelyn Waugh 1903-66   General

www.kirjasto.sci.fi/ewaugh.htm

T Coraghessan Boyle   Glen Duncan   Paul Micou
Michael Carson   Matthew Kneale   Anthony Powell
Justin Cartwright   David Lodge   William Sutcliffe
Joseph Connolly   Pauline Melville   Angus Wilson

Teresa Waugh 1940-   General

Beryl Bainbridge   Linda Grant   Alison Lurie
Jane Gardam   Susan Hill

James Webb US   War

www.jameswebb.com

Shaun Clarke   Jack Higgins
W E B Griffin   Johnny 'Two Combs'
Robert Harris   Howard
Eric L Harry   Robert Jackson

Sarah Webb 1969- Ire   Chick Lit

www.sarahwebb.info

Susannah Bates   Anne Dunlop   Marian Murphy
Francesca Clementis   Donna Hay   Andrea Semple
Clare Dowling   Shari Low   Stephanie Zia

Jennifer Weiner US   Chick Lit

www.jenniferweiner.com

Maggie Alderson   Susan Isaacs   Adele Parks
Jenny Crusie   Amy Jenkins   Morag Prunty
Tara Heavey   Sarah Mason   Daisy Waugh

Arabella Weir   Chick Lit

Sherry Ashworth   Laurie Graham   Sarah Mason
Mavis Cheek   Sue Limb   Carole Matthews
Imogen Edwards-Jones   Louise Marley   Lynne Truss

Margaret Weis 1948- US Fantasy: Epic

www.margaretweis.com

Terry Brooks	Elizabeth Moon	R A Salvatore
Steven Brust	Melanie Rawn	Jan Siegel
David A Drake	Mickey Zucker Reichert	

Jane Welch 1964- Fantasy: Epic

www.janewelch.com

David Farland	Julia Gray	Stephen R Lawhead
David Gemmell	Simon R Green	Adam Nichols
Terry Goodkind	Guy Gavriel Kay	K J Parker

Fay Weldon 1933- General

www.fantasticfiction.co.uk/authors/Fay_Weldon.htm

Beryl Bainbridge	Janet Frame	Emma Tennant
Elizabeth Buchan	Edna O'Brien	Jeanette Winterson
Angela Carter	Wendy Perriam	

H G Wells 1866-1946 Science Fiction: Space and time

also wrote as **Reginald Bliss**
www.kirjasto.sci.fi/hgwells.htm

Stephen Baxter	Tim Powers	Jules Verne
E M Forster	Christopher Priest	John Wyndham
Greg Keyes		

Rebecca Wells 1963- US General
Louisiana

www.ya-ya.com

Justin Cartwright	Karen Joy Fowler	Anne Rivers Siddons
Louise Erdrich	Elinor Lipman	Sarah Willis
Fannie Flagg	Jodi Picoult	

Irvine Welsh 1958- Sco General

www.fantasticfiction.co.uk/authors/Irvine_Welsh.htm

Des Dillon	Sean Hughes	Kevin Sampson
Roddy Doyle	James Kelman	Alan Warner
Niall Griffiths		

Patricia Wendorf Historical
The Patteran Trilogy

Diana Gabaldon	Caroline Harvey	Harriet Hudson
Cynthia Harrod-Eagles	Anne Haverty	Caroline Stickland
		T R Wilson

Louise Wener — Humour

www.fantasticfiction.co.uk/authors/Louise_Wener.htm

Sue Limb
Allison Pearson
Libby Purves
Lynne Truss

Jane Wenham-Jones — Chick Lit

www.fantasticfiction.co.uk/authors/Jane_Wenham-Jones.htm

Anita Anderson
Valerie-Anne Baglietto
Rebecca Campbell
Jenny Colgan
Anne Dunlop
Imogen Edwards-Jones
Monica McInerney
Tara Manning

Patricia Wentworth — 1878-1961 — Crime: Amateur sleuth

was **Dora Amy Elles**

🏃 Miss Maud Silver

www.fantasticfiction.co.uk/authors/Patricia_Wentworth.htm

Margery Allingham
Agatha Christie
Elizabeth Ferrars
Michael Innes
Ngaio Marsh
Gladys Mitchell
Gwen Moffat
Dorothy L Sayers

Mary Wesley — 1912-2002 — Aga saga

www.fantasticfiction.co.uk/authors/Mary_Wesley.htm

Clare Chambers
Victoria Clayton
Elizabeth Falconer
Adèle Geras
Kate Hatfield
Elinor Lipman
Nora Naish
Karen Nelson
Kathleen Rowntree
Kate Saunders
Diana Saville
Amanda Eyre Ward

Valerie Wilson Wesley — 1947- — US — Crime: PI

www.tamarahayle.com

🏃 Tamara Hayle - Newark, New Jersey

Charlotte Carter
Janet Evanovich
Sparkle Hayter
Laura Lippman
Terry McMillan
Alexander McCall Smith
Cath Staincliffe

Christopher West — 1954- — Crime: Police work - China

www.fantasticfiction.co.uk/authors/Christopher_West.htm

🏃 Insp Wang Anzhuang

Tony Hillerman
Roderic Jeffries
Peter May
Barbara Nadel
Eliot Pattison
Laura Joh Rowland
Lisa See
Qiu Xiaolong

Morris West — 1916-1999 — Aus — General

www.fantasticfiction.co.uk/authors/Morris_West.htm

Colin Andrews
Graham Greene
David Malouf
John Masters
W Somerset Maugham
Brian Moore
Nevil Shute
Leon Uris

Nigel West   1951-   Adventure/Thriller
is Rupert Allason
www.nigelwest.com

Len Deighton	Peter Rawlinson	Gerald Seymour
Philip Kerr	Tim Sebastian	Michael Shea
Charles McCarry		

Donald E Westlake   1933-   US   Crime: Humour
also writes as Tucker Coe, Richard Stark   🚶 John Dortmunder, Burglar
www.donaldwestlake.com

Tim Dorsey	Elmore Leonard	Charles Spencer
Carl Hiaasen	John D Macdonald	Sarah Strohmeyer
José Latour	Robert B Parker	

Edith Wharton   1862-1937   US   General
www.fantasticfiction.co.uk/authors/Edith_Wharton.htm

Jane Austen	Thomas Hardy	Alison Lurie
Penelope Fitzgerald	Henry James	Joyce Carol Oates
E M Forster		

Edmund White   1940-   US   General
www.edmundwhite.com

Michael Carson	Alan Hollinghurst
Patrick Gale	Armistead Maupin

Gillian White   General
also writes as Georgina Fleming
www.fantasticfiction.co.uk/authors/Gillian_White.htm

Helen Dunmore	Shirley Hazzard	Graham Swift
Lesley Glaister	Deborah Moggach	

Gillian White   Adventure/Thriller: Psychological
also writes as Georgina Fleming
www.fantasticfiction.co.uk/authors/Gillian_White.htm

Harlan Coben	Carol Goodman
Sarah Diamond	Joanna Hines

Kirsty White   Saga
Scotland

Christine Marion Fraser	Elisabeth McNeill	Frances Paige
Gwen Kirkwood	Isobel Neill	Jessica Stirling
		Anne Vivis

Patrick White 1912-90 Aus — General

www.fantasticfiction.co.uk/authors/Patrick_White.htm

Peter Carey
Robert Drewe
Nadine Gordimer
Henry James
Thomas Keneally
David Malouf
V S Naipaul
Tim Winton

W

Robin White US — Adventure/Thriller

www.fantasticfiction.co.uk/authors/Robin_White.htm

Ted Allbeury
Eric Ambler
Dale Brown
John Le Carré
Patrick Robinson

Stephen White US — Crime: Psychological

www.authorstephenwhite.com

Alan Gregory, Psychologist
Boulder, Colorado

Jeffery Deaver
Tess Gerritsen
Daniel Hecht
Tami Hoag
John Katzenbach
Alex Kava
Jonathan Kellerman
Val McDermid
Jonathan Nasaw
Meg O'Brien
Andrew Pyper
Erica Spindler

T H White 1906-64 — Fantasy: Myth

www2.netdoor.com/~moulder/thwhite

Sylvie Germain
Ursula K Le Guin
C S Lewis
William Sarabande
Judith Tarr
J R R Tolkien
Sarah Zettel

Stella Whitelaw 1941- — Crime: PI

www.fantasticfiction.co.uk/authors/Stella_Whitelaw.htm

Jordan Lacey - Sussex

Simon Brett
Judith Cutler
Liz Evans
Lauren Henderson
Joyce Holms
David Roberts
Cath Staincliffe
Scarlett Thomas
Rebecca Tope

Jeanne Whitmee — Saga

London

Pamela Evans
Patricia Grey
Elizabeth Lord
Jenny Oldfield
Pamela Oldfield
Gilda O'Neill

Barbara Whitnell — Saga

Cornwall

Rosemary Aitken
Iris Gower
Claire Lorrimer
Cynthia S Roberts
Malcolm Ross
Sarah Shears
Nicola Thorne
Barbara Wood

Matt Whyman
Lad Lit

www.mattwhyman.com

Matthew Beaumont	John Harding	Tony Parsons
Mike Gayle	Nick Hornby	Willy Russell

W Madeleine Wickham 1969-
Aga saga

also writes as **Sophie Kinsella**

Judy Astley	Hazel Hucker	Jean Saunders
Anne Atkins	Elizabeth Noble	Amanda Eyre Ward
Amanda Brookfield		

Ann Widdecombe 1947-
General

www.annwiddecombemp.com

Sybil Marshall	Kathleen Rowntree	Mona Simpson
Pam Rhodes	Rebecca Shaw	Amanda Eyre Ward

Marianne Wiggins 1947- US
General

A S Byatt	Michael Ondaatje	Carol Shields
William Golding	Salman Rushdie	

Marcia Willett
Saga

also writes as **Willa Marsh** ⅄ Chadwick Family
www.devonwriters.co.uk

Adèle Geras	Julia Lisle	Santa Montefiore
Rebecca Gregson	Kate Long	Karen Nelson
Julie Highmore	Sarah MacDonald	Rosamunde Pilcher

Sabin Willett
Adventure/Thriller: Legal/financial

David Baldacci	John Grisham	Scott Turow
James Grippando	Christopher Reich	

David Williams 1926- Wales
Crime: Police work - UK

is **Robert Paul Williams** ⅄ DCI Merlin Parry & Sgt Gomer Lloyd -
www.fantasticfiction.co.uk/authors/David_Williams.htm Wales
Mark Treasure - Banking

Ann Cleeves	Janet Laurence	Charlotte MacLeod
Jonathan Gash	Roy Lewis	Andrew Taylor
Bill James		

Go to back for lists of:
Authors by Genre • Characters and Series • Prize Winners • Further Reading

Dee Williams
www.fantasticfiction.co.uk/authors/Dee_Williams.htm

Saga
East End, London

Helen Carey	Gwen Madoc	Alison Stuart
Harry Cole	Connie Monk	June Tate
Brenda McBryde	Sheila Newberry	Anne Vivis

W

Gerard Williams

Crime: Historical - C19th
⚡ Dr James Mortimer & Dr Violet Branscombe
C19th London

Arthur Conan Doyle	Laurie King	David Pirie
John Maclachlan Gray	Gillian Linscott	Barrie Roberts
Ray Harrison	Anne Perry	M J Trow

Niall Williams   1958-   Ire

General
www.niallwilliams.com

Dermot Bolger	Simon Mawer	Joseph O'Connor
Jennifer Johnston	Edna O'Brien	Colm Toibin
Bernard MacLaverty		

Nigel Williams   1948-

Humour

David Baddiel	John Lanchester	Sue Townsend
Jonathan Coe	Geoff Nicholson	Mark Wallington
Stephen Fry	David Nobbs	P G Wodehouse

Tad Williams   1957-   US

Fantasy: Epic
www.tadwilliams.com

Terry Brooks	Robin Hobb	Adam Nichols
David A Drake	Greg Keyes	Michael Scott Rohan
David Eddings	Stan Nicholls	J R R Tolkien

Tad Williams   1957-   US

Science Fiction: Near future
www.tadwilliams.com

Steve Aylett	Nick Sagan	Bruce Sterling
Jon Courtenay Grimwood	Lucius Shepard	David Zindell

Connie Willis   1945-   US

Science Fiction: Space and time
www.fantasticfiction.co.uk/authors/Connie_Willis.htm

Jasper Fforde	Tim Powers	Jan Siegel
William Gibson	Christopher Priest	Robert Charles Wilson
Diana Norman		

Sarah Willis   US   General

Anita Diamant   Maggie O'Farrell   Rebecca Wells
Sue Miller   Anne Tyler

W Tim Willocks   1957-   Adventure/Thriller
www.fantasticfiction.co.uk/authors/Tim_Willocks.htm

Thomas Harris   Dean R Koontz
Andrew Klavan   David Lindsey

Audrey Willsher   Saga
London • Leicestershire

Harriet Hudson   Mary Jane Staples   Elizabeth Waite
Meg Hutchinson   Alison Stuart   Sally Worboyes
Lynda Page

A N Wilson   1950-   General

Kingsley Amis   Iris Murdoch   Mail 1978
Julian Barnes   Anthony Powell
Malcolm Bradbury   Bernice Rubens

Angus Wilson   1913-1991   General
www.fantasticfiction.co.uk/authors/Angus_Wilson.htm

Anthony Burgess   J B Priestley   Evelyn Waugh
A S Byatt   Piers Paul Read

Derek Wilson   1935-   Crime: Historical - C18th
also writes as Jonathan Kane   ⚘ George Keene, Spy
www.derekwilson.com   Nathaniel Gye, Parapsychologist
                                                  Tim Lacy - Art world

Janet Gleeson   Roy Lewis   Hannah March
Daniel Hecht   John Malcolm   Iain Pears

Laura Wilson   Crime: Psychological
www.laura-wilson.co.uk

Karin Alvtegen   Carol Goodman   Ruth Rendell
Andrea Badenoch   Phil Lovesey   Chris Simms
Carol Anne Davis   Margaret Murphy   Carol Smith
Sarah Diamond   Gemma O'Connor   Andrew Taylor

Go to back for lists of:
Authors by Genre • Characters and Series • Prize Winners • Further Reading

Robert Wilson   1957-   Adventure/Thriller

www.robertcharleswilson.com   ⃰ Bruce Medway - Portugal
                                                        Insp Javier Falcon

James Adams   Alan Furst   J Wallis Martin CWA 1999
Raymond Chandler   Philip Kerr   Henry Porter
Dan Fesperman

W

Robert Charles Wilson   1953-   Can   Science Fiction: Space and time

www.robertcharleswilson.com

David Brin   Linda Nagata   Connie Willis
Wil McCarthy   Ian Watson   David Wingrove

T R Wilson   1962-   Saga

also writes as **Tim Wilson**; *is* **Hannah March**   East Anglia

Tessa Barclay   Mary Mackie   Graham Swift
Margaret Dickinson   Caroline Stickland Patricia Wendorf
Malcolm Macdonald

Tim Wilson   1962-   Horror

also writes as **T R Wilson**; *is* **Hannah March**
www.fantasticfiction.co.uk/authors/Tim_Wilson.htm

Mark Burnell   Stephen Laws   Scott Nicholson
Peter James   Mark Morris   Phil Rickman

R D Wingfield   Crime: Police work - UK

www.fantasticfiction.co.uk/authors/R_D_Wingfield.htm   ⃰ DI Jack Frost - 'Denton'

Robert Barnard   Jeff Gulvin   Peter Robinson
Deborah Crombie   M R D Meek   Andrew Taylor

David Wingrove   1954-   Science Fiction: Space and time

www.fantasticfiction.co.uk/authors/David_Wingrove.htm

Greg Egan   Paul J McAuley   Linda Nagata
Jon Courtenay Grimwood   Wil McCarthy   Robert Charles Wilson
Gwyneth Jones

Don Winslow   1953-   US   Crime: Amateur sleuth

                                                    ⃰ Neal Carey - Nevada

Robert Crais   Carl Hiaasen   Elmore Leonard
Denise Danks   José Latour   Shane Maloney

Jeanette Winterson 1959- General

www.jeanettewinterson.com

Angela Carter	Bernice Rubens	Whitbread 1985
Emma Donoghue	Colin Thubron	Mail 1987
Laura Esquivel	Sarah Waters	
Michèle Roberts	Fay Weldon	Virginia Woolf

Tim Winton 1960- Aus General

www.fantasticfiction.co.uk/authors/Tim_Winton.htm

Peter Carey	Brian Moore
Thomas Keneally	Patrick White

David Wishart 1952- Sco Crime: Historical - Ancient

www.david-wishart.co.uk

⚐ Marcus Corvinus - Ancient Rome

Lindsey Davis	Allan Massie	Steven Saylor
Margaret Doody	Rosemary Rowe	Marilyn Todd

Mary Withall Sco Saga

Eisdalsa Island Trilogy - Scotland

Maggie Craig	Nora Kay	Eileen Ramsay
Christine Marion Fraser	Gwen Kirkwood	Anne Vivis
Evelyn Hood		

P G Wodehouse 1881-1975 Humour

www.fantasticfiction.co.uk/authors/P_G_Wodehouse.htm

⚐ Jeeves, Butler • Bertie Wooster

George Macdonald Fraser	Tom Holt	David Nobbs
Stephen Fry	John Mortimer	Nigel Williams

Joan Wolf 1951- US Crime: Historical - Medieval

www.joanwolf.com

⚐ Hugh Corbaille - C12th England

Simon Beaufort	Sylvian Hamilton	Viviane Moore
Alys Clare	Michael Jecks	Ellis Peters

Laura Wolf US Chick Lit

Sarah Ball	Andrea Semple
Sue Haasler	Stephanie Zia

Go to back for lists of:
Authors by Genre • Characters and Series • Prize Winners • Further Reading

Gene Wolfe   1931-   US   Fantasy: Literary
www.fantasticfiction.co.uk/authors/Gene_Wolfe.htm

John Crowley	Julian May	BSFA 1981
Robert Holdstock	Tim Powers	
Ursula K Le Guin	Adam Roberts	Roger Zelazny

W

Tom Wolfe   1931-   US   General
www.tomwolfe.com

T Coraghessan Boyle	Colin Harrison	Thomas Pynchon
Charles Dickens	Tama Janowitz	Alice Randall
Bret Easton Ellis	Norman Mailer	Anthony Trollope
Alan Gurganus	Paul Micou	Gore Vidal

Isabel Wolff   Humour
www.isabelwolff.com

Raffaella Barker	Wendy Holden	Josie Lloyd & Emlyn Rees
Faith Bleasdale	Amy Jenkins	Sue Margolis
Claire Calman	India Knight	

Tobias Wolff   1945-   US   General
www.fantasticfiction.co.uk/authors/Tobias_Wolff.htm

Don DeLillo	Patrick McGrath	Tom Robbins
Richard Ford	Richard Powers	John Updike
John Irving		

Meg Wolitzer   US   General

Penelope Lively	Lorrie Moore	Jane Smiley
Alison Lurie	Libby Purves	

Barbara Wood   Historical
www.barbarawood.com

Janet Dailey	Joanne Harris	Nicola Thorne
Iris Gower	E V Thompson	Barbara Whitnell

Valerie Wood   Saga
www.valeriewood.co.uk

Catherine Cookson	Audrey Howard	Wendy Robertson
Inga Dunbar	Erin Kaye	Kay Stephens
Evelyn Hood	Mary McCarthy	

Sarah Woodhouse   1950-   Historical

Elizabeth Buchan   Cynthia S Roberts   Romantic 1989
Pamela Oldfield   Patricia Shaw
Elizabeth Palmer   Susan Vreeland

W Richard Woodman   1944-   Sea: Historical
www.richardwoodman.com   ⋆ Nathaniel Drinkwater
                                                C18th/19th England

Brian Callison   Jonathan Lunn   Dudley Pope
Tom Connery   Philip McCutchan   Showell Styles
Alexander Fullerton   Jan Needle   Victor Suthren

Janet Woods   Aus   Saga
http://members.iinet.net.au/~woods   C19th Dorset

Tessa Barclay   Louise Brindley   Malcolm Macdonald
Anne Bennett   Julia Bryant   Connie Monk
Rose Boucheron   Claire Lorrimer   Pamela Oldfield

Stuart Woods   1938-   US   Adventure/Thriller
www.stuartwoods.com   ⋆ Stone Barrington, PI - New York
                                        Chief Holly Barker, Police - Florida

Ace Atkins   Stuart Harrison   David Lindsey
Martina Cole   Patricia Highsmith   Michael Malone
John Gilstrap   Douglas Kennedy   Jefferson Parker
James Grippando   Andrew Klavan   Joseph Wambaugh

Virginia Woolf   1882-1941   General
www.utoronto.ca/IVWS

Martin Amis   E M Forster   Michèle Roberts
Joseph Conrad   James Joyce   Jeanette Winterson
Margaret Drabble   Iris Murdoch

Sally Worboyes   Saga
www.fantasticfiction.co.uk/authors/Sally_Worboyes.htm   London • Kent

Harry Cole   Lena Kennedy   Victor Pemberton
Elizabeth Daish   Anna King   Audrey Willsher
Harriet Hudson   Jenny Oldfield

Go to back for lists of:
Authors by Genre
Characters and Series
Prize Winners
Further Reading

Anne Worboys   1920-   Saga

also writes as **Annette Eyre, Vicky Maxwell**

Virginia Andrews   Anne Melville   Elvi Rhodes
Sheelagh Kelly   Mary E Pearce   Mary Stewart
Lena Kennedy   Miss Read

W

Deborah Wright   Chick Lit

www.deborahwright.co.uk

Maggie Alderson   Jenny Eclair   Victoria Routledge
Lisa Armstrong   Freya North   Liz Young
Sarah Ball

Glover Wright   Adventure/Thriller

James Follett   Pete Hamill   Kenneth Royce
Jeff Gulvin   Jack Higgins

T M Wright   1947-   US   Horror

also writes as **F W Armstrong**
www.fantasticfiction.co.uk/authors/T_M_Wright.htm

Ramsey Campbell   Richard Laymon   Robert McCammon
Stephen Gallagher   Brian Lumley   Peter Straub
Stephen King

Janny Wurts   1953-   US   Fantasy: Epic

www.paravia.com/JannyWurts

Steven Brust   Louise Cooper   Elizabeth Moon
Chris Bunch   Raymond E Feist   Mickey Zucker Reichert
Jonathan Carroll   L E Modesitt Jr

Jonathan Wylie   1953-   Fantasy: Epic

also writes as **Julia Gray**; *is* **Mark & Julia Smith**
www.fantasticfiction.co.uk/authors/Jonathan_Wylie.htm

Jonathan Carroll   L E Modesitt Jr
Paul Kearney   Michael Scott Rohan

John Wyndham   1903-69   Science Fiction: Near future

was **John Wyndham Harris**
www.fantasticfiction.co.uk/authors/John_Wyndham.htm

Brian W Aldiss   Philip K Dick   H G Wells
Isaac Asimov   Robert A Heinlein   Roger Zelazny

Grace Wynne-Jones Ire   General
www.irishwriters-online.com/gracewynnejones.html

Sarah Harrison	Judith Summers
Marian Keyes	Laura Zigman

Qiu Xiaolong China   Crime: Police work - China
⚐ Insp Chen - Shanghai
www.fantasticfiction.co.uk/authors/Qiu_Xiaolong.htm

Andrea Camilleri	Peter May	Lisa See
Luiz Alfredo Garcia-Roza	Barbara Nadel	Christopher West
Donna Leon	Eliot Pattison	

Jane Yardley   Aga saga

Marika Cobbold	Elizabeth Noble	Amanda Eyre Ward
Preethi Nair	Ann Swinfen	Sophia Watson

Margaret Yorke 1924-   Crime: Psychological
⚐ Patrick Grant
www.fantasticfiction.co.uk/authors/Margaret_Yorke.htm

Jane Adams	Gerald Hammond	CWA 1999
Louise Doughty	Julie Parsons	Louis Sanders
Elizabeth Ferrars	Danuta Reah	Alison Taylor

Liz Young   Chick Lit
also writes as **Elizabeth Young**
www.fantasticfiction.co.uk/authors/Liz_Young.htm

Claire Calman	Lisa Jewell	Sheila Norton
Francesca Clementis	Jill Mansell	Deborah Wright

Louisa Young   General
⚐ Evangeline Gower,
ex Belly dancer
www.contemporarywriters.com/authors/?p=auth02C22K362412627021

James Hawes	Zadie Smith
Hanif Kureishi	Meera Syal

Roger Zelazny 1937-1995 US   Fantasy: Epic
http://zelazny.corrupt.net

Poul Anderson	Larry Niven	Gene Wolfe
Ray Bradbury	Robert Silverberg	John Wyndham
Steven Brust	Kurt Vonnegut	

Sarah Zettel 1966- US | Fantasy: Myth

www.sff.net/people/sarah-zettel

Ashok K Banker	Ursula K Le Guin	J R R Tolkien
David Eddings	C S Lewis	T H White

Stephanie Zia 1955- | Chick Lit

Sue Haasler	Stephanie Theobald	Sarah Webb
Carmen Reid	Kate Thompson	Laura Wolf
Andrea Semple		

Z

Laura Zigman US | Chick Lit

Lisa Jewell	Kathy Lette	Tina Reilly
Marian Keyes	Freya North	Grace Wynne-Jones
Sophie Kinsella	Claudia Pattison	

David Zindell 1952- | Science Fiction: Space and time

www.fantasticfiction.co.uk/authors/David_Zindell.htm

Iain M Banks	Stephen Donaldson	Brian Stableford
Orson Scott Card	Lucius Shepard	Tad Williams
Mark Chadbourn		

Authors listed by Genre

It is almost impossible to identify accurately individual authors with one particular section of genre fiction; often there is no 'cut off' point between, for instance, **War** and **Adventure**; between **Fantasy**, **Science Fiction** and **Horror**; or between **Historical** and **Saga**. So, although in the main sequence this Guide indicates under the names of each author the genre in which they usually write, and these names are repeated again in the lists that follow, it is suggested that readers also refer to linking genres — and in particular to the main list — to discover new names that could become firm favourites.

Some categories — **Adventure/Thriller**, **Crime**, **Fantasy**, **Science Fiction**, **Sea Stories** and **War** — have been sub-divided to help readers find novelists they will enjoy. Do remember that some authors use a different name when they write in another genre, and others will produce an occasional book which is quite different in character to their usual style. Always look at the book jacket and the introduction before you borrow or purchase.

Stories with fast moving plots, exotic settings and usually larger-than-life main characters and with the action full of thrilling and daring feats. Many of these authors specialised in stories set in the period of the cold war but increasingly now they have a political, financial industrial espionage or terrorist background.

Paul Adam
James Adams
Ted Allbeury
Eric Ambler
Colin Andrews
Russell Andrews
Geoffrey Archer
Campbell Armstrong
Michael Asher
Desmond Bagley
David Baldacci
Raymond Benson
Tim Binding
Alice Blanchard
Martin Booth
Tom Bradby
Suzanne Brockmann
Dale Brown
Dan Brown
James Buchan
John Buchan
Mark Burnell
Stephen J Cannell
Lorenzo Carcaterra
John Case
Lee Child
Lincoln Child
Tom Clancy
James Clavell
Nicholas Coleridge
Stephen Coonts
Michael Cordy
Bryce Courtenay
Harold Coyle
Conor Cregan
Clive Cussler
Murray Davies
John Gordon Davis
Len Deighton
Nelson DeMille
June Drummond
Brendan Dubois
Daniel Easterman
Clive Egleton

Barry Eisler
Colin Falconer
Duncan Falconer
Dan Fesperman
Joseph Finder
Sean Flannery
Ian Fleming
Vince Flynn
James Follett
Ken Follett
Alan Folsom
Colin Forbes
Frederick Forsyth
Clare Francis
Brian Freemantle
Alexander Fullerton
John Fullerton
Alan Furst
Joseph R Garber
John Gardner
Lisa Gardner
Lury Gibson
John Gilstrap
Robert Goddard
Jean-Christophe Grangé
Jeff Gulvin
David Hagberg
Brian Haig
Pete Hamill
Robert Harris
Colin Harrison
Stuart Harrison
Jack Harvey
Humphrey Hawksley
Paul Henke
Richard Herman
Jack Higgins
Tobias Hill
Philip Hook
Gwen Hunter
Stephen Hunter
Graham Hurley
Greg Iles
Hammond Innes

Donald James
Laurent Joffrin
Alan Judd
Joseph Kanon
John Katzenbach
Thomas Kelly
Judith Kelman
Douglas Kennedy
Gordon Kent
Philip Kerr
Michael Kimball
John Lawton
John Le Carré
Stephen Leather
Robert Littell
Sam Llewellyn
James Long
Robert Ludlum
Eric Lustbader
Gavin Lyall
Amin Maalouf
Charles McCarry
Alistair MacLean
Michael Marshall
David Mason
John R Maxim
Jenny Maxwell
Glenn Meade
Patricia Melo
David Michie
Kyle Mills
David Morrell
John J Nance
Bill Napier
John Nichol
Christopher Nicole
Hilary Norman
Gareth O'Callaghan
Chris Paling
James Pattinson
Henry Porter
Stanley Pottinger
Douglas Preston
Anthony Price

Adventure/Thriller *(cont)*

A J Quinnell
Julian Rathbone
Matthew Reilly
Kenneth Royce
Chris Ryan
Robert Ryan
Lawrence Sanders
Julian Jay Savarin
Tim Sebastian
Gerald Seymour
Sidney Sheldon
Nevil Shute
James Siegel
Daniel Silva
Paullina Simons
Scott Smith
Wilbur Smith
Mark T Sullivan
James Thayer
Craig Thomas
Nigel West
Robin White
Tim Willocks
Robert Wilson
Stuart Woods
Glover Wright

Amateur sleuth
Caroline Carver

Historical
Arturo Pérez-Reverte

Horse racing
Lyndon Stacey

Legal/financial
Jeff Abbott
Harry Bingham
John Burdett
Alafair Burke
Linda Davies
Brad Meltzer
Michael Ridpath
Sabin Willett

Medical
Robin Cook
Michael Palmer

Modern
Thomas Harris

Police work
Jon Cleary *Australia*
David Lindsey *US*

Psychological
Keith Russell Ablow
Lisa Appignanesi
Suzanne Berne
Mary Higgins Clark
Jeremy Dronfield
Leslie Forbes
Nicci French
Joanna Hines
Andrew Klavan
J Wallis Martin
Julie Parsons
Christina Schwarz
Gillian White

Spy
Evelyn Anthony

Aga Saga

A phrase that came into being in the early 1990s, the Aga Sagas are novels based upon the middle-class surroundings of the type of person that typically owns an Aga cooker, but who is not immune to the emotional dilemmas that can confront all classes of society.

Diana Appleyard
Judy Astley
Anne Atkins
Maeve Binchy
Amanda Brookfield
Elizabeth Buchan
Sarah Challis
Lucy Clare
Victoria Clayton
Marika Cobbold
Anne Doughty
Nina Dufort
Elizabeth Falconer
Patricia Fawcett

Kate Fenton
Katie Fforde
Kate Fielding
Adèle Geras
Rebecca Gregson
Julia Hamilton
Julie Highmore
Hazel Hucker
Kate Long
Sarah MacDonald
Charlotte Moore
Stevie Morgan
Nora Naish
Elizabeth Noble

Elizabeth Palmer
Robin Pilcher
Rosamunde Pilcher
Kathleen Rowntree
Jean Saunders
Kate Saunders
Diana Saville
Ann Swinfen
Peta Tayler
Joanna Trollope
Amanda Eyre Ward
Sophia Watson
Mary Wesley
Madeleine Wickham
Jane Yardley

Stories written by young women for other young women, usually with a central plot of boyfriend mishaps and the problems of staying in shape.

Jessica Adams
Cecelia Ahern
Maggie Alderson
Catherine Alliott
Anita Anderson
Lisa Armstrong
Trisha Ashley
Valerie-Anne Baglietto
Louise Bagshawe
Sarah Ball
Zoë Barnes
Emily Barr
Lynne Barrett-Lee
Susannah Bates
Susie Boyt
Colette Caddle
Dawn Cairns
Claire Calman
Rebecca Campbell
Alexandra Carew
Jaye Carroll
Francesca Clementis
Victoria Colby
Jenny Colgan
Victoria Corby
Jenny Crusie
Claudine Cullimore
Martina Devlin
Clare Dowling
Anne Dunlop
Sabine Durrant
Jenny Eclair
Imogen Edwards-Jones
Helen Fielding

Jane Green
Sue Haasler
Sarah Harvey
Louise Harwood
Donna Hay
Tara Heavey
Suzanne Higgins
Melissa Hill
Wendy Holden
Amy Jenkins
Lisa Jewell
Christina Jones
Louise Kean
Cathy Kelly
Marian Keyes
Sophie Kinsella
Dorothy Koomson
Amanda Lees
Kathy Lette
Josie Lloyd & Emlyn Rees
Laura Lockington
Shari Low
L McCrossan
Jacinta McDevitt
Monica McInerney
Serena Mackesy
Marissa Mackle
Chris Manby
Tara Manning
Jill Mansell
Sue Margolis
Louise Marley
Sarah Mason
Carole Matthews

Anna Maxted
Sharon Mulrooney
Amanda Murphy
Marian Murphy
Melissa Nathan
Claire Naylor
Freya North
Sheila Norton
Anita Notaro
Tyne O'Connell
Sheila O'Flanagan
Adele Parks
Claudia Pattison
Alexandra Potter
Morag Prunty
Carmen Reid
Tina Reilly
Kathy Rodgers
Victoria Routledge
Patricia Scanlan
Andrea Semple
Stephanie Theobald
Kate Thompson
Fiona Walker
Daisy Waugh
Sarah Webb
Jennifer Weiner
Arabella Weir
Jane Wenham-Jones
Laura Wolf
Deborah Wright
Liz Young
Stephanie Zia
Laura Zigman

Crime

This type of novel is usually characterised by the clues which gradually lead the reader to the final solution, often within an atmosphere of rising tension or danger. Although there are basically two types of detective, the private investigator *(PI)* and the official policeman, there are an increasing number of subgenres within these two broad headings. The style of crime writing has been divided, in the majority of cases, into separate headings, and under each is shown the list of authors who usually but not always write in that vein.

Amateur sleuth
Margery Allingham
Ace Atkins
Marian Babson
C J Box
Lilian Jackson Braun
Simon Brett
Edna Buchanan
Jan Burke
Charlotte Carter
Sarah Caudwell
Agatha Christie
Harlan Coben
Tim Cockey
Natasha Cooper
Judith Cutler
Denise Danks
Eileen Dewhurst
Anabel Donald
Martin Edwards
Ruth Dudley Edwards
Ron Ellis
Elizabeth Ferrars
Dick Francis
John Francome
Frances Fyfield
Jonathan Gash
Denise Hamilton
Gerald Hammond
Janis Harrison
Carolyn G Hart
Veronica Heley
Lauren Henderson
Joyce Holms
Hazel Holt
Alison Joseph
Jim Kelly
Jonathon King
Janet Laurence
Roy Lewis
Marianne MacDonald

Charlotte MacLeod
John Malcolm
Shane Maloney
Liza Marklund
Margaret Maron
M R D Meek
Denise Mina
Gladys Mitchell
Gwen Moffat
Fiona Mountain
Chris Niles
Iain Pears
Jenny Pitman
Richard Pitman
Ann Purser
Mike Ripley
Betty Rowlands
Dorothy L Sayers
Zoë Sharp
Simon Shaw
Charles Spencer
Veronica Stallwood
Scarlett Thomas
Rebecca Tope
M J Trow
Patricia Wentworth
Don Winslow

Forensic
Max Allan Collins
Patricia D Cornwell
Jeffery Deaver
Iris Johansen
Keith McCarthy
Nigel McCrery
Kathy Reichs
Karin Slaughter

Hardboiled
Jake Arnott
Nicholas Blincoe
Lawrence Block

Anthony Bourdain
Ken Bruen
James Lee Burke
Jeremy Cameron
Jerome Charyn
James Hadley Chase
Martina Cole
David Cray
Alan Dunn
James Ellroy
Robert Ferrigno
G M Ford
Mandasue Heller
Vicki Hendricks
George V Higgins
Jon A Jackson
Bill James
Russell James
Simon Kernick
Elmore Leonard
Walter Mosley
Chuck Palahniuk
David Peace
George P Pelecanos
Richard Price
Robert T Price
James Sallis
John B Spencer
Jason Starr
Boston Teran
Jim Thompson
Martyn Waites

Historical
Rennie Airth
Boris Akunin *C19th*
Bruce Alexander *C18th*
Simon Beaufort *Medieval*
Alys Clare *Medieval*
Barbara Cleverly *C20th*
Michael Clynes *C16th*
Judith Cook *C16th*

Lindsey Davis *Ancient*
David Dickinson *C20th*
Paul Doherty
Margaret Doody *Ancient*
Patricia Finney *C16th*
Margaret Frazer *Medieval*
Janet Gleeson *C18th*
Philip Gooden *C16th*
John Maclachlan Gray *C19th*
Richard Grayson *C19th*
Susanna Gregory *Medieval*
Sylvian Hamilton *C13th*
Ray Harrison *C19th*
Jane Jakeman *C19th*
J Robert Janes *C20th*
Michael Jecks *Medieval*
Stuart M Kaminsky *C20th*
Laurie King *C20th*
Alanna Knight *C19th*
Bernard Knight *Medieval*
Deryn Lake *C18th*
Gillian Linscott *C20th*
David Liss *C18th*
Joan Lock *C19th*
Peter Lovesey *C19th*
Hannah March *C18th*
Edward Marston *Medieval*
Andrew Martin *C19th*
Viviane Moore *Medieval*
Fidelis Morgan *C17th*
Amy Myers *C19th*
Rebecca Pawel *C20th*
Michael Pearce *C20th*
Anne Perry *C19th*
Elizabeth Peters *C19th*
Ellis Peters *Medieval*
John Pilkington *C16th*
David Pirie *C19th*
Candace Robb *Medieval*
Barrie Roberts *C19th*
David Roberts *C20th*
Roberta Rogow *C19th*
Rosemary Rowe *Ancient*
Laura Joh Rowland *C17th*
Norman Russell *C19th*
C J Sansom *C16th*
Steven Saylor *Ancient*
Kate Sedley *Medieval*

Martin Stephen *C17th*
Charles Todd *C20th*
Marilyn Todd *Ancient*
Peter Tonkin *C16th*
Peter Tremayne *Medieval*
Gerard Williams *C19th*
Derek Wilson *C18th*
David Wishart *Ancient*
Joan Wolf *Medieval*

Humour
Dave Barry
Marc Blake
Christopher Brookmyre
Christopher Buckley
Tim Dorsey
Janet Evanovich
Jasper Fforde
Bill Fitzhugh
Christopher Fowler
Kinky Friedman
Peter Guttridge
Sparkle Hayter
Carl Hiaasen
Danny King
Joe R Lansdale
Douglas Lindsay
Pauline McLynn
Daniel Pennac
Scott Phillips
Malcolm Pryce
Zane Radcliffe
Laurence Shames
Sarah Strohmeyer
Donald E Westlake

Legal/financial
William Bernhardt
Po Bronson
D W Buffa
Jonathan Davies
William Diehl
Linda Fairstein
James Grippando
John Grisham
Craig Holden
Paul Kilduff
John T Lescroart
John McLaren

Phillip Margolin
Steve Martini
Perri O'Shaughnessy
Richard North Patterson
Christopher Reich
Nancy Taylor Rosenberg
Lisa Scottoline
Susan R Sloan
Robert K Tanenbaum
Scott Turow

Medical
Paul Carson
Tess Gerritsen
Ken McClure
Leah Ruth Robinson

Private Investigator (PI)
John Baker
Linda Barnes
Adam Baron
Cara Black
Raymond Chandler
Carol Higgins Clark
Robert Crais
James Crumley
Stephen Donaldson
Arthur Conan Doyle
Stella Duffy
Robert Edric
Loren D Estleman
Liz Evans
Reg Gadney
Meg Gardiner
Sue Grafton
James Hall
Steve Hamilton
Dashiell Hammett
Paul Johnston
Frank Lean
Laura Lippman
John D MacDonald
Ross Macdonald
Manuel Vázquez Montalbán
Marcia Muller
Reggie Nadelson
Sara Paretsky
Robert B Parker
Eliot Pattison

293

Crime

PI *(cont)*
John Shannon
Alexander McCall Smith
Michelle Spring
Dana Stabenow
Cath Staincliffe
Mark Timlin
Valerie Wilson Wesley
Stella Whitelaw

Police work - UK
Catherine Aird
Vivien Armstrong
Jeffrey Ashford
Meg Elizabeth Atkins
Jo Bannister
Robert Barnard
M C Beaton
Pauline Bell
Mark Billingham
Janie Bolitho
W J Burley
Gwendoline Butler
Paul Charles
Ann Cleeves
John Connor
Brian Cooper
Deborah Crombie
Clare Curzon
Freda Davies
Colin Dexter
Margaret Duffy
Marjorie Eccles
Kate Ellis
Geraldine Evans
Anthea Fraser
John Gardner
Elizabeth George
Caroline Graham
Ann Granger
Alex Gray
J M Gregson
Martha Grimes
Georgie Hale
Patricia Hall
Cynthia Harrod-Eagles
Roy Hart
John Harvey
Reginald Hill

Lesley Horton
Graham Hurley
Michael Innes
Graham Ison
P D James
Quintin Jardine
H R F Keating
Susan B Kelly
Bill Knox
Frederic Lindsay
Peter Lovesey
Iain McDowall
Jill McGown
Barry Maitland
Ngaio Marsh
Priscilla Masters
Maureen O'Brien
Nick Oldham
Stuart Pawson
Ellis Peters
Ian Rankin
Ruth Rendell
Nicholas Rhea
Peter Robinson
Dorothy Simpson
Sally Spencer
Andrew Taylor
Josephine Tey
Leslie Thomas
June Thomson
Peter Turnbull
David Williams
R D Wingfield

Police work - US
Michael Connelly
Paula Gosling
W E B Griffin
Donald Harstad
William Heffernan
Lynn Hightower
Tony Hillerman
J A Jance
Faye Kellerman
Jonathan Kellerman
Lynda La Plante
Thomas Laird
Dennis Lehane
Ed McBain

Michael McGarrity
Michael Malone
Archer Mayor
Theresa Monsour
Carol O'Connell
Jefferson Parker
Ridley Pearson
J D Robb
John Sandford
Jess Walter
Joseph Wambaugh

Police work - other foreign
Giles Blunt *Canada*
Andrea Camilleri *Italy*
Michael Dibdin *Italy*
Karin Fossum *Norway*
Luiz Alfredo Garcia-Roza
  Brazil
Bartholomew Gill *Ireland*
Juan Goytisolo *Spain*
Juliet Hebden *France*
Mark Hebden *France*
David Hewson *Italy*
Roderic Jeffries *Spain*
José Latour *Cuba*
Donna Leon *Italy*
Jim Lusby *Ireland*
Claire McNab *Australia*
Henning Mankell *Sweden*
Peter May *China*
Magdalen Nabb *Italy*
Barbara Nadel *Turkey*
Lisa See *China*
Georges Simenon *France*
Maj Sjöwall and
  Per Wahlöö *Sweden*
Martin Cruz Smith *Russia*
Fred Vargas *France*
Christopher West *China*
Qiu Xiaolong *China*

Psychological
Jane Adams
Karin Alvtegen
Andrea Badenoch
Ingrid Black
Hilary Bonner
Stephen Booth

John Connolly
Thomas H Cook
Carol Anne Davis
Sarah Diamond
Roger Jon Ellory
Joy Fielding
Carol Goodman
Gregory Hall
Mo Hayder
Daniel Hecht
Frances Hegarty
Christiane Heggan
Patricia Highsmith
Tami Hoag
Morag Joss
Alex Kava

Gay Longworth
Phil Lovesey
Sharyn McCrumb
Val McDermid
Elizabeth McGregor
Pierre Magnan
Margaret Murphy
Jonathan Nasaw
Meg O'Brien
Ed O'Connor
Gemma O'Connor
James Patterson
Andrew Pyper
Sarah Rayne
Danuta Reah
Patrick Redmond

Liz Rigbey
Pernille Rygg
Louis Sanders
Jenny Siler
Chris Simms
Carol Smith
Erica Spindler
Boris Starling
Tony Strong
Alison Taylor
P J Tracy
Barbara Vine
Minette Walters
Stephen White
Laura Wilson
Margaret Yorke

Fantasy

Fantasy novels — as distinct from Science Fiction — deal with the impossible, being based on magic or the supernatural. They follow no scientific 'rules', only the whim of the author. While there are many sub-divisions in the world of Fantasy, we have used six sub-genres to help readers find the kind of book they most enjoy: **Contemporary** – the intrusion of the fantastic into modern life; **Dark** – Fantasy which incorporates a sense of horror; **Epic** – books in which heroes and heroines wage epic combat with forces of evil; **Myth** – authors who place their stories in worlds of myth, saga and legend, particularly Celtic; **Humour** – not all fantasy is dark, and these authors write light and humorous stories, often including elements of familiar folk tales; **Literary** – the characters of fiction and literature in general take on reality in a fantasy world rich in literary allusion. A few crossover children's authors have now been included to represent the growing interest in this younger section of the genre.

Barbara Hambly
Philip Pullman
Michael Scott Rohan

Contemporary
Gene Brewer
Mark Chadbourn
John Crowley
Charles de Lint
Neil Gaiman
Tim Powers

Dark
Jonathan Carroll
Storm Constantine
Jonathan Green
Tanith Lee

Epic
Mark Anthony
Sarah Ash
Robert Asprin
James Barclay
Carol Berg
Joanne Bertin
Marion Zimmer Bradley
Terry Brooks
Steven Brust
Chris Bunch
Trudi Canavan
James Clemens
Eoin Colfer
Louise Cooper
Stephen Donaldson

Sara Douglass
David A Drake
David Eddings
Kate Elliott
Steven Erikson
David Farland
Raymond E Feist
Jude Fisher
Maggie Furey
David Gemmell
Mary Gentle
Terry Goodkind
Julia Gray
Simon R Green
Elizabeth Haydon
Robin Hobb

Fantasy

Epic (cont)
Ian Irvine
Kate Jacoby
J V Jones
Robert Jordan
Guy Gavriel Kay
Paul Kearney
Greg Keyes
Katherine Kurtz
Mercedes Lackey
Ursula K Le Guin
Valery Leith
Megan Lindholm
Holly Lisle
Juliet E McKenna
John Marco
George R R Martin
Julian May
L E Modesitt Jr
Elizabeth Moon
Michael Moorcock
Robert Newcomb
Stan Nicholls
Adam Nichols
William Nicholson

K J Parker
Melanie Rawn
Mickey Zucker Reichert
J K Rowling
Sean Russell
R A Salvatore
Jan Siegel
Sheri S Tepper
J R R Tolkien
Harry Turtledove
Freda Warrington
Margaret Weis
Jane Welch
Tad Williams
Janny Wurts
Jonathan Wylie
Roger Zelazny

Humour
Piers Anthony
Craig Shaw Gardner
Andrew Harman
Tom Holt
Terry Pratchett
Martin Scott

Literary
Robert Holdstock
C S Lewis
Gene Wolfe

Myth
Ashok K Banker
Alice Borchardt
C J Cherryh
Cecilia Dart-Thornton
Sylvie Germain
Katharine Kerr
Stephen R Lawhead
Juliet Marillier
Caiseal Mor
Garth Nix
Ricardo Pinto
William Sarabande
Judith Tarr
T H White
Sarah Zettel

Glitz & Glamour

This genre features the modern world of big business and entertainment, with generous proportions of sex, violence and avarice.

Maria Barrett
Sally Beauman
Celia Brayfield
Sandra Brown
Candace Bushnell
Alexandra Campbell
Jackie Collins
Joan Collins
Jilly Cooper
Jenn Crowell

Jude Deveraux
Lucinda Edmonds
Julie Ellis
Olivia Goldsmith
Judith Gould
Judi James
Judith Krantz
Jayne Ann Krentz
Roberta Latow
Susan Lewis

Johanna Lindsey
Frankie McGowan
Judith Michael
Fern Michaels
Una-Mary Parker
Harold Robbins
Madge Swindells
Caroline Upcher
Penny Vincenzi

Another very popular category, where fictional characters are set against an actual historical perspective, with close and realistic links between fiction and fact. Some are based on real people and events, while others are purely imaginary.

Elizabeth Aston
Jean M Auel
Margaret Bacon
Geraldine Brooks
Elizabeth Chadwick
Joy Chambers
Marion Chesney
Tracy Chevalier
Gloria Cook
Catherine Coulter
Teresa Crane
Will Davenport
Sara Donati
June Drummond
Dorothy Dunnett
Robert Edric
Margaret Elphinstone
Barbara Erskine
Michael Curtis Ford
Diana Gabaldon
Julie Garwood
Pauline Gedge
Margaret George
Winston Graham
Philippa Gregory
Sandra Gulland
Cynthia Harrod-Eagles

Caroline Harvey
Anne Haverty
Elizabeth Hawksley
Georgette Heyer
Joanna Hines
Jane Aiken Hodge
Helen Hollick
Sheri Holman
Victoria Holt
C C Humphreys
Conn Iggulden
Christian Jacq
Elizabeth Jeffrey
Ross King
Matthew Kneale
Rosalind Laker
Morgan Llywelyn
Genevieve Lyons
Colleen McCullough
Valerio Massimo Manfredi
Allan Massie
Robin Maxwell
Rosalind Miles
Andrew Miller
Diana Norman
Edith Pargeter
Christopher Peachment

Margaret Pemberton
Sharon Penman
Maureen Peters
Steven Pressfield
Amanda Quick
Julian Rathbone
Mary Renault
Cynthia S Roberts
James Robertson
James Runcie
Edward Rutherfurd
Simon Scarrow
Manda Scott
Anya Seton
Patricia Shaw
Wilbur Smith
Jane Stevenson
Reay Tannahill
E V Thompson
Nigel Tranter
Kate Tremayne
Barry Unsworth
Susan Vreeland
Peter Watt
Patricia Wendorf
Barbara Wood
Sarah Woodhouse

Horror

This section includes authors who frequently write suspense and horror, where the storyline involves pursuit and eventual escape — often from the supernatural, demonic or the occult.

David Ambrose
Kelley Armstrong
Jonathan Aycliffe
Richard Bachman
Clive Barker
David Bowker
Chaz Brenchley
Poppy Z Brite
Ramsey Campbell
Jonathan Carroll
Simon Clark
Douglas Clegg
Nancy Collins
John Farris
Christopher Fowler
Stephen Gallagher
Muriel Gray
Laurell K Hamilton

Charlaine Harris
James Herbert
Tom Holland
Tanya Huff
Shaun Hutson
Peter James
Graham Joyce
Jeanne Kalogridis
Stephen King
Dean R Koontz
Stephen Laws
Richard Laymon
Bentley Little
H P Lovecraft
Brian Lumley
Robert McCammon
David Martin

Graham Masterton
Richard Matheson
Mark Morris
Gloria Murphy
Kim Newman
Scott Nicholson
Christopher Pike
Anne Rice
Phil Rickman
John Saul
Dan Simmons
S P Somtow
Steven Spruill
Peter Straub
Whitley Strieber
Tim Wilson
T M Wright

Humour

A select group of authors whose novels are mainly written to amuse.

Sherry Ashworth
Nicholson Baker
Colin Bateman
Faith Bleasdale
T Coraghessan Boyle
Marius Brill
Mavis Cheek
Jonathan Coe
Joseph Connolly
Roddy Doyle
George Macdonald Fraser
Michael Frayn
Stephen Fry
Maggie Gibson

James Hawes
Charles Higson
Tom Holt
Sean Hughes
Garrison Keillor
Sue Limb
Robert Llewellyn
John McCabe
Magnus Mills
John Mortimer
Geoff Nicholson
David Nobbs
Joseph O'Connor
Kate O'Riordan

Allison Pearson
Alexei Sayle
Tom Sharpe
William Sutcliffe
Linda Taylor
Alan Titchmarsh
Sue Townsend
Lynne Truss
Mark Wallington
Keith Waterhouse
Louise Wener
Nigel Williams
P G Wodehouse
Isabel Wolff

Nick Hornby and Tony Parsons began the male equivalent to Chick Lit. Written about men in the same age range who have trouble expressing their emotions.

David Baddiel
Mark Barrowcliffe
Matthew Beaumont
Dougie Brimson
Colin Butts
Nick Earls
Ben Elton
Cy Flood
Mike Gayle
Alex George

Nick Hornby
John King
Tim Lott
David Nicholls
Tony Parsons
Kevin Sampson
Sean Thomas
Matt Thorne
Matt Whyman

Humour
Simon Armitage
Richard Asplin
Paul Burke
James Delingpole
John Harding
Ben Hatch
Mil Millington
John O'Farrell
Damien Owens
Paul Reizin
Willy Russell

Saga

A popular genre, frequently set against an historical background, telling the story of two or more generations of a family, with the plot often revolving around the purchase of property or the development of a family business.

Elizabeth Adler
Rosemary Aitken
Vanessa Alexander
Lyn Andrews
Aileen Armitage
Anne Baker
Donna Baker
Tessa Barclay
Anne Bennett
Maggie Bennett
Emma Blair
Jessica Blair
Philip Boast
Rose Boucheron
Harry Bowling
Clare Boylan
Barbara Taylor Bradford
Rita Bradshaw
Louise Brindley
Benita Brown
Julia Bryant
Anita Burgh
Betty Burton
Helen Cannam

Helen Carey
Irene Carr
Jean Chapman
Brenda Clarke
Harry Cole
Catrin Collier
Alexandra Connor
Catherine Cookson
Josephine Cox
Maggie Craig
Elaine Crowley
Janet Dailey
Elizabeth Daish
Emma Dally
Elizabeth Darrell
Doris Davidson
Margaret Thomson Davis
Frank Delaney
R F Delderfield
Margaret Dickinson
Inga Dunbar
Elizabeth Elgin
Pamela Evans
Katie Flynn

Helen Forrester
June Francis
Christine Marion Fraser
Sara Fraser
Elizabeth Gill
Iris Gower
Margaret Graham
Patricia Grey
Ruth Hamilton
Lilian Harry
Meg Henderson
Elizabeth Ann Hill
Evelyn Hood
Una Horne
Audrey Howard
Susan Howatch
Harriet Hudson
Meg Hutchinson
Sara Hylton
Anna Jacobs
Sheila Jansen
Joan Jonker
Penny Jordan
Marie Joseph

Saga (cont)

Margaret Kaine
Nora Kay
Erin Kaye
Sheelagh Kelly
Lena Kennedy
Anna King
Beryl Kingston
Gwen Kirkwood
Mary A Larkin
Maureen Lee
Judith Lennox
Freda Lightfoot
Elizabeth Lord
Claire Lorrimer
Brenda McBryde
Mary McCarthy
Malcolm Macdonald
Mary Mackie
Elisabeth McNeill
Gwen Madoc
Beryl Matthews
Margaret Mayhew
Anne Melville
Mary Minton
Connie Monk
Catrin Morgan
Elizabeth Murphy
Annie Murray
Isobel Neill
Sheila Newberry
Geraldine O'Neill
Gilda O'Neill

Joan O'Neill
Jenny Oldfield
Pamela Oldfield
Sharon Owens
Lynda Page
Frances Paige
Mary E Pearce
Victor Pemberton
Belva Plain
D M Purcell
Alexandra Raife
Eileen Ramsay
Claire Rayner
Miss Read
Elvi Rhodes
Pam Rhodes
Denise Robertson
Wendy Robertson
Malcolm Ross
Liz Ryan
Susan Sallis
Judith Saxton
Sarah Shears
Anne Rivers Siddons
Linda Sole
LaVyrle Spencer
Sally Spencer
Eileen Stafford
Mary Jane Staples
Danielle Steel
Kay Stephens
Sally Stewart

Caroline Stickland
Jessica Stirling
Alison Stuart
Jean Stubbs
Sue Sully
Janet Tanner
June Tate
Alice Taylor
Michael Taylor
Rosie Thomas
Grace Thompson
Nicola Thorne
Margaret Thornton
Eileen Townsend
Adriana Trigiani
Janet MacLeod Trotter
Anne Vivis
Elizabeth Waite
Elizabeth Walker
Kirsty White
Jeanne Whitmee
Barbara Whitnell
Marcia Willett
Dee Williams
Audrey Willsher
T R Wilson
Mary Withall
Valerie Wood
Janet Woods
Sally Worboyes
Anne Worboys

Although Science Fiction (SF) and Fantasy are often mixed, SF deals with the possible, and is based (often tenuously) on scientific knowledge obeying the laws of nature in the universe — however fantastic some of the stories may seem. The literature of SF is substantial and we have used five subgenres to help you find the type of author you want to read: **Near future** – stories concerning all pervasive technologies, their use and misuse, normally set within the next hundred years; **Space opera** – space adventure stories of extravagant dimensions, often involving galactic empires and space battles; **Space and time** – travel into either the past or the future, exploring history as it might have been, or the future as the author sees it; **Technical** – SF novels with an overriding emphasis on the technical and scientific achievement, usually involving flight into outer space; **Humour** – authors whose books highlight the humorous aspects of SF.

Humour
Douglas Adams
Rob Grant
Harry Harrison
Robert Rankin

Near future
Neal Asher
Steve Aylett
Eric Brown
Pat Cadigan
Greg Egan
William Gibson
Jon Courtenay Grimwood
Gwyneth Jones
James Lovegrove
Richard Morgan
Jeff Noon
Richard Powers
Kim Stanley Robinson
Justina Robson
Nick Sagan
Lucius Shepard
Michael Marshall Smith
Neal Stephenson
Bruce Sterling
Tad Williams
John Wyndham

Space and time
Brian W Aldiss
Isaac Asimov
Ben Bova
Ray Bradbury
Philip K Dick
Harlan Ellison
Robert A Heinlein

Anne McCaffrey
Jack McDevitt
Ian McDonald
Ken MacLeod
China Miéville
Larry Niven
Christopher Priest
Kristine Kathryn Rusch
Robert Silverberg
Jules Verne
Kurt Vonnegut
Ian Watson
H G Wells
Connie Willis
Robert Charles Wilson
David Wingrove
David Zindell

Space opera
Dan Abnett
Kevin J Anderson
Poul Anderson
Iain M Banks
David Brin
John Brosnan
Lois McMaster Bujold
Orson Scott Card
C J Cherryh
Ben Counter
David Feintuch
Alan Dean Foster
Colin Greenland
Joe Haldeman
Peter F Hamilton
Brian Herbert
Frank Herbert

Michael P Kube-McDowell
Robert Reed
Alastair Reynolds
Adam Roberts
Dan Simmons
Charles Stross

Technical
J G Ballard
Stephen Baxter
Greg Bear
Gregory Benford
Arthur C Clarke
K W Jeter
Paul J McAuley
Wil McCarthy
John Meaney
Linda Nagata
Brian Stableford

Sea

A popular category where many authors have made a well-deserved reputation for writing about the sea either in an historical or a modern setting. Many novelists in this genre will also be found under **Adventure/Thriller** and also under **War stories**.

Historical
Tom Connery
David Donachie
C S Forester
Alexander Kent
Jonathan Lunn
Jan Needle
James L Nelson
Patrick O'Brian
Marcus Palliser
Dan Parkinson
Julian Stockwin
Showell Styles
Victor Suthren
Richard Woodman

Historical & Modern
Philip McCutchan
Dudley Pope

Modern
Brian Callison
James Cobb
Duncan Harding
Nicholas Monsarrat
Douglas Reeman
Patrick Robinson
Justin Scott
Peter Tonkin
Antony Trew

War

Authors who have written widely but not exclusively about war, generally within the 19th and 20th centuries. Many books about war will also be found under **Adventure/Thriller** and also under **Sea stories**. Some **General** novelists have also written individual books about war.

Guy Walters
James Webb

Historical
Bernard Cornwell
Garry Douglas
Daniel Hall
Richard Howard
Allan Mallinson
Patrick Rambaud

Modern
Shaun Clarke
Francis Cottam
W E B Griffin
Eric L Harry
Johnny 'Two Combs'
   Howard
Robert Jackson
Leo Kessler
Mike Lunnon-Wood
Andy McNab
Robert Radcliffe
David L Robbins
Derek Robinson
Alan Savage
Terence Strong

Characters and Series

This section lists all the Characters, Series and Family names which appear in the main A–Z sequence of the guide.

A

Ben Abbott	Justin Scott
Abdouf	Jean-Christophe Grangé
Jack Absolute	C C Humphreys
Johnny Ace	Ron Ellis
Laura Ackroyd	Patricia Hall
Adams Family	Mary Jane Staples
Commissaire Adamsberg	Fred Vargas
Sister Agnes Bourdillon	Alison Joseph
Captain Alatriste	Arturo Pérez-Reverte
Albany Series	William Kennedy
Alexander the Great	Paul Doherty
Alexander the Great	Valerio Massimo Manfredi
DS Khalid Ali	Lesley Horton
DI Roderick Alleyn	Ngaio Marsh
Alpiew	Fidelis Morgan
DI Enrique Alvarez	Roderic Jeffries
Amerotke	Paul Doherty
Simon Ames	Patricia Finney
Robert Amiss	Ruth Dudley Edwards
Peter Amsterdam	Laurence Shames
Fitzroy Maclean Angel	Mike Ripley
Anno Dracula Series	Kim Newman
Joseph Antonelli	D W Buffa
Insp Wang Anzhuang	Christopher West
DI John Appleby	Michael Innes
Appletree Saga	Mary E Pearce
Lew Archer	Ross Macdonald
Owen Archer	Candace Robb
Comm Jan Argand	Julian Rathbone
Jonathan Argyll	Iain Pears
Aristotle	Margaret Doody
Sheriff Spenser Arrowood	Sharyn McCrumb
Arthurian Trilogy	Helen Hollick
Countess Ashby-de-la-Zouche	Fidelis Morgan
Peter Ashton	Clive Egleton
DI Carol Ashton	Claire McNab
Askham Family	Nicola Thorne
Brother Athelstan	Paul Doherty
Jack Aubrey	Patrick O'Brian
Dr David Audley	Anthony Price
Kurt Austin	Clive Cussler
Mick Axbrewder	Stephen Donaldson

B

Dr Frank Clevenger	Keith Russell Ablow
Com John Coffin	Gwendoline Butler
Artie Cohen	Reggie Nadelson
Insp Robert Colbeck	Edward Marston
Elvis Cole	Robert Crais
Lewis Cole	Brendan Dubois
Hap Collins	Joe R Lansdale
The Continental Op	Dashiell Hammett
Conway Family	Jessica Stirling
Alexandra Cooper	Linda Fairstein
DC Ben Cooper	Stephen Booth
PC Den Cooper	Rebecca Tope
Coppins Bridge Series	Elizabeth Daish
Hugh Corbaille	Joan Wolf
Sir Hugh Corbett	Paul Doherty
Cordwainer Series	Iris Gower
Det John Corey	Nelson DeMille
Lord Edward Corinth	David Roberts
Grace Cornish	Simon Shaw
Corps Series	W E B Griffin
Frank Corso	G M Ford
Corvill Family	Tessa Barclay
Marcus Corvinus	David Wishart
Det Nic Costa	David Hewson
Covert-One Series	Robert Ludlum
Craddock Family	R F Delderfield
Melissa Craig	Betty Rowlands
Craigallan Family	Tessa Barclay
Alan Craik	Gordon Kent
Francis Crawford of Lymond	Dorothy Dunnett
Tildy Crawford	Sara Fraser
Creasy	A J Quinnell
Sgt Cribb	Peter Lovesey
DI Mike Croft	Jane Adams
DS Crosby	Catherine Aird
Det Alex Cross	James Patterson
Sgt Jack Crossman	Garry Douglas
DI John Crow	Roy Lewis
Crowner John	Bernard Knight
Dave Cunane	Frank Lean
John Cunningham	Gerald Hammond
Richard Cypher	Terry Goodkind

D

Josse D'Acquin	Alys Clare
Supt Adam Dalgleish	P D James
Isabel Dalhousie	Alexander McCall Smith
Eve Dallas	J D Robb
Quintilian Dalrymple	Paul Johnston
Patrick Dalton	Dan Parkinson
DI Dalziel	Reginald Hill
The Dark Tower Series	Stephen King
Annie Darling and Max Darling	Carolyn G Hart

Lucas Davenport	John Sandford
'Dangerous' Davies	Leslie Thomas
Hugh de Lac	James Patterson
Chevalier Galeran de Lesnevan	Viviane Moore
Sir John de Wolfe	Bernard Knight
Lt Pete Decker	Faye Kellerman
Officer Cindy Decker	Faye Kellerman
Evan Delaney	Meg Gardiner
Alex Delaware	Jonathan Kellerman
Ralph Delchard	Edward Marston
John Delmas	Raymond Chandler
Det Lisa Delorme	Giles Blunt
Frank Dempsey	Paul Burke
Sgt Denny	Gwendoline Butler
Harry Devlin	Martin Edwards
Det Paul Devlin	William Heffernan
DI Alison Dexter	Ed O'Connor
Peter Diamond	Peter Lovesey
Eve Diamond	Denise Hamilton
Auguste Didier	Amy Myers
Sean Dillon	Jack Higgins
Trixie Dolan	Marian Babson
DS Cal Donovan	Jo Bannister
John Dortmunder	Donald E Westlake
Arthur Conan Doyle	Roberta Rogow
Arthur Conan Doyle	David Pirie
Family Dracul	Jeanne Kalogridis
Nathaniel Drinkwater	Richard Woodman
DI Jessie Driver	Gay Longworth
Drummond Family	Emma Blair
Philip Dryden	Jim Kelly
Mike Dukas	Gordon Kent
Steven Dunbar	Ken McClure
Eve Duncan	Iris Johansen
Roger of Durham	Simon Beaufort

E

Easter Empire	Beryl Kingston
Tam Eildor	Alanna Knight
Eisdalsa Island Trilogy	Mary Withall
John Eisenmenger	Keith McCarthy
DI Elder	John Harvey
Emma	Elizabeth Daish
Insp Espinosa	Luiz Alfredo Garcia-Roza

F

Fairacre	Miss Read
Robert Fairfax	Hannah March
Marcus Didius Falco	Lindsey Davis
Insp Javier Falcon	Robert Wilson
Thomas the Falconer	John Pilkington
Erast Fandorin	Boris Akunin
DI Joe Faraday	Graham Hurley
DI Jeremy Faro	Alanna Knight

Characters & Series

G

Evangeline Gower	Louisa Young
Rear Admiral Jake Grafton	Stephen Coonts
Davina Graham	Evelyn Anthony
DI Liz Graham	Jo Bannister
DI Alan Grant	Josephine Tey
Patrick Grant	Margaret Yorke
Cordelia Gray	P D James
Alan Gregory	Stephen White
Henry Gresham	Martin Stephen
Lew Griffin	James Sallis
Gil Grissom	Max Allan Collins
Marshal Guarnaccia	Magdalen Nabb
Lt Joe Gunther	Archer Mayor
Nathaniel Gye	Derek Wilson

St Vincent Halfhyde	Philip McCutchan
Sid Halley	Dick Francis
Judy Hammer	Patricia D Cornwell
DI Handford	Lesley Horton
Sigrid Harald	Margaret Maron
DI Hardcastle	Graham Ison
Hardie Family	Anne Melville
Dismas Hardy	John T Lescroart
Robert Harland	Henry Porter
Steve Harmas	James Hadley Chase
Ch Supt Colin Harpur	Bill James
Emma Harte	Barbara Taylor Bradford
DS Barbara Havers	Elizabeth George
Det Al Hawkin	Laurie King
Hawksmoor Series	Aileen Armitage
Det Stuart Haydon	David Lindsey
DS Roger Hayes	Vivien Armstrong
Nanette Hayes	Charlotte Carter
Tamara Hayle	Valerie Wilson Wesley
Heart of Gold Series	Catrin Collier
Zatopek "Zed" van Heerden	Deon Meyer
Abbess Helewise	Alys Clare
DCI Hennessy	Peter Turnbull
Heron Saga	Pamela Oldfield
Matthew Hervey	Allan Mallinson
DI Judy Hill	Jill McGown
Dr Tony Hill	Val McDermid
Hillsbridge Family	Janet Tanner
Kate Hilton	Margaret Dickinson
Dido Hoare	Marianne MacDonald
Billy-Bob Holland	James Lee Burke
Sherlock Holmes	Arthur Conan Doyle
Sherlock Holmes	Laurie King
Sherlock Holmes	Barrie Roberts
Max Holt	Janet Evanovich
Det Bert Hook	J M Gregson
Alison Hope	Susan B Kelly

DS Lloyd Hopkins	James Ellroy
Ward Hopkins	Michael Marshall
Horatio Hornblower	C S Forester
Dep Sheriff Carl Houseman	Donald Harstad
Howarth Chronicles	Jean Stubbs
Robin Hudson	Sparkle Hayter
Insp Liu Hulan	Lisa See
DI Sheldon Hunter	Meg Elizabeth Atkins

I

Sano Ichiro	Laura Joh Rowland
Cetin Ikmen	Barbara Nadel
ACC Desmond Iles	Bill James
Kate Ivory	Veronica Stallwood

J

DS Ken Jackson	Anthea Fraser
DI Saul Jackson	Norman Russell
DCI Jacobson	Iain McDowall
Sgt Gemma James	Deborah Crombie
Jeeves	P G Wodehouse
Sam Jones	Lauren Henderson
Constable Sunset Jones	Joe R Lansdale
DCI Carol Jordan	Val McDermid
DCI Richard Jury	Martha Grimes

K

Dmitri Kameron	Michael Pearce
India Kane	Caroline Carver
Kane Family	Frank Delaney
Roger 'Butch' Karp	Robert K Tanenbaum
Kevin Kearney	Michael McGarrity
George Keene	Derek Wilson
John Keller	Lawrence Block
Sarah Kelling	Charlotte MacLeod
Irene Kelly	Jan Burke
Clare Kelso	Jessica Stirling
Commodore Kemp	Philip McCutchan
Lennox Kemp	M R D Meek
DI Christy Kennedy	Paul Charles
Jerry Kennedy	George V Higgins
Patrick Kenzie	Dennis Lehane
Harry Keogh	Brian Lumley
Margaret Kerr	Candace Robb
DS Kerr	Iain McDowall
Kershaw Sisters	Anna Jacobs
Kidd	John Sandford
Sal Kilkenny	Cath Staincliffe
Kit Killigrew	Jonathan Lunn
Supt Duncan Kincaid	Deborah Crombie
DDA Samantha Kincaid	Alafair Burke
Willow King	Natasha Cooper
Kings Series	Christine Marion Fraser
Louie Knight	Malcolm Pryce
Deborah Knott	Margaret Maron

Hermann Kohler	J Robert Janes
Koko (Siamese cat)	Lilian Jackson Braun
DS Kathy Kolla	Barry Maitland
DS Mike Korpanski	Priscilla Masters
Takeshi Kovacs	Richard Morgan
Big Herbie Kruger	John Gardner
Thomas Paine Kydd	Julian Stockwin

L

Jordan Lacey	Stella Whitelaw
Tim Lacy	Derek Wilson
Det John Lambert	J M Gregson
Arnold Landon	Roy Lewis
Professor Robert Langdon	Dan Brown
Ingrid Langley	Margaret Duffy
Lilac Larkin	Katie Flynn
Stephen Larkin	Martyn Waites
Dr Samantha Laschen	Nicci French
John Latymer	Judith Cook
Sgt Alain Lausard	Richard Howard
CS Vernon Lavelle	David Bowker
Lavender Road Series	Helen Carey
Rina Lazarus	Faye Kellerman
DI Tim Le Page	Eileen Dewhurst
Joe Leaphorn	Tony Hillerman
Dr Hannibal Lecter	Thomas Harris
Aimée Leduc	Cara Black
John Lempriere	Lawrence Norfolk
Det Supt Sholto Lestrade	M J Trow
Stone Lewis	John Baker
Libertus	Rosemary Rowe
Jack Liffey	John Shannon
DS Lineham	Dorothy Simpson
Nicholas Linnear	Eric Lustbader
Sara Linton	Karin Slaughter
Darina Lisle	Janet Laurence
Sgt D Llewellyn	Geraldine Evans
DCI Lloyd	Jill McGown
Sgt Gomer Lloyd	David Williams
Matthew Loftus	Marcus Palliser
Ben London	Philip Boast
London Sequence	Margaret Pemberton
Lord of the Two Lands Trilogy	Pauline Gedge
Lorimer Family	Anne Melville
DCI Lorrimer	Alex Gray
Loveday Series	Kate Tremayne
Lovejoy	Jonathan Gash
CI John Lubbock	Brian Cooper
Harry Ludlow	David Donachie
LuEllen	John Sandford
DCI Thomas Lynley	Elizabeth George
Lyons Corner House Series	Lilian Harry
Lytton Trilogy	Penny Vincenzi

M

PC Hamish MacBeth	M C Beaton
DI Cal McCadden	Jim Lusby
Terry McCaleb	Michael Connelly
Sharon McCone	Marcia Muller
Insp Peter McGarr	Bartholomew Gill
Travis McGee	John D MacDonald
McGrath Family	Frances Paige
DCI Michael McKenna	Alison Taylor
Joanna Mackenzie	Margaret Duffy
MacKintosh Sisters	Frances Paige
Peter Macklin	Loren D Estleman
Alex McKnight	Steve Hamilton
Patrick McLanahan	Dale Brown
Archie McNally	Lawrence Sanders
Andrina McPherson	Margaret Thomson Davis
Elizabeth McPherson	Sharyn McCrumb
Rose McQuinn	Alanna Knight
DI John Madden	Rennie Airth
Kenny Madigan	Robert T Price
Paul Madriani	Steve Martini
Nick Madrid	Peter Guttridge
Trish Maguire	Natasha Cooper
Commissaire Jules Maigret	Georges Simenon
Benjamin Malaussène	Daniel Pennac
Lord Ambrose Malfine	Jane Jakeman
Sgt Kathleen Mallory	Carol O'Connell
Vic Malloy	James Hadley Chase
Insp Scobie Malone	Jon Cleary
Sheila Malory	Hazel Holt
Chief Cuddy Mangum	Michael Malone
Sir Geoffrey Mappestone	Simon Beaufort
Mariner Series	Peter Tonkin
Div Supt Alan Markby	Ann Granger
George Markham	Tom Connery
Philip Marlowe	Raymond Chandler
Thomas Marlowe	James L Nelson
Miss Marple	Agatha Christie
DS Charles Marriott	Graham Ison
DCI Harriet Martens	H R F Keating
Saz Martin	Stella Duffy
Det Kate Martinelli	Laurie King
Daphne Matthews	Ridley Pearson
Stephen Maturin	Patrick O'Brian
Alex Mavros	Paul Johnston
Harry Maxim	Gavin Lyall
Peter Maxwell	M J Trow
John May	Christopher Fowler
Caroline Maybry	Jess Walter
Kate Mayfield	Nelson DeMille
Supt Gil Mayo	Marjorie Eccles
Lois Meade	Ann Purser

Major Mearns	Gwendoline Butler
Bruce Medway	Robert Wilson
DI Jim Meldrum	Frederic Lindsay
Kinsey Millhone	Sue Grafton
Milo Milodragovitch	James Crumley
Paris Minton	Walter Mosley
DI Benny Mitchell	Pauline Bell
Meredith Mitchell	Ann Granger
Mitford Series	Jan Karon
Tess Monaghan	Laura Lippman
Seraphin Monge	Pierre Magnan
Insp William Monk & Hester Monk	Anne Perry
Monkton Family	Margaret Thomson Davis
Insp Salvo Montalbano	Andrea Camilleri
Britt Montero	Edna Buchanan
Monty (dog)	Iris Johansen
Phyllida Moon	Eileen Dewhurst
DI Abigail Moon	Marjorie Eccles
Morland Dynasty	Cynthia Harrod-Eagles
DI Morse	Colin Dexter
Dr James Mortimer	Gerard Williams
PC Morton	Ray Harrison
DI Phil Moss	Bill Knox
DS Angus Mott	Clare Curzon
DS Suzie Mountford	John Gardner
Charlie Muffin	Brian Freemantle
Sgt 'Fang' Mulheisen	Jon A Jackson
Det Paris Murphy	Theresa Monsour
Tom Musgrave	Peter Tonkin

N

Vicki Nelson	Tanya Huff
Net Force Explorers	Tom Clancy
Newman	Colin Forbes
Thursday Next	Jasper Fforde
Neyler Family	Judith Saxton
Nicholson Family	Jessica Stirling
Pierre Niemans	Jean-Christophe Grangé
Noble Series	Christine Marion Fraser
Nugent Family	Betty Burton

O

Det Petra O'Connor	Jonathan Kellerman
Maggie O'Dell	Alex Kava
Maureen O'Donnell	Denise Mina
O'Hara Family	Elaine Crowley
Det Supt Oddie	Robert Barnard
Capt James Ogilvie	Philip McCutchan
Billy Oliphant	Alan Dunn
Michael Osbourne	Daniel Silva
Outlander Series	Diana Gabaldon
Gareth Owen (The Mamur Zapt)	Michael Pearce

S

Tim Simpson	John Malcolm
Evangeline Sinclair	Marian Babson
Joe Sixsmith	Reginald Hill
Jacob Skarre	Karin Fossum
DCI Bob Skinner	Quintin Jardine
DI Bill Slider	Cynthia Harrod-Eagles
DI Sloan	Catherine Aird
Drew Slocombe	Rebecca Tope
Henry Smart	Roddy Doyle
George Smiley	John Le Carré
Grace Smith	Liz Evans
Bretta Solomon	Janis Harrison
Sam Spade	Dashiell Hammett
Spenser	Robert B Parker
St Benet's Trilogy	Susan Howatch
Sookie Stackhouse	Charlaine Harris
DI Vera Stanhope	Ann Cleeves
Staples Family	Mary Jane Staples
Nathaniel Starbuck	Bernard Cornwell
David Stark	Lisa See
Dan Starkey	Colin Bateman
Clarice Starling	Thomas Harris
Jean-Louis St-Cyr	J Robert Janes
Nick Stefanos	George P Pelecanos
Stephanos	Margaret Doody
Stevenson Family Series	Malcolm Macdonald
Nick Stone	Andy McNab
Chief Jesse Stone	Robert B Parker
Stone of Light Trilogy	Christian Jacq
Stonemoor Series	Kay Stephens
Serge Storms	Tim Dorsey
Sir Richard Straccan	Sylvian Hamilton
Derek Strange	George P Pelecanos
Strathannan Series	Anne Vivis
Pearl Street	Maureen Lee
Leo Street	Pauline McLynn
Jim Stringer	Andrew Martin
Lt Jack Stryker	Paula Gosling
Det Milo Sturgis	Jonathan Kellerman
C W Sughrue	James Crumley
Sheriff John Victor Sully	Boston Teran
Supt Gregory Summers	Susan B Kelly
Dr Evelyn Sutcliffe	Leah Ruth Robinson
Sutton Family	Elizabeth Elgin
Swann Family	R F Delderfield
Sweet Rosie Series	Iris Gower
Jack Swyteck	James Grippando
Hilary Tamar	Sarah Caudwell
Alex Tanner	Anabel Donald
Tanner Trilogy	Harry Bowling
Tanquillan Series	Louise Brindley

T

Gerry Tate .... Marian Babson
DC Jennie Taylor .... Pauline Bell
Jack Taylor .... Ken Bruen
Taylor Family .... Sally Spencer
Carlos Tejada .... Rebecca Pawel
Telamon .... Paul Doherty
CI Mark Tench .... Brian Cooper
DCI Jane Tennison .... Lynda La Plante
Frank Terrell .... James Hadley Chase
DCI Michael Thackeray .... Patricia Hall
PC Thackeray .... Peter Lovesey
DCI Colin Thane .... Bill Knox
DI Luke Thanet .... Dorothy Simpson
Thomas the Falconer .... John Pilkington
Barney Thomson .... Douglas Lindsay
Thorn .... James Hall
DI Tom Thorne .... Mark Billingham
DI Richard Thornhill .... Andrew Taylor
Charles Thoroughgood .... Alan Judd
Three Sisters Island Trilogy .... Nora Roberts
Thrush Green .... Miss Read
Leslie Titmus .... John Mortimer
Tramont Family .... Tessa Barclay
Nick Travers .... Ace Atkins
Mark Treasure .... David Williams
Supt Perry Trethowan .... Robert Barnard
DCI Nick Trevellyan .... Susan B Kelly
Rose Trevelyan .... Janie Bolitho
Prof Kate Trevorne .... Paula Gosling
Tilly Trotter .... Catherine Cookson
Baroness Troutbeck .... Ruth Dudley Edwards
DS Troy .... Caroline Graham
Frederick Troy .... John Lawton
Capt Trujillo .... José Latour
Sam Turner .... John Baker
Turnham Malpas Series .... Rebecca Shaw
Tweed .... Colin Forbes
DI Keith Tyrell .... Freda Davies
Chris Tyroll .... Barrie Roberts

U
DI John Underwood .... Ed O'Connor
Francis Urquhart Trilogy .... Michael Dobbs
US Navy 'Seal' teams .... Suzanne Brockmann

V
Inspector Vadim .... Donald James
Martin Vail .... William Diehl
Valley Series .... Grace Thompson
Vampire Chronicles .... Anne Rice
Fran Varady .... Ann Granger
Lord Miles Vorkosigan .... Lois McMaster Bujold

Literary Prizes and Awards

There are over 250 literary prizes and awards available in the United Kingdom of which some 30 relate to fiction. These are listed in this section with a brief description of each award followed by the names of the winning authors and titles, generally from 1990 or when the award commenced. Earlier winners can be found in the 4th edition of this guide. Further details of all awards can be found by contacting the Book Trust at Book Trust House, 45 East Hill, London, SW18 2QZ or at www.booktrust.org.uk/prizes.

Authors Club First Novel Award

Introduced by Laurence Meynell in 1954. This is awarded to the most promising First Novel published by a writer in Great Britain.

1990	Alan Brownjohn	*The Way You Tell Them*
1991	Zina Rohan	*The Book of Wishes and Complaints*
1992	David Park	*The Healing*
1993	Nadeem Aslam	*Season of the Rainbirds*
1994	Andrew Cowan	*Pig*
1995	T J Armstrong	*Walter and the Resurrection of G*
1996	Yinka Adebayo	*A Kind of Black*
1997	Rhidian Brook	*The Testimony of Taliesin Jones*
1998	Mick Jackson	*The Underground Man*
1999	Jackie Kay	*Trumpet*
2000	Ann Harries	*Manly Pursuits*
2001	Brian Clarke	*The Stream*
2002	Carl Tighe	*Burning Worm*
2003	Dan Rhodes	*Timoleon Vieta Come Home*

James Tait Black Memorial Prizes

The James Tait Black Memorial Prizes, founded in memory of a partner in the publishing house A & C Black Ltd, were instituted in 1918. Two prizes are awarded annually; one for the best biography or work of that type and the other for the best work of fiction published during the calendar year. The prizes are the UK's oldest continuous book awards.

1990	William Boyd	*Brazzaville Beach*
1991	Iain Sinclair	*Downriver*
1992	Rose Tremain	*Sacred Country*
1993	Caryl Phillips	*Crossing the River*
1994	Alan Hollinghurst	*The Folding Star*
1995	Christopher Priest	*The Prestige*
joint winners { 1996	Graham Swift	*Last Orders*
1996	Alice Thompson	*Justine*
1997	Andrew Miller	*Ingenious Pain*
1998	Beryl Bainbridge	*Master Georgie*
1999	Timothy Mo	*Renegade or Halo 2*
2000	Zadie Smith	*White Teeth*
2001	Sid Smith	*Something Like a House*
2002	Jonathan Franzen	*The Corrections*
2003	Andrew O'Hagan	*Personality*

British Fantasy Awards

The British Fantasy Society, founded in 1971, sponsors a number of awards including the August Derleth Award for the best novel of the year. Winners are selected by members of the Society at their annual Fantasy Convention.

Year	Author	Title
1990	Dan Simmons	*Carrion Comfort*
1991	Ramsey Campbell	*Midnight Sun*
1992	Jonathan Carroll	*Outside the Dog Museum*
1993	Graham Joyce	*Dark Sister*
1994	Ramsey Campbell	*The Long Lost*
1995	Michael Marshall Smith	*Only Forward*
1996	Graham Joyce	*Requiem*
1997	Graham Joyce	*The Tooth Fairy*
1998	Chaz Brenchley	*Tower of the King's Daughter*
1999	Stephen King	*Bag of Bones*
2000	Graham Joyce	*Indigo*
2001	China Miéville	*Perdido Street Station*
2002	Simon Clark	*The Night of the Triffids*
2003	China Miéville	*The Scar*
2004	Christopher Fowler	*Full Dark House*

British Science Fiction Association Awards

Awarded annually after a ballot of members, by the British Science Fiction Association (BSFA). Winners of the Best Novel prize are listed below.

Year	Author	Title
1990	Colin Greenland	*Take Back Plenty*
1991	Dan Simmons	*The Fall of Hyperion*
1992	Kim Stanley Robinson	*Red Mars*
1993	Christopher Evans	*Aztec Century*
1994	Iain M Banks	*Feersum Endjinn*
1995	Stephen Baxter	*The Time Ships*
1996	Iain M Banks	*Excession*
1997	Mary Doria Russell	*The Sparrow*
1998	Christopher Priest	*The Extremes*
1999	Ken MacLeod	*The Sky Road*
2000	Mary Gentle	*Ash: A Secret History*
2001	Alastair Reynolds	*Chasm City*
2002	Christopher Priest	*The Separation*
2003	Jon Courtenay Grimwood	*Felaheen*
2004	Ian McDonald	*River of Gods*

Arthur C Clarke Award

Established in 1986 the Arthur C Clarke award is supported and judged jointly by the British Science Fiction Association, the Science Fiction Foundation and the Science Museum. It is for a Science Fiction novel receiving its first British publication. Horror and Fantasy are excluded unless there is a strong Science Fiction element in the book.

1990	Geoff Ryman	*The Child Garden*
1991	Colin Greenland	*Take Back Plenty*
1992	Pat Cadigan	*Synners*
1993	Marge Piercy	*Body of Glass*
1994	Jeff Noon	*Vurt*
1995	Pat Cadigan	*Fools*
1996	Paul J McAuley	*Fairyland*
1997	Amitav Ghosh	*The Calcutta Chromosome*
1998	Mary Doria Russell	*The Sparrow*
1999	Tricia Sullivan	*Dreaming in Smoke*
2000	Bruce Sterling	*Distraction*
2001	China Miéville	*Perdido Street Station*
2002	Gwyneth Jones	*Bold as Love*
2003	Christopher Priest	*The Separation*
2004	Neal Stephenson	*Quicksilver*
2005	China Miéville	*Iron Council*

Prizes

Commonwealth Writers Prize

Established in 1987 by the Commonwealth Foundation in association with the Book Trust and the Royal Overseas League, the award is administered annually within one of four regions of the Commonwealth. Entries submitted by publishers must be novels or short stories in English.

1990	Mordecai Richler	*Solomon Gursky*
1991	David Malouf	*The Great World*
1992	Rohinton Mistry	*Such a Long Journey*
1993	Alex Miller	*The Ancestor Game*
1994	Vikram Seth	*A Suitable Boy*
1995	Louis de Bernières	*Captain Corelli's Mandolin*
1996	Rohinton Mistry	*A Fine Balance*
1997	Earl Lovelace	*Salt*
1998	Peter Carey	*Jack Maggs*
1999	Murray Bail	*Eucalyptus*
2000	J M Coetzee	*Disgrace*
2001	Peter Carey	*True History of the Kelly Gang*
2002	Richard Flanagan	*Gould's Book of Fish*
2003	Austin Clarke	*The Polished Hoe*
2004	Caryl Phillips	*A Distant Shore*
2005	Andrea Levy	*Small Island*

Crime Writers' Association

The first meeting of the Association was convened by John Creasey in November 1953 and awards have been presented since 1955. Awarded in the following categories: **Gold Dagger** for the best thriller, suspense novel or spy fiction published in the UK in the English language; **Silver Dagger** for the runner-up; **Cartier Diamond Dagger** for outstanding contribution to the genre of crime writing; **John Creasey Memorial Dagger** (in commemoration of the first chairman of the CWA), sponsored by BBC Audio, for the best crime novel by an author who has not previously published a full-length work of fiction; the **Last Laugh Award** for the funniest crime book of the year was awarded from 1989 1995; the **Ellis Peters Historical Dagger**, the **Ian Fleming Steel Dagger** for thrillers and the **Dagger in the Library**, a new award for 2003, awarded to "the author of crime fiction whose work has given most pleasure to readers" as nominated by UK libraries.

1990	Gold Dagger	Reginald Hill	Bones and Silence
	Silver Dagger	Mike Phillips	The Late Candidate
	JCMA	Patricia D Cornwell	Postmortem
	Last Laugh Award	Simon Shaw	Killer Cinderella
1991	Gold Dagger	Barbara Vine	King Solomon's Carpet
	Silver Dagger	Frances Fyfield	Deep Sleep
	JCMA	Walter Mosley	Devil in a Blue Dress
	Last Laugh Award	Mike Ripley	Angels in Arms
1992	Gold Dagger	Colin Dexter	The Way Through the Woods
	Silver Dagger	Liza Cody	Bucket Nut
	JCMA	Minette Walters	The Ice House
	Last Laugh Award	Carl Hiaasen	Native Tongue
1993	Gold Dagger	Patricia D Cornwell	Cruel and Unusual
	Silver Dagger	Sarah Dunant	Fatlands
	JCMA	No award	
	Last Laugh Award	Michael Pearce	The Mamur Zapt and the Spoils of Egypt
1994	Gold Dagger	Minette Walters	The Scold's Bridle
	Silver Dagger	Peter Hoeg	Miss Smilla's Feeling for Snow
	JCMA	Doug J Swanson	Big Town
	Last Laugh Award	Simon Shaw	The Villain of the Earth
1995	Gold Dagger	Val McDermid	The Mermaid's Singing
	Silver Dagger	Peter Lovesey	The Summons
	JCMA	Janet Evanovich	One for the Money
	Last Laugh Award	Laurence Shames	Sunburn
1996	Gold Dagger	Ben Elton	Popcorn
	Silver Dagger	Peter Lovesey	Bloodhounds
	JCMA	No award	
	Last Laugh Award	No award	

1997	*Gold Dagger*	Ian Rankin	*Black & Blue*
	Silver Dagger	Janet Evanovich	*Three to Get Deadly*
	JCMA	Paul Johnston	*Body Politic*
1998	*Gold Dagger*	James Lee Burke	*Sunset Limited*
	Silver Dagger	Nicholas Blincoe	*Manchester Slingback*
	JCMA	Denise Mina	*Garnethill*
1999	*Gold Dagger*	Robert Wilson	*A Small Death in Lisbon*
	Silver Dagger	Adrian Matthews	*Vienna Blood*
	JCMA	Dan Fesperman	*Lie in the Dark*
	Historical Dagger	Lindsey Davis	*Two for the Lions*
2000	*Gold Dagger*	Jonathan Lethem	*Motherless Brooklyn*
	Silver Dagger	Donna Leon	*Friends in High Places*
	JCMA	Boston Teran	*God is a Bullet*
	Historical Dagger	Gillian Linscott	*Absent Friends*
2001	*Gold Dagger*	Henning Mankell	*Sidetracked*
	Silver Dagger	Giles Blunt	*Forty Words for Sorrow*
	JCMA	Susanna Jones	*The Earthquake Bird*
	Historical Dagger	Andrew Taylor	*The Office of the Dead*
2002	*Gold Dagger*	Jose C Samoza	*The Athenian Murders*
	Silver Dagger	James Crumley	*The Final Country*
	JCMA	Louise Welsh	*The Cutting Room*
	Historical Dagger	Sarah Waters	*Fingersmith*
	Steel Dagger	John Creed	*The Sirius Crossing*
2003	*Gold Dagger*	Minette Walters	*Fox Evil*
	Silver Dagger	Morag Joss	*Half Broken Things*
	JCMA	William Landay	*Mission Flats*
	Historical Dagger	Andrew Taylor	*The American Boy*
	Steel Dagger	Dan Fesperman	*The Small Boat of Great Sorrows*
2004	*Gold Dagger*	Sara Paretsky	*Blacklist*
	Silver Dagger	John Harvey	*Flesh and Blood*
	JCMA	Mark Mills	*Amagansett*
	Historical Dagger	Barbara Cleverly	*The Damascened Blade*
	Steel Dagger	Jeffrey Deaver	*Garden of Beasts*

Encore Award

Awarded to the best second novel of the year published in that calendar year. The winner is chosen by a panel of judges from entries submitted by publishers. The award is administered by the Society of Authors.

joint winners {	1990	Peter Benson	*A Lesser Dependency*
	1990	Paul Watkins	*Calm at Sunset, Calm at Dawn*
	1991	Carey Harrison	*Richard's Feet*
	1992	Iain Sinclair	*Downriver*
	1993	Colm Toibin	*The Heather Blazing*
	1994	Amit Chaudhuri	*Afternoon Raag*
	1995	Dermot Healy	*A Goat's Song*
	1996	A L Kennedy	*So I Am Glad*
	1997	David Flusfeder	*Like Plastic*
joint winners {	1998	Timothy O'Grady	*I Could Read the Sky*
	1998	Alan Warner	*These Demented Lands*
	1999	Christina Koning	*Undiscovered Country*
joint winners {	2000	John Burnside	*The Mercy Boys*
	2000	Claire Messud	*The Last Life*
	2000	Matt Thorne	*Eight Minutes Idle*
	2001	Phil Whitaker	*Triangulation*
	2002	Ali Smith	*Hotel World*
	2003	Jeremy Gavron	*The Book of Israel*
	2004	Michelle de Kretser	*The Hamilton Case*

Prizes

Geoffrey Faber Memorial Prize

As a memorial to the founder and first Chairman of the firm, Faber and Faber Limited established the prize in 1963. Awarded annually, it is given in alternate years for a volume of verse and for a volume of prose fiction published originally in this country by writers who are under 40 years of age. The following is the list of fiction prize winners:

1991	Carol Birch	*The Fog Line*
1993	Will Self	*The Quantity Theory of Insanity*
1995	Livi Michael	*Their Angel Reach*
1997	Emily Perkins	*Not Her Real Name*
1999	Gavin Kramer	*Shopping*
2001	Trezza Azzopardi	*The Hiding Place*
2003	Justin Hill	*The Drink and Dream Teahouse*

Foster Grant Romantic Novel of the Year

Established in 1960 the award, now sponsored by Foster Grant, is for the best romantic novel of the year by a United Kingdom citizen.

1990	Reay Tannahill	*Passing Glory*
1991	Susan Kay	*Phantom*
1992	June Knox-Mawer	*Sandstorm*
1993	Cynthia Harrod-Eagles	*Emily*
1994	Elizabeth Buchan	*Consider the Lily*
1995	Charlotte Bingham	*Change of Heart*
1996	Rosamunde Pilcher	*Coming Home*
1997	Sue Gee	*The Hours of the Night*
1998	Angela Lambert	*Kiss and Kin*
1999	Clare Chambers	*Learning to Swim*
2000	Maureen Lee	*Dancing in the Dark*
2001	Cathy Kelly	*Someone Like You*
2002	Philippa Gregory	*The Other Boleyn Girl*
2003	Sarah Mason	*Playing James*
2004	Jojo Moyes	*Foreign Fruit*
2005	Katharine Davies	*A Good Voyage*

Guardian Fiction Prize

Awarded annually from 1965 to 1999 for a work of fiction by a British or Commonwealth writer and published in the United Kingdom. Succeeded by the Guardian First Book Award which is open to fiction and non-fiction titles.

1990	Pauline Melville	*Shape-shifter*
1991	Alan Judd	*The Devil's Own Work*
1992	Alasdair Gray	*Poor Things*
1993	Pat Barker	*The Eye in the Door*
1994	Candia McWilliam	*Debatable Land*
1995	James Buchan	*Heart's Journey into Winter*
1996	Seamus Deane	*Reading in the Dark*
1997	Anne Michaels	*Fugitive Pieces*
1998	Jackie Kay	*Trumpet*

Guardian First Book Award

This award replaced the Guardian Fiction Prize from 1999 onwards. It recognises and rewards new writing by honouring an author's first book, which may be fiction or non-fiction.

1999	No award to fiction	
2000	Zadie Smith	*White Teeth*
2001	Chris Ware	*Jimmy Corrigan: The Smartest Kid on Earth*
2002	Jonathan Safran Foer	*Everything is Illuminated*
2003	No award to fiction	
2004	No award to fiction	

Hawthornden Prize

Founded in 1919 by Miss Alice Warrender, it is the oldest of the famous British literary prizes. Awarded annually to an English writer for the best work of imaginative literature, it is especially designed to encourage young authors, and the word 'imaginative' is given a broad interpretation.

The following dates are the years for which the award was given to a work of fiction:

1992	Ferdinand Mount	*Of Love and Asthma*
1993	Andrew Barrow	*The Tap Dancer*
1994	Tim Pears	*In the Place of Fallen Leaves*
1996	Hilary Mantel	*An Experiment in Love*
1997	John Lanchester	*The Debt to Pleasure*
2001	Helen Simpson	*Hey Yeah Right Get a Life*

David Higham Prize for Fiction

As this prize was discontinued after 1998, please see the 4th edition of this guide for prize winners.

Winifred Holtby Memorial Prize

See Ondaatje Prize (page 336)

Independent Foreign Fiction Award

Funded by the Arts Council & Champagne Taittinger and promoted by *The Independent* newspaper, an annual prize for the best contemporary work of prose fiction translated into English from any other tongue and published between 1 January and 31 December each year.

2001	Marta Morazzoni translated from the Italian by Emma Rose	*The Alphonse Courriér Affair*
2002	W G Sebald translated from the German by Anthea Bell	*Austerlitz*
2003	Per Olov Enquist translated from the Swedish by Tiina Nunnally	*The Visit of the Royal Physician*
2004	Javier Cercas translated from the Spanish by Anne McLean	*Soldiers of Salamis*
2005	Frédéric Beigbeder translated from the French by Frank Wynne	*Windows on the World*

International IMPAC Dublin Literary Award

Established in 1996 and awarded to a work of fiction written and published in the English language or written in a language other than English and published in English translation. The Award, an initiative of Dublin City Council, is a partnership with IMPAC, a productivity improvement company, and is the largest and most international prize of its kind. The winner is chosen by nominations made by selected public libraries.

1996	David Malouf	*Remembering Babylon*
1997	Javier Marias	*A Heart So White*
1998	Herta Müller	*The Land of Green Plums*
1999	Andrew Miller	*Ingenious Pain*
2000	Nicola Barker	*Wide Open*
2001	Alistair MacLeod	*No Great Mischief*
2002	Michel Housellebecq	*Atomised*
2003	Orhan Pamuk	*My Name is Red*
2004	Taher Ben Jelloun	*This Blinding Absence of Light*

Irish Times International Fiction Prize

Awarded biennially to the author of a work of fiction written in the English language and published in Ireland, the United Kingdom or the United States. The winner is selected by an international panel of judges.

1989	Don DeLillo	*Libra*
1990	A S Byatt	*Possession*
1991	Louis Begley	*Wartime Lies*
1992	Norman Rush	*Mating*
1993	E Annie Proulx	*The Shipping News*
1995	J M Coetzee	*The Master of Petersberg*
1997	Seamus Deane	*Reading in the Dark*
1999	Lorrie Moore	*Birds of America*
2001	Michael Ondaatje	*Anil's Ghost*

This prize has now been discontinued

Jewish Quarterly / Wingate Literary Prize for Fiction

Sponsored by the Harold Hyman Wingate Foundation and awarded to a work of fiction and non-fiction which stimulates an interest in themes of Jewish concern.

	1996	Alan Isler	*The Prince of West End Avenue*
joint winners	1997	W G Sebald	*The Emigrants*
	1997	Clive Sinclair	*The Lady with the Laptop*
	1998	Anne Michaels	*Fugitive*
	1999	Dorit Rabinyan	*Persian Brides*
	2000	Howard Jacobson	*The Mighty Walzer*
	2001	Mona Yahia	*When the Grey Beetles Took Over Baghdad*
	2002	W G Sebald	*Austerlitz*
	2003	Zadie Smith	*The Autograph Man*
	2004	David Grossman	*Someone to Run With*
	2005	David Besmozgis	*Natasha and Other Stories*

Mail on Sunday / John Llewellyn Rhys Prize

Founded in 1942 by Jane Oliver, the widow of John Llewellyn Rhys, a young writer killed in action in World War II. Open to writers aged under 35, the work may be any form of literature: fiction, short stories, poetry, drama, biography or literary non-fiction written by a British or Commonwealth writer. The following dates are the years for which an award was given to a work of fiction:

1992	Matthew Kneale	*Sweet Thames*
1994	Jonathan Coe	*What a Carve Up!*
1995	Melanie McGrath	*Motel Nirvana*
1996	Nicola Barker	*Heading Inland*
1997	Phil Whitaker	*Eclipse of the Sun*
1998	Peter H Davis	*The Ugliest House in the World*
1999	David Mitchell	*Ghostwritten*
2000	Edward Platt	*Leadville*
2001	Susanna Jones	*The Earthquake Bird*
2003	Charlotte Mendelson	*Daughters of Jerusalem*

Man Booker Prize for Fiction

Established in 1968 by Booker McConnell Ltd. Eligible novels must be written in English by a citizen of Britain, the Commonwealth or the Republic of Ireland. Since 2002 sponsorship has been by the Man Group and the prize is now known as the Man Booker Prize.

1990	A S Byatt	*Possession*
1991	Ben Okri	*The Famished Road*
1992	Michael Ondaatje	*The English Patient*
1992	Barry Unsworth	*Sacred Hunger*
1993	Roddy Doyle	*Paddy Clarke Ha Ha Ha*
1994	James Kelman	*How Late It Was, How Late*
1995	Pat Barker	*The Ghost Road*
1996	Graham Swift	*Last Orders*
1997	Arundhati Roy	*The God of Small Things*
1998	Ian McEwan	*Amsterdam*
1999	J M Coetzee	*Disgrace*
2000	Margaret Atwood	*The Blind Assassin*
2001	Peter Carey	*True History of the Kelly Gang*
2002	Yann Martel	*Life of Pi*
2003	D B C Pierre	*Vernon God Little*
2004	Alan Hollinghurst	*The Line of Beauty*

joint winners { 1992, 1992

Prices

Somerset Maugham Awards

The purpose of these annual awards is to encourage young writers to travel, and the emphasis of the founder is on originality and promise. Authors must be under 35 years of age, a British subject by birth, and ordinarily resident in the United Kingdom. Poetry, fiction and non-fiction are all eligible. The fiction winners from 1990 are listed below.

	1990	Nicholas Shakespeare	*The Vision of Elena Silves*
joint winners	1991	Peter Benson	*The Other Occupant*
	1991	Lesley Glaister	*Honour Thy Father*
	1991	Helen Simpson	*Four Bare Legs*
	1992	Geoff Dyer	*But Beautiful*
	1993	Duncan McLean	*Bucket of Tongues*
	1994	A L Kennedy	*Looking For The Possible Dance*
	1995	No award to fiction	
	1996	Alan Warner	*Morvern Callar*
joint winners	1997	Rhidian Brook	*The Testimony of Tailiesin Jones*
	1997	Philip Hensher	*Kitchen Venom*
	1998	Rachel Cusk	*The Country Life*
	1999	Andrea Ashworth	*Once in a House on Fire*
joint winners	1999	Paul Farley	*The Boy from the Chemist is Here to See You*
	1999	Giles Foden	*The Last King of Scotland*
	1999	Jonathan Freedland	*Bring Home the Revolution*
	2000	Sarah Waters	*Affinity*
	2001	Ben Rice	*Pobby and Dingan*
joint winners	2002	Charlotte Hobson	*Black Earth City*
	2002	Marcel Theroux	*The Paper Chase*
	2003	Hari Kunzru	*The Impressionist*
	2004	Charlotte Mendelson	*Daughters of Jerusalem*

McKitterick Prize

Endowed by the late Tom McKitterick the award is made to a first novel (published or unpublished) by an author over the age of 40.

1990	Simon Mawer	*Chimera*
1991	John Loveday	*A Summer to Halo*
1992	Alberto Manguel	*News from a Foreign Country Came*
1993	Andrew Barrow	*The Tap Dancer*
1994	Helen Dunmore	*Zennor in Darkness*
1995	Christopher Bigsby	*Hester*
1996	Stephen Blanchard	*Gagarin and I*
1997	Patricia Duncker	*Hallucinating Foucault*
1998	Eli Gottlieb	*The Boy who Went Away*
1999	Magnus Mills	*The Restraint of Beasts*
2000	Chris Dolan	*Ascension Day*
2001	Giles Waterfield	*The Long Afternoon*
2002	Manil Suri	*The Death of Vishnu*
2003	Mary Lawson	*Crow Lake*
2004	Mark Haddon	*The Curious Incident of the Dog in the Night-Time*

Ondaatje Prize

The Royal Society of Literature launched in 2004 this new award worth £10,000 for writing 'that evokes the spirit of a place'. It has been funded by business man and philanthropist Christopher Ondaatje with extra backing from *Conde Nast Traveller* magazine. It will be open to fiction and non-fiction works and was presented for the first time in May 2004. This award is a successor to the Winifred Holtby prize for regional fiction which has been discontinued.

The Orange Prize

Founded in 1996, this award is open to women authors of any nationality, provided that entries have been published in the United Kingdom. Administered by the Book Trust. From 2005 there will be a new prize worth £10,000 — the Orange Award for New Writers. It will be open to any first work of fiction by a woman of any nationality and published in the UK in the preceding year. Books can be entered for both the new Award and the main Orange Prize.

1996	Helen Dunmore	*A Spell of Winter*
1997	Anne Michaels	*Fugitive Pieces*
1998	Carol Shields	*Larry's Party*
1999	Suzanne Berne	*A Crime in the Neighbourhood*
2000	Linda Grant	*When I Lived in Modern Times*
2001	Kate Grenville	*The Idea of Perfection*
2002	Ann Patchett	*Bel Canto*
2003	Valerie Martin	*Property*
2004	Andrea Levy	*Small Island*

Pulitzer Prize for Fiction

Joseph Pulitzer, reporter, editor, publisher and a founder of the Graduate School of Journalism at Columbia University, established in 1903 a system of prizes to encourage 'public service, public morals, American literature and the advancement of education'. The Fiction Prize was first awarded in 1948.

1990	Oscar Hijuelos	*The Mambo Kings Play Songs of Love*
1991	John Updike	*Rabbit at Rest*
1992	Jane Smiley	*A Thousand Acres*
1993	Robert Olen Butler	*A Good Scent from a Strange Mountain*
1994	E Annie Proulx	*The Shipping News*
1995	Carol Shields	*The Stone Diaries*
1996	Richard Ford	*Independence Day*
1997	Steven Millhauser	*Martin Dressler: The Tale of an American Dreamer*
1998	Philip Roth	*American Pastoral*
1999	Michael Cunningham	*The Hours*
2000	Jhumpa Lahiri	*Interpreter of Maladies*
2001	Michael Chabon	*The Amazing Adventures of Kavalier and Clay*
2002	Richard Russo	*Empire Falls*
2003	Jeffrey Eugenides	*Middlesex*
2004	Edward P Jones	*The Known World*
2005	Marilynne Robinson	*Gilead*

Saga Award for Wit

This new award worth £20,000 sponsored by *Saga Magazine* is for humorous writing, whether fiction or non-fiction, by authors aged 50 or over. Publishers may submit up to four titles each. The first winner was announced at the Folkestone Literary Festival in September 2003.

2003 Alexander McCall Smith   *The Full Cupboard of Life*
2004 No award to fiction

Sagittarius Prize

Awarded to a first novel by a writer over 60 years of age, first published in the United Kingdom during the year preceding the year in which the award is presented. Administered by the Society of Authors.

1991	Judith Hubback	*The Sea Has Many Voices*
1992	Hugh Leonard	*Parnell and the English Woman*
1993	Brian O'Doherty	*The Strange Case of Mademoiselle P*
1994	George Hummer	*Red Branch*
1995	Fred Plisner	*Gravity is Getting Me Down*
1996	Samuel Lock	*As Luck would Have it*
1997	Barbara Hardy	*London Lovers*
1998	A Sivanandan	*When Memory Dies*
1999	Ingrid Mann	*The Danube Testament*
2000	David Crackanthorpe	*Stolen Marches*
2001	Michael Richardson	*The Pig Bin*
2002	Zvi Jagendorf	*Wolfy and the Strudelbakers*
2003	Margaret Kaine	*Ring of Clay*
2004	William Newton	*The Two Pound Tram*

WHSmith Literary Award

Awarded from 1959 to the book that, in the opinion of the judges, has made the most outstanding contribution to literature in the year under review. There are no age limits for the author and the award is open to all types of literature including foreign works in translation.

1990	V S Prichett	*A Careless Window and Other Stories*
1991	Derek Walcott	*Omeros*
1992	No award to fiction	
1993	Michèle Roberts	*Daughters of the House*
1994	Vikram Seth	*A Suitable Boy*
1995	Alice Munro	*Open Secrets*
1996	No award to fiction	
1997	No award to fiction	
1998	No award to fiction	
1999	Beryl Bainbridge	*Master Georgie*
2000	Melvyn Bragg	*The Soldier's Return*
2001	Philip Roth	*The Human Stain*
2002	Ian McEwan	*Atonement*
2003	Donna Tartt	*The Little Friend*
2004	Richard Powers	*The Time of our Singing*
2005	Philip Roth	*The Plot Against America*

Sunday Times Young Writer of the Year Award

Awarded to a writer who is under the age of 35 on the strength of the promise shown by a full-length published work of fiction, non-fiction or poetry.

1991	Helen Simpson	*Four Bare Legs in a Bed*
1992	Caryl Phillips	*Cambridge*
1993	No award to fiction	
1994	No award to fiction	
1995	Andrew Cowen	*Pig*
1996	Katherine Pierpoint	*Truffle Beds*
1997	Francis Spufford	*I May Be Some Time*
1998	Patrick French	*Liberty or Death*
1999	No award to fiction	
2000	Sarah Waters	*Affinity*
2001	Zadie Smith	*White Teeth*
2002	No award to fiction	
2003	No award to fiction	
2004	No award to fiction	

Thumping Good Read Book Award

Awarded to a novel that is judged by a panel of WHSmith's customers to be an "accessible and page-turning good read".

1992	Robert Goddard	*Into the Blue*
1993	Robert Harris	*Fatherland*
1994	Dominick Dunne	*A Season in Purgatory*
1995	Thomas Eidson	*St Agnes' Stand*
1996	Andrew Klavan	*True Crime*
1997	David Baldacci	*Absolute Power*
1998	Douglas Kennedy	*The Big Picture*
1999	Lee Child	*Die Trying*
2000	Boris Starling	*Storm*
2001	Jeffery Deaver	*The Empty Chair*
2002	Mo Hayder	*The Treatment*
2003	Harlan Coben	*Gone For Good*
2004	No award	

Betty Trask Awards

Started in 1984 and administered by the Society of Authors, the awards are for the benefit of young authors (under 35), and are given on the strength of the manuscript of a first novel of a romantic or traditional — rather than experimental — nature. The winners are required to use the money for foreign travel. The principal winners are:

1990	Robert McLiam Wilson	*Ripley Bogle*
1991	Amit Chaudhuri	*A Strange and Sublime Address*
1992	Liane Jones	*The Dream Stone*
1993	Mark Blackaby	*You'll Never Be Here Again (Unpublished)*
1994	Colin Bateman	*Divorcing Jack*
1995	Robert Newman	*Dependence Day*
1996	John Lanchester	*The Debt to Pleasure*
1997	Alex Garland	*The Beach*
1998	Kiran Desai	*Hullabaloo in the Guava Orchard*
1999	Elliot Perlman	*Three Dollars*
2000	Jonathan Tulloch	*The Season Ticket*
2001	Zadie Smith	*White Teeth*
2002	Hari Kunzru	*The Impressionist*
2003	Jon McGregor	*If Nobody Speaks of Remarkable Things*
2004	Louise Dean	*Becoming Strangers*

Whitbread Book of the Year and Literary Awards

Established in 1971, the Whitbread PLC prizes now reward five categories of book. These are: Novel; First Novel; Children's Novel; Poetry and Biography. Writers must have been resident in Great Britain or the Republic of Ireland for three years or more. Nominations are selected by the panel of judges from each category and one of the category winners is then voted Whitbread Book of the Year. The awards are administered by the Booksellers Association.

1990	Novel & 'Book of the Year'	Nicholas Mosley	Hopeful Monsters
	First Novel	Hanif Kureishi	The Buddha of Suburbia
1991	Novel	Jane Gardam	The Queen of the Tambourine
	First Novel	Gordon Burn	Alma Cogan
1992	Novel	Alasdair Gray	Poor Things
	First Novel & 'Book of the Year'	Jeff Torrington	Swing Hammer Swing!
1993	Novel & 'Book of The Year'	Joan Brady	Theory of War
	First Novel	Rachel Cusk	Saving Agnes
1994	Novel & 'Book of The Year'	William Trevor	Felicia's Journey
	First Novel	Fred D'Aguiar	The Longest Memory
1995	First Novel	Kate Atkinson	Behind the Scenes at the Museum
	Novel	Salman Rushdie	The Moor's Last Sigh
1996	First Novel	John Lanchester	The Debt to Pleasure
	Novel	Beryl Bainbridge	Every Man For Himself
1997	First Novel	Pauline Melville	The Ventriloquist's Tale
	Novel	Jim Crace	Quarantine
1998	First Novel	Giles Foden	The Last King of Scotland
	Novel	Justin Cartwright	Leading the Cheers
1999	First Novel	Tim Lott	White City Blue
	Novel	Rose Tremain	Music and Silence
2000	First Novel	Zadie Smith	White Teeth
	Novel & 'Book of The Year'	Matthew Kneale	English Passengers
2001	First Novel	Sid Smith	Something Like a House
	Novel	Patrick Neate	Twelve Bar Blues
2002	First Novel	Norman Lebrecht	The Song of Names
	Novel	Michael Frayn	Spies
2003	First Novel	D B C Pierre	Vernon God Little
	Novel & 'Book of the Year'	Mark Haddon	The Curious Incident of the Dog in the Night-Time
2004	Novel & 'Book of the Year'	Andrea Levy	Small Island

Prizes

341

Further Reading
and
Websites

Books

This short list contains books which should be readily available in most public library systems. They form an invaluable complement to **Who Else Writes Like...?** and will help the reader explore a particular genre, pursue the reading of a series, or follow up a more detailed path from one specific author and title to another.

Bloomsbury Good Reading Guide
by Kenneth McLeish, *Bloomsbury Publishing plc*,
6th rev edition edited by Nick Rennison 2003
A natural 'follow up' to *Who Else Writes Like...?* It contains articles on some 375 authors describing the type of books they write – listing over 3,500 individual books, suggesting alternative and 'follow up' authors and titles.

Bloomsbury Good Reading Guide to Crime Fiction
edited by Nick Rennison, *Bloomsbury Publishing plc*, 2003
A complementary guide, arranged in a similar format and featuring over 200 authors covering many subgenres of crime fiction.

Bloomsbury Essential Guide for Reading Groups
by Susan Osborne, *Bloomsbury Publishing plc*, 2002
Offers advice on finding, joining or setting up a reading group plus a list of 50 books to stimulate discussion.

Chambers Dictionary of Literary Characters
Chambers, 2nd edition, 2004
First published in 1994 this greatly enlarged second edition contains entries for more than 6,500 of the most famous and influential characters from novels, plays and poetry.

Cumulated Fiction Index
Career Development Group of CILIP
1945-1960	by G B Cotton and Alan Glencross
1960-1969	by Raymond Smith
1970-1974	by Raymond Smith and Anthony J Gordon
1975-1979	by Marilyn E Hicken
1980-1989	by Marilyn E Hicken
1990-1994	by Marilyn E Hicken
1995-1999	by Marilyn E Hicken

This series indexes the majority of novels published in the United Kingdom since the end of the Second World War. The subject headings indicate places, persons, and periods of history as well as showing genres and techniques. It is particularly helpful to readers of crime fiction as the index divides this genre into thirteen groups.

Dictionary of Literary Pseudonyms in the English Language
compiled by Terence Carty, *Mansell*, 1995
Lists 12,000 English language literary pseudonyms to give the real names of around 7,500 authors, from the early seventeenth century to the present day.

Encyclopaedia of Fantasy
edited by John Clute and John Grant, *Orbit*, 1999
A companion volume to the Encyclopaedia of science fiction, it contains over 4,000 entries covering every aspect of fantasy in literature, films, television, opera, art and comics.

Encyclopaedia of Science Fiction
edited by John Clute and Peter Nichols, *Orbit, 2nd ed,* 1993
(rev paperback ed, 1999)
The essential reference work on science fiction due to its coverage and scholarship.

Good Fiction Guide
edited by Jane Rogers, *OUP*, 2002
Features over 1,000 writers from Maeve Binchy to Emile Zola, each entry recommends alternative authors and also suggests new areas of literature to explore.

Mammoth Encyclopaedia of Modern Crime Fiction
compiled by Mike Ashley, *Constable and Robinson*, 2002
A welcome addition to the reference shelves, and the first title to include all the major new discoveries of the last couple of decades.

Science Fiction: The Illustrated Encyclopaedia
edited by John Clute, *Dorling Kindersley*, 1995
Covers the history of the genre in all its forms. Lavishly illustrated. Over 100 short biographies of SF writers.

Sequels Vol 1: Adult Books
compiled by Mandy Hicken, Career Development Group, CILIP,
13th ed 2004
Lists novels in which the same characters appear; sequences of novels connected by theme; sequences of novels with a geographical or historical connection; and non-fiction, mainly autobiographical, which is intended to be read in sequence. The arrangement is primarily under the author, with an index of series and characters. Invaluable if you want to read a series in order.

Who's Who of Twentieth Century Novelists
edited by Tim Woods, *Routledge*, 2001
Contains 1,000 biographical entries of novelists who have influenced 20th century fiction. Drawn from a broad range of countries, genres and styles including writers of popular genre fiction. The emphasis is on post 1945 writers.

Who Wrote What? A Dictionary of Writers and their Works
edited by Michael Cox, *OUP*, 2002
A selective listing of over 25,000 titles from nearly 3,000 well known British, American & Commonwealth authors including major European and Classical figures.

Websites

With the growth of the Internet there is an increasing range of websites which can assist the reader to expand their interest in particular authors and their works. Here are some sites which should prove useful but please note that although they were accurate at the time of going to press, they may very well change during the life of this edition.

General Interest
www.contemporarywriters.com
www.fantasticfiction.co.uk
www.kirjasto.sci.fi
www.reader-development.com/wordofmouth
www.whichbook.net

Crime
www.crimefiction.com
www.thrillingdetective.com
www.ex.ac.uk/~RDavies/bankfiction (financial thrillers)

Historical Fiction
www.histfiction.net

Horror
www.horrorworld.org

Science Fiction
http://isfdb.tamu.edu/sfdbase.html
www.fantasticmetropolis.com
www.infinityplus.co.uk
www.sfwa.org

Romance
www.theromancereader.com

Western
www.readwest.com

Chick Lit
www.chicklit.co.uk